BATTLEGROUND
SPORTS

BATTLEGROUND
SPORTS

VOLUME 1 (A–O)

Edited by Michael Atkinson

GREENWOOD PRESS
Westport, Connecticut • London

Library of Congress Cataloging-in-Publication Data

Battleground sports / edited by Michael Atkinson.
 v. cm.
 Includes bibliographical references and index.
 ISBN 978–0–313–34024–6 ((set) : alk. paper) — ISBN 978–0–313–34025–3 ((vol. 1) : alk. paper) — ISBN 978–0–313–34026–0 ((vol. 2) : alk. paper)
 1. Sports—Social aspects—Encyclopedias. 2. Sports—Economic aspects—Encyclopedias. I. Atkinson, Michael, 1971–
 GV706.5.B375 2009
 306.483—dc22   2008030544

British Library Cataloguing in Publication Data is available.

Copyright © 2009 by Michael Atkinson

All rights reserved. No portion of this book may be reproduced, by any process or technique, without the express written consent of the publisher.

Library of Congress Catalog Card Number: 2008030544
ISBN: 978–0–313–34024–6 (set)
     978–0–313–34025–3 (vol. 1)
     978–0–313–34026–0 (vol. 2)

First published in 2009

Greenwood Press, 88 Post Road West, Westport, CT 06881
An imprint of Greenwood Publishing Group, Inc.
www.greenwood.com

Printed in the United States of America

The paper used in this book complies with the Permanent Paper Standard issued by the National Information Standards Organization (Z39.48–1984).

10 9 8 7 6 5 4 3 2 1

CONTENTS

Guide to Related Topics   *ix*
Series Foreword   *xiii*
Introduction   *xv*

Entries

Academic Misconduct Among Athletes	1
Adventure Racing	7
Animal Blood Sports	12
Antidoping Rules and Policies	18
Antitrust Violations in Professional Sports	22
Athlete Unions	29
"At-Risk" Youth in Sports	37
Biology and Athlete Performance	43
Cheating During Competition	53
Collective Protests and Social Movements	60
Commercializing Ethnic Athletes	65
Cool Pose	72
Corporate Branding	76

Corporate Stadiums	83
Criminal Violence During Competition	88
Disability Sports	97
Drafting Amateur Athletes	103
Eating Disorders	111
Environmental Impacts of Sports	117
Equipment Manufacturing in the Third World	125
Ergogenics	131
Erythropoietin (EPO)	138
Ethnic Coaches, Managers, and Owners	143
Field Invasions	151
Funding Equality Legislation	156
Gambling	161
Gay Games	167
Gender and Educational Opportunities	171
Gender and Game Rules	177
Gene Manipulation	185
Governments, Laws, and Gambling	191
Government Sponsorship of Teams	197
Hazing	203
Homophobia	208
Hooliganism	215
Illness	221
International Olympic Committee (IOC)	228
Labor Migration	235
LGBT Sports Leagues	240
Marijuana, Alcohol, and Illicit Drugs	247
Marketing Female Athlete Sexuality	253
Mascots	260
Media Broadcasting Rights	266
Media Coverage of Women's Sports	271

Men in Women's Sports	278
Militarism and the Olympics	284
Missile Throwing	289
Openly Gay Athletes	295
Parent Misconduct	301
Parkour (Free Running)	307
Partner Abuse Among Athletes	312
Player–Fan Fighting	317
Postevent Riots	321
Private vs. Public Sports Spaces	326
Pseudosports	331
Publicity in Sports	336
Racial Profiling and Stacking	343
Rape and Sexual Assault	348
Referee Abuse	354
Religious Expression	360
Rights of Young Athletes	366
Salaries of Professional Athletes	371
Sexual Abuse Among Athletes	377
Skateboarding	383
Snowboarding	389
Soccer Tragedies	398
Sports Doctors, Trainers, and Drugs	403
Sports for All	407
Steroid Use By Athletes	412
Surfing and "New" Water Sports	418
Taunting	425
Terrorism and the Olympics	430
Ticket Distribution and Scalping	436
Transsexual Athletes	443
Ubersexuality	449

Ultraendurance Running	454
Urban Planning and Gentrification	459
Video Games	465
Virtual Sports	472
Whistle-Blowers and Drugs	477
Women and the Apologetic	482
Women Coaches and Owners	488
Women in Men's Sports	491
Women Sportscasters	498
X Games	503
Yoga and Alternative Fitness	509
Bibliography	*515*
About the Editor and Contributors	*535*
Index	*539*

GUIDE TO RELATED TOPICS

ALTERNATIVE SPORTS
Adventure Racing
Parkour (Free Running)
Pseudosports
Skateboarding
Snowboarding
Surfing and New Water Sports
Ultraendurance Running
X Games
Yoga and Alternative Fitness

DRUGS
Antidoping Rules and Policies
Ergogenics
Erythropoietin (EPO)
Marijuana, Alcohol, and Illicit Drugs
Sports Doctors, Trainers, and Drugs
Steroid Use by Athletes
Whistle-Blowers and Drugs

ECONOMICS
Antitrust Violations in Professional Sports
Corporate Branding
Corporate Stadiums

Gambling
Governments, Laws, and Gambling
Marketing Female Athlete Sexuality
Salaries of Professional Athletes
Ticket Distribution and Scalping

EDUCATION
Academic Misconduct Among Athletes
Funding Equality Legislation
Gender and Educational Opportunities

GENDER
Gender and Educational Opportunities
Gender and Game Rules
Men in Women's Sports
Women and the Apologetic
Women Coaches and Owners
Women in Men's Sports
Women Sportscasters

HEALTH AND WELLNESS
Biology and Athlete Performance
Disability Sports
Eating Disorders
Illness

MEDIA
Media Broadcasting Rights
Media Coverage of Women's Sports
Publicity in Sports
Women Sportscasters

OLYMPICS
International Olympic Committee (IOC)
Militarism and the Olympics
Terrorism and the Olympics

POLITICS, IDEOLOGY, AND PUBLIC POLICY
Drafting Amateur Athletes
Government Sponsorship of Teams
Labor Migration
Militarism and the Olympics
Private vs. Public Sports Spaces
Religious Expression
Urban Planning and Gentrification

RACE AND ETHNICITY
"At-Risk" Youth in Sports
Commercializing Ethnic Athletes
Cool Pose
Ethnic Coaches, Managers, and Owners
Labor MigrationRacial Profiling and Stacking

RIGHTS MOVEMENTS
Athlete Unions
Collective Protests and Social Movements
Environmental Impacts of Sports
Equipment Manufacturing in the Third World
Rights of Young Athletes
Sports for All and Fair Play Leagues

SEXUALITY
Gay Games
Homophobia
LGBT Sports Leagues
Openly Gay Athletes
Transsexual Athletes
Ubersexuality

SPECTACLES
Cheating During Competition
Field Invasions
Mascots
Missile Throwing
Publicity in Sports
Taunting

TECHNOLOGY
Biology and Athlete Performance
Gene Manipulation
Video Games
Virtual Sports

VIOLENCE
Animal Blood Sports
Criminal Violence During Competition
Hazing
Hooliganism
Missile Throwing
Parent Misconduct
Partner Abuse Among Athletes

Player–Fan Fighting
Postevent Riots
Rape and Sexual Assault
Referee Abuse
Sexual Abuse Among Athletes
Soccer Tragedies

SERIES FOREWORD

Students, teachers, and librarians frequently need resources for researching the hot-button issues of contemporary society. Whether for term papers, debates, current-events classes, or to just keep informed, library users need balanced, in-depth tools to serve as a launching pad for obtaining a thorough understanding of all sides of those debates that continue to provoke, anger, challenge, and divide us all.

The sets in Greenwood's *Battleground* series are just such a resource. Each *Battleground* set focuses on one broad area of culture in which the debates and conflicts continue to be fast and furious—for example, religion, sports, popular culture, sexuality and gender, science and technology. Each volume comprises dozens of entries on the most timely and far-reaching controversial topics, such as abortion, capital punishment, drugs, ecology, the economy, immigration, and politics. The entries—all written by scholars with a deep understanding of the issues—provide readers with a non-biased assessment of these topics. What are the main points of contention? Who holds each position? What are the underlying, unspoken concerns of each side of the debate? What might the future hold? The result is a balanced, thoughtful reference resource that will not only provide students with a solid foundation for understanding the issues, but will challenge them to think more deeply about their own beliefs.

In addition to an in-depth analysis of these issues, sets include sidebars on important events or people that help enliven the discussion, and each entry includes a list of "Further Reading" that help readers find the next step in their research. At the end of volume 2, the readers will find a comprehensive Bibliography and Index.

INTRODUCTION

There is little debate that sport itself is constructed as a physical and psychological battleground. Competitive athletic struggles against an opponent to "score" or to beat a time are ancient human practices transcending time and space. Sports contests can be incredibly draining physical and mental ordeals, where bodies, selves, emotions, and psyches intentionally clash as part of the game. But sport is also, and perhaps more consequentially, a social battleground that routinely involves the clashing of ideologies and cultural values. *Battleground: Sports* is a panoramic review and discussion of some of the major cultural battles in sport that play out on fields, in arenas, and through the media.

A basic premise is underwritten in the entries that span both volumes of *Battleground: Sports*. What occurs on the field of play is meaningful to players locked in competitive struggle, but what happens in sport is defined as meaningful by audiences for cultural reasons that mainly transcend the context of sport. Consider the following examples: Between 1926 and 2007 nearly every NCAA basketball game involving players from the University of Illinois involved a mascot named Chief Illiniwek (a student dressed in American Indian–style garb). Illiniwek was the brainchild of a young Eagle Scout from Urbana, Illinois, and a university band director who hoped to bring some excitement to the "Marching Illini" (the university's band that played at school sports events) musical halftime shows. Illiniwek was intended as a simple, uncontroversial one-off gimmick. He performed "ritual" Native American dances for the audience. The gimmick caught on, and within a decade, the faux Sioux chief became a university icon and was known across the country as a symbol of mainstream college basketball. During the 1960s, critical discussion about the appropriateness of using indigenous peoples' symbols and rituals in college sports stirred. History professor and antichief activist Fred Hoxie argues that a rise in vocal, well-educated

American Indian activists and the country's own increasing diversity combined to bring the mascot issue to the forefront. Across America, colleges and high schools began shedding American Indian imagery in their sports programs as antimascot lobbyists described them more as discriminatory effigies of Native American culture than symbols of honor and respect. Groups such as I-Resist and the Progressive Resource/Action Cooperative actively campaigned against the chief and other mascots, and the NCAA eventually instituted a sanctions policy of banning universities who use American Indian imagery in their sports programs from national tournaments. On February 21, 2007, the University of Illinois decided to discontinue their use of Chief Illiniwek in any and all representational forms.

In June 2008, the Canadian Broadcast Company (CBC) announced that it would cease using the theme song to its iconic television program *Hockey Night in Canada*. The theme song, known in Canada as the country's second national anthem, is among the most recognized tunes in the country's music history. The composition was originally written by Dolores Claman in 1968 and became one of the longest-running theme songs in broadcasting history. The CBC refused to enter into a new license agreement with respect to the use of the theme (a cost to CBC of approximately $500 for each game broadcast of Hockey Night in Canada) in June of 2008. Because the song is considered a piece of Canadian heritage by people from all walks of life in Canada, public outrage against the decision resulted. Rival broadcasters, CTV Inc., quickly purchased the rights to the song. The theme will be used in NHL broadcasts on CTV beginning in the autumn of 2008. Rick Brace, president of Revenue, Business Planning, and Sports for CTV said, "The song has a long and storied history in Canadian sports and has become ingrained in the hearts and minds of hockey fans across the country. It is an iconic tune, embraced by Canadians everywhere, and we felt it was imperative to save it. We know we will be in hockey forever … it's an honour and a privilege to own such a cherished piece of Canadiana … 'The Hockey Theme' means so much to Canadians, and we know it's in good hands with CTV" (www.ctv.ca).

On their surface, the use of a Native American mascot or the termination of the Hockey Night in Canada theme song seems rather insignificant in the practice of sports such as basketball or ice hockey. Indeed, the mascot or the song had absolutely no impact, one might argue, on how sports matches actually unfolded. But sports insiders will tell you that anything that happens in, near, around, and between playing fields is multilayered with cultural meanings, uses, and purposes. The use of Native American imagery to sell college sports, predominantly by and for white people, provokes questions regarding the historical exploitation and oppression of Native populations in the United States and elsewhere. The sanction tactic adopted by the NCAA, and the University of Illinois's eventual discontinuance of the mascot, are important gestures that signify changing racial ideologies in sports and challenge racially insensitive practices outside of sports. The removal of a television song that brings diverse people together (in a highly fragmented nation) to share in a form of collective identification has clear significance and consequences. The massive public reaction had little to do with the song's role in framing the beginning of the actual games and more to do with how it is a symbol of Canadian heritage and identity.

When considering how sport is culturally significant and socially contested, we must remember that first and foremost it is a social institution. As a social institution, sport is defined and organized by collective ways of thinking that pertain to how games are played, by whom, how they are represented to people, and how the business of sports is operated. Historically, the cultural logics underpinning sports have followed closely along with the ideologies, statuses, identities, and worldviews of the dominant group: white, Christian males in the middle and upper classes. One needs only to think of mainstream sports such as football, baseball, basketball, ice hockey, and golf to find examples of sports that have been utilized as social spaces to reproduce dominant cultural codes and practices of masculinity or Christianity, for example. For nearly 200 years, organized sport has been a place of not only athletic "games" but also a site for transmitting shared values and worldviews between dominant groups. In sociological terms, sport has long been a territory of socialization wherein dominant cultural ways of thinking are transmitted generationally to others.

Involvement in a social practice such as sport has been heavily contoured by cultural logics of problem solving. Until rather recently organized competitive sports have been almost exclusively designed as a cultural training ground for young men; intended to teach them important lessons such as perseverance under pressure, the value of camaraderie and collective problem solving, the benefit of emotional control, the centrality of fairness and justice in everyday life, the importance of assertion and dominance, and the value of hard work and sacrifice in the pursuit of rational and rule-bound goals. Each of these lessons were not accidentally emphasized through sports, they were deliberately inserted into its performance to produce in young men the cultural worldviews they would need to succeed as future husbands, fathers, and community and business leaders. From a culture-as-problem solving perspective, then, sport served a functional role in reproducing masculine hegemony in society. Women, ethnic minorities, religious minorities, and others were either explicitly or implicitly excluded on this basis.

What happens in sport, and the forms of sport, is therefore related to both the structure of a society and the cultural logics transmitted through its institutions. Consider the following. Most social analysts and critics of sports might argue that contemporary sport is a heavily commercial, mass-mediated, transnational/global corporate, body-disciplining social practice. That is, what we even think about as "sport," how sport is organized and played, how it is represented, and how it is often inserted into social institutions such as school, the family, and governmental agencies and appendages, is heavily tied to the ways in which contemporary social life is organized on a large scale and the metalogics that structure our societies (such as competition, power, economic authority, and conquest). Sport is not merely a series of "games" played between people, it is a microcosm of our very social structures and the ideological foundation of their operation.

Additionally, sport—if we take a fully panoramic view of both amateur and professional sports—still tends to be a place where dominant social identities are reproduced. Cultural logics about masculinity, heterosexuality, Christianity, middle-class work, and propriety still abound as underpinning logics about who plays, how they play, and how sport serves a functional role in society. Sport is a place where dominant identities are reaffirmed as the norm and where alternative identities are often muted, ignored, or resisted. Even though women, ethnic minorities, members of the gay and lesbian community, and others are now more represented in sports worlds than ever before, there is little evidence to suggest that the majority of sports are socially and ideologically structured by codes of femininity, socially alternative forms of spirituality, minority ethnic expression, or homosexuality. A long list of sports played in North America that includes lacrosse, swimming, cycling, wrestling, skiing, distance running, auto racing, diving, squash, tennis, bowling, archery, polo, rugby, rowing, sailing, volleyball, triathlon, water polo, equestrian, surfing, fencing, extreme sports, and others indicates that sport may very well remain a social space where dominant cultural logics about normative, mainstream identities prevail.

Notwithstanding the previous comments, if we think critically about the entire social performance of sport and its significance to people, we immediately realize that sport has become a culturally contested space; that is, it is a social battleground where cultures and ideologies are both reproduced over time but also challenged and resisted. Sport in the twentieth century increasingly became a publicly mass-mediate battle site where struggles against racial prejudice, sex and gender discrimination, economic disadvantage, and religious oppression were waged. Due to the mass interest in sport, its insertion into popular culture, its role in schools, its presence in local communities, its global mass mediation, and key pieces of legislation in North America designed to "open up" athletics for all, sport has become a centerpiece social practice where dominant cultural logics are debated, resisted, and changed. In this way, sport is now a site for not merely reproducing dominant cultural logics, but destabilizing them and generating new ones.

The cultural and ideological battles that are fought through sport closely mirror those that are waged in institutions other than sport. As struggles for better educational opportunities, equal access to economic power positions, protection of basic civil and human rights, and freedoms of expression were being waged in schools, workplaces, families, churches, governments, and in the media by marginalized groups of people, so too were they being played out in sports. In looking back at the twentieth century and reviewing landmark cultural battles in sport, we see how they closely linked with collective political struggles in particular eras. The fight to include women in the Olympics had ostensible links to the suffrage movement; Jackie Robinson's crossing of the color line in baseball links with the Civil Rights movement; Billie Jean King's "Battle of the Sexes" match against Bobby Riggs dovetailed with the women's liberation movement; Mohammad Ali's refusal to enlist in the Army to fight in the Vietnam war intersected with student radical, amnesty, and black militancy movements; and the rise of gay and lesbian sports leagues through the 1970s clearly overlapped with

Gay Rights lobbies for basic civil liberties. As a result of sport's mass mediation through the twentieth century and the public nature of many of sport's core cultural battles, victories for minority groups in sport became some of the defining moments in social and civil rights movement on the continent.

At the same time, sport is a cultural space where both long-term and emergent social problems infiltrate its parameters and seriously challenge social constructions of its overall value and purpose. In this instance, sport is not seized as a site for doing collective, politically conscious identity or social rights work; it becomes a place where crime, deviance, and antisocial behavior become rife. The rise of gambling, performance-enhancing or illicit drugs, rape or sexual assault, and cheating cultures in college and professional sports such as basketball and baseball in the United States over the past 60 years raises important questions about what social values sport teaches to young people. Public discussion of brutal hazing cultures in sports, the physical abuse of children at the hands of coaches, and racial profiling and exploitation in particular sports cultures have each undermined the many revered images of athletes we all share. Stories about athlete hubris, the common disrespect and abuse of referees and officials, abusive parents and fans, and other unsavory practices among sports insiders all indicate that there might be pathological cultural logics at work in many sports leagues, organizations, communities, and structures.

Sport has also become a battleground wherein culturally "questionable" or contested social practices that are diffuse in a society receive tremendous spotlight. The subject of player salaries, the corporate branding of sports spaces, the rise of transnational sports corporations, the media's colonization of sport, the heavy emphasis on technology in sport training and performance, and the export and import of athletes into sports leagues around the world are often used as examples of how Western societies such as the United States and Canada have become aggressively corporate, over-mediated, and technologically driven nation-states. These central features are referred to as of "late modern" social life, where all social practices and cultural logics are framed by economic-media-technological forces. From this perspective, late modern sport is nothing more than a site for corporations and mass media agents to generate income, wherein scientific and technological innovation may be tested and implemented.

Sport is also a social place that is not immune to other problems that have deep roots in other institutions but nevertheless infiltrate sports cultures and practices. Diseases and biological threats in society, such as cancer and HIV/AIDS, problems of violent crime and substance abuse among youth, sedentary lifestyles and associated obesity rates, societal trends toward isolation and personal alienation from others, tensions between religious groups, and other external problems to sport, have fundamentally challenged how athletics are structured and performed over the past 50 years. In many ways, sport is progressively used as method of social problem solving and as inoculants against noxious social conditions associated with late modern life. The rise of midnight basketball leagues as safe havens for inner-city youth, "Sport for Peace" or "Sport for All" programs designed to reconcile ethnic or nationalist groups that have been split along religious or class lines, and the emergence of marathon cultures aimed at raising money and awareness about illness through sports are relatively new cultural logics about the functional role of athletics in a society. Such movements illustrate that sport is not only a battleground wherein groups seek to change the structures and cultures of sport to be more inclusionary, but also how sport can be employed as a vehicle for combating outside problems that create divisions between people.

HOW TO READ AND USE THIS BOOK

The entries that comprise *Battleground: Sports* provide a review, description, and analysis of how sport is a cultural battleground in a host of ways. Authors who have contributed to the volumes are educators, activists, historians, and others who are deeply fascinated by how sports can create, negotiate, or potentially solve social problems. Entries across the volumes, which by no means cover every potential battleground issue in sport, provide a relative chronology of sport's social importance in the history of North American identity politics and cultural identification. The entries are intended to prompt questions, stir emotions, disrupt taken-for-granted assumptions about sports, and encourage a new generation of sports enthusiasts to understand how sports is inextricably interlaced with social forces, processes, and trends that exist far away from the playing fields. The entries assert how sport matters as a dominant form of cultural expression and site of ongoing socialization. In the end, the contributors hope readers will dissect, contemplate, and critique the arguments and analyses presented across the volumes. Readers are ultimately encouraged to use information in the book as a point of departure in the ongoing debate about the significance and impacts of battles in sport.

Further Reading: Althusser, L. *Lenin and Philosophy and Other Essays.* London: New Left Books, 1971; Andrews, D. *Sport-Commerce-Culture.* New York: Peter Lang, 2006; Marx, K. *Das Capital,* Volume 1. New York: Penguin, 1863/1992; Miracle, A. and Rees, C. *Lessons of the Locker Room.* New York: Prometheus Books, 1994; Williams, R. *Marxism and Literature.* Oxford: University of Oxford Press, 1977.

Michael Atkinson

ACADEMIC MISCONDUCT AMONG ATHLETES

Academic misconduct in sports occurs when a member of a school team or league willfully and knowingly violates the rules structuring one's involvement in sports. Academic misconduct has many faces and manifestations, ranging from players being paid to play, to players who are "given" grades in order to maintain their status in a school program, to gambling rings involving players and coaches, and to player violence and sexual abuse against others. In particular cases, those involved in academic misconduct are individual "bad apples" in otherwise clean sports cultures. But in many other instances, entire teams or leagues develop into organizations that promote, facilitate, or condone academic misconduct.

BACKGROUND

The reporting and presence of a broad spectrum of deviant behaviors in contemporary school sports conflicts with an ideology that has been used to justify the place of sports in the educational curriculum for nearly 200 years. Because of the complex interplay between competition codes, physical rigor, and personal restraint demanded in highly rule-bound sports, physical educators promoted the idea that sports could foster positive personal characteristics and morals in young people. Specifically, sports could help young people (predominantly young boys) develop high levels of perseverance, confidence, self-restraint, leadership, respect of self and others, resolve, and altruism. By the mid-1800s, athletics were increasingly inserted into North American educational curricula because educators felt that rigorous forms of physical activity played a pivotal role in developing personal character, fostering patriotism and community pride. Christian educators also felt that sports taught students to embody the central tenets of Christianity through competition. Young boys' abilities to work, sacrifice, focus, be dedicated, and to respect a "gentleman's" code of moral conduct were deliberately nurtured through athletics.

In 1857, educators and social reformers in the United States and the United Kingdom started to speak of the need for creating a new generation of young, "muscular Christians." College sports in particular were to be the sites in which Christian values would be reinforced among athletes as a key component in their athletic training. British author Thomas Hughes published his novel *Tom Brown's Schooldays* in 1857, in which he praised the benefits of not only devoting one's heart and mind to God, but the benefits of building a strong body through sports such as rugby, cricket, and soccer to do God's will. Leading the muscular Christian crusade in sports cultures, and publicly promoting the need to link athletics with Christianity in college sport, was the Young Men's Christian Association (YMCA). The YMCA was founded as a Christian outreach movement in industrial America that strived to ensure young Christians possessed the requisite skills to lead new generations at the turn of the twentieth century. One of America's most notable "muscular Christians" was the Victorian-era evangelist D. L. Moody, who brought the YMCA's message to the nation. Interestingly, the sport of basketball had YMCA origins. Canadian-born James Naismith invented the sport at the International Training School of the YMCA in Springfield, Massachusetts. Naismith believed that basketball served as a perfect social ritual for teaching young men Christian values and encouraging young men to socialize and bond with others like them.

Muscular Christianity survived as an ethos in the educational system in North America until the 1960s, during which ideologies of secular humanism (i.e., using sports to produce civic character in athletes without an overt religious link) and more scientifically dominant, kinesiological ways of understanding the need for physical training as a facilitator to good health emerged. Still, however, the idea that sports plays a causal role in fostering positive personal characteristics had been firmly entrenched in educational and popular cultural logics.

To this day, many socialization myths surround high school and university athletics especially in regard to the relationship between sports and personality development, academic success, and future career trajectories. One of the most pervasive myths is that participation in sports is causally linked to academic achievement, dedication, and overall satisfaction. From this perspective, school boards are well justified in promoting extensive sports programs because they are believed to help develop well-rounded students. Organized sports in school is also seen as a pathway to advanced education as recruiters and admission board members might look favorably on someone who is an athlete. Psychologists of sports often add that the increased self-esteem experienced as a result of socialization within sports cultures is also likely to be carried within students even beyond college.

From the 1970s onward, the notion that sports plays a unique role in character and personality development has been the target of much social criticism and academic debate. In 1994, Miracle and Rees published their landmark book *Lessons of the Locker Room,* which systematically deconstructed "the myth" about school sports (i.e., that it plays an incontrovertible role in character development). They reminded people that British and American school headmasters in the nineteenth century used organized sports to socialize their boys into the dominant values of the ruling class. These organized sports were progressively introduced into American public schools as a way of integrating an influx of immigrants into society during both post–World War periods. In cities such as New York, Chicago, Boston, and Philadelphia, social reformers promoted the Public School Athletic League to "Americanize" the growing numbers of immigrant youth. By the 1950, the school sports emphasized American capitalist goals and ideologies (winning, dominance, aggression, and external rewards) over British morality and virtue development through sports. Thus, school sports, according to Miracle and Rees, reflected a leisure-based capitalist training ground saturated by discourses and practices of accumulation, success, and power.

Contemporary research comparing athletes with nonathletes in terms of character traits, personality attributes, or scholastic achievement provide inconsistent and contradictory results, and thus, sports' role or placement within school has come under intense fire. Research into high school sports has revealed that participation in athletics may increase one's educational aspirations (logical, given the work ethos underpinning youth sports) but not necessarily one's grade point average. On the subject of personality development, there is little evidence to substantiate the pervasive claim that sports cultures breed especially gifted moral youth. When such research findings are considered alongside pressures within schools to produce children that are technologically, linguistically, and scientifically savvy, there is a rapidly developing "anti-sports" social movement within educational circles—even in the face of the contemporary moral panic about rising obesity rates among youth.

In 1992, U.S. presidential hopeful Ross Perot started a wave of criticism of sports programs within schools when he publicly grieved that parents are generally concerned more with their children's sporting success than their academic development. He, among others in the 1990s' public debate about school sports, patently rejected the claim that sports builds character or aids in the process of keeping children academically motivated or socially "safe." Others to follow have argued that as the global economy has changed and American industry faces hypercompetition from emerging markets such as India, China, and Germany, the education of American youth should not be riddled with sports.

Miracle and Rees revealed consistent evidence that involvement in sports may actually be detrimental to one's social, emotional, and psychological development. Because athletes are occasionally treated as immensely special and thus catered to in a multitude of ways, they develop unrealistic attitudes regarding their own impunity in any social situation. Following years of coddling, special handling, ego stroking, and accommodation, some athletes perceive there to be few limits on what they can do in their social life, including a full battery of rule/law/norm transgressions. Miracle and Rees's research, conducted before the proverbial lid had been blown off of scandals and deviancy trends in school sports in the United States, foreshadowed current trends of deviancy in school sports by pointing to these consequences of socialization, particularly at the National Collegiate Athletic Association (NCAA) level.

A seemingly endless stream of scandals has been reported in school sports over the past two decades, and each has unquestionably challenged the long-standing cultural ideal that sports serves a functional, prosocial role within educational spheres. For example, stories about athlete deviance within schools, including cases of academic fraud, economic crime, violence, and sexual assault, are unfortunately common in the current era. Here is a small selection of highly publicized cases of deviance in school sports. Consider how they potentially challenge the "myth" that participation in sports fosters special qualities in participants.

KEY EVENTS

The legacy of academic fraud involving athletes at the college or university level in North America is indeed long. It has been pointed out that over the course of the twentieth century, colleges and universities have treated student athletes more like athletes who are students with special privileges. Because they are seen as athletes who play for a university (and who just happen to be students as well), certain academic liberties or leniencies are granted to them from time to time. For example, universities and colleges in the United States and Canada have received formal reprimand for "shepherding" athletes through courses or entire degree programs. Jan Ganglehoff blew the whistle in 1999 on the University of Minnesota's athletics department for the questionable "special treatment" of their athletes. Ganglehoff, who worked as a former basketball office manager at Minnesota, allegedly wrote over 400 term papers or other assignments for Gophers' basketball players. During an internal investigation prompted by Ganglehoff's claims, Minnesota uncovered what its university president called "the most serious case of academic fraud ever reported to the NCAA." Basketball head coach Clem Haskins "voluntarily" resigned, along with several members of the athletics department's executive team. In one of the harshest punishments levied by the NCAA to date, the school's basketball records (from 1993 to 1999) were expunged from the national records.

James Gundlach, a professor at Auburn University, blew the whistle on his university athletics department in a 2004 story printed in the *New York Times*. Gundlach exposed the university's secret system of developing "reading" (one-on-one) courses for star athletes. Gundlach had blown the whistle on a long-term practice in universities and colleges of designing courses especially for athletes so that they would pass them without substantial effort. Among the most legendary of such courses are so-called "rocks for jocks" modules offered in Geology departments. Gundlach's claims prompted an internal school investigation, and Auburn eventually altered the manners by which directed readings courses (most notably in its sociology and education departments) could be offered and administered. The Minnesota and Auburn cases illustrate the complex web of interdependence involved in the ongoing performance of academic fraud involving athletes and how such fraud develops both structurally and culturally within a school over time.

THE "FAB FIVE" SCANDAL

The starting five players on the University of Michigan's basketball team are often referred to as the "Fab Five." In 2002, federal prosecutors (FBI and IRS), NCAA officials, and members of the University of Michigan discovered that long-time Michigan financial booster Ed Martin had illegally given money to Fab Five players as part of a complex gambling and money laundering operation in which he was involved in the 1980s and 1990s. After nearly three years of testimony, it was discovered that four players, Chris Webber (in 1988), Maurice Taylor (from 1996 to 1997), Robert Traylor (in 1994), and Louis Bullock (from 1995 to 1999), had each received tens of thousands of dollars from Martin while playing basketball at Michigan. In one of the biggest gestures of self-punishment to date in college sports, Michigan imposed its own sanctions against the basketball team—targeted at its very legacy—in 2002. The University excused itself from postseason play in 2003; erased from the record books its entire 1992–1993, 1995–1996, and 1998–1999 seasons and its NCAA tournaments records in 1992, 1993, 1996, 1998, and 1999; returned nearly half a million dollars in revenue earned from postseason play in the 1990s; and stripped its own division/playoff titles (and their commemoration around the school) from the records. Sports insiders argue that the University of Michigan may never fully recover from the scandal and neither may the image of college sports.

The Baylor University basketball scandal stands as one of the most intriguing college sports controversies to date. The university's men's basketball program came under intense scrutiny in 2003 when player Carlton Dotson plead guilty to charges of murdering fellow player Patrick Dennehy. Dotson received 35 years in prison for the crime. The investigation into the murder uncovered a legacy of academic fraud within Baylor's basketball program. Investigators discovered that players, including Dennehy, had portions of their tuitions illegally paid for by members of the coaching staff; the team had frequently violated NCAA recruiting rules; coaching staff provided gifts to players; drugs (marijuana and alcohol) existed in the school, and positive drug tests among athletes were not reported; and head coach David Bliss had been heavily involved in the promotion and cover up of rule violations among the players. As a result of the investigation, Baylor imposed preliminary sanctions on its basketball program. Initial sanctions imposed by the school included two years' probation and no postseason play for the 2003–2004 season, and players from the team were transferred to other colleges. The NCAA imposed further penalties on the school in 2005 by extending the university's probation until 2010.

The Baylor University case illustrates the importance of a relatively new NCAA rule designed to severely punish schools who cultivate rule violations and cheating. The so-called death penalty rule was instituted in the NCAA prior to the 1985 season. The rule takes aim at college and university sports programs that have been identified as repeat offenders. Arguably the harshest punishment against a sports culture of academic offending, the death penalty rule allows the NCAA to ban a college or university sports team (from any participation at the postsecondary level) if a second major violation of NCAA rules is discovered among them within five years after being initially placed on probation. Prior to the development of the official death penalty rule, the University of Kentucky's men's basketball team was the first recipient of a death penalty–like sentence. Basketball players Alex Groza, Ralph Beard, and Dale Barnstable were each found guilty in 1951 of point shaving during the 1949 season. As a result of the case, the Southeastern Conference of the NCAA banned Kentucky from conference play in 1952–1953. In November 1951, at the height of the investigation, National Basketball Association (NBA) President Maurice Podoloff declared that all the players involved in the scandal were barred from the league for life.

The second, and only other, death penalty sentence was given to the Southern Methodist University football team in 1986. The team had already been placed on three years' probation in 1985, but merely one year later, they faced allegations that nearly two dozen players were receiving compensation to play. As a result, the 1987 season was cancelled, all home games in 1988 were cancelled, the program would not be allowed to participate in Bowl games or appear on television between 1988 and 1989, new coaches and assistant coaches were hired, players were redistributed to other universities, and the university rescinded 55 new football scholarships. In deciding the case, the NCAA cited a need to break the historical cultural of academic fraud and wrongdoing at the university. Of note, SMU had been placed on probation a staggering seven times before receiving their final death penalty in 1986. Since the SMU case, the NCAA came close to administering the death penalty to the University of Kentucky's basketball program in 1986 and to the University of Alabama's football program in 2002 (in both cases for alleged player payment and recruiting violations).

In 2004, the national media highlighted another chilling instance of academic misconduct among athletes, that of sexual assault. For quite some time, allegations of sexually abusive behavior by athletes, and its tolerance by university staff, have plagued school sports programs. In 2004, three members of the La Salle University men's basketball program were accused of rape on two separate occasions. Gary Neal and Mike Cleaves were accused, and later acquitted, of raping a 19-year-old University of New Haven student. Dzaflo Larkai was accused, and also later acquitted, of raping a member of La Salle's women's basketball team. As a result of the incidents, all three players were suspended indefinitely from the university. The head coaches of both the men's and women's basketball team, Billy Hahn and John Miller, were forced to resign their posts after their knowledge of the incidents, but failure to report them, surfaced during the investigations.

Each of these scandals are indeed shocking due to their scale, the duration, and the extent to which insiders attempted to conceal athlete, coach, administrator, and sponsor wrongdoing for extended periods. These examples and others have accomplished more in the recent past to undermine the cultural ideology that school sports programs are especially virtuous social grounds.

FUTURE PROSPECTS

Among the most frightening realizations made when reviewing cases of academic fraud and misconduct within school systems is that while reported cases are certainly disheartening for sports enthusiasts, there simply may be more egregious deviant cultures in school sports yet to be discovered. If the recent past is any indicator, members of college and university sports programs may be deterred from engaging in considerable deviance from time to time following highly publicized cases of punishment, but even rules such as the NCAA's death penalty do not seem effective enough to eradicate fraud from academic sports cultures. School sports may have finally reached a historical point in which only the scarcest trace of character-building through sports is emphasized within its culture.

See also Cheating During Competition; Criminal Violence During Competition; Gambling; Governments, Laws, and Gambling; Marijuana, Alcohol, and Illicit Drugs; Partner Abuse Among Athletes; Salaries of Professional Athletes; Whistle-Blowers and Drugs.

Further Reading: Lapchick, R. (1987). *On the Mark: Putting the Student Back in Student-Athlete.* Massachusetts: Lexington Books; Maloney, M. (1993). An Examination of the Role that Intercollegiate Athletic Participation Plays in Academic Achievement: Athletes' Feats in the Classroom. *Journal of Human Resources* 28: 555–570; Miracle, A., and Rees, C. R. (1994). *Lessons of the Locker Room.* New York: Prometheus Books.

Michael Atkinson

ADVENTURE RACING

Adventure racing is performed as a combination of two or more athletic disciplines, such as orienteering (wilderness navigation over a set time and distance), cross-country running, mountain biking, paddling, and rock climbing. An adventure race can span 10 days or more, while "sprint" races can be completed in a matter of hours. Adventure racing historically required teams to be of a specified size and to include both men and women, but many races no longer restrict team size and include single-sex divisions. Some also include age-based categories. The general purpose of an adventure race is to test competitors' abilities to withstand intense physical and emotional ordeals during a sports contest. The "untamed" wilderness settings in which the races occur add elements of risk or danger to the overall atmosphere for competitors.

BACKGROUND

The roots of adventure racing are relatively deep, and people debate the origin of the modern adventure race in North America. Some argue that modern so-called extreme adventure racing is an offshoot of the Australian sport of rogaining. Rogaining is a form of adventure racing wherein either individuals or teams compete to travel a preset distance in the wilderness that covers a variety of terrain and requires participants to employ a variety of physical skills (such as hiking, running, climbing, descending, and often, swimming). In a garden-variety race, participants are required to navigate to specific check points on the course as they make their way to a preestablished finish point. The word *rogaining* is derived from the names of three of the founders, Rod Phillips, Gail Davis, and Neil Phillips (RoGaiNe, hence *rogaining* or *rogainer*) who were all members of the now famous Surrey-Thomas Rover Crew.

Yet rogaining can trace its roots back to 1947 when the first of many events featuring rogaining was organized by the Melbourne University Mountaineering Club. These events led to the birth of the sport of rogaining in April 1976 in Melbourne, Australia. The sport was named, rules were adopted, and the world's first rogaining association was formed (the Victorian Rogaining Association). Therefore, quite some time before other (and now more globally influential) extreme or counter-cultural sports like surfing, skateboarding, and snowboarding had surfaced, rogaining had been well established as a radical sports alternative for adventure and adrenaline seekers. Growth of the association and the sport occurred rapidly through the 1980s, as new cultural tastes and preferences from extreme sports were developing around the globe. Here, adventure racers and rogainers viewed most of mainstream sport as overly controlled, hierarchical, dominated by coaches, and emotionally contained. By contrast, new outdoor sports eschewed the notion of doing athleticism within tight confines of the gym, or the artificial playing field. Instead, rogaining events deliberately placed people in often unpredictable and risk-filled natural environments.

Rogaining was introduced to North America by Canadian orienteer Jim Force who toured Australia during the World Orienteering Championship (WOC) in 1985. The first rogaining competition in North America was in Canada in September 1986 at Lake Minnewanka, Alberta, in the Canadian Rockies near Calgary; it was hosted by Kitty Jones, Andy Newson, and Jim Force. Winners were Stuart Wood and John Laycock, and there were 89 participants in 30 teams. The first U.S. rogaining competition was in May 1989 at Buck Meadows, Wenatchee National Forest, in Washington State in the Cascades near Ellensburg; it was hosted by the Washington State Orienteering Association with Bob Reddick, Carl Moore, Knut Olson, and many others from four area clubs. When the U.S. Orienteering Federation (USOF) adopted rogaining and created a Rogaine Committee, many other rogaines followed in North America.

In 1994, the Australian Rogaining Association (ARA) President Peter Taylor visited the United States and developed the concept of an annual North American Rogaining Championship. This event has provided a focus for North American rogaining and increased expertise in competing in and organizing 24-hour rogaines. On June 25, 1994, the first North American Rogaining Championship was run by Sage Orienteering Club (Canada); the 1995 event was run by Columbia River Orienteering Club (USA); the third championship on July 20, 1996, was organized by Central New York Orienteering (USA); and the March 1997 event was run by Tucson Orienteering Club (USA).

In discussing the origins of modern adventure racing, other historians point to the two-day Karrimor International Mountain Marathon, first held in 1968, as the birth of the sport; or at least, the widespread recognition of its presence in alternative-sport cultures. The Karrimor Marathon required two-person teams to traverse mountainous terrain while carrying all the supplies required to sustain themselves through the double-length marathon run. In 1980, the Alpine Ironman was held in New Zealand. Individual competitors ran, paddled, and skied to a finish line over 100 miles away. Later that year, the Alpine Ironman's creator, Robin Judkins, launched the better-known Coast-to-Coast race, which involved most of the elements of modern adventure racing: trail running, cycling, and paddling. Independently, a North American race, the Alaska Mountain Wilderness Classic, debuted in 1982 and involved six days of unsupported wilderness racing (carry all food and equipment, no roads, no support) over a 150-mile course.

In 1989, Gerald Fusil launched the Raid Gauloises in New Zealand. Inspired by the Paris-Dakar Rally dune buggy race, Fusil envisioned an expanded expedition-style race in which competitors would rely on their own strength and abilities to traverse great and challenging terrain. The race included all the modern elements of adventure racing, including mixed-gender teams competing in a multiday, 400-plus–mile race. Building on Fusil's concept, the inaugural Southern Traverse was held in New Zealand in 1991.

KEY EVENTS

Adventure racing was a relatively fringe sports activity until the early 1990s. After purchasing the rights from Gerald Fusil to the Raid race, American Mark Burnett launched the first Eco-Challenge race in 1995. The Eco-Challenge was held from 1995 to 2002. With the Eco-Challenge also came the widely promoted public name *adventure race,* a term coined by American journalist and author Martin Dugard to describe the class of races embodied by the Raid and Eco-Challenge.

The Eco-Challenge was designed as a multiday race in which teams of four competed. Eco-Challenge creator Mark Burnett had competed in two Raid Gauloises events and decided to fashion his own version of the race. Each Eco-Challenge team comprised a mandatory mix of both men and women who raced nonstop, 24-hours a day, over a rugged 300-mile (500-km) course, participating in trekking, white water canoeing, horseback riding, sea kayaking, scuba diving, mountaineering, and mountain biking. Teams originally consisted of five members, but the team size was eventually reduced to four members.

Each Eco-Challenge was broadcast on cable television. The 1995 Utah race was shown as a 45-minute feature, produced by and broadcast on MTV. The 1995 Maine/New England event was broadcast in segments as part of the X Games broadcast on ESPN. Starting in 1996, Eco-Challenge was aired on the Discovery Channel, and the production enjoyed a significantly expanded budget. The 1996 British Columbia production, broadcast on the Discovery Channel, won an American Emmy Award. In 2000, the USA Network agreed to a three-year contract to broadcast the Eco-Challenge. Later that year, the show was nominated for a Prime-Time Emmy Award. USA did not renew the show after the 2002 Fiji race due to poor ratings.

ECO-CHALLENGE TIMELINE

1995 USA
1995 USA (as part of the X Games adventure race)
1996 Canada
1997 Australia
1998 Morocco
1999 Argentina
2000 Sabah, Borneo
2001 New Zealand
2002 Fiji

The first major expedition-length race to be held exclusively in the United States was launched in 2002 and called Primal Quest. Primal Quest quickly became the premier U.S. expedition race and has been held each year since its launch. In 2004, the death of veteran racer Nigel Aylott overshadowed the race and raised debates about the safety of Primal Quest and adventure racing. Aylott was killed during an orienteering section of the Primal Quest race. However, Aylott's death may have unintentionally stirred increased interest in the sport as a risk activity among athletic thrill seekers.

Indeed, adventure racing has been plagued with participant injury since its inception in North America. As a result, progressive rule systems have been designed in major adventure races in order to protect participants from harm. While the rules of adventure racing vary by length of race or organizing company, virtually all races include the three main rules of racing: no motorized travel; no outside assistance except at designated transition areas (assistance from competing teams is generally permitted at all times); and teams must carry all mandatory gear designated by race officials. Primal Quest races include penalties for: unsportsmanlike conduct, public protest, or "displays of disgust" with race rules; failing to travel as a team; traveling outside of the field's boundaries; destruction of property; damage to race equipment; testing positive for banned substances; losing or not wearing your race bib; and administration of IV fluids other than by race medical staff. Longer races may also involve skill or even fitness tests; such as requiring team members to swim 50 meters, tread water, or ascend a vertical cliff.

Three deaths of adventure racers intensified debates about the safety of the sport. In June 2003, Dominique Robert was killed when she was pinned underwater during a canoe section of the Raid Gauloises. On September 21, 2004, as previously noted, Nigel Aylott was killed by a falling boulder during an orienteering section of Primal Quest. Eduardo Delgado Rosas died on February 24, 2005, while completing a one-kilometer swimming leg of the Extreme Adventure Hidalgo. The death of these athletes has enhanced scrutiny and fueled debate regarding the purpose of adventure racing, with some participants calling for international regulation of the sport in order to better ensure the safety of racers.

In some more exotic locales, danger of contact with unusual pathogens should be taken into account. In the Borneo Eco-Challenge (2000), dozens of participants were hospitalized with leptospirosis. Renal shutdown and heat stroke are other common health concerns during endurance events. The Canadian Adventure Racing Association (a registered amateur athletic association) has drafted comprehensive safety guidelines for use in Canada. The safety guidelines are a working document and have been revised several times by industry experts and government agencies. They serve as the benchmark for adventure racers across Canada and are being considered as a template for the rest of the adventure racing world.

The allure of adventure racing to participants is very common to other extreme sports that ascended in popularity through the 1990s. Adventure racing is often described as a "liminal" event (Turner, 1969) or threshold event, in which an individual finds his or her limits and pushes through them. Racing often takes participants out of their comfort zone by challenging competitors with unfamiliar surroundings, often while sleep deprived and physically exhausted. In this sense, the true battleground in an adventure race is one's own body and mind.

Adventure races such as Eco Challenge and Primal Quest rose to popularity during a cultural period in which growing numbers of North Americans were dissatisfied with mainstream sports experiences. Many of the first generation adventure racers were also endurance athletes from other sports who were either seeking cross-training opportunities or more thrilling, and team based, sports experiences. Scores of adventure racers were former triathletes or marathoners (and ultramarathoners) looking for new challenges. Aging athletes in these fields discovered that while they could no longer keep up with 20 year olds in a foot race, in a 24+ hour race, they held competitive advantages gleaned through years of experience with endurance events.

FUTURE PROSPECTS

Public appetite for risk or edge sports seems to be increasing with every year. Sports including rock climbing, sky diving, back country or cliff skiing, BASE jumping, and a full range of other extreme sports have become part of popular culture in North America. As one of these socially alternative and risky sports, adventure racing continues to be attractive for people who seek out grueling tests of endurance in the leisure sphere.

See also Snowboarding; Surfing and New Water Sports; Ultraendurance Running; X Games; Yoga and Alternative Fitness.

Further Reading: Dugard, M. (1999). *Surviving the Toughest Race on Earth.* Whitby, ON: Ragged Mountain Press; Marais, J., and de Speville, L. (2004). *Adventure Racing.* Champaign, IL: Human Kinetics; Tuner, V. (1969). *The Ritual Process: Structure and Anti-Structure.* Chicago: Aldine; Wheaton, B. (2004). *Understanding Lifestyle Sports.* London: Routledge.

Michael Atkinson

ANIMAL BLOOD SPORTS

Animal blood sports are competitions or games involving animals (and sometimes humans) where there is an implicit risk or probability that one of the participants will be harmed, wounded, or killed during the course of events. Typically, animal blood sports are those in which animals are subject to being chased and killed (e.g., foxhunting) or those that place participants in direct physical combat with one another (e.g., dogfighting). They are called "blood sports" because, as part of the competition, blood is drawn from at least one of the participants involved.

BACKGROUND

Animal blood sports have a long tradition in human cultures. Roman gladiators (ca. 260 B.C.) were known to fight wild animals such as lions and tigers at the Coliseum and Circus Maximus in contests called *venationes*. It is also believed that the practice of "baiting" animals for sport originated around the same time in Rome. *Baiting* refers to the practice of tormenting (typically chained or confined) animals by encouraging another animal (most frequently a dog) to attack them. A baiting contest ends when the chained or subdued animal is killed. Until the mid-nineteenth century in countries such as Great Britain, a full range of animals was used in baiting contests: donkeys, tigers, bulls, horses, bears, monkeys, lions, and even boars, in some rare cases. Until the turn of the twentieth century, forms of cricket baiting could be found in China and camel baiting in several northern African countries. In the Americas, badgers have been used in baiting contests, as have hogs and rats. Most Western nations banned the practice of baiting in the mid-nineteenth century.

A modern-day remnant of baiting culture is dogfighting. Dogfighting, traceable back to both ancient Rome and Japan, can be defined as the act of combat between two dogs for the entertainment and financial profit of spectators. The sport, historically popular in the United States, the United Kingdom, Afghanistan, Australia, Japan, Argentina, South Africa, Honduras, Colombia, and Brazil, involves placing two dogs into a fighting "pit." Their handlers then release the dogs and they scratch, claw, and bite one another until one dog either quits or dies. In addition to the dogs, there are typically two handlers and a referee in the pit during the contest. The battles are watched by spectators who bet on the outcome of the fights. American historians of dogfighting, such as Hanna Gibson, tell us that the modern-day version of the sport was, for all intents and purposes, "born" in 1835 in England (ironically, the same year British officials passed the Humane Act prohibiting baiting), with the widespread introduction and popularization of the Staffordshire Bull Terrier—and later the American Pit Bull terrier—into the sport. Through the nineteenth century, these breeds were trained to be two of the most aggressive on earth. They joined the ranks of other historical vicious fighting dogs such as the Great Dane, Tibetan Mastiff, Molossus, Old English Bulldog, and the Dogo Argentino.

Even though the sport of dogfighting is now illegal in 48 American states, the culture of dogfighting continues to thrive in states such as Louisiana.

Problematically, the sport there has been linked to forms of street crime such as drug trafficking, homicide, illegal gambling, assault, rape, weapons trafficking, and cruelty to animals. The Humane Society of the United States estimates that, in 2006, there were 45,000 dogfighters in the United States alone, generating over $5 million in illegal revenue from dogfight matches. In addition to the brutal violence the dogs face in the ring, they are often subject to intense and painful training programs by their handlers, are physically abused and neglected by their handlers when not performing "well" in competition, and are often force fed performance-enhancing drugs by trainers (Atkinson and Young, 2008).

An even older and more globally popular form of animal pit fighting is cockfighting. It is widely believed that the practice of cockfighting—similar to dogfighting, except that a special breed of an Indian rooster takes the place of dogs—is perhaps the oldest spectator sport, dating back 6,000 years to ancient Persia (modern-day Iran). It is difficult, in the study of human history, to find a more widely practiced and watched blood sport than cockfighting. The sport historically flourished in India (where it is known as *aseel*), China, and along the Mediterranean during the fourth century B.C. and spread throughout the world over the course of sea exploration and colonization. Famous military leaders throughout time, including Alexander the Great and George Washington, were reputed cockfighting enthusiasts, as were many generations of British royalty from the twelfth to the nineteenth centuries. By the mid-1700s, British nobility once referred to cockfighting as the "sport of kings."

Today, the blood sport of cockfighting is especially popular in Belgium, France, Spain, Mexico, the Philippines, Puerto Rico, Guam, the United States, and Haiti. In several of these countries, public stadiums have been constructed to house cockfight matches. Just like the dogs involved in pit-fighting contests, gamecocks suffer intensely through competition. Animal rights advocates have therefore targeted the sport for termination. The gamecocks are bred and "designed" to be especially combative and aggressive. Parts of their bodies may be cut off (including the wattle at their necks) to prevent injury during matches, and they may be fitted around the legs with metal spurs (called "cockspurs") for gouging their opponents during fights. They are often given drugs to boost their aggression, and they may even have parts of their skin burned with chemicals to harden their flesh and protect them from injury in the game ring. Despite the extent of cruelty in the sport, cockfighting continues to be an important part of social expression and identity in cultures around the world.

While some baiting sports and animal pit fighting such as dogfighting and cockfighting have partly gone "underground" over time, traditional English forms of foxhunting and hare coursing are blood sports that remained publicly legitimate until quite recently (ca. 2005). Foxhunting, the practice of using scent hounds such as Beagles to track and kill a fox, dates back to ancient Egypt. Through the fourteenth and fifteenth centuries, foxhunting ascended in popularity in Britain especially, eventually being viewed by the British elite as a noble and civilized form of sports. Through colonization, the English exported foxhunting to countries such as Canada, the United States, India, and Ireland.

Hare coursing—the chasing of a rabbit by two dogs in an open field or space with the intention of catching it or making it turn in a particular direction—is believed to have originated in ancient Greece and has a long history in countries such as England, Ireland, and the United States. The oldest form of hare coursing simply involved two dogs pursuing a live hare with the winner being the dog that caught and killed the hare. There are two main forms of "open" hare coursing: "driven coursing" and "walk-up coursing." In driven coursing hares were flushed out of cover by "beaters" (i.e., one or several men who literally beat the bushes or grasses with sticks and rods) to run toward a designated coursing field. As they entered the field, a person known as a "slipper" released two dogs at the same time to chase the hare. In walk-up coursing, a line of people walk through the countryside, and a pair of dogs is released once a hare runs out of the woods on its own. The practice of coursing fell into considerable disrepute in the United Kingdom and America in the 1970s. By 2002, British and Scottish governments banned open coursing through national legislation. However, in both Northern Ireland and the United States, attempts made by anticoursing lobbyists such as the Irish Council against Bloodsports (Ireland), People for the Ethical Treatment of Animals (PETA, U.S.), and Animal Place (U.S.) have been unsuccessful in convincing federal legislators to criminalize the practice.

KEY EVENTS

One of the most well-known animal blood sports in the Western world is a close sporting cousin to hare coursing. Greyhound racing, a predominantly legal practice in countries where it occurs, is one of the most globally popular animal blood sports, along with cockfighting, and game hunting or fishing.

By the 1720s, greyhounds had been imported in great numbers to the American colonies as the favored dogs in the sport of hare coursing. Noblemen from England brought the emerging tradition of hare coursing to the Americas around 1840 and exposed audiences to greyhounds in the process—soon after, they began racing the dogs for sport by themselves (Branigan, 1997). After a series of failed attempts to create an even bloodier coursing culture, Owen Patrick

---

DID YOU KNOW

The ancient Egyptians, Romans, and Greeks revered the greyhound—the world's oldest purebred dog—as a companion, hunter, and religious icon. Pharaohs, including Sesotris, Tutankhamen, Amenhotep II, and Ramses IV, were even buried with greyhounds. Early Christian respect for the breed was so high that the greyhound is the only dog mentioned by name in the Holy Bible. The Irish, in particular, embraced the greyhound as a mythic and poetic creature. Following suit, British and other European (e.g., French, Spanish, and German) noble classes adopted the greyhound as a distinguished companion during the Middle Ages. British monarchs from the sixth to the eighteenth centuries (e.g., King Canute, King Harold, and King Edward III) elevated the greyhound's status through legal code as *the* companion and trusted hunting animal.

Smith helped establish the first modern greyhound racetrack in 1910 in Oakland, California. Smith introduced a primitive form of coursing/racing several years earlier, staging contests where greyhounds were released in sealed pens with live hares. In response to the crowd's horror to the sight of the killings, Smith, an engineer, developed the first electronic lure—a device he called the "Inanimate Hare Conveyor"—to stage a more humane race.

Until the 1990s, greyhound racing served as a staple of American sports cultures, ranking as the sixth most popular spectator sport during the period. Through the majority of the twentieth century, greyhound racing held a central position in the American gambling cultures and as a tourist attraction, especially in the southern United States. With this said, the sport of greyhound racing has come under intense scrutiny in the past two decades for the manner in which dogs are treated at tracks and in races.

According to the National Greyhound Association (NGA), there are, on average, approximately 34,000 racing greyhounds born in the United States each year, and 28,000 are registered to race every year. Estimates suggest that approximately 50,000 to 60,000 greyhounds are used as racers. At the present time, 46 tracks are in operation in 16 American states, generating over $100 million in revenue per year. A greyhound track, at any given time, may house up to 1,000 dogs through a series of kennels. A kennel operator is in charge of all dogs in a specific kennel (anywhere from 10–100 plus dogs). The dogs are often kept in rows of stacked cages (some cages are only 24 inches wide) and are housed and muzzled up to 22 hours per day. The dogs are taken out several (1–4) times per day to urinate/defecate and usually once to eat and receive water. Due to the stacking approach to kenneling, the wire mesh nature of the kennels, and the lack of proper flooring in each, greyhounds at the bottom rows are showered with the waste of others. At some of the more disreputable tracks, music is blasted in the kennels to drown out the constant barking or whining of the dogs (Atkinson and Young, 2005).

Over a dozen cases of transportation-related deaths involving greyhounds have been reported since 1993 by animal rights advocacy groups. Deaths occur when greyhounds are left unattended in small caravans or wagons (when being transported between race tracks) in extreme heat conditions. In such cases, the dogs die of either heat exhaustion or dehydration. From overuse in races and the intensity of the races themselves, pain and injury inevitably occur. Some greyhounds live through pain on a daily basis—broken bones, torn ligaments or muscles, back and neck injuries, lacerations, and facial abrasions caused by muzzling are common. Rather than feeding the dogs a high-caliber diet, some tracks utilize what has been termed "4-D" (dead, dying, downed, diseased) meat to temporarily sustain the greyhounds' bodies. This meat is often full of E-coli toxins and may not be sold commercially according to USDA standards. It is illegally purchased for pennies per pound, and its consumption may lead to a skin condition in the dogs referred to by dog handlers as "Alabama rot" (open lesions and ulcers) or an intestinal problem referred to as "blow-out" (chronic vomiting and diarrhea leading to death from dehydration).

Due to dismal sanitary conditions at some of the low-budget tracks, greyhounds may suffer from hookworm, tapeworm, whipworm, and giardia. In the past six years, outbreaks of kennel cough in several American racetracks have killed several dozen greyhounds. Many die each year from on-track collisions and falls (often smaller females are trampled in races with large males) or from electrocution by electric lure systems. The disposal (i.e., getting rid of them when they no longer win races) of the dogs varies considerably, but two main trends appear to occur most frequently. First, greyhounds may be individually killed following their retirement as racers. Colloquially referred to as "going back to the farm," a greyhound's life may be ended in a rather unceremonious manner. Although such disposal methods do not appear to represent an industry standard, racing greyhounds in the United States may be bludgeoned, hung, starved to death, abandoned in a field or woods, decapitated, electrocuted (known as a "Tijuana hotplate"), sold to local fishermen (to be used for shark chum), given to a local hunter, or sold to a medical laboratory for research purposes. Tracks may employ the services of a "for hire" killer, who will terminate a greyhound for a fee ($10 to $20 per dog).

An even more disturbing trend is the mass killing of racing hounds. Since the mid-1990s, antiracing organizations have reported the discovery of so-called killing fields of dog carcasses in the United States and Europe. Greyhounds have been found dead in rural grasslands, tied to railway tracks, or stacked in local dumpsters. Medical laboratories and a handful of American universities have been targeted as "mass murderers" of greyhounds, and the entire racing figuration has been labeled by animal rights groups as abusive and inhumane.

Throughout the late twentieth century, groups such as the Society for the Prevention of Cruelty to Animals (SPCA), PETA, and the Animal Liberation Front (ALF) have consistently and quite publicly raised ethical concerns about the treatment of greyhounds, and greyhound racing has fallen into moderate disrepute in North America. Since 1993, dozens of tracks have closed in the 16 American states still permitting greyhound racing, although these have been primarily business decisions in response to rapidly declining profits.

American adoption and rescue agencies such as Wings for Greyhounds, Second Chance for Greyhounds, Operation Greyhound, and the Greyhound Protection League have helped place retired racers in private homes, and antiracing groups such as the national Greyhound Protection League and Pennsylvania's Citizens Against Greyhound Racing, continue to call for the outright termination of the sport.

The sport of bullfighting is one of the most culturally revered and ritualistic of all animal blood sports. Indeed, the author Ernest Hemingway immortalized the sport in his 1932 book, *Death in the Afternoon.* Traced back to the Minoa Crete sport of "bull jumping"—where youths sought to hop over charging bulls (a sport now popular in the southwestern United States and Mexico)—modern bullfighting is a popular sport in Spain, France, Portugal, Peru, Colombia, Venezuela, India, Ecuador, and Mexico. Spain alone has over 400 bullfighting venues and is regarded as the cultural center of the sport in our time. It is also recognized as the modern birthplace of bullfighting as a sport.

A bullfight in Spain (called *corrida de toros*), like in Portugal and France, is a massive spectator event and deeply patterned by pageantry, ritual, and custom. Bullfights in the country are directly linked to times of cultural festival, such as the city of Pamplona's famous "running of the bulls" in the city's streets.

In a traditional Spanish bullfight, the matador confronts the bull in a circular arena that is encased by walls four- to five-feet tall. The matador may be supported by a crew of up to six assistants on horseback. These assistants help deliver initial wounds to the bull using spears, lances, or swords in highly scripted and ritualistic ways. The matador is responsible for delivering the "death blow"—referred to as the *escotada*—at which time the confrontation ends. Following its death, the bull is normally tied to, and dragged from the ring by, mules. Subtle variations on the sport's performance are evident around the world; for example, in Portugal, the bull is not killed in the ring but rather taken away from the audience's view and then slaughtered by a professional butcher. In countries such as France, even the bulls (those successfully surviving a match) become legendary figures. Since gorings of matadors are not uncommon, French bullfighters often meet their deaths on the horns of a bull. One of the most celebrated bulls of all time in France was Islero, who supposedly killed many bullfighters including the popular matador Manolete.

Estimates suggest that 50,000 bulls are killed yearly in matches around the world. As a result of the inhumane treatment of the bulls in the sport, and the painfully slow manner by which they die, anti-bullfighting groups such as the League Against Cruel Sports have lobbied for the sport's criminalization. By claiming that the law in European countries is "speciesist" (prejudice against a certain species) and unfair to animals, groups such as No Mas Violencia in Spain have urged economic boycotts against any organization or government supporting the practice. In Brazil and Argentina, animal welfare reformists successfully encouraged their governments to ban the sport. Greenpeace and The International Movement Against Bullfights have also urged, on a global scale, for the termination of all bullfights and similar animal sports. In California, American bullfighters have responded by pioneering a "bloodless" bullfight, where a large piece of Velcro fabric is attached to the back of the bull, and a Velcro-tipped spear is struck against the bull by a matador to symbolically represent a death strike.

FUTURE PROSPECTS

In the past three or four decades, global animal rights activists have challenged the cultural legitimacy of sports such as bullfighting, greyhound racing, dogfighting, and others. The recent banning of foxhunting in the United Kingdom—a centuries-old tradition—perhaps shows how our sensitivities to the care or suffering of animals in sports are changing. Groups such as PETA in the United States have argued that, culturally, we need a new view on the role of animals in sports and entertainment. Among other things, PETA argues that animals are not placed on earth for our entertainment, torture, or amusement. They, like all other creatures, are subjects of their own independent lives with physical and emotional needs. In fact, as creatures with the capacity for caring and nurturing, it is our social responsibility to protect, PETA argues, rather than injure animals. PETA members suggest that if we view animals as equal to humans in nature, and if we approach our coexistence with them from a "let's do them minimal harm" perspective, we would simply not want to participate in or witness any form of blood sports in the future (see www.peta.org).

See also Environmental Impacts of Sports; Mascots.

Further Reading: Atkinson, M., and Young, K. (2005). Reservoir Dogs. *International Review for the Sociology of Sport* 40: 335–356; Atkinson, M., and Young, K. (2008). *Deviance and Social Control in Sport.* Champaign, IL: Human Kinetics; Branigan, J. (1997). *The Reign of the Greyhound.* New York: Howell Book House; Hemingway, E. (1932). *Death in the Afternoon.* New York: Scribner.

Michael Atkinson

ANTIDOPING RULES AND POLICIES

The word *doping* is probably derived from the Dutch word *dop,* the name of an alcoholic beverage made of grape skins used by Zulu warriors in order to enhance their prowess in battle. The term became well-known in sports cultures around the turn of the twentieth century, originally referring to illegal drugging of racehorses. The practice of enhancing performance through foreign substances or other artificial means, however, is as old as competitive sports itself. Ancient Greek athletes, for example, are believed to have used special diets and "stimulating potions" to fortify themselves. Strychnine, caffeine, cocaine, and alcohol were often used by cyclists and other endurance athletes in the nineteenth century. Olympic sports legend suggests that Thomas Hicks ran to victory in the Olympic marathon of 1904 in St. Louis by help of raw egg, injections of strychnine, and doses of brandy administered to him during the race. By the 1920s, it had become evident that restrictions regarding drug use in sports were necessary. It was not until 1982, however, that the World Anti-Doping Association (WADA) was created to set and enforce doping rules in global sports culture.

BACKGROUND

In 1928, the International Amateur Athletic Federation (IAAF) became the first international sports federation to ban the use of athlete doping (use of stimulating substances). Members of the IAAF believed that doping violated the ethos of fair play underpinning amateur sports. Many other global sports federations followed suit, but their restrictions remained ineffective because tests to detect foreign substances in the body were not pioneered or administered with consistency. During this period, the problem of doping was made worse by the invention and mass distribution of synthetic hormones (invented in the 1930s and increasingly used for doping purposes since the 1950s). The death of Danish cyclist Knud Enemark Jensen during competition at the Olympic Games in Rome in 1960 increased the pressure for sports authorities to introduce drug tests (the autopsy revealed traces of amphetamine in Jensen's system). In 1966, the International Cycling Union (UCI, Union Cycliste Internationale) and the International Federation of Association Football (FIFA, Fédération Internationale de Football Association; the governing body of soccer) were among the first international federations to introduce doping tests in their respective World Championships. In 1967, the death of cyclist Tom Simpson during the Tour de France, attributed to the overconsumption of stimulants, served to highlight the need for stronger antidoping policies; the same year, the International Olympic Committee (IOC) instituted its Medical Commission and set up its first list of prohibited substances. Drug tests were introduced for the first time at the Olympic Winter Games in Grenoble and at the Olympic Games in Mexico in 1968.

Most international sports federations implemented drug testing by the 1970s. The use of anabolic steroids was becoming widespread in Olympic strength events because there was no way of detecting them yet. A reliable test method was finally introduced in 1974, and the IOC added anabolic steroids to its list of prohibited substances in 1976. This resulted in a marked increase in the number of drug-use disqualifications in the late 1970s, notably in strength-related sports such as throwing events and weightlifting. Antidoping regulation was complicated in the 1970s and 1980s due to suspicions of state-sponsored doping being practiced in some countries.

The most famous doping case of the 1980s concerned Ben Johnson, the 100-meter champion who tested positive for stanozolol (anabolic steroid) at the Olympic Games in Seoul in 1988. Johnson's case focused to an unprecedented degree the world's attention on the doping problem, and the need for greater institutional control of doping. There is an evident connection between more effective test methods and a remarkable drop in the level of top results in some sports in the 1990s, notably in track and field athletics. While the fight against stimulants and steroids was producing results, the main front in the antidoping war was rapidly shifting to blood doping. "Blood boosting," removal and subsequent reinfusion of the athlete's blood in order to increase the level of oxygen-carrying hemoglobin, has been practiced since the 1970s. The IOC banned blood doping as a method in 1986, but the practice continues today.

KEY EVENTS

Over the course of time, pivotal events in sports underlined the need for more substantial institutional mechanisms that could control, and possibly prevent, athlete doping. Among the most influential was the revelation that East German (GDR) Olympic athletes were unwittingly given performance-enhancing drugs over the course of some 30 years. Between 1960 and 1990, East Germans ran, swam, and shot-putted their way to glory, winning Olympic gold medals and setting world records. The proverbial "lid" was blown off the practice in the 1990s, when several groups of athletes sued East German government agencies and pharmaceutical companies. Approximately 190 East German competitors launched a case against the German pharmaceutical company Jenapharm. They claimed that the East German firm knowingly supplied the steroids that were given to them by trainers and coaches from the 1960s onwards until East Germany's official state demise in 1989. Jenapharm executives argued that it was not responsible for the doping scandal and blamed sports leaders, officials, doctors, and coaches within the former East German communist system. In lieu of the scandal, Germany's athletics federation announced that it would check 22 national records set by East German athletes through the 1960s to the 1990s. The investigation also came after Ines Geipel, a member of the record-holding East German women's 4x100-meter relay team, asked for her record from the Summer Games of 1984 to be struck. She revealed she had been doped by team doctors with anabolic steroids. In a separate case, another former East German swimmer Karin König sued the German Olympic committee for damages, claiming that she was also a victim of doping between 1982 and 1987.

This state-sponsored doping regime played a decisive role in the success of East German athletes in international competitions in the Cold War era; most notably at the 1976 Montreal Olympics and the 1980 Moscow games. The athletes who came forward claimed to have all received the steroid Turinabol, an anabolic agent containing testosterone made by the company Jenapharm. The infamous "blue bean" pills the athletes were given (that they were told contained vitamins) accelerated muscle build-up and boosted recovery times. Their subsequent side effects were catastrophic: in women, infertility, embarrassing hair growth, breast cancer, and heart problems; and in men, testicular cancer. An estimated 800 East German athletes developed serious steroid-related ailments.

East Germany's secret police kept meticulous records of the impact the drugs had on performance. A top-secret sporting medical committee including members of the Parteibüro, East Germany's communist leadership body, met to decide which members of the national squad were to be given the drugs. The aim was to show the superiority of the communist regime to its capitalist neighbor West Germany. In the 1972 Munich Olympics, East Germany—a country of 17 million—reached the top three in the medals table with the United States and the Soviet Union. Four years later, East German women won 11 of the 13 swimming events. Leaked documents suggest that Jenapharm scientists collaborated with the secret police, the Stasi, regarding the use of steroids in sports. In the late 1990s, criminal cases were brought against Manfred Ewald, the former East German team doctor, and Dr. Manfred Hoppner, a former team medical consultant. They were given suspended sentences.

In 1998, a large number of prohibited medical substances were found by police in a raid of Team Festina's hotel rooms and vehicles during the Tour de France. The "Festina case" became the biggest doping scandal in cycling history after the entire Festina team was thrown out of the 1998 tour following the discovery of 40 bottles of doping products, including EPO, in a team car. French police stepped in and arrested riders and team managers for conspiracy to distribute illegal drugs. The scandal led to a major reappraisal of the role of public authorities and institutional sports bodies in antidoping affairs. As early as 1963, France had been the first country to enact antidoping legislation. Other countries followed suit, but international cooperation in antidoping affairs was long restricted to the Council of Europe. In the 1980s, there was a marked increase in

THE GREATEST DOPING SCANDAL EVER?

Performance-enhancing steroids were nothing new to international athletics in the 1980s but had become most associated with state-run Eastern Bloc sports programs. When the world learned of sprinter Ben Johnson's positive test for anabolic steroids in 1988, some argue the innocence of the Olympic Games was lost forever. That year, Ben Johnson became world champion and touted as the fastest man in the world when he set a world record in the 100-meter sprint. At the world championships in Rome in 1987, Johnson, a Jamaican-born Canadian, had smashed the 100-meter world record by winning in 9.83 seconds. He smashed his own record the following year in the Seoul Olympics, running a 9.79 100-meter race. Three days later, the IOC stripped Johnson of his medal, and he was sent home in disgrace after he tested positive for performance-enhancing drugs. Immediately declared a cheat by the Canadian media, the affair was described as a national tragedy by Prime Minister Brian Mulroney. Johnson was banned from competition for two years. He returned to the Olympics in 1992 in Barcelona, but failed even to make the 100-meter final.

Following the Johnson drug scandal in 1988, the Canadian federal government established the Commission of Inquiry Into the Use of Drugs and Banned Practices Intended to Increase Athletic Performance. Ontario Appeal Court Chief Justice Charles Dubin was appointed to conduct the inquiry. Several months of shocking testimony about the rampant use of performance-enhancing substances among athletes led Dubin to criticize the testing policies and procedures of both the Canadian federal government and the Canadian Olympic Association in his report released in June 1990. As a result, Canada strengthened its drug-testing program with the creation of the independent nonprofit Canadian Anti-Doping Organization in April 1991. The organization is responsible for drug-testing policy, practice, and implementation in Canada. Canada is now an internationally recognized leader in the fight against performance-enhancing substances, but the commission's findings have been largely ignored in other countries.

cooperation between international sports authorities and various governmental agencies, partly due to revelations about East German doping and allegations of widespread Russian, Chinese, and American doping cultures in sports. Before 1998, debate was still taking place in several discrete forums (IOC, sports federations, individual governments), resulting in differing definitions, policies, and sanctions regarding doping. One result of this confusion (i.e., about, precisely, what doping is and how it should be policed), was that doping sanctions were often disputed between sport agencies and/or civil authorities and sometimes overruled across national or international sport federations or in civil courts.

The 1998 Tour de France scandal highlighted the need for an independent international agency that would set unified standards for antidoping work and coordinate the efforts of sports organizations and public authorities. The IOC took the initiative and convened the World Conference on Doping in Sport held in Lausanne, Switzerland, in February 1999. Following the proposal of the Conference, WADA was established in Lausanne on November 10, 1999. This agency is structured on the basis of equal representation of the Olympic

Movement and Public Authorities. In 2001, WADA voted to move its headquarters to Montreal.

During its first years of existence, WADA reached agreements with 34 international sports federations governing Olympic summer and winter sports to conduct unannounced, out-of-competition tests. The agency developed a harmonized universal antidoping code by the Olympic Games of 2004 in Athens. Sports outside the scope of the Olympic Movement are still a problem, however. Professional sports, notably major leagues in the United States such as the National Football League and Major League Baseball, operate under their own antidoping rules and policies, which are often not as strict as those upheld by WADA. To this day, WADA creates and distributes lists of banned substances in sports, establishes international standards for athlete testing, and informs international rules and punishment systems in amateur sports federations.

FUTURE PROSPECTS

World Anti-Doping Agency was viewed as fully instituted in 2002 as an independent organization to oversee all doping control matters for all sports throughout the world. Dependent upon IOC funding, it has now reached a maturity whereby nearly all amateur sports that are played in the world have ratified the code and protocols it has produced. In the future, for WADA's mandate to be successful and to counter cultures of doping evident in amateur sports, it is generally believed that members of international and national sports federations should aid in the enforcement of WADA rules by: helping to fund scientific research to develop new detection methods; educating athletes about doping through the athlete outreach programs; monitoring the acceptance of and compliance with the World Anti-Doping Code; conducting unannounced, out-of-competition doping tests among elite athletes; observing the doping control and results management programs of major events; and fostering the development of national antidoping organizations (NADOs) to assist with the implementation of WADA antidoping protocols.

See also Cheating During Competition; Ergogenics; Gene Manipulation; Sports Doctors, Trainers, and Drugs; Steroid Use by Athletes; Whistle-Blowers and Drugs.

Further Reading: Houlihan, B. (1999). *Dying to Win: Doping in Sport and the Development of Anti-Doping Policy.* Strasbourg, Austria: Council of Europe; Senn, A. (1999). *Power, Politics and the Olympic Games.* Champaign, IL: Human Kinetics; Waddington, I. (2000). *Sport, Health and Drugs: A Critical Sociological Perspective.* London: Taylor and Francis.

Michael Atkinson

ANTITRUST VIOLATIONS IN PROFESSIONAL SPORTS

Professional sports leagues have had a long-standing experience with challenges to antitrust and anticompetition laws. While each country has developed its own methods of regulating industry, the United States has featured perhaps the most high-profile and controversial antitrust decisions regarding professional sports. In many ways the current structure and functioning of sports leagues and other industry stakeholders has been largely determined by the unique recognition that Major League Baseball (MLB) and, by extension, other leagues have received vis-à-vis antitrust scrutiny.

Professional sports leagues have a unique operating structure. Observers have described them as monopolies, or as cartels. A monopoly is a single firm that supplies a product or service to a market. In the case of professional sports leagues, a single league is the sole provider of the highest caliber of sporting competition in a given sport. For example, the National Basketball Association (NBA) is the sole provider of elite professional basketball in North America. A cartel is a group of firms that comes together to provide a product or service. This can be an issue where the firms conspire to control the supply of the product or the price it is sold at. For example, the NBA comprises 30 independently owned franchises that come together to decide issues such as franchise expansion and relocation, negotiate with the National Basketball Players Association (NBPA) for player rights, and award league-wide television contracts. There are typically four groups who are impacted by monopoly or cartel behavior in professional sports leagues: (1) fans who are forced to pay higher ticket prices due to the lack of substitute forms of entertainment; (2) media companies who are forced to bid against one another for the right to broadcast games; (3) players who have less negotiating leverage due to the absence of other comparable employment opportunities; and (4) individual franchises who may have interests that diverge from the leagues that they play in. Antitrust law has developed as a means of protecting consumers and other stakeholders in the marketplace from behaviors by monopolies, and the aforementioned activities have all received antitrust scrutiny. In fact, the National Football League (NFL) alone faced over 60 different antitrust suits from the mid-1960s through the start of this century.

BACKGROUND

The roots of antitrust laws have their basis in concerns over business conglomerates, or trusts, that emerged during the latter part of the nineteenth century. At that time, single individuals or businesses owned or controlled large elements of certain industries, including the supply of raw materials, transportation networks, production, and distribution. Because they controlled such a wide scope of the industry, there were concerns that these firms could manipulate prices and control supply. As a result, governments were called upon to create laws to protect consumers from these potential practices.

The response was the Sherman Antitrust Act enacted by Congress in 1890. The Act prohibits activities by two or more entities to restrain trade commerce and also bars monopolistic activities by any one firm. Antitrust lawsuits can be brought by the U.S. Justice Department or individuals and are often heard by juries. The Clayton Act was introduced in 1914 and expanded and clarified some of the issues addressed by the Sherman Act. Most importantly for the operations of sports leagues, the Clayton Act allowed for labor unions to be considered excluded from antitrust scrutiny. This was important because it allowed unions to engage in strikes without fear of violating antitrust laws, through the nonstatutory labor exemption.

The Sherman Act has two key sections. The first addresses illegal restraints of trade. This occurs when two or more firms conspire to restrict competition or control pricing. The second addresses illegal monopolies. Activities have to both affect interstate commerce and unreasonably restrain trade in order for them to receive consideration. The punishment for violations is steep—any damages are tripled. Other countries have developed similar regulations, such as the UK Monopolies and Restrictive Practices Act (1948) and Canada's Competition Act (1976).

When professional sports leagues have been scrutinized by antitrust laws, the key issue has been in deciding whether the harm to competition that results from the collective behavior of teams outweighs the benefits that reducing competition has for consumers. For example, the creation of player drafts is anticompetitive because it reduces the opportunities that players have to sell their services to different teams. However, by implementing a draft that has the weakest teams obtain the rights to the best prospects, leagues argue that competitive balance is more likely to occur. This then leads to more closely contested games, which is in the best interests of fans. Thus, drafts could be deemed acceptable because the alleged benefits to improved competitive balance outweigh the negative or anticompetitive consequences (restricted mobility and negotiating leverage for players).

The first serious confrontation between sports leagues and antitrust law that had an enduring effect on the industry as a whole was the *Federal Baseball* decision that effectively gave MLB immunity from antitrust laws. The Federal League of Baseball Players (FLBP) operated for two seasons in 1914 and 1915. In order to attract top players, the FLBP persuaded 81 MLB players to leave their existing teams to play in the new league.

With competition between rival leagues, player salaries escalate and profits erode; as a result, leagues have an incentive to merge or get a rival league to cease operations. In the case of FLBP, the leagues did eventually reach a settlement, and existing teams in MLB agreed to buy out FLBP owners. However, MLB was only interested in stopping head-to-head competition in major cities—where franchises from both MLB and the FLBP played—and the settlement offered to FLBP teams in non-MLB cities was less. One owner, Ned Hanlon of the FLBP Baltimore Terrapins, felt that the settlement was unfair.

In response, Hanlon brought a suit against the other FLBP teams and organized baseball, claiming that other teams colluded to resolve the issue in a way that excluded him from obtaining the settlement he deserved. In a trial in federal court, Hanlon was awarded $80,000. This amount was trebled according to federal antitrust laws. However, in appeal, organized baseball argued that baseball was a "spontaneous output of human activity … not in its nature commerce" and, therefore, not subject to antitrust laws. The District of Columbia Court agreed, and the decision was reversed. *Federal Baseball* eventually reached the U.S. Supreme Court, where representatives of MLB argued that baseball could not exist without exemption from antitrust laws. This occurred in the wake of the Chicago Black Sox gambling scandal, and there were concerns about the future of baseball—at that time truly "America's pastime." In this context, Justice Oliver Wendell Homes concluded that baseball, although a business, did not impact interstate commence. Although teams clearly traveled across state lines to play against one another, games were "purely state affairs." In addition, he noted that games were the result of the personal efforts of players and not related to production. Thus, baseball was "not a subject of commerce."

According to Roger Abrams, "the Supreme Court's decisions exempting the baseball business from the nation's antitrust laws are archaic reminders of judicial decision making at its arthritic worst" (1999, p. 307). Despite the fact that many like Abrams have been highly critical of baseball's immunity status, other sports leagues have also received some respite from antitrust scrutiny. One of the most contested discussions relates to whether leagues are defined as cartels or as single firms. Those that argue the latter have used the notion of single entity theory to argue their position.

Leagues can be considered a single entity for a number of reasons. First, many leagues extensively share revenues, including media, gate, and sponsorship. In addition, decisions related to franchise allocation and relocation are made at the league level. One could also argue that the appeal of individual teams would be virtually nonexistent without other league teams to compete against and that it requires a league to create interest in not just the outcome of a single game (which requires two teams to come together to produce), but also the series of games that culminates in a championship. Also, unlike other businesses, teams have a vested interest in the financial and competitive well-being of other league franchises.

Arguments against considering a league as a single entity include the fact that leagues are unincorporated associations of separately owned clubs. In addition, individual teams make independent decisions regarding player acquisition and openly compete for players and managers. In other words, teams are separate legal entities, and therefore, leagues should be viewed as cartels of individual businesses that come together to produce games and a league season.

KEY EVENTS

Antitrust law has been applied in a number of different contexts in professional sports leagues. Typically, courts will assess whether or not the benefits of a rule or restriction—such as the draft described previously—are greater than the restrictions on competition that result. To do so, courts will use what is called the "rule of reason." Thus, courts will determine if a restriction does not unreasonably restrict competition.

The first issue relates to restrictions on the mobility of players. Since the 1870s, when baseball introduced its reserve clause, players have been bound to their teams. Prior to the advent of players associations and antitrust challenges in the 1970s, a player would be bound to the club that held his rights forever. The player could retire and return years later, but the team would still own that player's rights. As a result, player salaries were far lower than they would be in a more competitive labor market. Meanwhile, teams had the ability to release and trade players at will.

The breakthrough antitrust case that challenged the reserve clause was *Philadelphia World Hockey Club v. Philadelphia Hockey Club*. In that case, the World Hockey Association (WHA), which had commenced operations in 1972, was having difficulty signing players because virtually all talented hockey players were under contract with National Hockey League (NHL) clubs. This was because NHL teams had historically signed young players to "C" form contracts that bound them to an NHL team. As a result, it was difficult for the WHA to fill out team rosters, even with players not already playing in the NHL. A claim under Section 1 of the Sherman Antitrust Act alleged that the NHL's reserve clause constituted an unlawful boycott against players, while a Section 2 challenge claimed that the NHL's monopoly position made it impossible for a new league to begin and sustain operations due to the NHL's control of playing talent. Judge Higginbotham agreed with the WHA, effectively ending the ability of the NHL to enforce the terms of its reserve clause. This allowed the WHA to legally sign players who were from the NHL and whose rights were retained by NHL teams.

While this victory was obtained by the WHA, it was really the players who benefited most from the challenge to the reserve clause. A few years later, the MLB Players Association also was able to break the reserve clause, and free agency was introduced, driving up player salaries. Another area where leagues come under antitrust scrutiny is in the league-wide negotiation of television contracts. Prior to the early 1960s, individual teams would negotiate with local television and radio stations to air games. In larger markets with more than one franchise, teams would be competing with each other to establish a relationship with a given media outlet. However, the American Football League (AFL), and later the NFL, realized that by pooling television rights, leagues could then get television networks to compete against each other to air games, thereby driving up rights fees for teams.

However, teams that conspired to withhold their rights fees in an attempt to increase overall profits were clearly in violation of antitrust laws. To circumvent this issue, the Sports Broadcasting Act was passed in 1961. This allowed the NFL to negotiate an exclusive broadcasting contract with television network Columbia Broadcast System (CBS). Since that time, the NFL (which does not have local television coverage), has seen its rights fees skyrocket.

Another antitrust issue that has arisen has occurred where leagues have merged. The American Basketball Association (ABA) operated for nine seasons from 1967 through 1976. The ABA was an innovative league that introduced the three-point shot and the slam dunk contest and featured many star players, including Julius Irving and Connie Hawkins. However, the league was very unstable financially, and competition for players drove up salaries in both the ABA and the more established NBA. Not long after the league began operations, the ABA began discussion with the NBA regarding the prospects of merging the two leagues (four ABA franchises eventually joined the NBA in 1976). However, merging the two leagues would clearly re-establish the NBA's monopoly position, which would violate antitrust laws. In order to merge, the NBA and ABA would need the permission of the NBPA.

As mentioned previously, the Clayton Act (1914) was created to redefine and build on the Sherman Antitrust Act (1890). One significant development was to exempt unions from antitrust scrutiny. In addition, the nonstatutory labor exemption was introduced, which allowed for restrictions in competition to occur in industries where they had been agreed upon through the process of collective bargaining. In other words, in order for the NBA to resume its monopoly position, it needed the NBPA to agree to a merger through the process of collective bargaining. Following the conclusion of the first collective bargaining agreement (CBA) in 1970, 14 NBA players, led by Oscar Robertson, challenged the NBA's reserve clause and college draft. In addition, the suit also challenged a proposed merger between the ABA and NBA. Eventually, NBA players agreed to allow the merger in exchange for greater player mobility. This was part of a new CBA that was agreed upon in 1976. Thus, the ABA–NBA merger was delayed for several years as the NBPA used antitrust laws to gain further concessions from the NBA.

Perhaps the most significant impact that antitrust law has had on professional sports in recent decades emanates from the *Raiders* decision, which saw the Oakland Raiders challenge the NFL's refusal to allow the Raiders to move to Los Angeles. The decision has resulted in a greater freedom for franchises to decide where to move and has led to an era of "franchise free agency" in the NFL. The Raiders franchise had been operating in the city of Oakland since it was an AFL team in the 1960s. In 1980, Raiders owner, Al Davis, signed a memorandum of agreement to move the team to Los Angeles to play in the Los Angeles Memorial Coliseum. On March 10 of that year, NFL owners met to discuss the possible move and voted 22–0 (with 5 abstentions) to deny the move. Davis himself did not attend the meeting because he did not feel that he needed permission from the league to move.

The Raiders and Los Angeles Memorial Coliseum Commission brought an antitrust suit against the NFL, claiming that the NFL's refusal to allow the team to relocate was an unreasonable restraint of trade; more specifically, the NFL's franchise relocation rule, which required the approval of 75 percent of owners, violated the Sherman Act. The first trial was declared a mistrial and no decision. A new trial began in 1982, and a decision in May of that year determined that indeed the NFL had violated the Sherman Act. As a result, the Raiders were free to move to Los Angeles.

The NFL chose to use a "single entity" defense in order to avoid having to pay damages to Raiders' owner, Al Davis. If successful, the NFL would not be subject to antitrust scrutiny under Section 1 of the Sherman Act. The NFL argued that the league, although comprised of separately owned teams, really acted as a single business, and decisions were made at the league level. Thus, teams were completely interdependent economically and, therefore, should be considered a single business entity. They pointed to the amount of revenues that were shared as evidence that teams were not economic competitors. However, the Raiders successfully argued that in voting to control franchise movement, the restriction did not promote league stability and could be used to block teams from moving for reasons other than preserving the viability of the league. In addition, the court could not look past the fact that teams were independently owned and concluded that teams maintained sufficiently distinct identities that made them separate entities for antitrust consideration. In addition, there was some concern raised that if the court acknowledged the NFL as a single entity, this might create a precedent that would allow the NFL to avoid antitrust scrutiny for a variety of other activities.

FUTURE PROSPECTS

Due to their unique characteristics, professional sports leagues, players' associations, and other league stakeholders will continue to carefully navigate and negotiate antitrust laws in order to maximize their personal interests. Although professional baseball has enjoyed antitrust immunity, the recent Curt Flood Act

CHALLENGING THE ROZELLE RULE

John Mackey played for the Baltimore Colts from 1963 to 1972. In 1992, he was inducted into the Pro Football Hall of Fame, and in 1999, he was voted one of the 100 greatest NFL players of all time by *The Sporting News*. He was the first president of the NFL Players Association following the merger of the NFL and rival AFL. While he was a player, the NFL had implemented the "Rozelle Rule," which compensated teams who lost players that other teams signed as free agents. However, the compensation was usually so steep that it effectively gave teams no incentive to sign players. As a result, free agency was virtually nonexistent in the NFL.

Mackey and 15 other current and former NFL players challenged the Rozelle Rule, claiming that it violated the Clayton and Sherman Antitrust Acts. This marked the first time that a major sports-related antitrust suit made it to the U.S. Court of Appeals. The NFL argued that without the rule, players would move to teams in larger cities, and this would destroy competitive balance in the NFL. However, the courts sided with the players. In the process, the court created a three-pronged test to determine whether nonstatutory immunity from antitrust laws should be granted in professional sports: (1) any restraint would only impact the two sides that agreed to the restraint—in this case, the NFL and NFLPA; (2) any restraint had to be negotiated and agreed upon through the process of collective bargaining; and (3) the restraint had to be the product of bona fide arm's length bargaining between the two sides. It was in this final test that the Rozelle Rule failed, and the NFL was deemed in violation of antitrust laws—the rule had been created by the NFL and not with the input of the NFLPA.

Despite the victory, the NFLPA negotiated away much of the possible gains made through the *Mackey* case during the 1977 collective bargaining agreement. Because these new restrictions were now negotiated through a bona fide collective bargaining process, they would be immune to antitrust scrutiny. It wouldn't be until the early 1990s that players in the NFL would enjoy greater mobility as free agents.

has partially lifted baseball's antitrust immunity with regards to labor relations. In the future, leagues will continue to work with players' associations in order to ensure that any restrictions are agreed upon in the process of collective bargaining, and they will use a single-entity defense in order to justify placing restrictions on individual league franchises.

Further Reading: Abrams, R. (1999). Before the Flood: The History of Baseball's Antitrust Exemption. *Marquette Sports Law Journal* 9: 307–313; Duquette, J. J. (1999). *Regulating the National Pastime: Baseball and Antitrust.* Westport, CT: Praeger; Kurlantzick, L. S. (1983). Thoughts on Professional Sports and the Anti-Trust Laws: Los Angeles Memorial Coliseum Commission v. National Football League. *Connecticut Law Review* 15: 183–208; Lowe, S. R. (1995). *The Kid on the Sandlot: Congress and Professional Sports, 1910–1992.* Bowling Green, OH: Bowling Green State University Popular Press; Weistart, J. C. (1984). League Control of Market Opportunities: A Perspective on Competition and Cooperation in the Sports Industry. *Duke Law Journal* 1984: 1013–1070.

Daniel S. Mason

ATHLETE UNIONS

Athlete unions are official bargaining units representing the collective interests of players in negotiations with professional sports leagues. Called players' associations, these units have emerged as formidable adversaries to leagues who have historically held a significant power advantage over players with regards to salaries and labor mobility. All four major leagues in North America, including the National Football League (NFL), Major League Baseball (MLB), the National Basketball Association (NBA), and the National Hockey League (NHL), have witnessed work stoppages due to strikes or lockouts resulting from negotiations.

BACKGROUND

While leagues have been in operation for in excess of 100 years, players' associations have only emerged as powerful adversaries to management since the early 1970s. A powerful tool used by teams to keep player salaries low and restrict player movement was the reserve clause. Introduced by MLB teams in the late nineteenth century—with variations adopted by other leagues—the reserve clause effectively bound a player to a team that held the player's rights in perpetuity. Unless a player was released, the player could only play for the club that held his rights. At the end of each season, the team could exercise its reserve option and re-sign the player. As a result, player salaries were low compared to the revenues they generated for the teams they played for. For example, a study by Gerald Scully showed that players were only paid about 10 to 20 percent of the revenues they generated for their respective teams (called Marginal Revenue Product).

Players were often left in the dark regarding what their rights were and were told that their respective leagues really were not designed as businesses—players should play for the love of the game, and paternalistic owners were only breaking even financially. Players who questioned this were relegated to the minors or traded. If an athlete thought to consult an agent, team management would refuse to meet with them; they would even trade players to other teams to get rid of the problem. However, eventually players began organizing to get more access to information and other benefits, such as meal money and pensions. Today, player unions have substantial bargaining leverage because they recognize that players have specialized, unique skills that are difficult to replace. Thus, while it might be relatively easy for a team to replace any one player, together players wield significant bargaining power. Each of the players' associations in the four major professional leagues are detailed here.

The Major League Baseball Players Association (MLBPA) was formed in 1952 but did not become an active force until 1966, when it hired Marvin Miller to replace Judge Robert Cannon. Cannon had aspired to be the next commissioner of baseball and was not opposed to the reserve clause. Today, the MLBPA is considered one of the most successful unions in any industry.

The National Football League Players Association (NFLPA) formed in 1956. Like the MLBPA, the NFLPA did not mobilize quickly; however, it did become the first players' association to register as a labor union with the U.S. Department of Labor in 1968. The biggest breakthrough in the NFLPA occurred when it decertified and filed an antitrust suit against the NFL. This resulted in more widespread free agency for players starting in the early 1990s. Rosters for the NFL are larger than those found in most other sports. As a result, average salaries are much lower than in baseball or basketball. In addition, most player salaries are not guaranteed in the NFL—this allows teams to release players and does not give players the same kind of financial stability as in other sports.

The NBA began operations in 1946. Through the late 1950s, interest in professional basketball increased, resulting in the creation of a rival league, the American Basketball League (ABL), in 1961. Although operating for only two seasons, player salaries increased with competition for players between the two leagues, and players became more aware of their bargaining position. In 1962, the National Basketball Players Association (NBPA) was formed. However, the ABL folded after two seasons, and the NBA reacquired its monopoly position on elite basketball. This changed in 1967 with the advent of the American Basketball Association (ABA). With greater mobility and more leverage, the NBA finally officially recognized the NBPA in 1967. Prior to that time, there were no minimum player salaries, no pension plans, and no health, accident, or life insurance benefits for NBA players.

In 1976 a collective bargaining agreement (CBA) was reached that resulted in concessions to the players in exchange for the association allowing the two leagues to merge. The NBPA has also successfully challenged the salary cap *(Lanier v. National Basketball Ass'n),* and the restrictions of the player draft and salary cap *(Bridgeman v. National Basketball Ass'n; Wood v. National Basketball Ass'n).*

The National Hockey League Players Association (NHLPA) has had a tumultuous history since its inception. Interest in forming an association was first championed in the 1950s by NHL stars Ted Lindsay and Doug Harvey. The two were bitter rivals but joined forces when they began to question issues related to the players' league-controlled pension plan and the low salaries paid to players. The association did not achieve its goals when it failed to gain support from the players on the powerful Detroit Red Wings. However, it was able to gain some concessions from the NHL. The NHLPA became more formally established in 1967 when Alan Eagleson became its first executive director. After a prolonged period of meager bargaining gains, many of which could be attributed to indifference, conflicts of interest, or even outright fraud (see sidebar), Eagleson was eventually ousted in the early 1990s and replaced by Bob Goodenow. Goodenow took a much more militant stance in his and the association's relationship with the NHL. Soon after Goodenow started his position as executive director, the players had their first strike, at the onset of the 1992 Stanley Cup playoffs. The strike was short lived, and owners, upset with NHL president John Zeigler's performance, replaced him with hockey's first commissioner, Gary Bettman. The two sides played without a CBA through the 1993–1994 season, and in the fall of 1994, the NHL locked out the players. Once described by observers as the weakest union in professional sports, the NHLPA has made significant gains for players as salaries escalated through the 1990s and into the next century. Following a lost season in 2004–2005 due to another league-imposed lockout, the NHLPA accepted a salary cap and replaced Bob Goodenow with Ted Saskin. Saskin was removed as NHLPA head after a scandal related to the process of his hiring and his monitoring of player emails. In the fall of 2007, the NHLPA hired its newest director, Paul Kelly.

The primary role of the players' associations is to look after the interests of members of the association and to collectively bargain with their respective leagues. In addition, associations will seek out revenue opportunities from licensing and sponsorship and provide a means of monitoring player agents. Early gains made by associations were in establishing and raising minimum salaries, pensions, and insurance and improving conditions of employment. In recent decades, the relationship between labor and management in professional sports has been highly contested. After overcoming the restraints that had been placed upon them for decades through mechanisms such as the reserve clause, players remain highly suspicious of owner interests. In addition, management has traditionally been unwilling to share any information on the financial performance of teams, which created an atmosphere of distrust.

Players' associations have been granted the authority to represent players as a whole. According to U.S. labor law, leagues may not implement any substantive changes to the working conditions of players without getting approval from the union. Typically this occurs through good-faith bargaining. At times, negotiations may reach an impasse. There are also several issues and characteristics that make players' associations unique. First, most other unions negotiate a basic wage for their members. In professional sports, associations negotiate minimum wages and other benefits, but individual players—usually with the assistance of agents—negotiate their own salaries. In other industries, unions often work to try to restrict the number of people who become union members and try to limit competition for their services in order to protect their members. In sports, unions encourage competition for player services by seeking less restrictive free agency rules.

RISE AND FALL OF ALAN EAGLESON

For 25 years, the NHLPA was controlled by R. Alan Eagleson. Eagleson held multiple roles while operating the NHLPA, including as an agent and as a negotiator for Hockey Canada. This resulted in several conflicts of interest. In addition, Eagleson was considered too close to members of NHL management, including former NHL president John Zeigler and Chicago Blackhawks owner, Bill Wirtz.

Eagleson was an attorney who had social and business contacts with several prominent Toronto Maple Leaf players of the early 1960s. He began to assist several players with their contractual affairs and made a huge splash in the industry when he signed Bobby Orr to a multiyear agreement with the Boston Bruins. He then used his contacts and influence to develop a burgeoning agency practice and became the executive director of the NHLPA in 1967. However, Eagleson did not devote all of his time to the NHLPA.

He was credited for his involvement with the 1972 Summit Series between the Soviet Union and Canada, where top professional hockey players were able to compete against the Soviet national team. This led Eagleson to create the Canada Cup, a tournament of national teams that was staged in 1976, 1981, 1984, 1987, and 1991. Eagleson was able to convince professional players that participating in the tournament was in their best interests because profits would go toward player pensions. However, it soon became apparent that the tournaments, despite their popularity, were not resulting in any significant gains for players, and it later was revealed that Eagleson was redirecting money—specifically from rinkboard advertising—for his own personal use.

A broader investigation into Eagleson's activities by journalist Russ Conway revealed a number of issues and problems with Eagleson's affairs, eventually leading to an FBI investigation. Issues that were explored were conspiring with NHL teams to suppress player salaries, taking kickbacks from insurance claims he received on behalf of NHL players, spending NHLPA funds on friends and family, and loaning NHLPA and individual player funds to friends. He was charged with 34 counts of fraud, racketeering, embezzlement, and obstruction of justice in 1994, and he eventually served 6 months in prison.

Another interesting element of players' associations and collective bargaining relates to the entry draft and restrictions on rookie salaries. Associations negotiate these restrictions, which serve to limit the ability of incoming players to earn higher salaries.

Both the NHL and MLB have developed a means of assisting teams and individual players after they have reached a negotiations impasse—salary arbitration. Arbitration rights have been collectively bargained for and allow players to seek out the opinion of an independent third party (the arbitrator) who will then make a decision on the amount. In this case, arbitration is binding—both the league and players agree to abide by the decision of the arbitrator. While the process varies between the two leagues and has evolved over time, players seek to maximize their salaries by highlighting their strengths and comparing their salaries to other players of similar caliber. Team managers then try to downplay the abilities of the player, but they must be careful not to offend or alienate the player and damage their relationship.

There are two basic types of arbitration. The first involves the team and player each pleading their case and suggesting a specific financial figure. The arbitrator then decides on an amount somewhere at or between these two figures. For example, a team might be offering a player $2 million per season, while the player is seeking $4 million. After hearing each side, a salary of $3 million might be awarded. The second type of arbitration is called final offer arbitration, and it has been used in MLB. In final offer arbitration, the arbitrator hears both cases and then must choose one of the two amounts—either the team's offer or the players' desired wage. This system is designed to encourage both sides to reach an agreement prior to arbitration because each side risks having the other side's contract offer accepted. It also reduces the likelihood of the team making an offer that is too low, and a player making an outlandish salary demand. Salary arbitration was introduced in MLB in 1969, with final offer arbitration instituted in 1973. Scholars have argued that the ability to take a team to arbitration provides a player with as much negotiating leverage as does being a free agent.

Issues of contention in contemporary collective bargaining between players and leagues include free agency restrictions, arbitration, and luxury taxes and salary caps. Obviously, players want to increase player mobility. This can be achieved by lowering the age or years of service required before free agency is granted, reducing compensation in the case of restricted free agency (to encourage teams to make offers to players), and reducing the number of rounds of the draft (which gives more player flexibility to seek out playing opportunities). Both luxury taxes and salary caps serve to suppress player salaries; however, the difference is that with a cap, teams are unable to spend more than a certain limit, while luxury taxes penalize teams that exceed a certain salary threshold. Thus, although the players do not like either system, they prefer a luxury tax to a cap because it gives teams more flexibility to spend on salaries.

When it comes to collective bargaining, players in all four sports typically have several underlying issues that form their negotiating stance. The first is that they view any restriction on salaries (such as a cap or luxury tax) as simply a mechanism that is forcing the players to help owners from overspending on player salaries. In other words, why should the players have to fix a problem that is the owners' fault? Second, owners often claim that players must accept cost certainty (i.e., a cap or tax) in order to assist smaller market franchises who lack the same revenue streams as larger market teams. In this case, players argue that simply sharing more revenues among league clubs will solve this problem and that caps and other salary restrictions are therefore unnecessary.

Another issue relates to restrictions on player mobility. Players wonder why they lack the freedom to choose where they can play, while in other industries the most gifted and sought-after workers can sell their services to the highest bidder and choose who they want to work for. A final issue relates to trust—players simply do not believe that the owners are losing as much money as they claim to be. This is exacerbated by the owners' unwillingness to share the details of their financial operations.

In representing the players, players' associations also face several concerns that differentiate sports from other industries. For example, how does the association represent the interests of such a diverse group of athletes, where careers are short and some players make salaries far greater than others? Associations must also consider when the interests of some players may be compromised in order to meet the interests of the entire group. For example, putting restrictions on incoming player salaries might be conceded to the league in order to create less restrictive free agency for veteran players. Another problem facing associations relates to the career span of professional athletes, where the average player might play five seasons. This creates pressure on unions when there is a prolonged work stoppage, such as from a strike or lockout, because players are losing a significant portion of their career earnings. This gives leagues more leverage during prolonged work stoppages.

From the owners' perspective, they feel that they own multimillion dollar businesses and, as a result, should have the right to a reasonable return (profit) from their operations. Because teams are privately owned firms, owners do not feel that they should have to share their independent financial information. It can also be difficult for large-market and more profitable team owners to accept the notion of sharing their revenues with weaker teams. They feel that they have paid fair market value for their teams, and sharing revenues will reduce their franchise values and team profits. In addition, despite the cooperation between teams to produce the league product, on-the-field competitiveness can sometimes spill over into team management and ownership, which creates less willingness for team owners to cooperate. In addition, team owners are dependent on the rational behavior of other teams. Where one team goes out and overpays for a player, all the other teams suffer because players of similar caliber will demand a similar wage. Thus, team owners argue that having restrictions on salaries allows teams to save them from other incompetent owners or team managers. Finally, team owners can be motivated by a desire to win and/or to make a profit. As a result, win-maximizing owners will often be willing to pay more for a player's services, which drives up player salaries for all teams.

KEY EVENTS

Perhaps the key event in the history of organized labor in professional sports was the hiring of Marvin Miller by MLBPA in 1966. He was instrumental in gaining considerable concessions for players. He generated new revenues through licensing and sponsorship agreements and worked with players to challenge longstanding rules and regulations, including the reserve clause. Despite baseball's antitrust exemption, Miller was able to radically improve the bargaining position of baseball players, and some consider MLBPA to be one of the most successful unions in any industry. Today, MLB remains the only league of the four major leagues to operate without a salary cap.

Miller worked with several MLB players to attempt to remove the restrictions imposed by the reserve clause. For example, in 1974, star pitcher Catfish Hunter signed an agreement with the Oakland Athletics. As part of the contract, the owner of the Athletics, Charlie Finley, was supposed to pay money into an insurance annuity. When Finley failed to do so, Hunter and Miller claimed that the Athletics had violated the terms of the contract and therefore Hunter should become an unrestricted free agent. The grievance went before a three-person arbitration panel who voted in favor of Hunter, making him a free agent. Hunter ended up signing a deal with the Yankees that was for a total of $3.75 million, giving players a clear indication of how free agency could impact their salaries.

Another prominent event in the history of the MLBPA occurred when two pitchers, Andy Messersmith and Dave McNally, worked with the MLBPA to challenge the reserve clause. In 1975, both players were not satisfied with their contract offers from their teams, the Los Angeles Dodgers and Montreal Expos, respectively. As a result, they refused to sign their new contracts, which teams had the right to offer. At that time, baseball contracts were usually for one year with the team having the option to renew for one additional year. By doing this every year, a player's rights could be tied to the team indefinitely. This changed in 1973 when a provision of the contract was changed to state that players could play without having a signed contract. Thus, in challenging this new wording, the two players played the entire season without having signed their contracts, and at the end of the 1975 season, they claimed to have met the conditions of their contracts and were now free agents. The issue also went to arbitration, where it was declared on December 21, 1975, that the players were indeed free agents. With this ruling, players could play out the terms of their contracts without signing them and then declare themselves free agents. If all players did this, then baseball would have total free agency. However, Miller was shrewd enough to know not to flood the market and instead negotiated a new collective bargaining agreement that saw players become free agents after a specified number of years of service. This allowed for a finite number of free agents to appear each year who would drive up player salaries due to demand for their services.

Another major event associated with these challenges was the advent of free agency. In baseball, free agency allowed player salaries to grow dramatically. Teams signed players to more multiyear contracts, and free agents were paid more for their services than comparable players who were not free agents. Starting in 1976, a player with six years of service in MLB could become an unrestricted free agent. The impact on salaries was immediate; the average MLB salary nearly tripled between 1976 and 1980.

Players in other sports did not enjoy the same freedom. In the NFL, free agency existed in principle but not in practice. Players who signed with new teams were forced to pay compensation. From 1977 through 1993, a player who had completed his second year in the league and had played out his contract was considered a conditional free agent. However, the compensation was so steep (the team the player had been with could match any offer, and compensation included two first-round draft picks) that it deterred teams from making offers to players. Thus, only two players changed teams during this 26-year period.

In 1987, frustrated NFL players went on strike. The collective bargaining agreement (originally negotiated in 1982) had expired, and the players were concerned about restrictions on player mobility. However, the strike did not result in any bargaining resolutions, so the players returned to work and launched a class action lawsuit against the NFL, where an effort was made to stop the ability of the NFL to impose the player restrictions from the previous CBA. As a result of this, an "impasse standard test" was developed. The test determined that an antitrust exemption occurred until it was apparent that there was no possibility that a fruitful bargaining solution would occur. Thus, as long as the league could show that it was making an effort to negotiate a solution to the bargaining impasse, the NFL could continue to operate under the restrictive practices of the expired agreement. Thus, leagues would be protected by the labor exemption even in the absence of a collective bargaining agreement. The labor exemption allows sports leagues to develop mechanisms that might otherwise violate antitrust laws as long as they have been agreed to by labor unions through the process of collective bargaining. In other words, the antitrust exemption gives unions protection from antitrust laws and allows for restriction practices in their industry as long as they consent to them.

Subsequent suits eventually resulted in the development of a "beyond impasse" standard where it was determined that, if there was a bargaining impasse, the conditions of the previous bargaining agreement could continue to be imposed, even if there was a stalemate. This shifted a significant amount of power to the owners because they could now avoid settling with players and continue with the same restrictions from the earlier agreement. In response, on December 5, 1989, player representatives of NFL teams voted to decertify; that is, the NFLPA ceased to be the recognized bargaining unit for the players of the NFL by changing its structure and becoming a volunteer professional organization. In doing so, the NFL would no longer be protected by the labor exemption, and the players could then file an antitrust suit against the NFL. On February 1, 1990, eight NFL players filed a suit alleging that the NFL's Plan B free agency system violated Section 1 of the Sherman Antitrust Act. The suit was successful, and a series of ensuing suits filed by other groups of NFL players resulted in the possibility of 1,100 NFL players being awarded damages. This encouraged the NFL to resume negotiations with the players, and the result was far less restrictive rules regarding player mobility in the NFL. On January 6, 1993, an agreement was reached to settle the lawsuits, and by March, the NFLPA had recertified. The league had been operating without a current CBA for five years.

As evidenced by the struggles faced in professional football, collective bargaining can be acrimonious and a struggle. As a result, all four major professional sports leagues have witnessed work stoppages in recent years due to strikes and lockouts. The NFL had strikes in 1982 (lasting 57 days) and 1987 (24 days) before the NFLPA used antitrust laws to obtain more gains from the NFL. Hockey witnessed a lockout in 1994–1995, and the entire 2004–2005 season was canceled as a result of a league-imposed lockout. The NBA had been relatively unscathed until more recently, when it lost part of the 1998–1999 season due to a lockout. Finally, only recently has MLB seen more harmony between labor and management; there was a period of several decades where there was some kind of work stoppage at the conclusion of every collective bargaining agreement. In 1994, a strike led to the cancellation of the 1994 MLB season and the widespread alienation of fans across the country. The results were devastating in many respects—for example, MLB games averaged 36,612 per game in paid attendance in 1994 leading up to the strike and only 25,021 in 1995.

FUTURE PROSPECTS

While leagues and players' associations continue to posture and fight for their respective sides, it appears that both sides understand that more collaborative initiatives are in their best interests. Recent negotiations in MLB have not had the same level of animosity, and as salaries become increasingly tied to league revenues (as in the NBA, NFL, and NHL), there is a strong incentive for both sides to work together to increase revenues to the benefit of all. Today, player unions are formidable adversaries to leagues, and the uneven balance of power does not favor owners as it did in the days of the reserve clause.

See also Antitrust Violations in Professional Sports; Drafting Amateur Athletes; Salaries of Professional Athletes.

Further Reading: Conway, R. (1995). *Game Misconduct: Alan Eagleson and the Corruption of Hockey.* Toronto: Macfarlane Walter & Ross; Harris, D. (1986). *The League: The Rise and Decline of the NFL.* New York: Bantam Books; Jennings, K. M. (1990). *Balls and Strikes: The Money Game in Professional Baseball.* Westport, CT: Praeger; McDonough, E. R. (1997). Escaping Antitrust Immunity—Decertification of the National Basketball Players Association. *Santa Clara Law Review* 37: 821–863; Miller, M. (1991). *A Whole Different Ballgame: The Inside Story of the Baseball Revolution.* New York: Birch Lane Press.

Daniel S. Mason

"AT-RISK" YOUTH IN SPORTS

Sports organizers in the second half of the twentieth century created a new method of social intervention for groups of inner-city youth besieged with drug, violence, and poverty problems. Sports programs were created to provide these inner-city youth—who came to be called "at-risk" youth—with safe havens from the harsh realities of street life, a social context for developing strong community bonds and prosocial personalities, and a set of physical cultural practices designed to protect their bodies from disease. The programs were funded and overseen by public and private institutions and were predominantly targeted at working-class, ethnic minority youth who were often profiled by police, social workers, and court officials as future criminals or social welfare recipients.

BACKGROUND

The use of sports to insulate youth from negative social influences and at the same time instill in them positive moral/social values is not an invention of the late twentieth century. Indeed, criminologists have argued since the 1920s that the structuring of leisure time for youth is a central tactic for combating a range of delinquent behaviors. Much of the rationale for including youth sports and physical education classes in school and the creation of community clubs such as the Boy Scouts and the Young Men's Christian Association (YMCA) during the early twentieth century was grounded in the idea that sports and athletics could instill positive social values in youth. Sports became a right and a rite for predominantly white, middle-class American boys in the process of their socialization into structurally and culturally integrated men. But social reformists in cities such as Chicago, New York, and Boston also spearheaded the American "play movement" (essentially a social program designed to create more parks and recreation spaces for inner-city immigrant youth) of the early 1900s as a tool for breaking the cycle of gang formation and juvenile delinquency among the underprivileged.

Until the late stages of the twentieth century, consistent evidence illustrates a "separate and unequal" model for youth sports. On the one hand, youth sports became widely structured into the education and socialization of members of the middle class for their socialization and integration into mainstream society. They were either sponsored directly by the government or by philanthropic organizations such as the YMCA. On the other hand, sports programs were not developed within the working-class, poor, or ethnic minority concentrated zones of cities until sports were heralded as vehicles for curing, or at least combating, problems of violence, drugs, and theft. Competing social philosophies for sports development showed that some members of the population had a simple right to sports and play, while others possessed the right to sports when it was determined that they needed to be protected from the social conditions of their own lives. The latter ideologies would become central in the creation of new, multi-institutional youth programs in the late 1990s explicitly oriented toward fighting "risk" conditions in the city.

Concerns about the risks youth faced in cities in the late part of the twentieth century mainly revolved around issues with drugs, gangs, interpersonal violence, pregnancy, disease, and educational attrition. Whereas young individuals were targeted as problematic in communities as serial recidivists (especially young, black males), discourse was emerging as early as 1988 about an entirely new category of at-risk youth. Essentially, an at-risk youth is one who falls into a series of social categories that are statistically related to criminal offending, such as low socioeconomic status, low educational attainment, and ethnic minority membership. However, one does not have to be a delinquent, deviant, or criminal to be lumped into the at-risk category. In a culturally proactive and socially protectionist maneuver, legislators across the United States decided that sports could be used to combat the conditions of risk in these areas for youth and thus improve their lives.

The agenda for recognizing, labeling, and seeking to help people at risk became a hallmark of Clinton-era social democratic public programs. *Risk* turned into a social and political buzzword in an era booming economically but preoccupied with threats of AIDS and other diseases, racial conflict, urban decay, drugs, violent crime, handguns, and obesity. Republican philosophies of "just say no" and protect yourself had not ostensibly succeeded in the 1980s, and legislators were left searching for viable alternatives to fight spreading social problems and the further growth of "dangerous populations." Social theorists often categorize this as the development of a total "risk society" in an era where governments statistically documented myriad social and personal risks North

Americans were facing, and mass media served a dominant role in amplifying them. While everyone became a subject of risk discourses, some populations were identified as more at risk than others.

During the discussion of a 1994 federal crime bill, Republicans and Democrats engaged in what is arguably the first sustained debate about whether sports could be employed as a tool for fighting inner-city crime in the risk era. The debate helped usher in a new era of social problems–oriented sports initiatives championed by urban crime experts, youth counselors, and educators. A subtheme in the crime bill debate was that local communities could neither assess the extent, nor root causes of, "risk" in their own backyards. Indeed, for (youth) problems and sources of risk to be eradicated from cities, it would take the concerted efforts of government experts. Such is the model of problem-solving, risk-preoccupied societies, where governments, scientists, and a vast array of social experts exert power over citizens by diagnosing the conditions of risk faced by them and then proposing cures. Sports had been scarcely used in this respect for the majority of the twentieth century and had only sporadically been inserted into debates about crime control after the 1940s.

The central task would be to find the financial, institutional, and social resources needed to create sports programs and leisure activities in inner-city spaces where risks abound. By 1997, sports for young people in underprivileged areas were being discussed in the United States as part of the crime-fighting provisions section of the federal budget. Three dominant goals of introducing sports to young people at risk in cities featured prominently in the government plans: to use sports as a means for reducing crime, to prevent violence between young people, and to engender greater public trust in communities where a sense of togetherness and common fate had been shattered by the presence of many social problems and personal risks (Collingwood, 1997).

In the early planning of how sports could be a central crime- and risk-combating technique for the government, few people seemed to question whether or not sports could actually improve, cure, or eradicate the risks young people encounter in their local communities. Sports leagues might provide temporary shelter from drugs or violent offenders on city streets, but they certainly cannot correct the problems of racism, poverty, poor educational opportunities, and other forms of deeply structured social inequality. Nevertheless, a spate of crime-fighting sports programs were introduced in the United States in the late 1990s. These programs, armed by the same philosophies as a decade earlier, increase in number practically every year regardless of the empirical evidence that suggests they have no discernable impact on overall crime rates.

KEY EVENTS

The pinnacle event in the creation of the at-risk youth sports movement in the United States is unquestionably the foundation of midnight basketball. The Chicago Housing Authority received a grant from the U.S. Department of Housing and Urban Development in 1989 to organize a basketball league in two high-crime areas in the city. Their line of attack was based on an old crime/juvenile delinquency philosophy promoted by some North American criminologists that if young people in marginalized social groups are not provided with safe, supervised, educational, and morally underpinned activities in their leisure time, they could turn to more socially harmful activities. These ideas were extended by G. Van Standifer, the ex-mayor of Glenarden, Maryland, who believed that boys from these communities needed extra attention during the peak crime hours of 10:00 P.M. to 2:00 A.M. Van Standifer proposed the formation of a midnight basketball league in Washington, D.C. (noted at the time as being one of America's most violent cities). Participants were to be between the ages of 17–21 (without due acknowledgment of crime literature that suggests that the enduring personality characteristics criminals tend to share are formed much earlier in life), games would start at 10:00 and continue all evening; there would be police presence at each game. They would later add educational classes and mentoring and peer tutoring agendas to each evening of play. Crime rates in the communities dropped nearly 30 percent that year, and Van Standifer attributed it to the league. Only a year later, he created the Midnight Basketball League, Inc. and then the National Association of Midnight Basketball (comprised of 38 chapters across the country). The program created an immediate media frenzy around the idea of using sports to fight crime and resulted in dozens of copycat leagues, day camps, and drop-in centers in the United States and Canada showcasing a variety of sports. The programs appealed to city, state/province, and federal crime control advocates because they cost very little to run since corporations such as Nike, McDonald's, and Snapple, along with generous benefactors and businesses in cities, fund them almost entirely. Interestingly, major corporations and local businesses now have one of the mandates to police risk in American cities in conjunction with official agents of social control.

By 1994, a federal report called "Beyond Fun and Games" commissioned by the National Recreation and Parks Association (NRPA) noted that nearly two dozen sports programs had been established to help fight substance abuse, disease, teenage pregnancy, crime, and gang membership. Congresswoman Patricia Schroeder from Colorado and Senator Carol Mosely-Braun from Illinois proposed the widespread implementation of midnight basketball in inner-city areas in a 1994 education bill "Goals 200: Educate America Act." Further searching by the NRPA revealed that, by 1997, over 600 new sports programs had been created for at-risk youth in U.S. cities. Basketball leagues, baseball leagues, and street hockey leagues were most popular. Critics have argued that the programs would not have been required if the U.S. government had not cut funding for the development of parks and recreation facilities in the 1970s and reduced funding for after-school sports programs and physical education classes in the 1980s.

Critics of the midnight basketball initiative also argue that several major problems were inherent in the sports-as-a-social-safety-valve model. First, it once again reinforced racist crime and social problems ideologies that race is significantly linked to crime. The overwhelming target communities for basketball leagues are African American dominated. By encouraging the establishment of sports and not education or work programs for young men in these

THE CANADIAN SOMALI YOUTH BASKETBALL LEAGUE

In 2004, the Somali Youth Basketball League (SYBL) was founded in Ontario, Canada, as a volunteer, not-for-profit basketball league designed to offer a fun and competitive environment for youth and to maintain a drug- and violence-free environment. The league welcomes a diverse group of youth participants. The first season saw the participation of 144 young boys and girls. Here are its stated goals:

- Establishing leadership and mentorship activities that will help youth skills that can be used anywhere, including the school environment.
- Teaching youth how to effectively communicate, debate, and help address some of the challenges and issues that youth face in school and the community.
- There will be positive role models introduced to the youth in efforts to encourage youths and build unity within the community.
- Enhanced leadership and communication skills through sports will help increase chances for future employment.

communities (which are more linked to the root conditions of criminality), the programs do little to address the true sources of risk for them. Crime statistics through the late 1990s and early 2000s presented a series of sobering realities in this regard; notwithstanding the extraordinary claims made in communities with midnight basketball leagues about their effectiveness in reducing crime (and their surging popularity across the continent), police data over the long term in most cities do not support the idea that sports leagues can significantly reduce the risks facing youth today.

Corporations jumped onto the "sports for at-risk youth" bandwagon. For example, in 1993, Nike created the PLAY campaign. The PLAY (Participate in the Lives of American Youth) campaign sought to draw public attention to the right of every child to play and have access to sports as a vital part of their safe social development. Corporations such as Nike were focusing attention on how social problems emerge and how sports can help at-risk youth. Nike replicated enduring cultural associations between race and crime in their PLAY campaign and even used African American sports icon Michael Jordan as its main spokesperson.

FUTURE PROSPECTS

The popularity of sports programs in crime- and risk-fighting agendas continues to bloom; indeed, a new category of sports programs is being developed for another category of at-risk youth, the obese. Although there may be a lack of consistent, concrete evidence that sports programs combat street crime or the risks that inner-city children face, we cannot discount the potential physical, social, and psychological benefit of sports for so-called youth at risk. However, whether or not sports should be a central social welfare provision for people in deeply marginalized and disadvantaged communities beset with crime and violence is worth debate. By focusing on a "sports as the solution" model for upward mobility and the safety of young black males in the inner city, sponsors of the programs may be inadvertently advocating one of the most racially divisive ideologies of the twentieth century—that sports is the best, and only, avenue for black males to achieve success.

See also Cool Pose; Government Sponsorship of Teams; Private vs. Public Sports Spaces; Rights of Young Athletes; Sports for All and Fair Play Leagues; Urban Planning and Gentrification.

Further Reading: Cole, C. L. (1996). American Jordan: PLAY, Consensus and Punishment. *Sociology of Sport Journal* 13: 366–397; Collingwood, T. (1997). *Helping at Risk Youth Through Physical Fitness Training.* Champaign, IL: Human Kinetics; Hartmann, D. (2001). Notes on Midnight Basketball and the Cultural Politics of Recreation, Race and At-Risk Urban Youth. *Journal of Sport and Social Issues* 25: 339–371.

Michael Atkinson

B

BIOLOGY AND ATHLETE PERFORMANCE

Human performance in sports is predominantly measured along rational, quantified, and objective lines. How high an athlete can jump or run, how fast they can move, the consistency of their play, or their clarity of mental focus can all be scientifically measured, mapped, and analytically dissected. In the realm of elite amateur and professional sports, while social and psychological factors are appreciated as key predictors of athletic success, elite training and coaching interventions now focus almost exclusively on how the physical/biological body can be "reworked" to improve its functioning. But at the same time, through critical debates about beliefs that certain people (i.e., men from particular racial groups) are born with "naturally" better genes for becoming top athletes, alternative understandings of the body's role in relation to sports performance have emerged.

BACKGROUND

The publication of and subsequent controversy relating to Herrnstein and Murray's *The Bell Curve* (1994) was a watershed moment in cultural debates about the genetic foundations of personal behaviors, abilities, and attitudes, including those in the world of sports. *The Bell Curve,* and later books such as Rushton's (1997) highly controversial *Race, Evolution and Behavior,* asserted that people are born with particular phenotypic and genotypic differences that partially determine how they, for example, run, jump, swim, climb, or even how they are able to train and recover. Such interests on and statements about the "essential" differences between people (e.g., according to sex and race) are indeed central in ancient debates about the determined nature of the body and self.

The late modern scientific interest in genetics and their link to human physical attributes and behaviors is arguably linked to Sir Francis Galton's eugenicist expositions on Charles Darwin's (Galton's own cousin) evolutionary theory. Galton (1865) argued, among other things, that there were certain genetically determined types of people (healthy, intelligent, morally virtuous) who should be the preferred "reproducers" in a society; while weak and inferior others should not be encouraged to reproduce. Galton wrote that personal traits were inherited rather than developed socially, and therefore, these social groups should be allowed to flourish as the genetic backbone of a society. In his book *Hereditary Genius*, he argued that in order for a society (or any other scale social group) to survive over time, they needed to practice a policy of "artificial selection," or, the deliberate amalgamating and arranging of social groups with the "best" genes.

Within sports circles, debates about the naturally/genetically gifted athlete have fallen along very similar eugenicist lines. Driving part of the interest in genetic differences between athletes, and their ostensible relationship to sports performance, is the casual observation that black athletes dominate in particular American and global sports cultures (i.e., such as track and field, basketball, football, and distance running, among others) due to their genetic characteristics. John Hoberman and Jon Entine are among those who suggest that black athletes as a racial group share particular skeletal and muscle structures that predispose them to being better athletes than whites. While acknowledging the complexities of racial categories and classifications (which are often decided by something as subjective as skin color), a considerable community of scholars and others continue to believe that one's racial background determines sports performance ability.

The twentieth century witnessed, of course, the rise in sciences devoted to the medicalized surpassing of a person's (black or not) natural athletic abilities. The advance of doping in sports cultures is primarily a phenomenon predicated on the desire to overcome the natural limits of the genetic body through pharmaceutical intervention. Cultural, political, economic, and social pressures to produce better athletes in sports worlds helped drive those involved in the sports medicine field to discover ways of stimulating muscle growth, oxygen use, blood flow, and tissue and cellular recovery in decisively unnatural ways, such as by doping. Doping is presently a global problem in sports cultures and was arguably first brought to light by steroid abuse among East German athletics teams.

Shocking was the revelation that East German (GDR) Olympic athletes were unwittingly given performance-enhancing drugs over the course of some 30 years. Between 1960 and 1990, East Germans ran, swam, and shot-putted their way to glory, winning Olympic gold medals and setting world records. The proverbial "lid" was blown off the practice in the 1990s, when several groups of athletes sued East German government agencies and pharmaceutical companies. Approximately 190 East German competitors launched a case against the German pharmaceutical company Jenapharm. They claimed that the East German firm knowingly supplied the steroids that were given to them by trainers and coaches from the 1960s onwards until East Germany's official State demise in 1989. Jenapharm executives argued that it was not responsible for the doping scandal and blamed sports leaders, officials, doctors, and coaches within the former East German communist system. In lieu of the scandal, Germany's athletics federation announced that it would check 22 national records set by East German athletes through the 1906s to the 1990s. The investigation also came after Ines Geipel, a member of the record-holding East German women's 4x100 meters relay team, asked for her record from the Summer Games of 1984 to be struck. She revealed she had been doped by team doctors with anabolic steroids. In a separate case another former East German swimmer Karin König sued the German Olympic committee for damages, claiming that she was also a victim of doping between 1982 and 1987.

This state-sponsored doping regime played a decisive role in the success of East German athletes in international competitions in the Cold War era; most notably at the 1976 Montreal Olympics and the 1980 Moscow games. The athletes who came forward claimed to have all received the steroid Turinabol, an anabolic agent containing testosterone made by the company Jenapharm. The infamous "blue bean" pills the athletes were given (that they were told contained vitamins) accelerated muscle build-up and boosted recovery times. Their subsequent side effects were catastrophic: infertility among women, embarrassing hair growth, breast cancer, heart problems, and testicular cancer. An estimated 800 East German athletes developed serious steroid-related ailments.

The most public face of the doping scandal is Andreas Krieger—a shot-putter who took so many male hormones she decided to have a sex change. One of the few other victims to have spoken publicly about her plight is the swimmer Rica Reinisch, who at the age of 15 won three gold medals in the 1980 Moscow Olympics.

East Germany's secret police kept meticulous records of the impact the drugs had on performance. A top-secret sporting medical committee including members of the Parteibüro, East Germany's communist leadership body, met to decide which members of the national squad were to be given the drugs. The aim was to show the superiority of the communist regime to its capitalist neighbor West Germany. In the 1972 Munich Olympics, East Germany—a country of 17 million—reached the top three in the medals table with the United States and the Soviet Union. Four years later, East German women won 11 of the 13 swimming events. Leaked documents suggest that Jenapharm scientists collaborated with the secret police, the Stasi, regarding the use of steroids in sports. In the late 1990s, criminal cases were brought against Manfred Ewald, the former East German team doctor, and Dr Manfred Hoppner, a former team medical consultant. They were given suspended sentences.

The legacy of the East German scandal should be one that awakens sports insiders and outsiders to the dangers of doping in sports (and the unbridled use of sports science technologies to create physically better athletes) and frightens athletes about the social and physical consequences pertaining to drug use. Yet, through the final third of the twentieth century, the interest in the links between genes, doping, and athlete performance have grown stronger and more controversial.

Ideas about the genetic foundation of human performance abilities were again brought to the public discussion through research conducted under the auspices of the Human Genome Project (HGP). Begun formally in 1990, the U.S.-led HGP was a 13-year collaborative research effort coordinated by the U.S. Department of Energy and the National Institutes of Health. The HGP mandate and goals were to:

- identify all the approximately 20,000–25,000 genes in human DNA;
- determine the sequences of the 3 billion chemical base pairs that make up human DNA;
- transfer related technologies to the private sector (including sports), and;
- address the ethical, legal, and social issues (ELSI) that may arise from the project.

A genome is the entirety of DNA in an organism, including its genes. Genes carry information for making all the proteins required by all organisms to grow and thrive. These proteins determine, among other things, how the organism looks, how well its body metabolizes food or fights infection, how the body moves, and, some researchers believe, even how it thinks and behaves. The HGP was launched as a means of exploring the relationship between DNA variations among individuals and different physical strengths and (especially) weaknesses between them. In learning about DNA sequences, logic followed that scientists would be able to more thoroughly understand the genetic origin of human capabilities. With knowledge of how physical capabilities operate at a genetic level, researchers could then either seek to "fix" faulty genes in people (gene therapy) or replace "poor" DNA in people (gene doping) with more effective DNA.

Among the HGP findings published in 2004 were descriptions of how a handful of the 25,000 genes detected in the human body were found to play a role in athletic performance. One example is the "IGF-1," or insulin growth factor, gene that when manipulated will increase the number and size of muscle cells in the body (steroids, by contrast, will only increase the size). Other findings indicate that genetically "boosting" the expression of the gene for "MGF," the mechano-growth factor, in the body could limit fatigue and improve muscle repair. Researchers for the HGP further learned that the "AMPK" gene affects how muscles accumulate and use glycogen (energy for the performing body) and, therefore, how its manipulation or restructuring impacts endurance. The "ACE-1," or angiotensin-converting enzyme gene, can actually be deleted in the body to increase strength or, by contrast, inserted for greater endurance (i.e., by having an effect on blood pressure and how muscles use oxygen). Troubling, however, is that only a few of these genes and/or their manipulation have been extensively tested for long-term side effects.

As a result of the HGP findings and other research on the genetic basis of performance, one common method of improving performance is increasing red blood cell numbers, which boosts the transport of oxygen from the lungs to the muscles, improving stamina and performance. The conventional but illegal method of boosting red blood cell count among athletes is with the hormone erythropoietin (EPO). The popularity of EPO and its link to doping scandals in the world of professional cycling have placed it on the World Anti-Doping Agency's (WADA) most wanted list. As a result, doctors and athletes have explored new forms of gene doping with "HCP" (a gene that regulates blood cell distribution) and Repoxygen (a drug that works by increasing levels of the body's own EPO). The subject of gene doping in sports was once more thrust into the public consciousness when German athletics coach Thomas Springstein was accused of attempting to obtain it prior to the 2006 Winter Olympics in Turin, Italy. Springstein and another trainer in Germany went under investigation by WADA, which banned gene doping outright in 2003. Approximately $8 million has been spent in WADA programs and initiatives designed to screen for gene doping, and WADA officials, including former WADA president Dick Pound, believe that gene doping will eventually surpass drug use as the main method of illegal performance enhancement in sports. One WADA-pioneered idea to fight gene doping and therapy in amateur sports is to "genetically map" athletes and then periodically rescreen them to detect any changes. Such a program would not be able to tell, however, whether or not an individual athlete received gene doping or therapy before entering into sports. But this does not mean genetically modified athletes avoid detection. The WADA rules allow samples to be tested for up to eight years after an event.

A frightening tendency in contemporary sports cultures is, then, the social and institutional pressure placed on elite athletes to remedy their genetically "deficient" bodies through scientific intervention. For athletes without the supposed "best" genetic gifts to excel at a particular sport, they may, from an early age, receive rounds of gene therapy to make them run swiftly, jump high, and be strong. By either legally or illegally having a doctor manipulate their DNA for a range of benefits, from increased stamina and reduced fat to larger muscles, athletes who receive genetic treatments may be able to cheat even their own physiological heritage. Yet, gene therapy and doping are together a modern Pandora's box in the world of sports because many risks face the athlete who decides to manipulate their genes. The first risk is that a manipulated gene might mutate into something pathological. The second major risk is that gene therapy might be carcinogenic over the long term (causing, especially, leukemia) or trigger another type of fatal illness.

KEY EVENTS

The expansion of medical–scientific ways of knowing and seeing the body in Western societies has certainly played a role in the framing of athletic performance along almost exclusively biological lines. The development and formal institutionalization of sports sciences throughout the twentieth century has ushered in a new paradigm for conceptualizing precisely the sporting body and its performance. With roots in physical education pedagogy in North American schools, the discipline of kinesiology has transformed how people approach sports performance. The (kinesiological) science of manual muscle testing was first developed in the early twentieth century by a Boston orthopedic surgeon named Robert Lovett. Lovett used muscle testing to analyze disabilities resulting from polio and nerve damage. He applied muscle testing to trace spinal nerve damage because muscles that tested weak often had a common spinal nerve. Henry and Florence Kendall modified and systematized Lovett's ideas, and in 1945 published their pioneering book *Muscle Testing and Function*. Dr. George Goodheart, a chiropractor, observed Kendall and Kendall's work and found that muscle testing was not only promising as a diagnostic method but could enhance physical training and therapy methods as well. By combining his discoveries, Goodheart pioneered a system that brought together work advanced by his predecessors including theories of lymphatic function, vascular function, the origin/insertion technique for muscular problems, ancient eastern meridian and acupuncture methods, and muscle testing for feedback in both diagnosis and therapeutic benefits. Kinesiological techniques and methods for analyzing the sporting body flourished in health, physical education, and other biological sciences programs in universities throughout the second half of the twentieth century. Influential first- and second-generation kinesiologists were John Thie, Alan Beardall, John Barton, Paul Dennison, Charles Krebbs, and Andrew Verity. Within the emerging kinesiological discipline, researchers developed keen interests in how human physiology, biomechanics, and psychology separately and collectively influence athlete performance. The burgeoning scientific approach to sports performance promulgated by schools of kinesiology has progressively explored the genetic parameters and foundations of sports performance along physical and psychological lines. Controversial in this area is the often researched link between genetic markers of "race" and their much believed link with sports performance.

In all the discussions about the genetic foundations of physical ability and their believed link to "race genes," the African dominance in distance running since the 1970s is stereotypically cited as a primary empirical indicator that particular races of people are more naturally equipped to excel in certain sports than others. Proponents of racial-genetic theory often point out that not only do East Africans (Kenyans) dominate in distance running but that of the more than 35 tribal groups in Kenya, a single (common genetic) tribe, the Kalenjins, has produced the greatest endurance runners of all-time, including Lelei, Loroupe, Kiptanui, Keino, Kiprotich, Cheromei, Sang, and Rono. The Kalenjins were traditionally an agrarian people who walked extensively through the Rift Valley of Kenya shepherding livestock. Evolutionist arguments have thus followed that centuries of physical cultural practice (long-distance farming) have helped to cultivate genes within the Kalenjins that have enhanced their ability to move across long distances efficiently. From studies of the Kalenjin dominance in distance running and others, kinesiologists increasingly lobbied that African runners (and black athletes in general) are genetically superior to white athletes. Compared to whites, they argued, black athletes (based on their regional origins and historical lifestyles) are not only better suited for sports that involve short, explosive bursts of energy because their bodies naturally contain higher concentrations of fast-twitch fibers than whites, but that other racialized black populations such as the Kalenjins are better suited for endurance events because their bodies have been conditioned, on a genetic/evolutionary basis, to endure.

Proponents of the black "super-gene" theory in sports have not been able to explain exactly how Africans (and not other black "racial" groups) managed to genetically evolve. Others have pointed out that the sporting success of other "raced" or "ethnicized" groups have not been attributed to genes. For example, the Finnish success in distance running through the 1920s to the 1970s would not be ascribed to genetics; instead, researchers discussed the merits of the high-protein Finnish diet and its relationship to sports performance. When white, British men dominated middle-distance running in the 1950s and 1980s, no one proclaimed superior genetics to be the source; by contrast, insiders ascribed British success, as documented in films such as *Chariots of Fire,* to the values of hard work, determination, and resolve shared by the athletes. Throughout the latter half of the twentieth century, black athlete success has rarely been attributed to psychological skills, diet, work effort, or moral values but rather genetics or illegal drug-taking. In this debate, one must question whether or not centuries-old racist ideologies about the uncivilized and inherently savage, powerful black body are still at work in the realm of sports.

A significant problem with genetic-based arguments, as researchers discovered in the 1980s and 1990s, is that despite the efforts of the Human Genome Project and many other researchers, scientists are yet to pinpoint which "racial" genes are necessary for topflight performances in sports. In a study carried out by Claude Bouchard at Laval University in Quebec, 23 black male students and 23 Caucasian male students were compared. The black students hailed from Cameroon, Senegal, Zaire, the Ivory Coast, and Burundi (mainly, that is, from the western and central parts of Africa), while the Caucasians were born in Canada and were of French descent. While the researchers found number and density differences between the groups' muscle fibers, they argued that muscle fiber type is not tightly regulated by genes and that an individual's muscle-fiber composition can change over time. In a separate study, Tim Noakes and his colleagues at the University of Capetown, South Africa, compared elite black versus elite white South African runners. Although both groups had similar 5K running times (about 13:45), the blacks were considerably faster in 10K and half-marathon races. Noakes and his colleagues examined both training and genetic differences between the groups, finding that the latter had far more explanatory power than the former. Perhaps the most revealing study on this topic was carried out by Swedish exercise physiologist Bengt Saltin, who compared sedentary adolescent Kenyans, Kenyan high school runners, and elite Kenyan runners with top-level Scandinavian runners. Saltin unearthed a number of important facts. First, relatively sedentary adolescent Kenyans had exactly the same aerobic capacities as sedentary Danish teenagers. If the Kenyans are genetically superior, one would expect them to have higher aerobic capacities than their Scandinavian counterparts (unless their "superhuman" genes only revealed themselves in response to training). Second, young Kenyan runners train with incredible intensity; about 50 to 60 percent of their total mileage was done at heart rates of 90 percent of maximum or higher. This was significantly higher than the Scandinavians' total and is much higher than the training habits of European and American runners in general.

Culturally based studies of how Kenyans train reveal far more empirically consistent documentation about physical performance. The African approach to training differs considerably from the American–European method in a number of ways, including intensity (Africans usually train more intensely but with less mileage), the amount of hill training completed, periodization (Africans vary their training more and rest more than North Americans or Europeans), and diet (Africans eat more carbohydrate, less protein, and less fat than North American athletes). Africans also benefit from a decade-long base period—running back and forth to school at moderate speeds in childhood—before they take up serious running, while Americans and Europeans tend to enter into competitive running in senior school without a prolonged, strength-boosting build-up during childhood.

Arguments about the role of genes in sports performance and ability beyond the realm of race have also been highlighted in the past 20 years. In 1997, American professional golfer Casey Martin sued the PGA for disallowing him to use an electric golf cart during competition. Tour officials deemed his use of the cart provided him with an unfair competitive advantage because it reduced his overall work effort throughout a round of play. Martin's lawsuit against the PGA, however, sought to force the PGA Tour to accommodate his rare genetic disorder, Klippel-Trenaunay-Weber Syndrome, which makes it painful and even dangerous for him to walk. His doctors testified that undue stress on his withered right leg could cause it to break and may force amputation. U.S. Magistrate Thomas Coffin finally ruled in 2001 that during a tournament a golf course is a place of public accommodation and thus is covered under the federal *Americans with Disabilities Act*. Martin, despite PGA Tour resistance, won the right to use a cart during competition because the PGA Tour could not discriminate against him on the basis of his genetically inherited condition. Martin's case generated a national debate over the rights of the disabled to compete in professional sports and an eventual outpouring of support for him. One could argue that the PGA's resistance to Martin's initial argument illustrates more than a degree of hypocrisy in the sport, however, as players seek to extend and eclipse the "natural" abilities of their bodies to hit a golf ball through the use of high-tech clubs, balls, shoes, and gloves.

More recently, South African Paralympic runner Oscar Pistorius lost his right to compete against able-bodied athletes because of his over-reliance on technology. Known as the "Blade Runner," Pistorius is a double amputee world record holder in the 100-meter, 200-meter, and 400-meter Paralympic events and runs with the aid of carbon fiber transtibial artificial limbs (a commercial product named "Cheetah"). In 2007, Pistorius took part in his first international able-bodied competitions. However, his artificial lower legs, while enabling him to compete, generated claims from physiologists that he has an unfair advantage over able-bodied runners. The International Association of Athletics Federations (IAAF) agreed and amended its rules to ban the use of any technical device that incorporates springs, wheels, or any other element that provides a user with an advantage over another athlete not using such a device. Among other issues, the Pistorius case inadvertently raised another debate about the fairness of unequal access to technological advances in sports training and competition; such that critics cited the IAAF ruling as unjust and arbitrary in a world of sports where athletes from wealthy nations benefit from access to the best training and competition technology while others who come from impoverished nations are disadvantaged.

FUTURE PROSPECTS

As long as ideologies about sports performance are buttressed by medical–technical and scientific understandings of the human body, we can expect to witness only heightened interest in the biology of performance. As the race to produce the perfect athlete rages on, scientists explore the inner/genetic operations of the body and how to physically train the body in highly technological ways in order to push the boundaries of nature. Case studies in sports illustrate, however, that even scientific constructions of the natural body are not neutral but rather replete with cultural constructions, and often times discriminatory stereotypes, about the best or most natural bodies.

See also Antidoping Rules and Policies; Eating Disorders; Ergogenics; Erythropoietin (EPO); Gene Manipulation; Men in Women's Sports; Racial Profiling and Stacking; Steroid Use by Athletes; Transsexual Athletes; Women in Men's Sports.

Further Reading: Entine, J. (2000). *Taboo: Why Black Athletes Dominate Sports and Why We Are Afraid to Talk About It.* New York: PublicAffairs; Galton, F. (1865). *Hereditary Genius.* London: MacMillan & Co.; Herrnstein, R., and Murray, C. (1994). *The Bell Curve.* New York: Free Press; Hoberman, J. (1997). *Darwin's Athletes.* Boston: Houghton Mifflin; Noakes, T. (2002). *Lore of Running.* Champaign, IL: Human Kinetics; Rushton, J-P. *(1997). Race, Evolution and Behavior.* Port Huron, MI: Charles Darwin Research Institute.

Michael Atkinson

C

CHEATING DURING COMPETITION

Cheating in sports is the deliberate violation of the formal or informal rules and codes governing fair competition between athletes. Many athletes are both socially encouraged to cheat within particular sports cultures and internally motivated to sometimes win at all costs. While often undertaken individually by athletes, cheating can also occur as a group effort involving several players, coaches, trainers, and even team owners. Cheating is perhaps as organized as sports and can be difficult to police by authority agents.

BACKGROUND

Among the most obvious rationales offered for athlete cheating is extrinsic motivation, especially at the elite amateur and professional levels. With the ongoing commercialization of sports and the sheer profit to be made by succeeding, the financial incentive to cheat has never been greater. The very structure of modern sports places such a great emphasis on competition, excellence, and the exaltation of winners that few see little merit in Vince Lombardi's old adage that "it is not whether you win or lose, it is how you play the game." Corporate sponsorships, status markers, professional accomplishments such as championships, and the social kudos that all follow along with winning can be so alluring that athletes are motivated to break the rules of sports in order to win.

The pressure to produce a winning team, even in the realm of youth sports, is massive for coaches and administrators. In the 2001 Little League World Series, American player Danny Almonte became a household name as one of the most promising young hurlers of a generation. The media spotlight fell on him when, toward the end of the tournament, the young Dominican immigrant pitched a perfect game on national television. In a bizarre turn of fate, officials in his native land leaked information to the American press that Almonte was not a 12-year-old (the tournament age maximum) but was actually 14 years old.

One must also remember that professional athletes are paid workers in complex sports corporations (or elites who may represent their nation) and, as such, are sometimes incredibly pressured by fellow athletes, peers, coaches, and sponsors to produce results. It is difficult to accept, for instance, that all professional cyclists who have been caught doping in the past decade have each individually decided to cheat in the complete absence of social pressure. Important light has been shed on how athletes are socially pressured to cheat and learn to ideologically conceptualize the cheating process. Athletes in competitive amateur and professional sports are taught to unquestionably strive for social distinction as athletes, accept no limits as players, make sacrifices for their sports, and play through pain and injury as part of an overarching sports ethic. The belief in and pursuit of the sports ethic by athletes often takes on a pathological form, such that athletes will even break the rules in order to succeed. Of course, not all athletes are socialized quite so completely or assess all social interaction and athletic performances in relation to the principles of the sports ethic, but so ubiquitous and impacting is this ethic that most athletes must encounter and reconcile themselves to it at some point in their sports careers.

The bulk of athlete behavior during competition, training, or in social settings jibes with sports ethic requisites. Athlete behavior can be illustrated on a statistical "normal curve," and everyday athlete behavior can be located at the "heart" of the curve. Athlete behaviors that deviate from the sports ethic, such as cheating, are conceptually located at either of the two normal curve's tails. What we might call total "sports deviance" is rather statistically rare. On the one tail, a category of behaviors is placed that is referred to as positive deviance. These are athlete behaviors that pursue the principles of the sports ethic to an unhealthy extent. An example of positive deviance is losing weight dangerously quickly (for instance, through dehydration strategies) in order to make a weight category in, say, boxing or wrestling, or in order to please judges in an "appearance sports" such as gymnastics or figure skating. On the other tail, Hughes and Coakley (1991) also describe negative deviance, wherein cheating behaviors normally fall. These are athlete behaviors that overtly reject or dismiss the importance of the sports ethic frame.

Among the most common forms of cheating as negative deviance in sports are direct rule violations undertaken by players during the course of competition. For example, in 1987, while playing for Minnesota, Joe Niekro was accused by opposing players of doctoring the baseball with an emery board. An umpire made him empty his pockets on the mound, and an emery board and a piece of sandpaper fell out. Niekro denied doctoring the ball but accepted a 10-day suspension he received from the league. In December 1990, jockey Sylvester Carmouche finished first (as a 23–1 long shot) while riding horse Landing Officer at a Louisiana Delta Downs race. Landing Officer won the race by a staggering 24 lengths and crossed the finish line a mere 1.2 seconds off the track record. Race officials soon learned that Carmouche had steered the horse off the course while it was lost from view in the dense fog covering the infield that day, illegally cut across the middle of the track, only to rejoin the field as the leader of the pack.

One of the most prevalent and problematic forms of cheating in the modern era of sports is doping or the use illegal performance-enhancing drugs. Few sports are immune to doping problems, but few sports seem to have been plagued by this form of cheating as much as professional cycling. Jacques Anquetil, in a self-effacing manner, once said, "You don't ride the Tour [de France] on mineral water." Tour de France officials have increasingly found more than mineral water in competitor's systems. In 1978, they discovered that Michel Pollentier was not riding on mineral water, or at least, so they suspected. Officials disqualified Pollentier after a brilliant stage win in the race. They discovered he had been using someone else's urine (stashed cleverly within an elaborate bag and drainage system underneath his jersey) for each of his post-stage sample submissions. While the process of substituting uncontaminated urine for racer's "dirty" urine allegedly continues to this day, of far more concern in the sport is the use of performance-enhancing drugs undetectable through current technology.

In the 1904 Olympics in St. Louis, New Yorker Fred Lorz won the men's marathon in 3 hours and 13 minutes. A few short minutes after his victory, organizers discovered Lorz had cheated by hailing a passing car and riding 11 miles as a passenger. Lorz was stripped of his medal and received a lifetime ban from the Olympics. Only a year later, he amazingly won the Boston Marathon. Critics of sports cheats such as Lorz claim that one of the most common character traits among them is hubris. Hubris is a pride-driven arrogance, a belief that one is above any formal punishment systems in a social institution such as sports. Despite the contemporary punitive, zero-tolerance era in amateur and professional sports, the hubris one learns as an athlete leads the individual to believe that "I simply won't be the one who is caught." Sociologists and psychologists of sports note that because athletes are often treated in Western cultures as socially important, "special populations" of people with tremendous status, they are socialized into believing their own impunity.

A final and perhaps lesser known form of cheating in sports is the deliberate rigging of contests or collusion by those involved to determine the outcomes. Collusion to "fix" games or tournaments has been historically linked to gambling cultures in sports. Allegations of match fixing have dogged a cluster of sports including boxing, horse racing, baseball, dog racing, football, and basketball for well over 80 years. For example, after winning both the 1950 NCAA and NIT tournaments (the only school at the time in history to have accomplished such a double), the City College of New York fell into national disgrace in 1951. Seven players were indicted for conspiring to shave points from games or deliberately lose regular-season games. The scandal eventually spread to seven other schools around the country. Players from Long Island University, New York University, Bradley, Kentucky, and Toledo were all named in the gambling/point-shaving ring.

BASEBALL—THE HOME OF THE CHEAT?

Throughout the twentieth century, few sports have produced as many cheaters (perhaps outside of track and field) as baseball. Consider some of the more (in)famous cheaters in professional baseball.

1. New York Giants (1951)
   The Giants admitted they had an elaborate sign-stealing system in place at the Polo Grounds in 1951. Coach Herman Franks would sit in the Giants' clubhouse and use a telescope to steal the opposing catcher's signs to the pitcher.
2. John McGraw (Orioles, Cardinals, Giants, 1891–1906)
   John McGraw had a league-wide reputation of illegally blocking opposing players on the bases and attempting to injure them with illegal plays.
3. Gaylord Perry (Giants, Indians, Rangers, Padres, Yankees, Braves, Mariners, Royals, 1962–1983)
   Perry, a Hall of Fame inductee, was an expert at doctoring a baseball with Vaseline in order to throw "special" pitches. In 1982, he became one of the very few pitchers to be actually suspended for doctoring the ball.
4. Albert Belle (Indians, White Sox, Orioles, 1989–2000)
   Belle was among several players in major history to be caught using a corked bat.
5. Whitey Ford (Yankees, 1950–1967)
   Among Ford's contribution to the game was his invention of the "gunk ball," a baseball loaded with dirt that enabled it to move unpredictably when pitched.
6. The Bossard Family (groundskeepers, Cleveland Indians, Chicago White Sox, 1920s–present)
   Members of the Bossard family would illegally doctor the fields under their charge in order to counter opposing teams' strengths. They would water down base paths, alter the distance of outfield fences, and other tricks.
7. Norm Cash (White Sox, Tigers, 1958–1974)
   Cash used a corked bat during the 1961 season, a year in which he led the league in batting percentage with a .361 average, 41 home runs, and 132 runs batted in (RBI).
8. Graig Nettles (Twins, Indians, Yankees, Padres, Braves, Expos, 1967–1988)
   On September 7, 1974, New York Yankees' Graig Nettles broke his bat hitting a ball, after which six rubber "superballs" flew out of the remains. Nettles claimed innocence, arguing that Yankees fans had actually "donated" the bat to him.

KEY EVENTS

There are few "landmark" cases of cheating in sports that rival the 1919 Chicago White Sox scandal. Despite being incredible favorites in the 1919 World Series against the Cincinnati Reds, the White Sox astonishingly lost to them in eight games in a best-of-nine World Series. Sports fans, pundits, and insiders decried the Sox's lackluster play throughout the Series, and rumors about a potential fix tainted the games. After a series of insider tips to the police and team owners, players from the White Sox were called to a grand jury. The grand jury indicted eight White Sox players, including pitcher Eddie Cicotte and outfielder "Shoeless" Joe Jackson, who admitted that players on the team had received thousands of dollars from Chicago and New York gamblers to lose the series. In another twist, a higher court acquitted the players of conspiracy to defraud the public. But newly instated baseball commissioner Kenesaw Mountain Landis ignored the court's determination of player innocence and banned each for life. Several of the players, including Joe Jackson, were regarded at the time as among the best in the sport's young history. Such a case is a classic example, to sociologists of sports, of the culture of hubris among athletes.

In 1985, at Cincinnati's Riverfront Stadium, baseball icon Pete "Charlie Hustle" Rose broke the all-time hit record in professional baseball by notching his 4,192nd during a late-season game. Rose passed another icon, Ty Cobb, to become baseball's career leader in hits; one of the most coveted records in the sports. Rose's accomplishment more than secured his place in the professional baseball hall of fame in Cooperstown, New York. However, before the decade ended, Rose's career legacy was forever tainted when he was banned from the sport after a federal investigation found he had gambled thousands of dollars on baseball games as a player and a manager for the Cincinnati Reds. Twenty years after the incident, and repeated personal and public appeals to have Rose reinstated into professional baseball, Major League Baseball continues to stand on their side of the proverbial line that has been drawn in the sand regarding gambling and cheating in the sport. Rose's punishment and lifelong exile has become a symbol of warning to athletes in baseball and other sports.

On April 21, 1980, Rosie Ruiz, a 23-year-old New Yorker, crossed the finish line as the women's winner of the prestigious Boston Marathon. Not only did she win in her gender category, she set the third fastest time on record at the time for a female runner (2:31:56). Those involved in the event remarked how fit Ruiz appeared, especially because she approached the winner's podium relatively relaxed and free of sweat. Ruiz had been a virtual unknown in the world of distance running, had not been noticed as a front-runner during the race, and stunned the running world with her unexpected victory. However, spectators later approached race officials, offering testimony that they had witnessed the runner entering the race illegally during the final mile and sprinting to the finish line. Race officials disqualified Ruiz from the race and soon after discovered that she also cheated during the earlier New York marathon. Ruiz used the same tactic in New York, riding a subway car from the starting line to a stop near the finish line. In a shocking repeat of Ruiz's rule violation, in September 1991, spectators noticed that the winner of the Brussels marathon, Abbes Tehami, cheated to win the race by having his coach run nearly two-thirds of it for him. Tehami leapt into the marathon toward its end and claimed victory. He was also later disqualified.

At other times, the use of illegal equipment on the field can prove disastrous for players and teams. One of the most dramatic examples of a player being caught during a game using equipment that violates the sport's rules occurred in 1993 during the Stanley Cup Finals. The National Hockey League will only allow a certain degree of curve on a player's stick. If a player is caught using an illegal blade (which the opposing team can ask, at any point during a game to be checked by a referee) he receives a two-minute penalty. The best-known playoff stick-check came in the 1993 Stanley Cup finals between the Los Angeles Kings and the Montreal Canadiens. With the Kings leading 2–1 in the game and 1:45 away from going up 2–0 in the series, Canadiens coach Jacques Demers asked referee Kerry Fraser to measure the curve on Marty McSorley's stick. McSorley's stick was determined to be illegal, and the Canadiens were awarded a power play. Eric Desjardins scored on the ensuing power play, sending the game into overtime. Desjardins scored his third goal of the game a few seconds into overtime winning the game, and the Canadiens won the next three games to win the Cup. One of the issues to emerge in post-playoff discussions of the incident was the complex codes and rules of illegal stick use among players and how McSorley had seemingly "forgotten" one of the primary rules that instructs a player to always exchange his illegal stick for a legal one in the late stages of a game.

By 1988, Jamaican-born Canadian sprinter Ben Johnson had been named the "fastest man alive" and was favored to win the marquee 100-meter sprint at the Seoul Olympics that year. He fulfilled his media billing as the "chosen one" and became an Olympic champion by beating rivals Carl Lewis and Linford Christie in the final heat. Just three days later, Johnson tested positive for the banned anabolic steroid stanozolol. Olympic officials condemned Johnson and immediately stripped him of his gold medal. Following the Olympics, the Dubin Inquiry investigation into Canadian amateur sports was established to study, in part, the extent of drug cheating among athletes. The scandal and the Dubin Inquiry's final report were among the catalysts for the eventual organization and establishment of the World Anti-Doping Agency (WADA). Johnson's positive test also directed the international spotlight on the prevalence of performance-enhancing drugs in track and field and the role of sports doctors in promoting unsafe and illegal practices in sports, and it generated a new global interest in the role of doping in sports.

Yet, a decade and a half later, the 2003 investigation of the Bay Area Laboratory Co-Operative (BALCO) and its founder, Victor Conte, shocked the sports world once more. Journalists Lance Williams and Mark Fainaru-Wada investigated and exposed the company as a major distributor of illegal performance-enhancing drugs to professional athletes in the United States. In particular, BALCO marketed and sold Tetrahydrogestrinone (THG), a growth hormone, to elite sports cultures around the world. Ironically, BALCO also was a service business in the elite sports world for blood and urine analysis and food supplements. In effect, they had produced an illegal drug (THG) that their own tests would not detect. But, in 2003, after media allegations about the company's activities, the U.S. Attorney for the Northern District of California investigated BALCO further. U.S. sprint coach Trevor Graham had also supplied insider information to the U.S. Anti-Doping Agency (USADA) in June 2003. Toward the end of 2003, over two dozen athletes in the United States were found with the illegal steroid THG in their systems. On September 3, 2003, agents of the Internal Revenue Service, Food and Drug Administration, San Mateo Narcotics Task Force, and USADA raided BALCO facilities. Among the athletes implicated in the BALCO investigation were: baseball players Barry Bonds, Jason Giambi, Gary Sheffield, Benito Santiago, Jeremy Giambi, Bobby Estalella, and Armando Rios; hammer thrower John McEwen; shot putters Kevin Toth and C. J. Hunter; sprinters Dwain Chambers, Marion Jones, Tim Montgomery, Raymond Smith, and Kelli White; middle-distance runner Regina Jacobs; boxer Shane Mosley; cyclist Tammy Thomas; National Football League (NFL) players Bill Romanowski, Tyrone Wheatley, Barrett Robbins, Chris Cooper, and Dana Stubblefield; and, members of the 1998 U.S. Olympic Judo team. The BALCO scandal single-handedly blew the lid off of the vast culture of drug cheating in North American professional sports and the sheer amount of cooperation between players, doctors, trainers, corporate sponsors, and research companies in the cheating.

One of the more recent forms of cheating to receive intense public scrutiny is espionage among teams. As an example, think about the subject of spying on or scouting others players or teams as part of doing sports. While it is common practice to study videotaped footage of other teams in professional sports such as ice hockey, or to send team representatives to watch others practice and study their "secret" plays, in other sports, such as football, such activities constitute espionage. In 2007, the New England Patriots were caught videotaping other teams' defensive coordinators as they sent in hand signals to the players. The Patriots would study the signals in order to crack the codes and thereby anticipate the plays of defensive squads. The Patriots were fined $250,000, head coach Bill Belichick was fined $500,000, and perhaps most consequentially, the NFL removed the team's right to draft a player in the first round of the 2008 draft. Just a few weeks prior to the Patriots' "Spy Gate" scandal, Formula One racing team McLaren was assessed a staggering $100 million fine and stripped of team racing points by the World Motor Sports Council for possession of "leaked" technical information on rival team Ferrari's car designs.

FUTURE PROSPECTS

The current stance adopted by a majority of leagues and sports organizations toward identifying and catching cheats in sports cultures is still reactive rather than proactive. Despite a groundswell of insider and journalistic evidence pointing to deep-seated cultures of cheating in a vast array of sports, organizers have not typically considered the growing number of allegations regarding a huge array of cheating types and forms (perhaps save for the case of antidoping) as indicators of patterned cultural deviance among athletes. Cheaters tend to be painted as isolated offenders in sports rather than symbols of sporting cultures that often play "above the rules" of the game.

See also Academic Misconduct Among Athletes; Sports Doctors, Trainers, and Drugs.

Further Reading: Hughes, R., and Coakley, J. (1991). Positive Deviance Among Athletes: The Implications of Overconformity to the Sport Ethic. *Sociology of Sport Journal* 8: 307–325.

Michael Atkinson

COLLECTIVE PROTESTS AND SOCIAL MOVEMENTS

Collective protests in sports refer to group actions undertaken by individuals in either formal or informal social groups that are aimed at changing the ways in which sports is politically organized and practiced. Other social protests staged in and around heavily mass-mediated sports events may have little to do with the game or sport in question. Here, political and cultural protestors strategically seize the public platform created by spectator sports in order to promulgate their ideologies. Particular protests are one-off events, while others are staged repeatedly. In the case of the latter, when groups make concerted efforts over time to protest an issue in or around sports, the group may develop into what political scientists and sociologists refer to as new social movements.

BACKGROUND

The rise of social groups that have been referred to as "new social movements" occurred following the 1960s. Social movements prior to the 1960s, such as the labor union movement or the suffrage movement, were primarily focused on balancing out the political–economic disparities that existed between large groups of people. New social movements (NSM) that have developed from the 1960s onward share a greater interest on identity-rights politics. These movements, such as the feminist movement, environmental movement, LGBT movement, and disability rights movement, all promote changes in dominant social lifestyles and cultures that would lead to a greater appreciation and care for others (using their own group focal point as a case example). Fairness, equity, justice, tolerance, and diversity are often thematic philosophical undercurrents in each of the NSMs. Unlike political pressure groups or traditional social movements that have formal organizational structures and easily defined members, NSMs consist of an informal, loosely organized social network of supporters. Strict protest groups tend to be single-issue based and are often local in terms of the scope of change they wish to effect. By contrast, NSMs endure longer than single-issue protests and seek to effect change on an (inter)national level on various issues in relation to their set of beliefs and ideals. A NSM may, however, adopt the tactic of a protest campaign as part of its strategy for achieving wide-ranging change.

According to a theory called resource mobilization, new social movements come together as members recognize the collective benefit of pooling their material, intellectual, emotional, and social assets together in the quest for change. Additionally, change will only result through the new social movement's efforts if they, at some point in time, become enmeshed with dominant power structures from within. Simply, it is not enough to protest from the outside. To some, a new social movement will first contain a core group of charismatic members who harness the disaffected energies of many of the social movement's members and attract critical support from them. From there, other key agents within the NSM will capture the media's attention, forge alliances with those in power, and create an organizational structure. This theory assumes that without such resources NSMs cannot be effective and that dissent alone is not enough to engender any social change.

The world of sports has occasionally been a social battleground of NSM campaigning, protest, and attempted social change. By and large, NSMs in sports, such as the women's rights movements, LGBT rights movements, ethnic minority rights movements, disability movements, and others, have struggled to ensure that the people they represent are treated equitably in athletic contexts (i.e., arguing for their greater access to sports, their respectful treatment therein, and that shifts in social constructions of sports are needed to reflect a diverse range of participants' interests, backgrounds, and abilities). Members from each of these NSMs have become involved in dominant hierarchical sports structures to help lobby for their group. Thus, we can legitimately speak of the Paralymipc movement as an NSM because it not only creates a social place for athletes with disabilities to compete at an international level, but also because it seeks to crack the hegemony of able-bodied sports cultures, to work within major sports federations to promote inclusiveness, and one which designs international media campaigns to promote awareness about disability rights in all social spaces.

The social movements in sports mostly work behind the public scenes of sports in order to effect change. More visible are social movements that use the mass mediation of sports as a platform for doing identity politics; generally, politics based on nationhood, political paradigms, religion, or ethnicity. The taking hostage and murder of Israeli athletes at the 1972 Olympics in Munich by social movement Black September is a chilling example of how sports or its athletes become drawn into the politics of contest between warring ideological rivals. Although sports is often described as, and wished to be, a depoliticized zone where athletes may be free from intense social and cultural hostilities, the global mass mediation of many sports over the past four decades have transformed them into attractive targets for doing NSM work. Equally, because sports megaevents such as the World Cup and the Olympics bring international political rivals into close contexts, it makes sense that hostilities from the outside will become interlaced with competition on the inside.

KEY EVENTS

Just four years before the tragic events of Munich, events leading up to the 1968 Summer Games in Mexico contained a landmark example of how NSM may use sports as a backdrop for engaging in social protest. For more than six months prior to the opening ceremonies, a group of over 5,000 middle-class and pro-Marxist university student protesters (from the Universidad Autonoma de Mexico and the Instituto Politecnico Nacional) repeatedly gathered near Olympic venues to express anger against the Mexican government's massive spending on the Games. The student movement in Mexico, like that in the United States, did not form around the issue of sports but because they interpreted the Mexican government's spending on the Games as a trivial use of public money. According to these students, who were becoming the voices of a leftist middle-class youth population, the Mexican government led by President Gustavo Ordaz had wasted over $140 million on the event, money that could have been utilized to address problems of Mexican educational access, labor opportunities, and health care programs for the large Mexican working class. Often perceived as a source of cultural and economic success, the Olympics were seen (in this case) by Ordaz's government as a symbolic marker of Mexico's "success" in world sports and, for this reason, any negative sentiment surrounding the Games was suppressed.

Following a summer of outburst and hostilities between protesters and police, Ordaz's government sought to stop the student movement outright. Under government support, the Mexican army "cleared out" student protesters from the Plaza Tlatelolco on October 2, 1968 (just 10 days before the opening ceremonies of the Games), by firing upon demonstrators with machine guns. Thirty-two student deaths were reported by the Mexican government, with other death counts running as high as 300. Around 2,000 students were jailed following the protest, and the clearly depleted resistance movement went away before the start of the Games themselves. Despite the 1968 Olympics' status as the first internationally broadcast Games, only a few stories about the student movement reached public discourse during the event. But during the Games, the American civil rights/resistance movement found expression on the field of play when John Carlos and Tommie Smith raised their fists as signals of Black Power while standing on the podium receiving their medals after the men's 400-meter race.

Geopolitical hostilities between the capitalist United States and the communist Soviet Union were not hidden from public view in 1980, when the United States, along with a handful of other Western nations, refused to participate in the Winter Games in Moscow (ostensibly due to the Soviet Union's invasion of Afghanistan). But it is difficult to divorce the political move/protest from early political philosophies toward the Soviets in the late Cold War world. The boycott, one might argue, had little to do with sports or the invasion and everything to do with the resurfacing of military tensions between the two nation-states and clashes over political–economic philosophy. In 1984, the Soviet Union and other Eastern Bloc nations responded in kind by boycotting the Summer Games in Los Angeles.

During the early 1960s, an international across-sports social movement developed that ideologically clashed swords with the National Party's apartheid governmental regime in South Africa. Established in 1948, the white federal government apartheid policy was an affront to sports authorities and players around the world. Among the first organizations within sports to chastise the South African government was FIFA, who in 1961 suspended the South African team from play because black players from South Africa were barred from membership on their national team. In 1964, the International Olympic Committee (IOC) joined in by banning South Africa from the Tokyo Games. The United Nations eventually joined into the NSM when its general assembly called for a boycott of all South African sports bodies that practiced apartheid. Without any formal authority over sports worlds, the UN special committee promoted the ban, but some of its member nations and international committees continued to maintain sporting links with the country.

A sports tempest then brewed in 1970 when England hosted an exhibition tour in the United Kingdom that included the all-white South African team.

Only two years earlier, South Africa had outraged the international cricket community when its government refused to allow an England cricket team to visit the country because Basil D'Oliveira, a South African–born black player, was on the England team. By 1970, South Africa was barred from the International Cricket Council (ICC). England was subsequently pressured by members of the ICC to withdraw the South African cricket team's invitation to the UK exhibition tour. Additionally, England faced political pressure from African, Asian, and West Indian nations who threatened boycotts of the Commonwealth Games in Edinburgh later that year. The political swordplay between members of the anti-apartheid sports movement and others continued throughout the 1970s. In 1971, the Australian cricket team canceled a South African tour. In 1976, Tanzania lead 22 African nations in a boycott of the Montreal Olympics after the IOC refused to ban New Zealand from the Games after the All Blacks rugby team toured to South Africa that year. A decade later, a British Lions rugby tour to South Africa was canceled after rampant protests in the United Kingdom and elsewhere.

Starting in 1988, the Nike Corporation was criticized for contracting with, and outsourcing to, factories in countries such as Vietnam, Indonesia, and Mexico. Vietnam Labor Watch, an activist group, was among the first to document that factories contracted by Nike violated minimum wage and overtime laws in Vietnam. In the 1990s, Nike also faced damning criticism for use of child labor in Cambodia and Pakistan in factories it contracted to manufacture soccer balls. Among other violations alleged in reports about worker abuse was that most Nike shoe factories illegally paid workers wages less than the industry standard 86 cents per day. A slew of newspapers and magazines jumped onto the anti-Nike bandwagon, conducting and reporting their own first-hand investigations of labor practices in Indonesia, including the *Los Angeles Times, Boston Globe, New York Times, Chicago Tribune, USA Today, Wall Street Journal, The International Herald Tribune, Rolling Stone,* and *Jakarta Post.* In 1996, the Portland grassroots activist and antiglobalization organization "Justice, Do It Nike" began regular mass-mediated protests at Nike stores across the country. Partly due to a burgeoning anti-Nike movement in the United States, strikes by thousands of Nike-producing workers in Vietnam were initiated in 1997. The anti-Nike movement grew until the early 2000s, drawing together workers' advocacy groups around the globe to examine fair production and trade practices in sports. Included among them were Press for Change; Boycott Nike; the National Labor Committee; Global Exchange; Campaign for Labor Rights; National Organization of Women; Clean Clothes Campaign; Community Aid Abroad; The Living Wage Project; Justice, Do It Nike; and many other nongovernmental organizations (NGOs).

A collection of new social movements that take aim at sporting practices seeks to expose the exploitation of "voiceless" victims in sports. For example, in recognizing the impact of golf on the environment, an alliance of environmental NGOs, consumer groups, tourism critics, and concerned citizens in Japan formed the Global Anti-Golf Movement (GAG'M) to oppose the rapid proliferation of golf courses and golf tourism in Asia-Pacific. The group attracted public attention when it promoted the World Anti-Golf Day on April 29, 1993. The movement stirred a flurry of debate about the environmental impact of sports such as golf, skiing, snowboarding, boating, and others. The movement then spread to countries such as the United States, Canada, Brazil, and India through the mid-1990s, leading to public criticism of sports as environmentally unfriendly. Environmental designers have attempted to respond to the still-developing environmental movement in sports by constructing "green courses" through the later years of the twentieth century. Organizations such as GAG'M and others claim, however, that such courses, including the community-resisted Silvertip golf course in the town of Canmore, Alberta, are hardly more environmentally friendly than their nongreen counterparts. Dating back to an anticruelty movement started in 1802, The League Against Cruel Sports (UK) has been a global leader in promoting the termination of sports that use and abuse animals as participants. Originally formed through decades of consciousness-raising about the inhumanity involved in fox hunting, animal bating, and angling, the League has drawn together people from an array of social backgrounds and has become structurally associated with mainstream animal rights groups such as the Royal Society for the Protection of Animals. People involved with the League have successfully lobbied for landmark legal reform regarding animal abuse in British sports, including new laws protecting historically hunted animals such as otters, badgers, and most controversially, foxes.

A new social movement that is written about or analyzed in the popular media is not a collectively organized group per se, but more of an interconnected series of events that are conceptually labeled similarly. The movement is referred to as the "anti-Olympic movement," and its central actors are normally disenfranchised or historically marginalized groups within Olympic host cities or those concerned by the cultural politics of host cities and nations. They use the Olympic media platform to reach international audiences, placing pressure on local governments, businesses, police, or other officials in the process. For example, at the 2000 Olympic Games in Sydney, Aborigines, often representing the Nyungah Circle of Elders, staged protests in the weeks leading up to the Games as a method of drawing public attention to their land claims, historical racism in Australia, and the negative ecological impact of the Games on the local environment. Even before the IOC announced the city of Vancouver had won the bid to host the 2010 Winter Games, representatives of the Four Host First Nations and the Assembly of First Nations expressed strong resistance to the staging of the Games in and around Vancouver. Since then, groups such as the Native Youth Movement have decried the massive budget spent on the event (which could have been used to help address the economic disparities existing between Natives and white Canadians in the province), the appropriation of disputed Native land for venue sites (unceded Salish, St'at'imc, and Squamish territories), the selling of historic Native medicine and religious sites to foreign investors, the destruction of natural wildlife areas such as Eagleridge Bluffs and Callaghan through forest clear cutting, and the gentrification of Native peoples already caused by Olympic development and tourism.

There have been few Olympic Games to date, perhaps since at least the 1936 Berlin Games, as socially controversial as the Beijing 2008 Summer Olympics.

Following the IOC's announcement that China won the 2008 bid, anti-Olympic sentiment (in this instance directed both at the IOC for its choice and toward the host country, China) focused on China's military relationship with Tibet and the potential for boycotts from pro-Tibetan organizations, such as "Students for a Free Tibet," as well as from organizations such as Amnesty International, who disagree with China's involvement in the military crises in Darfur and Myanmar. Supporters of the Tibetan independence movement and the Dalai Lama disrupted the Olympic torch relay passage through Paris and London, creating shock and concern among the IOC and the Beijing organizing committee. China has also been battling problems with air and water pollution both in the city of Beijing and in neighboring areas, which anti-Olympians cited as a major health risk to athletes. Interpol also publicly issued statements in early 2008 that there was a "real possibility" that the Beijing Olympics would be targeted by terrorist groups as well as potentially violent disruption from pro-Tibet protestors. Defenders of the Beijing Games suggested that the international "concern" over the Games had more to do with racist anti-Chinese sentiment and political opposition to its developing economic power than anything to do with Tibet, water pollution, or sports. They were perhaps correct, as the Games were staged with only minor protests, no major disruptions, and no health scares.

FUTURE PROSPECTS

Given the global popularity and significance of sports as a cultural process and product, it comes as no surprise that identity rights battles are waged by new social movements in and around sports fields. The idea that sports are free from political and cultural jockeying between groups is now more historical thinking than contemporary reality. The mobilization of political action through or against the backdrop of sports calls into question the ideological foundations of sports organizations and institutions, along with the very social role of sports in contemporary local–global politics.

See also Animal Blood Sports; Environmental Impacts of Sports; Terrorism and the Olympics.

Further Reading: Howe, D. (2008). *The Cultural Politics of the Paralympic Movement: Through the Anthropological Lens.* London: Routledge; Melucci, A. (1991). *Challenging Codes: Collective Action in the Information Age.* Cambridge: Cambridge University Press; Tilly, C. (1978). *From Mobilization to Revolution.* Reading, MA: Addison-Wesley.

Michael Atkinson

COMMERCIALIZING ETHNIC ATHLETES

The commercialization of ethnic athletes refers to the manners by which athletes of color are used to sell sports teams, leagues, organizations, one-off games, their sponsors' products, or a range of other commodities. The active or mass commercialization of ethnic athletes in sports (present in one manifestation or another since the turn of the twentieth century) became a taken-for-granted norm in professional sports through the 1980s and into the 1990s. From one perspective, the use of African American and other ethnic minority athletes in the "selling" of sports is an economically progressive social turn in the culture of sports. But from another perspective, the commodification of ethnic athletes rings with an exploitative historical tendency to use expendable and easily renewable African American labor as a vehicle for generating profit for others.

BACKGROUND

It is tempting to cite the visible presence of ethnic minorities in contemporary sports cultures as a signifier of their colonization of the historically white terrain of sports. The shift toward ostensibly more inclusive sports is often heralded as a major racial/ethnic victory by minority groups in the twentieth century. Supposedly, the colonization of professional sports by principally African American and Latino athletes is a movement away from simple binary divisive racial categories such as white/other (or, simply, us/them). Bracketed within the logics of racial desegregation in sports has been the suggestion that greater demographic numbers of ethnic minorities within sports have also served to alter the mass media's representation of "color," "blackness," or "race" in sports and in the United States in that the increased place and importance of ethnic minorities in sports and the marketing of ethnic minority athletes leads to progressive portrayals of ethnic "others" in society. Such an assumption is potentially dangerous because there is little evidence to confirm that either the commercialization of modern sports or its marketing has shifted the representation of ethnicity (particularly "blackness") in the popular media away from its construction as the opposite of, or alternative to, mainstream white cultures and identities.

Why is the mass mediation of blackness or other racialized identities significant in the world of sports? Some argue that the mass commercialization and mediation of modern sports throughout the twentieth century played a particular role in altering the visible presence of African Americans in popular culture. The relatively rapid transformation of sports such as basketball, baseball, and football into commercial enterprises preoccupied with extending their brands has been facilitated by Western industrialism, migration to cities, the advent of visual electronic media, increased social affluence in the United States, and a growing cultural desire for pay-per-view leisure activities. As an economically driven institution that seeks to sell its people and practices to consuming audiences, professional sports simply could not operate without its extensive mass mediation, such that sports and the media are synonymously referred to as a "sports-media nexus."

In the day-to-day commercial business of modern sports, ethnic minority athletes are presently used more than ever before as talking heads or commercial embodiments for their sports, their teams, or simply themselves. Images of (mainly black) athletes as cool, innovative, socially responsible, rebellious, wholesome, or an endless list of other qualities are deliberately arranged and manipulated by sports marketers in an attempt to promote investment in sports by diverse audiences. For example, NBA defensive star Dennis Rodman received critical acclaim as a Detroit Pistons player in the late 1980s. However, it was not until Rodman was traded to the Chicago Bulls, colored his hair flamboyantly, tattooed his body extensively, engaged in sexual relationships with high-profile celebrities, dressed provocatively, and organized other deliberately staged techniques of self-promotion as a black "bad boy" that he became heavily mass mediated within popular culture and a commercial interest for corporate sponsors. As part of the selling of modern sports and its benefactors' products to consuming audiences, then, athletes such as Rodman become walking marketing billboards. It is interesting how athlete images and identities can shift from ad to ad, or campaign to campaign.

The twentieth century witnessed an explosion of both traditional and innovative representations of racial identity in sports in the process of selling it to new audiences. What laid much of the groundwork for increased audience consumption of "blackness" in sports, one might argue, had to do with the increased representation of African Americans in popular culture (rap, hip-hop, and popular film most notably). The representation of black masculinity became far more complex and contested through the late 1970s and 1980s as the essence of blackness was mediated in a range of popular cultural fields. As part of the process, in contemporary sports worlds African American athletes were not showcased by sports marketers as merely corporeal beings that struggled to win their on-field sports contests, they became what David Andrews called "floating signifiers" of racial identity.

A floating signifier is something that has no fixed or inherent meaning within a culture. It is an object, gesture, image, person, or action that can be multiply construed by audiences across space and time. One of the most fascinating trends in late-modern twentieth-century sports is the manner by which the images of ethnically or racially identified athletes were arranged to convey messages about sports (as a commodity) and the commercial products associated with it. The racial image of African American athletes (among others) were strategically manipulated and used in team, league, and sports sponsors' marketing campaigns in order to sell sports to both white majority and ethnic minority audiences. The process has taken on a global turn as well, with increased numbers of Asian players imported from China and Japan so that Western professional sports such as baseball and basketball can hold cultural significance in burgeoning Asian markets. Hideo Nomo, Yao Ming, Wang Zhizhi, Mengke Bateer, and Ichiro Suzuki have all extended the commercial enterprise of sports to the Pacific Rim and afforded their teams with a public image of diversity appreciation. In such a sports marketing process, race loses a sense of fixity or cultural determination because the images and identities of ethnic minority athletes are situationally constructed to meet whatever image the team or corporation using them is attempting to manufacture.

The employment/deployment of African American athletes and other racial minority athletes to sell sports and sports products is a relatively recent phenomenon. When considering that sports icons such as Willie Mays, Frank Robinson, Bill Russell, Carl Lewis, Althea Gibson, Wilt Chamberlain, Jackie Joyner-Kersey, Julius Erving, and others were rarely courted by corporate sponsors (i.e., compared to their white contemporaries), the multimillion dollar endorsement deals paid to athletes such as Bo Jackson, Earvin Johnson, Deion Sanders, and others in the 1980s seem monumental. Consider further that Sammy Sosa, during the 1998 "home run race" with Mark McGwire in Major League Baseball (MLB) baseball, secured multimillion dollar endorsement deals. This occurred only two and a half decades after Hank Aaron had received constant death threats (and rare offers for corporate sponsorship) from baseball fans while he chased legendary white baseball icon Babe Ruth's home run record. With respect to race and sports commercialization, then, the mass use of black athletes in the process of selling sports/teams/products is an invention of the last two decades.

Although there is an endless list of possible ways that ethnicity or race may be constructed in the commercialization of sports, there are four predominant themes used in the mass mediation of blackness in sports. For the sake of illustration, we will look at the case of African American athletes as commercially racialized groups.

First, black athletes are often depicted as racial *revolutionaries* in sports (and thus whatever they are being associated or marketed with, similarly revolutionary). In this instance, high-caliber African American athletes' successes become poached, cited, and represented in sports as part of a movement toward ethnic integration and civil harmony between racialized groups in athletics and elsewhere. Their roles and statuses are rarely associated with activism, any racial politics that would disrupt the authoritarian positions of white people in sports, and in many cases they become represented like whites in sports business ventures. These athletes are symbolically showcased as revolutionary in sports for representing how black athletes can be culturally assimilated into mainstream white, commercial business/popular culture through sporting success without overt political struggle. Hence, they signify a progressive, tolerant, liberal, and harmonious America. Second, African American athletes often adopt or are given the image of a sports *reformer* whose abilities to excel within a sport alter the course of how it is played. While close conceptually to the revolutionary, the image of the black athlete as reformer in sports is partially more politically charged because his or her sports involvement is regularly linked to the need for minority-group athletes to fight for inclusion and equity in their sport.

Third, the image of the African American athlete as a social radical in sports is widely used to sell contemporary sports. By drawing on historical images of the black male as an "outsider" racial figure, aggressively strong and confident rebel athlete, or socially "dangerous"/politically conscious person, the radical image of African American athletes in sports marketing and commercialization not only reaffirms enduring cultural stereotypes about black men (and women) as racial others, it taps white popular cultural youth markets who are eager to consume radical images of black masculinity in sports and elsewhere. Finally, images of the social *rogue* in sports are attributed to particular African American athletes, such as those who have encounters with the criminal justice system in one capacity or another. In these cases, particular athletes become identified as troublesome black athletes in highly stereotypical and discriminatory ways. The images of them tap into and hyperbolize racist stereotypes about black males in the process of marketing and selling images of them as sports deviants.

KEY EVENTS

Earvin "Magic" Johnson is among those athletes in the 1980s who could be considered as a representative, par excellence, of how revolutionary images of blackness have been represented in sports. Johnson entered the NBA in 1980, drafted by the Los Angeles Lakers after winning national high school and college championships. Between 1980 and 1990, Johnson led the Lakers to five NBA championships, won League MVP three times, and was selected to the All-Star team nine times. He was a member of the 1992 men's Olympic basketball "Dream Team," and he was known throughout the United States as an inspirational, and largely deracialized, figure in the sport. Even in his much-publicized, and perhaps media fabricated through ad campaigns such as the Converse Weapon shoe commercials, "racial rivalry" with Larry Bird of the Boston Celtics, Johnson would never be portrayed as an outsider racial figure in the sport. He endorsed countless practices during his tenure in the NBA and often carried the image of a formidable athlete and wholesome figure in basketball. Yet, Johnson, to the bewilderment of the nation, announced that he was HIV positive in 1991. Johnson became an outspoken advocate for the HIV/AIDS community in the United States (which he is to this day) and was publicly referred to as a "national hero" in 1992 by President George H.W. Bush. Sports critics were amazed that although Johnson did receive criticism within sports and by the media for playing while carrying HIV (as he did from 1992–1996), rarely did critics pounce on his racial background or denigrate black players for the type of behavior that lead to his contraction of HIV (Johnson admitted that he contracted the disease from multiple sex partners).

Much more critical attention has been given to the basketball player who arguably helped to rewrite the book on marketing race through sports, Michael Jordan. Regarded as the greatest basketball player of all time, Jordan's social significance in sports as a racial figure extends far beyond the court. Jordan became fully ingratiated in the sports marketing process, earning hundreds of millions of dollars by advertising for mega-brands such as Coca-Cola, Chevrolet, Gatorade, McDonald's, Disney, Wheaties, Hanes, and MCI over his career. In one of his commercials for Gatorade, children of diverse backgrounds sang out that they wanted to "be like Mike," an image and representation of blackness unprecedented at that point in history. Jordan's relationship with the Nike Corporation changed the face of the sports apparel industry after his signature shoe, the Air Jordan, was launched in 1985. Nike even created an entire division of "Air Jordan" products (again, an unprecedented gesture to a black athlete). He starred in the Disney movie "Space Jam" alongside Looney Tunes cartoon characters in 1996, acted as the Director of Basketball Operations for the Washington Wizards, and is currently part owner of the Charlotte Bobcats NBA franchise.

Michael Jordan symbolized how images of race can "float" within the world of sports. For example, at the annual NBA Slam Dunk contest, Jordan's representation of race closely paralleled expectations that black athletes would perform wild, aggressive, and spectacular movements that whites simply could not. He was, in this instance, sold as a circus side show as racially identifier others often are portrayed. But in Disney films and television commercials for Hanes underwear, Jordan represented a calm, racially pacified symbol of a "changing America" wherein ethnic minorities could succeed and exist harmoniously among whites. The Air Jordan campaign blurred and rearranged images of black masculinity as both street tough and yet integrated, corporate, and mainstream. Jordan's de- and re-racialized envelopment into popular culture, like Magic Johnson in the 1990s, survived an adultery scandal, gambling scandal, on- and off-again retirements, and ongoing suggestions from the African American communities in the United States that he had "sold out" to white, corporate America.

There are several dozen players who could be identified as racial reformers in the world of sports. Among those is tennis player Arthur Ashe. Ashe was an activist/author/tennis player who remains to date the only black male to win a Wimbledon Tennis Championship (which he accomplished in 1975). He also won the U.S. Open in 1968 and the Australian Open in 1970, and he was a member of the Davis Cup Team for 11 years. Throughout his career, Ashe struggled to raise awareness about the exclusion of African Americans in sports and elsewhere, and he was actively involved in sociopolitical protests against the South African government during its apartheid regime and U.S. immigration policies. Ashe was represented to many as a black intellectual in sports who was focused not only on achieving excellence in tennis but also strategically using his public platform to raise awareness about social struggle in the United States. Like Magic Johnson, Ashe faced HIV/AIDS in life, eventually losing his battle with it in 1993. For his reformist sports and social work he received countless accolades including: the naming of the main court at the USTA National Tennis Center as the Arthur Ashe Stadium; the city of Richmond, Virginia, erected a monument in his honor on Monument Avenue (a location traditionally reserved for legendary Confederate figures); the naming of the Arthur Ashe Student Health and Wellness Center at UCLA; and the creation of ESPN's annual Arthur Ashe Award for Courage.

The representation of radical blackness in sports found a landmark expression in 1968 when U.S. Olympic track and field stars Tommie Smith and John Carlos stood together on the podium as 200-meter medal winners, and each raised a gloved black fist (as a symbol of black power) into the air during the playing of the American national anthem. Members of the international media, the International Olympic Committee (IOC), and other American athletes vilified them, and they were unceremoniously removed from the U.S. Olympic team and expelled from the Games. Their gesture was one of the most visible and mass-mediated displays of racial resistance in sports, especially contextualized within the highly turbulent 1960s wherein black Americans fought desperately for equal rights in sports and elsewhere. Dissimilar to figures like Ashe who racially politicized sports while working within its confines, Carlos and Smith's gesture was generally interpreted by mainstream sports insiders and outsiders as (racially) irreverent and inexcusably confrontational. Smith and Carlos's act of resistance, of course, had been partially upstaged by other racially confrontational athlete gestures of the 1960s, such as those of boxing legend Muhammad Ali. Ali is one of the most complex, racially identified and mass-mediated figures in sports history (unlike Carlos and Smith) because of his black activism in sports. As another figure who would become represented and sold as a racially radical figure in sports, football player Jim Brown is often forgotten in historical analysis of African American representation in sports. As a college football player, Brown was allegedly denied the Heisman Trophy because of his color, but he went on to become one of the greatest running backs in the sport's history. When he retired from the National Football League (NFL) as the career-rushing leader, he held almost every rushing-related record on the books.

Finally, among the "rogue" athletes who have been most vilified, and in the process commodified, is professional boxer Mike Tyson. Tyson's meteoric rise and fall from the top echelons of professional boxing (and commercial endorsements) has been constantly underpinned by his categorization in public culture as a "black savage" and the "Baddest Man on the Planet." Across his fighting career, public brawls, violent rants, and aggressive threats to other boxers; bankruptcy declaration; controversial membership in the Nation of Islam; arrest and incarceration for sexual assault; the biting off of a fragment of fellow boxer Evander Holyfield's ear; alleged spousal abuse of Robin Givens; and drug possession arrests, Tyson's image of the uncontrollable black male has been used by boxing promoters as a means of stirring commercial interest in the sport and portraying African Americans in a historically derogatory light.

FUTURE PROSPECTS

The idea that blackness or other racial identities can help to sell sports in highly complex ways is a relatively recent stroke of marketing genius. The collective representation of the range of traditionally other racial and ethnic identities is cleverly used in contemporary sports worlds to convey sellable images to audiences. As a result, the representation of blackness in sports is more dynamic and multilayered than arguably any other social sphere. In the future, as North American sports worlds fuse further with corporations, the media, and countries from around the world, representations of race and ethnicity (and the commodification of race in sports) should be even more complex and floating.

See also Collective Protests and Social Movements; Cool Pose; Ethnic Coaches, Managers, and Owners; Professional Athletes and the Olympics; Racial Profiling and Stacking; Taunting.

Further Reading: Andrews, D. (1996). The Facts of Michael Jordan's Blackness: Excavating a Floating Racial Signifier. *Sociology of Sport Journal* 13: 125–158; Andrews, D. (2001). *Michael Jordan Inc: Corporate Sport, Media Culture and Late Modern America.* Albany: SUNY Press; Cashmore, E. (2003). *Encyclopedia of Race and Ethnic Studies.* London: Routledge; Cashmore, E. (2005). *Tyson: Nature of the Beast.* London: Polity; Hartmann,

D. (2004). *Race, Culture and the Revolt of the Black Athlete: The 1968 Olympic Protests and their Aftermath.* Chicago: University of Chicago Press; Rhoden, W. (2007). *Forty Million Dollar Slaves.* Pittsburgh: Three Rivers Press; Whanell, G. (1992). *Fields in Vision: Television Sport and Cultural Transformation.* London: Routledge; Wiggins, K. (1997). *Glory Bound: Black Athletes in a White World.* Syracuse: Syracuse University Press; Zirin, D. (2005). *What's My Name, Fool: Sports and Resistance in the United States.* Chicago: Haymarket Books.

Michael Atkinson

COOL POSE

Cool pose is a term that refers to a set of words, mannerisms, gestures, and movements that young black males in basketball developed in the 1960s and 1970s as components of a unique subcultural style. The essence of cool is to appear in control, whether through a fearless style of walking or running, a facial expression, the clothes one wears, a haircut, gestures, athletic moves, or the way one talks. Cool pose is intended to show dominant white culture in sports and elsewhere that the young black male is strong, unique, and proud, despite his marginalized status in American society. Flashy or provocative clothes are part of the cool pose. An unbuckled belt, expensive sneakers, and thick gold chains, for example, are part of the cool look. Some elements of the cool pose have been analyzed in terms of kinesics, the subtleties of body movements. One is a distinctive swaggering gait, almost a walking dance, which can include tilting one's head to one side while one arm swings to the side with the hand slightly cupped while the other hand hangs to the side or is in the pocket.

BACKGROUND

Although some might suggest that the first definitive instance of cool pose in sports was American track athletes Tommie Smith and John Carlos coordinated signal of "black power" while standing on the Olympic podium at the 1968 Summer Games in Mexico, Majors (1992) argues that cool pose in sports can be traced to players in the American Basketball Association (ABA) during the 1960s and 1970s. The ABA copied and showcased a flamboyant form of (predominantly black) street basketball played on inner-city courts in cities such as Detroit, New York, Philadelphia, and Chicago.

The original ABA was founded in 1967, competing with the well-established (and largely white) National Basketball Association (NBA) until reaching a merger agreement in 1976. Ultimately, four ABA teams were absorbed into the older league: the New York Nets, Denver Nuggets, Indiana Pacers, and San Antonio Spurs. Two other clubs, the Kentucky Colonels and the Spirits of St. Louis, were disbanded. A third, the Virginia Squires, had folded less than a month earlier, missing out on the opportunities that a merger might have provided.

The ABA distinguished itself from the NBA with a more wide-open, flashy style of offensive play adopted from street basketball, as well as differences in rules (a 30-second shot clock as opposed to the NBA 24-second clock and use of a three-point field goal arc). Also, the ABA used a colorful red, white, and blue ball instead of the NBA's traditional orange ball. The ABA showcased dazzling above-the-rim, slam dunking (a move illegal in the NBA) and players such as Julius (Dr. J) Erving, Connie Hawkins, George (Ice) Gervin, David Thompson, George McGinnis, Artis Gilmore, Moses Malone, Roger Brown, and Dan (The Horse) Issel. Each of these electric stars first played professional basketball in the ABA.

THE ABA TEAMS

Although the league always had 11 or 12 teams, many of the franchises moved around a lot due to the fact that the teams just couldn't seem to draw a crowd in certain markets. A list of ABA franchises and their moves between 1967 and 1976 includes:

Anaheim Amigos (1967–1968)
Los Angeles Stars (1968–1970)
Utah Stars (1970–1976)
Baltimore Hustlers (1975)
Baltimore Claws (1975)
Dallas Chaparrals (1967–1973)
San Antonio Spurs (1973–1976)
Denver Rockets (1967–1974)
Denver Nuggets (1974–1976)
Houston Mavericks (1967–1969)
Carolina Cougars (1969–1974)
Spirits of St. Louis (1974–1976)
Indiana Pacers (1967–1976)
Kentucky Colonels (1967–1976)
Minnesota Muskies (1967–1968)
Miami Floridians (1968–1972)
New Jersey Americans (1967–1968)
New Jersey Nets (1968–1976)
New Orleans Buccaneers (1967–1970)
Memphis Pros (1970–1972)
Memphis Tams (1972–1974)
Memphis Sounds (1974–1975)
Oakland Oaks (1967–1969)
Washington Caps (1969–1970)
Virginia Squires (1970–1976)
Pittsburgh Pipers (1967–1968)
Minnesota Pipers (1968–1969)
Pittsburgh Pipers (1969–1970)
Pittsburgh Condors (1970–1972)
San Diego Conquistadors (1972–1975)
San Diego Sails (1975)

The ABA was considered an illegitimate league by middle-class, white American basketball purists who claimed that ABA players were ruining the sport. In particular, the street style of dress, language, and play the players created starkly contrasted the clean-cut image of the (white) NBA. Indeed, the ABA was often referred to as the black American league. Yet, players in the ABA embraced the opportunity to showcase to the world a different, and empowered, image of the black male, one of control, confidence, style, athleticism, and self-determination. This, argues Majors (1992), was the birth of the cool pose style.

From 1971 to 1975 the two leagues played a series of interleague games. They both compromised on the rules, an orange NBA ball for one half and the multicolored ABA ball for another half; a 24-second shot clock for one half and a 30-second clock for another half. Although many critics claimed that ABA players were less skilled than their NBA counterparts, the ABA won the rivalry by winning the interleague series 79 games to 76. After the 1974–1975 regular season, the ABA Champion Kentucky Colonels challenged the NBA Champion Golden State Warriors to a "World Series of Basketball," with the winner to take a $1 million purse. The NBA and the Warriors refused the challenge.

Although some of the ABA teams managed to draw big crowds, most of them were barely able to stay afloat. During the early years, the Houston Mavericks averaged about 200 fans a game. Finally, the league as a whole disbanded after the 1976 season. The most popular ABA teams, the Denver Nuggets, San Antonio Spurs, Indiana Pacers and New Jersey Nets, were allowed to join the NBA, where they still play today. Regardless of the ABA's demise, the black, urban male style that became a signature of the league had an indelible impact on American sports, and popular, culture.

KEY EVENTS

While the NBA and its affiliations took every opportunity to decry the ABA and its style in the 1970s, by the early 1980s, basketball leagues and clothing companies sought to profit from the cool pose image. Early in 1984, Nike was a struggling shoe company. At the same time, rookie Chicago Bulls player Michael Jordan was already endorsing several products, but Nike hoped that his cool pose appeal would generate sales. Later that year, Nike offered to create a new line of shoes called "Air Jordan." In particular, Nike sought to align its image with pop culturally burgeoning images of cool pose emerging from rap cultures in inner cities and new generations of NBA players who had been influenced by the cool pose of the ABA players. Nike eventually signed Jordan to a $2.5 million deal for 5 years plus royalties and other fringe benefits. Peter Moore of Nike created the first Air Jordan logo with a basketball with wings lifting it. The introduction of the "Air Jordan I" turned the athletic shoe industry upside down. Before the shoe, most basketball shoes were white, but the bold black and red styling of the Jordan I—in typical cool pose style—flouted this convention. The NBA banned the shoe from the league in response, but Jordan wore them anyway, racking up serious fines of up to $5,000 a game.

Nike, of course, was more than happy to pay these to keep the shoes on Jordan's feet and in the public eye. All this controversy and Jordan's spectacular numbers that year served to put the Air Jordan line on the road to becoming a household name.

After winning the 1986–1987 Slam Dunk competition at Seattle Coliseum, the Jordan logo changed to the familiar "Jumpman" logo of today. At Michael Jordan's request, the Air Jordan III was a three-quarter cut basketball shoe made of high-quality, lighter than average materials. This nonstandard approach to the process of designing basketball shoes led the Air Jordan III to rocket off the charts. Air Jordan Shoes were a part of the Nike family until late in 1997 when Nike unveiled a new marketing plan, and Jordan became its own sub-brand of Nike. To mark this change, the new Jordan Brand released the Air Jordan XIII, Air Jordan Team, and Air Jordan Trainers. Air Jordan shoes have consistently been among the best-selling basketball shoes since their creation in 1985. The Jordan brand is a household name, and people of all ages and social strata line up eagerly for the release of the latest model. Perhaps more important is that in conjunction with the Air Jordan shoe success, Michael Jordan's extremely "street based and high flying" style of play, his success in the NBA's annual slam dunk competitions, his captaining of the Bulls to World Championships, and his countless record-setting efforts helped to transform the NBA into the home of cool pose. His cool pose image would be picked up and marketed across pop culture throughout the 1990s, and as such, he helped to market a new form of black masculinity to the world.

If Michael Jordan was the cool pose hero in the 1980s and 1990s, emergent bad boy stars such as the NBA's Dennis Rodman, Alan Iverson, and Latrell Sprewell were its antiheroes. These players critiqued the squeaky-clean corporate image of Jordan and sought to re-insert a more rugged, and some might argue "authentic," form of cool pose back in basketball. The players, and a host of others, tattooed their bodies, wore cornrow hairstyles, showcased their sexual escapades in the media, and were routinely associated with drug and gang cultures. Each were all-star players on the court, but public interest in them often related less to their athletic prowess and more to the supposed "thug culture" they represented in the NBA.

As cool pose styles and ideologies spread to other professional sports and became increasingly infused with rap, hip-hop cultures, music videos, and films, corporate elites in sports often took aim at particular cool pose players in particular sports. Players such as Rodman and Iverson were routinely fined, suspended, or dropped from corporate sponsorships for their "outlandish" behaviors. The National Football League (NFL) banned end-zone celebrations and forms of taunting (such as the notorious "throat slash") in order to sanitize the game from cool pose flavors. In 2005, NBA commissioner David Stern instituted a new dress code in the league in order to remove the "gangster" image from the league and to combat image problems associated with the Pistons–Pacer brawl of 2004 and the Kobe Bryant rape case of 2005. Players reacted negatively to the move, claiming the new policy to be overtly racist.

FUTURE PROSPECTS

Cool pose has become almost synonymous with NBA culture in the 2000s. To this end, critics have suggested that style is more of a corporate fabrication and marketing technique (even among sports antiheroes) than an authentic style representing young black masculinity. However, even if this is the case, it is clear that sports organizations such as the NBA and NFL (wherein black males predominate as players) will place definite limits on how cool pose may be expressed. Furthermore, one should expect to see a continued trend of incorporation and co-option of cool pose styles and forms by nonblack players and fans.

See also Corporate Branding; Racial Profiling and Stacking; Taunting; Video Games.

Further Reading: Majors, R. (1992). *Cool Pose: The Dilemmas of Black Manhood in America.* New York: Simon & Schuster; Wilson, B. (1997). Good Blacks and Bad Blacks: Media Constructions of African American Athletes in Canadian Basketball. *International Review for the Sociology of Sport* 32: 177–189.

Michael Atkinson

CORPORATE BRANDING

Corporate branding is the practice of using a company's title as the name of a commodity it produces; as in the case of Coca-Cola where both the company and the product share the same name. Corporate branding is also a technique of commercial marketing, as in the practice of paying an individual, group, or organization to publicly associate with or directly use (i.e., sponsor) a corporate product, logo, or image. The latter instance of corporate branding abounds in the world of professional sports, where product marketing and image manipulation have become central features in contemporary, professional athletics. We need only think of Nike's multimillion dollar corporate branding of Michael Jordan or Tiger Woods as marquee spokespersons for their organization; Discovery Channel's branding of an entire professional cycling team (including, most notably, 1999–2005 Tour de France winner Lance Armstrong and 2007 Tour de France winner Alberto Contador); and UK-based Barclay Bank's branding of the English Premier League of soccer as prime examples.

BACKGROUND

Corporations globally invest millions of dollars into sports for many reasons. Chief among these is that both professional and amateur sports are now heavily mass-mediated phenomena, attracting incredible consumer audiences worldwide. For example, the FIFA World Cup of soccer in 2006 attracted a cumulative global audience of 5.9 billion during the course of the tournament with the final alone bringing in 280 million viewers. In the United States, the 2006 Super Bowl brought in an audience of 98 million, and the opening ceremonies of the Winter Olympics from Torino, Italy, attracted 87 million viewers

(Bloomberg.com, December 19, 2006). The average total attendance at a major league baseball stadium nears 2.5 million yearly (the New York Yankees alone had over 4.2 million fans fill their stadium seats in 2006), and over 35 million Americans watched a NASCAR race in 2006. Considering these figures, it is difficult to locate any other social event or collection of people where corporations may reach such a large number of consumers at a given time. Couple this with how sports fans tend to attach personal affinity and loyalty to the products a league, team, or athlete endorses, and the fields of sports become ideal marketing and branding sites.

Strategically placed corporate logos and images in and around North American baseball, basketball, football, and ice hockey arenas, for instance, brand the games as corporate billboards. A recent report on ESPN.com (posted May 13, 2004) suggested that the average corporate advertisement at a baseball game will be shown on camera over 200 times during the course of a broadcast. Companies such as E-Trade, Hallmark, Home Depot, Nextel, Canadian Tire, and many others sponsor pregame, halftime, or postgame wrap-up and highlight shows on television to further imprint companies and their products or services in our subliminally sporting consciousness.

Many authors argue that sports itself is one of the largest commercial, global industries. Sports have become such a big business that it is difficult to separate it from the rest of the "capitalist industrial complex" (Andrews, 2006). For Andrews, sports organizations operate to support the interests of commercial product and service providers such as Coca-Cola, McDonald's, Chevrolet, and Visa or multinational media corporations such as Disney, Viacom, and News Corporation who broadcast and invest in professional athletics. In this way, there is a stream of "cross" marketing, branding, and promotion among corporations, media, and sports.

Products and images of corporations, media, and sports are so intertwined with one another (i.e., think of CBS television, the Super Bowl, and Budweiser

RECENT ENDORSEMENT DEALS

- A CNN report on February 4, 2007, stated that corporations such as Frito-Lay, PepsiCo, Anheuser-Busch, and Ford Motor Company all paid nearly $2.5 million for separate 30-second advertisements during the 2006 Super Bowl.
- *Forbes* magazine (March 22, 2006) estimated that U.S. corporations alone paid amateur and professional athletes over $1 billion to endorse products through television commercials, print advertisements, radio spots, voiceovers, and infomercials and at point-of-purchase sales locations.
- Tennis star Maria Sharapova reportedly earned over $18 million in 2006 from endorsement contracts with Canon, Motorola, Nike, and other companies.
- NBC paid $800 million for rights in the United States to broadcast the 2004 Olympic Summer Games from Greece.

beer for example), it is difficult to locate any one subject or purpose of the sports spectacle itself.

The use of sports, at either the professional or amateur levels, to promote companies and their products has of course been the subject of controversy and debates. Considering that sports in its preindustrial, essentialist form constituted a set of social activities and relationships designed to reaffirm community bonds, instill morality in youth, and serve as a collective representation of corporeal discipline and strength, it is easy to understand why critics lament the metamorphosis of mainstream North American sports into a blatantly commercial enterprise.

But as many authors and sports historians will teach us, the commercialization and corporate branding of sports is a relatively recent phenomenon. Dunning writes that commercialization and branding in sports occurred in the overall "sportization" process (originating largely in England), where traditional folk rituals, pastimes, and leisure activities such as soccer, rugby, and cricket became modeled as competitive, hierarchical, rule-bound, rational, and institutionally taught "formal" games. Dunning and others note that the English public school (EPS) system in the second half of the nineteenth century had a major, and unintended, influence on the sportization process. English secondary and grammar schools predominantly subscribed to the Greek and Roman belief that sports formed an important part of education. Participation itself was seen to hold importance over winning, and a class prejudice against being paid to play sports professionally (i.e., as a trade) reinforced the ideology. Professional athleticism was a contradiction of the central purposes of sports—that is, character development, physical vitality, and social bonding—rather than as a means of earning a crass living. However, the EPS created a standardized structure for sports, formalized its instruction, and created deep cultural associations between sports and the leisure sphere. This model and sets of cultural associations would be adopted around the world, including in the United States and Canada. These would each play a role in the commercialization of sports in the United Kingdom and around the world.

Through the industrial revolution and the collective migration from rural areas to cities in Western nations such as England, Scotland, Ireland, France, Germany, and the United States, both rural pastimes and school "sports" were increasingly desired by audiences. At the same time, rules and regulations devised at English public schools for sports were applied widely to forms of athletics by the end of the nineteenth century. On the one hand, sports played in schools continued to be bound by an ethos of gentlemanliness and "fair play," while sports such as boxing, hockey, football, and baseball were attractive to urban residents seeking more aggressive and publicly available forms of entertainment. Members of the middle and upper classes seized the latter desire to organize leagues and teams (involving men who paid to play) to make profit. Through the course of the twentieth century, urbanization, industrialism, and mass production brought increased leisure time, which allowed an increase in the growth of commercial spectator sports, less elitism in sports, and greater access for the public. With the advent of mass media and global communications, professionalism and commercialism became incredibly prevalent in sports.

Corporate branding in sports is therefore a rather logical and long-term outcome of a movement toward professionalism and commercialism in sports. Despite resistance from "traditionalists" in elite private school systems (who prefer the character-building model of sports), sports emerged as a pay-for-play, capitalistic activity pitched to mass audiences for evening and weekend entertainment value. Even the bastion of amateur sports, the Olympic Games, now allows professional athletes to participate in select sports such as basketball and ice hockey. Critics suggest that publicly played and watched sports have lost their unique ability to instruct morality and ethics; instead, sports have sold their soul to the almighty dollar.

KEY EVENTS

Corporate branding occurs now in sports through three predominant means: branding the playing field, branding players and their equipment, and, branding teams, leagues, organizations, and mega events.

Branding the Field

Over the past decade and a half, North American companies have spent nearly $1.9 billion to brand and rebrand 38 professional sports venues. In some cases, the names of these corporate stadiums have changed several times due to corporate reorganization, mergers, acquisitions, and failure.

Professional sports leagues and organizations have also produced sporting spaces saturated with corporate images and logos for spectators and television viewers. While corporate marketing and branding *around* amateur and professional playing fields has been commonplace since World War II, one of the last commercial taboos was the branding of actual playing surfaces of sports. The National Hockey League (NHL) was among the first of the pro sports organizations to endorse the use of corporate advertisements on the actual playing fields. At the onset of the 1980/1981 NHL season, teams were allowed to place corporate names and images on the boards encasing the ice surface in their home rinks. In the early 1990s, Major League Baseball (MLB) followed suit with more strategically placed corporate logos on outfield walls and, later, electronic/LCD advertisements on signs behind home plate. In the cash-strapped Canadian Football League, corporations such as Daimler Chrysler have prominently advertised their Dodge Ram vehicle line on the middle of playing fields in Calgary, Toronto, and Saskatchewan. Sports organizations such as NASCAR, Major League Soccer, the Arena Football League, and the Professional Golfers Association (PGA) have all followed suit by allowing organizations to market their products and veritably brand the respective playing fields.

REBRANDED SPORTS STADIUMS IN THE UNITED STATES

1. KeyArena (Seattle Center Coliseum)
2. Qwest Field (Seattle Seahawks Stadium)
3. AT&T Park (Pacific Bell Park, SBC Park)
4. McAfee Coliseum (Oakland-Alameda County Coliseum, Network Associates Coliseum)
5. Monster Park (Candlestick Park, 3Com Park)
6. HP Pavilion (San Jose Arena, Compaq Center)
7. Arrowhead Pond (Anaheim Arena)
8. Qualcomm Stadium (San Diego Stadium, Jack Murphy Stadium)
9. Chase Field (Bank One Ballpark)
10. US Airways Arena (America West Arena)
11. Pengrowth Saddledome (Olympic Saddledome, Canadian Airlines Saddledome)
12. Rexall Place (Northlands Coliseum, Edmonton Coliseum, Skyreach Centre)
13. Edward Jones Dome (Trans World Dome, Dome at America's Center)
14. Savvis Center (Kiel Center)
15. Gaylord Entertainment Center (Nashville Arena)
16. Ameriquest Field (The Ballpark at Arlington)
17. AT&T Center (SBC Center)
18. Minute Maid Park (Enron Field, Astros Field)
19. U.S. Cellular Field (Comiskey Park)
20. RCA Dome (Hoosier Dome)
21. Quicken Loans Arena (Gund Arena)
22. Mellon Arena (Civic Center)
23. HSBC Arena (Marine Midland Arena)
24. Rogers Centre (SkyDome)
25. Corel Centre (The Palladium)
26. Bell Centre (Molson Centre)
27. TD Banknorth Garden (FleetCenter)
28. Continental Airlines Arena (Brendan Byrne Arena)
29. Wachovia Center (CoreStates Center, First Union Center)
30. M&T Bank Stadium (Ravens Stadium, PSINet Stadium)
31. FedEx Field (Jack Kent Cooke Stadium)
32. RBC Center (Raleigh Entertainment and Sports Arena)
33. Bank of America Stadium (Carolinas Stadium, Ericsson Stadium)
34. Alltel Stadium (Jacksonville Municipal Stadium)
35. TD Waterhouse Centre (Orlando Arena)
36. Tropicana Field (Florida Suncoast Dome, Thunderdome)
37. St. Pete Times Forum (Ice Palace)
38. BankAtlantic Center (Broward County Civic Arena, National Car Rental Center, Office Depot Center)

Branding Players and Their Equipment

Practically every sport played in North America is a potential target for corporate sponsors. Individual athletes are among the first to be sought after in this branding process. In a sport such as the triathlon, branding individual athletes with corporate logos and equipment is standard practice. Amateur triathletes, like their colleagues in a majority of other sports fields, come to rely on corporate or private sponsorship just to be able to compete. Given that an elite triathlete's daily schedule will include nearly five hours of training and that an average athlete's "storehouse" of training and competition equipment might cost $10,000 per year, sponsors fill a vital role in the sport as income providers to individual athletes and teams. Manufacturers of bikes, helmets, wetsuits, running and cycling shoes, and performance clothing and apparel (e.g., hats, goggles, race belts, sunglasses, sun block, body gels, etc.) infuse huge sums of cash into the sport in order to have their products seen on elite-level competitors. Semi-pro or elite athletes are easily noticeable at a race; one need only look at their logo-filled competition suits or bikes and helmets emblazoned with a rash of corporate stickers. Just as in professional basketball, surfboarding, golf, tennis, or baseball, the corporations clamor to brand the "best" athletes with their products. Thus, some critics suggest that athletes have become merely the mannequins of billionaire corporate sponsors.

Notable sponsors in the sport of triathlon include the Ford Motor Company, Subaru, Timex, Visa, Michelin, and Michelob, among others. But ubiquitous among sponsors in triathlon are the makers of sports-related food and drink products such as Gatorade and Powerbar. Here, these companies extend their corporate identities as fuel providers to high-level athletes. Products such as Powerbar were once the exclusive food of endurance athletes, but they now reach markets inside and outside of the sport. Concern is occasionally raised, however, that triathletes, like other athletes, come to rely on sports nutrition as their only means of diet. That is to say, athletes become socialized into an eating culture where the majority of foods are provided by manufacturers of sports-performance products. The over-consumption of sports-related foods has been linked to eating disorders among male and female triathletes (Atkinson, 2007). Problematically as well, the athletes are often unsure that the products meet their daily dietary needs or meet antidoping standards established by the International Triathlon Union or the World-Anti-Doping Agency.

Not to be confused with corporate sponsorship deals are corporate endorsement contracts and services. Athletes who endorse a product are simply paid by a company to be a spokesperson for it in some capacity. While sponsorship may provide the "essentials" for athletes on a day-to-day basis, only a select few athletes are highly desired corporate endorsers. These athletes endorse a huge range of products, including toothpaste, cars, mobile phones, airlines, underwear, casinos, food and drink, cigars, insurance, and health care providers. While athletes garner impressive salaries commensurate with their abilities to perform on the field, their incomes are often tripled or quadrupled through endorsement deals. In 2006, the top 10 athletes sought for endorsement contracts were: Tiger Woods, Oscar de la Hoya, Michael Jordan, David Beckham, Kobe Bryant, Lance Armstrong, Phil Mickelson, Andre Agassi, Derek Jeter, and Jeff Gordon. However, one does not always need to be a champion in order to attract endorsements. In 2002, Anna Kournikova was professional sports' highest paid female athlete, with almost all of her yearly income stemming from endorsement. Kournikova failed to win a professional tournament during her single tennis career, but she earned over $10 million per year in endorsement money from companies including: Adidas, Charles Schwab, Lycos, Micorsoft, Multiway, Omega, Pegasus, and Yonex. Perhaps sponsors were keenly aware that during 1999–2002, more people typed in her name on Internet search engines than any other athlete on the planet.

BRANDING TEAMS, LEAGUES, ORGANIZATIONS, AND MEGA EVENTS

Related to the process of branding players through sponsorship and endorsements is of course the practice of branding entire teams, federations, and events. In English soccer, corporations such as Fly Emirates Air, AIG, Northern Rock, Carlsberg, and Samsung invest millions of British pounds per year to have their corporate logos featured on players' jerseys. In NASCAR racing, entire race series are sponsored by companies such as Busch and Nextel. In Canada, Tim Horton's coffee and donut producer is the major sponsor of the men's curling championships. Nearly every team, league, organization, and mega event such as the Olympics has a litany of "official" cars, drinks, banks, and clothing they endorse. For example, Coca-Cola is the official drink of the Olympics, Lenovo is the official computer of the NBA, and Reebok is the official clothing supplier of the National Football League (NFL).

Perhaps one of the most interesting, and in some ways bizarrely logical, intersections between corporate branding and sports is the case of the Anaheim Ducks franchise in the NHL. The team was originally called the Mighty Ducks of Anaheim when founded in 1993 by the Walt Disney Company. The team's original name copied the name given to the fictional children's ice hockey team in the Disney movie *The Mighty Ducks* starring Emilio Estevez. Their uniform logo consisted of a goalie mask morphed into the shape of a cartoon duck's head. They developed a mascot called "Wild Wing" who ritually descended to the ice via suspension wires prior to every home game amidst a laser light show and other pyrotechnics. To help promote the team in the United States, Disney then developed an animated television series called *Mighty Ducks,* featuring a team of cartoon duck hockey players. The team played in Arrowhead Pond (now Honda Center), located just a short driving distance east of Disneyland. Disney sold the team in 2005, and the new owners (the Samueli family) immediately changed the team name and logo to the Anaheim Ducks.

FUTURE PROSPECTS

There are no indicators that the ongoing corporatization of sports through branding or other means will quell in the near future. With its global media platform, sports are an ideal context for multinational corporate investors and entrepreneurs to market their wares. The only question remaining is how extensively the tone and content of sports will change as the culture of commercialism therein crystallizes further.

See also Commercializing Ethnic Athletes; Corporate Stadiums; Equipment Manufacturing in the Third World; Salaries of Professional Athletes.

Further Reading: Amis, J., and Bettina, T. (2005). *Global Sport Sponsorship:* New York: Berg; Andrews, D. (2006). *Sport-Commerce-Culture.* New York: Peter Land; Atkinson, M. (2007). "Triathlon, Suffering and Exciting Significance". *Leisure Studies* 27(2): 165–180; Dunning, E. (1999). *Sport Matters.* London: Routledge; Howell, C. (2001). *Blood, Sweat and Cheers.* Toronto: University of Toronto Press; Mangan, J. (1996). *Athleticism in the Victorian and Edwardian School.* London: Routledge.

Michael Atkinson

CORPORATE STADIUMS

Starting in the late 1970s, sports teams found great profit in selling the rights to name or "brand" their home stadiums to corporate investors. While only a few stadiums entered into commercial agreements with corporations at first, by the turn of the twenty-first century, nearly every professional sports stadium in North America is "branded" with a corporate name and logo.

BACKGROUND

The sale of "naming rights" to a corporation is an economically straightforward relationship. Professional or amateur sports teams will enter into a contract with a corporate sponsor, where the corporation pays a yearly sum to a team (averaging in North America around $10 million per year) to have their corporation's name become the official name of the team's stadium. Granting a corporation the right to brand their stadium provides a huge influx of income that can be used to help pay for the cost of a new stadium, broker better player deals, develop training programs for young players, and a list of other strategic investments. For the corporation the transaction is equally straightforward. By emblazoning the company's name on a sports stadium, the company is guaranteed thousands of references to it yearly in sports broadcasts. Additionally, "having" a stadium is a status marker in contemporary business circles, indicating that your company is wealthy enough to invest in sports. But in the end, the naming rights trade is a hallmark economic strategy of the 1980s and 1990s: cross-promotion. Corporate sponsors use sports to promote their corporate agendas, and sports teams use corporations to extend their publicity (i.e., teams advertise for corporations, and then corporations advertise for the teams as well).

What the corporate branding of stadiums signifies about the contemporary nature of professional sports is another matter entirely. Critics of sports commercialization argue that the branding of stadiums by corporations is yet another indicator of the political economic nature of sports and the degree to which sports are transforming into sites of business enterprise rather than pure athletics. From a political economic perspective, the form and structure of modern sports is designed to sell a vast array of products. Decisions are made about everything related to games, and critics argue such decisions are made based on economic considerations. It is not just the professionalization and commercialization of sports/games itself that is relevant (a trend, of course, that has existed for 100 years in North American sports) but that everything about the social process of playing and watching sports can be commodified as part of a megabusiness.

What the further extension of business into the world of sports through naming rights sales proves is that anything that exists in sports is an object of commodification and consumption. Sports is a social terrain, like all others that exist, upon which capitalist investors seek to restructure as a site of business. Commercial goods producers, media companies, universities, scientific research agencies, educational systems, and even governments all seek to make money from sports processes, and they all do so in varying ways. As both become dominated by an ideology and structure of business practice, everything about sports cultural rituals change. The meaning of sports changes from something that is local and organically owned by fans and spectators to that which is given and framed to them by business investors. Whereas the "old" Montreal Forum (storied and beloved home to the National Hockey League's (NHL) Montreal Canadiens between 1924–1999) served as a symbol of French Canadian identity, the Canadiens' new building, the Bell Centre (named after its corporate sponsor Bell Canada) retains little of the forum's old feel or meaning for fans, resembling more of a shopping center and entertainment complex than a traditional ice hockey building.

Critics of the economic basis and feel of most professional sports suggest that issues such as naming rights illustrate how Western countries such as Canada and the United States are indeed "late modern" capitalist societies. A late modern society is one in which certain social tendencies categorize most features of everyday life, such as rationalization, commodification, alienation, disenchantment, universalism, and decontextualism. In the case of naming rights, the very act of selling the rights to name a team's stadium illustrates how economic rationality underpins social actions (i.e., what is paid for, and how much, reflects a profit-making model of decision making adopted by people), and every aspect of sports, even the buildings in which they are played, is transformed into objects to be marketed and sold. Through the corporate labeling of stadiums, their symbolism is less overtly related to a specific geographic place in which they are situated. Also, more directly referential to the universal, transnational companies sponsoring them, towns and teams are increasingly alienated from defining the physical geography of their own communities, and the stadium itself is "decontextualized" from being a place where sports may be celebrated by fans and recontextualized as a center for economic activity.

Fans may not mind or devote much critical attention to the process of corporate branding. If political economic and late modernity theorists are indeed correct, fans' tolerance of the corporate branding of stadiums indicates a general desensitization to the conditions of commercialism in sports and its relative taken-for-granted aspects. In other cases, the revolving-door nature of naming that is common at many stadiums has become somewhat comic in sports circles. Viewed from a critical perspective, the instability of stadium names might suggest something about the instability of the economic basis of sports and its fragile relationship with corporate investors.

KEY EVENTS

The (late) modern era of stadium naming rights in North America began in 1953 when the Anheuser-Busch company proposed renaming the St. Louis Cardinals' Sportsman's Park as Budweiser Stadium. When this idea was rejected by Ford Frick, the commissioner of baseball, he did so because of its commercial essence. Anheuser-Busch then proposed the title Busch Stadium after one of the company's founding figures. Frick approved the new name, and Anheuser-Busch quickly released a product called Busch Bavarian Beer (now known as Busch Beer) to help promote their own corporate promotion of baseball. The name would later be shifted to Busch Memorial Stadium in 1966, then shortened again in the 1970s to Busch Stadium, which remained the stadium's name until it closed in 2005. By that time, the MLBA's policy had changed regarding corporate naming, and Anheuser-Busch (who retained the naming rights after selling the team) was finally able to use the straight corporate name for the Cardinals' new stadium, which opened on April 4, 2006. Historians contend, however, that the exclusive naming rights deal between the NFL's New England Patriots and Schaefer brewery in 1970 signaled the first overt corporate branding deal. The Patriots' stadium in Foxboro, Massachusetts was renamed to Schaefer Stadium.

While corporate sponsors' businesses vary, media/telecommunications firms, banks, breweries, car manufacturers, and investment brokerage companies are heavily represented in stadium names across the continent. Name changes of the stadiums are, of course, frequent as companies let their rights contract expire, as companies' names change through mergers and acquisitions, and as teams broker more financially lucrative deals with other sponsors. Of note is Boston's TD Bankworth Stadium, which has been renamed over 30 times since its opening in 1993; the 2002 expeditious renaming of Houston's Enron Field after the public scandal involving the Enron Corporation; Office Depot's termination of their naming contract with the NHL's Florida Panthers after the corporation's frustration over the NHL player's lockout of 2004–2005; and the altering of the Philadelphia Flyer's building from First Union Center (F.U. Center) to First Union Nation Bank Center after Flyers' team executives noted that fans would inevitably call the stadium the "F.U."

While the flip-flopping of stadium names takes a comical tone at times, only two types of name changes appear to create tension among fans. In the first instance, if a stadium with a long history and deep cultural meaning for a city is to be renamed, fans normally speak out. When Candlestick Park in San Francisco changed its name to 3Com Park, fans refused to refer to it as anything other than Candlestick. 3Com eventually pulled out of the contract, and fans were further

CORPORATE NAMES IN CANADIAN SPORTS

As of 2007, the number of Canadian sports stadiums and entertainment complexes with corporate names mushroomed. While the United States is often regarded as the commercial branding Mecca of the West, many countries like Canada are following suit. Here is a list of corporate stadiums in Canada:

- Air Canada Centre in Toronto, Ontario
- Barrie Molson Centre in Barrie, Ontario
- Bell Centre in Montreal, Quebec
- BMO Field in Toronto, Ontario
- Brandt Centre in Regina, Saskatchewan
- Canada Inns Stadium in Winnipeg, Manitoba
- CanWest Global Park in Winnipeg, Manitoba
- Centre Air Creebec in Val-d'Or, Quebec
- CN Centre in Prince George, British Columbia
- Colisée Desjardins in Victoriaville, Quebec
- Colisée Pepsi in Quebec City, Quebec
- Credit Union Centre in Saskatoon, Saskatchewan
- ENMAX Centre in Lethbridge, Alberta
- ENMAX Centrium in Red Deer, Alberta
- General Motors Centre in Oshawa, Ontario
- General Motors Place in Vancouver, British Columbia
- Hershey Centre in Mississauga, Ontario
- Interior Savings Centre in Kamloops, British Columbia
- John Labatt Centre in London, Ontario
- K-Rock Centre in Kingston, Ontario
- Mosaic Stadium at Taylor Field in Regina, Saskatchewan
- MTS Centre in Winnipeg, Manitoba
- Pengrowth Saddledome in Calgary, Alberta
- Powerade Centre in Brampton, Ontario
- Prospera Centre in Chilliwack, British Columbia
- Prospera Place in Kelowna, British Columbia
- Rexall Centre in Toronto, Ontario
- Rexall Place in Edmonton, Alberta
- Ricoh Coliseum in Toronto, Ontario
- Rogers Centre in Toronto, Ontario
- Save-On-Foods Memorial Centre in Victoria, British Columbia
- Scotiabank Place in Ottawa, Ontario
- Steelback Centre in Sault Ste. Marie, Ontario
- TD Waterhouse Stadium in London, Ontario
- Telus Field in Edmonton, Alberta

irritated when stadium owners sold the rights to the Web site Monster.com and renamed it Monster Park. A group later created a petition to have the name repealed. For these reasons and others, teams such as the New York Yankees and Boston Red Sox have refused to sell the naming rights to their stadiums (Yankee Stadium and Fenway Park), citing how such an act would tarnish the tradition and history of each. Economists of sports might argue that neither is in a financial position where they need to because they are among the top money-making sports teams on the continent.

The other instance in which fans may be angered by stadium renaming arises when corporations with foreign roots purchase the naming rights to a stadium. Sports fans in New York were not impressed by the 2007 purchase of the naming rights to a sports stadium yet to be built in New York City by a British company. Barclays Bank purchased the naming rights to the stadium for a $400 million price tag over 20 years. Barclay Center is slated to be opened in 2011 and will house the NBA's New York Nets. Sports fans in New York must not realize that American companies have purchased the naming rights to stadiums in countries such as South Africa, New Zealand, and the UK.

The trend toward corporatization through naming stadiums has filtered down from the professional to the college/university levels and even to the minor leagues of sports. Massive corporate stadiums on or near university campuses, such as Comcast Stadium at the University of Maryland and DePaul University's Allstate Arena, raise serious questions about the ability for corporations to further transform sports and education into commercial ventures. Through the naming process, economic and ideological boundaries are blurred between the corporations, sports, and education, and trends toward universalizing all aspects of life toward market capitalism are accelerated in the process often without public scrutiny.

FUTURE PROSPECTS

Given the sheer financial size and length of most sponsorships deals and the lack of concerted public opposition to the naming process, it is reasonable to assume that the corporatization of sports space will be extended in the future. Teams and owners require millions of dollars in operating capital to be competitive as franchises, and it appears as if they are willing to make considerable ideological concessions in commodifying every nook and cranny of their sports environments. Only if and when corporations collectively fail to reap profit from the practice will it be curtailed in any significant degree.

See also Antitrust Violations in Professional Sports; Commercializing Ethnic Athletes; Governments, Laws, and Gambling; Media Broadcasting Rights; Salaries of Professional Athletes; Ticket Distribution and Scalping.

Further Reading: Horne, J. (2006). *Sport in Consumer Culture*. New York: Palgrave Macmillan.

Michael Atkinson

CRIMINAL VIOLENCE DURING COMPETITION

With minor exceptions, sports organizations have successfully maintained their monopoly over episodes of violence occurring within their jurisdictions and kept the courts from prosecuting athletes, even when such conduct violates formal and informal rules prohibiting the use of violence or the law of the land. In many cases of flamboyant on-field sports violence, it may be difficult to comprehend why the perpetrators were not criminally prosecuted in a court of law. However, even flagrant forms of violence in professional or amateur—and especially contact—sports tend to be treated as something socially special or unthreatening and controlled principally by sports organizations.

BACKGROUND

A summary review of the existing North American case law on sports violence at the amateur and professional levels reveals one consistent tendency: Players almost always escape cultural definition as bona fide criminals. Given the litany of other, and perceptually more pressing, social problems to pursue, the police find little justification in actively controlling the form or content of aggressive play in sports even when serious injuries result. In an overly litigious society, collective sentiment may also be that even unwanted or somewhat atypical incidents of on-ice violence in ice hockey—occurring between highly paid and trained professional athletes—is simply not worthy of extended social control efforts that consume public resources. Recent public reaction to police intervention into sports in North America establishes that while some on-ice acts may be defined by sports fans as inexcusable and worthy of strong league reprimand, police control of violence in the sport would effectively ruin the excitement of some sports, such as football, ice hockey, basketball, or rugby, by stripping all forms of aggressive play from the games.

Malicious forms of player–player violence are not restricted to one sport or level of sports but are deeply patterned and culturally supported across many sports. A topographical review of violence in sports shows that cases of hyper-violence in sports might be more commonplace than we might imagine. Yet, on-field forms of sports violence remain curiously under-studied. Few people critically examine the ways in which criminal violence may be embedded in sports processes. While sociologists and criminologists attend to a wide range of formal rule-breaking behaviors and subsequently classify such behaviors into conceptual categories such as "white-collar crimes," "hate crimes," sex crimes," and "race crimes," "sports crimes," or the instituted means of their control, have yet to be taken seriously. Although the criminal activities of athletes away from the playing field (e.g., sexual assault, gambling, battery, and murder) have received some research attention in recent years, criminologists have been curiously reluctant to label violent behaviors occurring on the sports field as "crimes" worthy of scholarly attention.

Explanations of player violence offered by coaches, league executives, and broadcasters support dangerous physical practices in ice hockey and restrict the possibility of players being considered as victims of criminal violence. Players

PLAYERS AVOIDING ARREST

Consider the following incidents:

- (2006, January) In the NCAA Gator Bowl football game between Virginia Tech and Louisville University, college junior Marcus Vick of Virginia deliberately "cleated and stomped" Louisville player Elvis Dumervil. In response, Vick was permanently released from the team. No legal action was taken.
- (2006, June) In one of the most tragic cases of on-field athlete violence in recent memory, South African Rugby Union player Riann Loots of Rawsonville Rugby Club was kicked in the head, while prostrate on the ground, by two members of the opposing Delicious Rugby Club during a league match. Loots died on the field, and both of the accused players were immediately suspended from league play. No legal action was taken.
- (2006, July) As fans watched the FIFA World Cup Final played between France and Italy, they saw French superstar Zinedene Zidane maliciously head butt Italian defender Marco Materazzi in the chest, knocking him to the ground. Initial reports of the event alleged that Zidane's attack was a response to taunts from Materazzi regarding the French player's family origin. Zidane received a red card for the foul and was ejected from the remainder of the World Cup, thus ending an otherwise illustrious career in disgrace. Materazzi received a three-game suspension from FIFA for his on-field comments. No legal action was taken.
- (2006, August) Race car driver Paul Tracy of Canada was suspended and fined $25,000 for deliberately knocking French driver Sebastien Bourdais off course during the Denver Grand Prix. After the race, Tracy also confronted Bourdais and challenged him to a fist fight. No legal action was taken.
- (2004, November) A player–fan riot broke out during an NBA match between the Indiana Pacers and Detroit Pistons. The mini-riot emerged following an on-court foul and subsequent fist-fight between players Ron Artest of Indiana and Ben Wallace of Detroit. The fight spilled over into the arena as Artest and other players from both teams chased and assaulted fans who had thrown plastic cups of beer toward the team benches. Artest received a 73-game suspension for his role in the altercation and forfeited salary of nearly $5 million for missed playing time during his suspension. Eight other players in total were suspended for the evening's riotous behavior, totaling over 140 games of suspensions and nearly $11 million in lost salaries. No one was arrested.
- (2003, October) During an American League Championship Series baseball game between the Boston Red Sox and the New York Yankees, 32-year-old pitcher Pedro Martinez of the Red Sox grabbed and threw to the ground 72-year-old Don Zimmer, an assistant coach for the Yankees, during an on-field melee between the two teams in the game's seventh inning. Later that same evening, Karim Garcia and Jeff Nelson of the Yankees allegedly assaulted Fenway Park groundskeeper Paul Williams in the Red Sox's bullpen. Major League Baseball punished no one involved in any of the evening's events.

are viewed as heroes or weaklings, superstars or wimps, aggressors or losers, and men or sissies in reflection of their ability to be rugged players. The use of violent play can be informally rewarded within teams through salary and contract incentives, praise, and other forms of preferential treatment. Similarly, fans and media broadcasters draw attention to the toughness and durability of the violent player and his ability to withstand ongoing victimization, often mythologizing tough players of the past as legends. "Legal" and "illegal" forms of violence in sports such as fistfights and brutal hits causing injury are showcased on sports highlights shows—often in "Plays of the Day/Night" segments.

Perhaps most important is that legal experts have debated whether violence in the game is best policed from the outside through either criminal or civil channels. Criminal law in North America is, let us remember, defined as a nation's or territory's recognized body of statute law that establishes what constitutes a legal offense and punishment of criminal offenses. Criminal statutes are codified into documents that articulate the precise conditions constituting a crime. These circumstances are generally known as *the elements of the offense.* Unless all the elements are sufficiently established by the prosecuting authority, the accused is not guilty of the alleged offense. In most Western nations such as Canada or the United States, three elements define an act as criminal: the *actus reus* or "guilty act," the *mens rea* or "guilty mind," and the attendant circumstances.

By contrast, civil or *tort* law refers to the body of law that provides an injured person with a means to secure financial compensation from the person who caused them an injury. Under tort law, when someone is injured either intentionally or by negligence, the offender may be required legally to pay damages to the injured. For most intents and purposes, tort law provides a codified system of rules for allowing people to receive compensation for the physical, emotional, or psychological injuries they suffer at the hands of another. The system of tort law is often viewed to be a deterrent against risky behavior because there are often heavy financial penalties accrued by having to pay for one's socially irresponsible actions. We are less concerned with the use of tort law in sports contexts and instead focus on criminally prosecuting athletes for incidents of on-field violence.

History teaches us that while a majority of on-field violence is not defined as criminal behavior, a handful of violent acts occurring within sports result in charges of "criminal assault" or "assault with a weapon." In Canada (a country that has been moderately proactive in arresting and prosecuting athletes) athletes may be charged with assault under Section 265 of the *Canadian Criminal Code,* which states:

> A person commits an assault when: (a) without the *consent* of another person, he applies force *intentionally* to that person, directly or indirectly; (b) he attempts or threatens, by an *act of gesture,* to apply force to another person, if he has, or causes that other person to believe upon reasonable grounds that he has, present ability to effect his purpose; (c) while openly wearing or carrying a weapon or an imitation thereof, he accosts or impedes another person or begs. (emphasis added)

Section 267 of the *Criminal Code* defines assault with a weapon (pertinent in the case of ice hockey as players are often assaulted with sticks) as:

> Everyone who, in committing an assault: (a) carries, uses or threatens to use a weapon or an imitation thereof; or, (b) causes bodily harm to the complainant; (c) is guilty of an indictable offence and liable to imprisonment for a term not exceeding ten years.

Canadian ice hockey assault cases such as *Agar v. Canning* (1965), *Martin v. Daigle* (1969), *R v. Maki* (1970), *R v. Green* (1971), *R v. Prénoveau* (1971), *R v. Watson* (1975), *R v. Starrat* (1980), *R v. Ciccarelli* (1988), *R v. Cey* (1989), *R v. Leclerc* (1991), and *R v. Neeld* (2000) have all represented an attempt to curtail instances of perceived criminal violence occurring within the sport at the amateur and professional tiers.

For crime enforcement agents in North America, however, the two central and most problematic elements in defining a sports crime are the *intent to injure* another player and the *lack of consent* to violent play (parameters established under s.265 of the *Criminal Code*). Over the course of time, each of these criteria has proved difficult to establish in sports violence cases. A review of the case law on potential sports crimes underlines inconsistencies in judicial decisions on what is recognized as criminal behavior. Perhaps most problematically, in *R v. Leclerc* (1991), the Canadian Court ruled that players of contact sports offer "implied consent to those assaults which are inherent and reasonably incidental to the normal playing of the game at this [professional] level." In a similar case in the United States, *Hackbartt v. Cincinnati Bengals* (1979), American courts ruled that players not only consent to violence but that forms of rule-breaking producing injury should be foreseeable by athletes. So, when Evander Holyfield stepped into a boxing ring with Mike Tyson on June 28, 1997, legal logic/principle states that because Holyfield had experienced prior forms of assault in the sport that violated contest rules (i.e., such as a low blow or head butt), and because he was aware of Mike Tyson's history of patterned violence against athletes and others, he should not have been surprised or felt victimized when Tyson bit off a piece of Holyfield's ear during the third round.

Judicial decisions resulting from the majority of the cases plainly state that while the violent acts under scrutiny may not be acceptable, toughness and aggression as organizing principles in sports should not be put on trial; yet, nor should they be ignored when interpreting violence in the game as either criminal or normative. When athletes have been brought to criminal courts for excessively violent acts on the ice, court justices have seemingly rejected these cases on the grounds that players *consent to violent victimization* in the game through their acceptance of the codes of aggression structuring athletic competition. Once again, such decisions are paramount in confirming cultural attitudes around player violence in ice hockey as victimless. It is precisely at this point that the legal notion of *volenti non fit injuria* (voluntary assumption of risk) becomes implemented to rationalize harmful outcomes that occur. If players consent to the mere possibility of violent victimization there can be no requisite guilt act or guilty mind among offenders and, thus, no crimes in sports.

The definitive North American legal standard for analyzing attendant circumstances of violence in sports is arguably set out by the decision in *R v. Cey* (1989). The court, in deciding the case (about an on-ice incident in ice hockey), questioned the *nature of the game* (professional, fast, competitive, physically punishing), *regular acts and circumstances* (e.g., high sticking usual, striking head as reasonable, blows after whistle acceptable), *the nature of the violent act* and *potential to injure,* and the *spirit of the violence* underpinning the act (whether retaliatory or intimidating). In light of the perceived normalcy of violence in contact sports, lack of criminal act, and lack of guilty minds among players, practically every defense of players for on-field actions has established the sport as one in which even the most dangerous forms of violence are legally defendable as part of the normal circumstances of the game. Add to this the way in which acts of aggression-producing catastrophic injuries are described as accidental, in the heat of the moment, or atypical for players, and there are scarce grounds to consider that acts of violence in sports may ever be considered criminal.

KEY EVENTS

Not all cases of dramatic forms of on-field player violence reach public awareness through mass mediation, but some of the major events clearly illustrate how reluctant sports insiders and outsiders are to define violence in sports as criminal. The 2000 arrest and prosecution of Canadian ice hockey player Marty McSorley is a prime example.

On February 21, 2000, the National Hockey League (NHL) ice hockey team the Boston Bruins visited the Vancouver Canucks in a mid-season contest. With only two minutes elapsed in the first period, long-time NHL enforcers—Marty McSorley of the Bruins and Donald Brashear of the Canucks—clashed horns in a fist-fight. For the remainder of the evening, McSorley tried to goad Brashear into another fight. In the final seconds of the game, McSorley skated out of his team's end of the rink and approached Brashear. He reached Brashear just inside the Canucks' blue line and struck him from behind with a two-handed stick slash to the right temple. Brashear tumbled backwards to the ice unconscious. He lay prone and motionless. Trainers worked on a convulsing Brashear for over 10 minutes on the ice to stabilize him. McSorley was assessed a match penalty for "attempting to injure" and also a game misconduct penalty.

In response to an unprecedented public outcry for stern reprimand by the league, the NHL (led by President Gary Bettman and Executive Vice-President Colin Campbell) suspended McSorley indefinitely on March 22, 2000. One day later, the NHL further admonished McSorley by suspending him for the Bruins' remaining 23 games of the 1999–2000 season, costing him over $100,000 in lost wages. As the longest suspension for an on-ice incident in NHL history, the League believed the penalty would have a deterrent effect on future violence and send out the message that such flagrantly dangerous stick-work was unacceptable. However, a Vancouver police sergeant on duty at the February game filed a report about the incident and recommended that criminal assault charges be laid against McSorley by the Crown prosecutor's office in Vancouver. It had been

12 years (1988) since NHL player Dino Ciccarelli of the Minnesota North Stars was criminally charged for an on-ice stick-swinging incident with Luke Richardson of the Toronto Maple Leafs. Ciccarelli was arrested two days after the incident and found guilty of assault. At that time, Ontario Provincial Court Justice Sidney Harris cited the need to convey a message to the NHL that "violence in a hockey game or in any other circumstance is not acceptable in our society" (*R v. Ciccarelli,* 1988). Harris sentenced Ciccarelli to one day in jail and levied a CDN$1,000 fine against him.

The McSorley–Brasher incident, and reaction to it, needs to be understood in particular social context. It occurred only a few years after a widely reported example of player–referee violence in Canadian university ice hockey. On February 24, 1996, at the end of an overtime period in a championship game between the University of Moncton and the University of Prince Edward Island (UPEI), chief referee Brian Carragher was pinned to the boards and assaulted by eight players from the University of Moncton. The incident occurred after a controversial goal ended the hockey game in UPEI's favor. Moncton goaltender Pierre Gagnon initiated the assault by grabbing Carragher; his assistant coach, Patrick Daviault, and several other players joined in the attack by throwing punches at the referee. Carragher was repeatedly punched in the head and body by the Moncton players and speared in the groin with a stick. Eventually, Daviault removed a metal mooring from the net and threw it into a pane of glass in front of the goal judge, shattering the glass. Four players from the Moncton team were suspended from intercollegiate competition (suspensions ranged from 1–5 years), and assistant coach Daviault received a one-year suspension. Although police and Crown prosecutors in Charlottetown, PEI, initially threatened criminal intervention into the sport in response to the event, none ever materialized.

Two years later, Jesse "The Bull" Boulerice of the Plymouth Whalers in the Ontario Hockey League (OHL) swung his stick at Andrew Long of the Guelph Storm. The blow lacerated Long's face (requiring 20 stitches to close), fractured his skull, and produced a blood spot on his brain. Boulerice was suspended for the entire 1998–1999 season by the OHL and charged with felony assault by the Detroit, Michigan, police. The charge, which potentially carried a 10-year prison sentence, shocked amateur and professional hockey cultures in North America. Boulerice pleaded "no-contest" to the charge (not, in legal terms, an admission of guilt) and received a nine-month suspended sentence from a Detroit county court. The charge is now expunged from his record, and Boulerice plays professional ice hockey.

In the wake of both the University of Moncton and Boulerice incidents, and following considerable resistance from NHL league officials, executives, players, and coaches (and indeed, many sports fans), Vancouver Crown prosecutor, Michael Hicks, filed charges of assault with a weapon against McSorley on March 7, 2000. On September 25, 2000, McSorley (represented by legal counsel William Smart) appeared before the Provincial Court of British Columbia to face the charge. In a sports drama that would last five days, Marty McSorley, the NHL, and violence in professional ice hockey were placed on trial. The court proceedings attracted an international audience, and the trial brought to the fore issues of player violence, player consent to sports violence, and the role of the State in governing sports violence. On October 6, 2000, McSorley was found guilty of assaulting Brashear with a weapon under section 267(2) of the *Criminal Code of Canada*. Justice William Kitchen sentenced McSorley to an 18-month conditional discharge (essentially probation), and ordered that he not play in any future NHL games involving Brashear. McSorley does not have a criminal record as a result of the decision and thus no difficulty crossing international borders. McSorley's 18-month discharge clearly represented a more lenient outcome than the year and a half imprisonment allowable under Canadian law as punishment for the act.

McSorley's slash to Brashear's head would be a scene played, and replayed, on international sports television for an extended period of time. The incident and its legal outcomes stirred public emotion about ice hockey's place in North American culture and the social impact of hockey violence. The March 6, 2000, edition of Canada's news magazine *MacLean's*, for instance, referred provocatively to ice hockey as a "Blood Sport." When examined from every angle, debated by sports pundits, and dissected from a multitude of theoretical points of view, however, the incident underlined what many hockey fans have known for quite some time—that illegal stick-work and other forms of player violence in the NHL are simply not under control. And equally contested would be the wider social utility of the McSorley trial and the issue of whether or not the criminal justice system should have a mandate to control player violence in ice hockey or in sports in general.

Although earlier episodes of NHL violence had also led to criminal charges, the McSorley–Brashear incident arguably represented a turning point in the history of professional ice hockey in that a clear and final message had supposedly been delivered to the sport to "clean up" the game lest increased legal intervention would follow. Yet, only four years later, on March 8, 2004, another flamboyant case of on-ice violence took place during an NHL game, once more occurring in Vancouver. The event would once again illustrate the ability of sports to resist serious criminal intervention.

During a late-season contest, Todd Bertuzzi of the Vancouver Canucks grabbed Steve Moore of the Colorado Avalanche and punched him in the back of the head in the third period of the game. Bertuzzi viciously struck Moore just underneath his helmet and forced him face-first into the ice. Bertuzzi landed on top of Moore and continued to strike punches against his skull, as the Colorado player laid semiconscious on the ice. Avalanche teammates piled on top of both players, resulting in an on-ice brawl between the two teams. Moore suffered two cracked vertebrae, a concussion, and several lacerations as a result of the attack. Bertuzzi was immediately suspended by the NHL for the 2003–2004 season, but he was reinstated by the League on August 8, 2005. He was charged with common assault by the Provincial Crown in British Columbia but pleaded "no contest" and eventually received one year of probation. Steve Moore has yet to play professional ice hockey again. He pursued civil action against both Bertuzzi and the Canucks in 2006, but it was dismissed before it even reached a court.

FUTURE PROSPECTS

Despite over 100 years of debate concerning violence in sports and criminal intervention into games, relatively little has been done to systematically identify, target, and rectify through multi-institutional punishment the more serious forms of violence in North American sports. And, despite a spate of recent and historical evidence to suggest that even unwanted and serious forms of violence are products of deeply revered socialization processes in the game, insiders and supporters of the standard version of sports aggression and violence as safe, exciting, and victimless have resisted dramatic structural or cultural changes into sports. The pervasive mentality in North American sports cultures is to leave sports alone and, in fact, to prepare young players for violence in sports. Landmark cases such as *Hackbarrt v. Bengals* or *R. v. McSorley* are heralded as powerful deterrents against hyperviolence in sports, but there are no facts or figures to suggest that they have any positive effect on controlling player violence. If anything, they illustrate the legal futility of pursuing a criminal case against an athlete. If the last 100 years of North American sports history teaches us anything, we should not expect to see a herd of players in courtrooms any time soon.

See also Academic Misconduct Among Athletes; Animal Blood Sports; Antitrust Violations in Professional Sports; Gambling; Hazing; Hooliganism; Partner Abuse Among Athletes; Rape and Sexual Assault; Referee Abuse; Rights of Young Athletes.

Further Reading: *Agar V. Canning.* (1965). 54 W.W.R. 302 (M.Q.B); affd. 55 W.W.R. 384 (C.A.); Atkinson, M. (2006). It's Still Part of the Game: Violence and Masculinity in Canadian Ice Hockey. In *Sport, Rhetoric, Gender and Violence: Historical Perspectives and Media Representations,* edited by L. Fuller. New York: Palgrave MacMillan; Barnes, J. C. (1988). *Sport and the Law in Canada.* Toronto, ON: Butterworths; Bridges, J. (1999). *Making Violence Part of the Game.* Commack: Kroshka Books; *Hackbart v. Cincinnati Bengals, Inc. and Charles Clark,* 601 F.2d 516; 444 U.S. 931 [1979]; *Martin v. Daigle.* (1969). 1 N.B.R. (2d) 755, 6 D.L.R. (3d) 634 (N.B.C.A); *R v. Cey.* (1989). 48 C.C.C. (3d) 480 (Sask C.A.); *R v. Ciccarelli.* (1988). O.J. No 2388 (O.P.C).; *R v. Green.* (1971). O.R. 591, 2 C.C.C. (2d) 442, 16 D.L.R. (3d) 137 (Prov. Ct.); *R v. Maki.* (1970). 3 O.R. 780, 1 C.C.C. (2d) 333, 14 D.L.R. (3d) 164 (Prov Ct.); *R v. McSorley.* (2000). B.C.J. No. 0116 (B.C.P.C); *R v. Neeld.* (2000). B.C.J. No. 57676-01 (B.C.P.C); *R v. Prénoveau.* (1971). R.L 21 (C.s.p); *R v. Starrat.* (1980). 1 O.R. 227, 5 C.C.C. (2d) 32 (C.A); *R v. Watson.* (1975). 26 C.C.C. (2d) 150 (O.P.C); Weinstein, M., Smith, M., and Wiesenthal, D. (1995). Masculinity and Hockey Violence. *Sex Roles* 33: 831–847; Young, K. (1993). Violence, Risk, and Liability in Male Sports Culture. *Sociology of Sport Journal* 10: 373–396; Young, K. (2002). From Sports Violence to Sports Crime: Aspects of Violence, Law, and Gender in the Sports Process. In *Paradoxes of Youth and Sport,* edited by M. Gatz, M. Messner, and S. Ball-Rokeach. New York: SUNY Press; Young, K., and Wamsley, K. (1996). State Complicity in Sports Assault and the Gender Order in 20th Century Canada: Preliminary Observations. *Avante* 2: 51–69.

Michael Atkinson

D

DISABILITY SPORTS

Disability sports involve athletic competition between people with physical and intellectual disabilities or sensory impairments. Some of these sports are based on existing sports but are adapted to meet the needs of the people playing. As a result they are sometimes also known as "adapted sports." However, many sports played by disabled people are not adapted but variants of able-bodied sports. Prior to the mid-1900s, very few institutional opportunities existed for people with disabilities to participate in organized sports.

BACKGROUND

Centuries of research on deviant body forms and associated identities show how differences in appearance, shape, size, race, or functional ability may be used as the basis of one's prejudicial exclusion in a full spate of social settings and practices. What constitutes a normative or a deviant body is culturally bound and historically specific, and every culture contains examples of socially lauded and socially marginalized body types. When a person is labeled with body deviance, such as being called physically disabled, the identity attribute may significantly alter the bearer's life experiences. Some sociologists of the body argue that from the nineteenth century onward, Western cultures have increasingly defined physical ability and disability from scientific and medical perspectives. Particularly influenced by Foucault's theory of biopower, control, and surveillance, sociologists of scientized bodies point to how "abled" and "disabled" identities are largely formed in and disseminated from institutional sites of medicine. Medical experts wield enormous power to culturally define what constitutes an able or disabled body and how such a body should be treated. Once bodies are medically dominated, they become, as both Frank (1991) and Couser (1997) argue, docile in that people lose cultural agency to determine what a (deviant) body means to them.

But long before Western medicine claimed definitional ownership over the (dis)abled body and defined it as docile, athlete cultures served to set social standards of body normalcy, beauty, and power. For well over 3,000 years, the social image of athleticism has been closely linked with physical perfection: a body free from any disability. As such, ancient Greek and Roman sports cultures not only rejected participants on the basis of perceived (dis)ability, but the history of modern sports development (ca. 1850 onward) reveals a stark pattern of discrimination against those who fail to "measure up" according to sociomedical constructions of ability. Emergent organized sports in Europe and the Americas though the late nineteenth and early twentieth centuries were simply not designed (through rules, styles of play, ethics of competition, or technology employed) to accommodate for those differently able, such as the deaf or blind.

Although many North Americans are largely unaware of its prevalence, small cultures of sports for athletes with a disability have existed for more than 100 years. In the eighteenth and nineteenth centuries, physicians lobbied for the increased use of sports/athletic activities as means of rehabilitation for persons with a disability. The world organization of sports for the deaf, the Comité International Sports des Sourds, was founded in France in 1922 as an institution dedicated to promoting sports for all. They would, in 1924, become chief organizers of the first disability games in Western nations called the "Silent Games" (now known as the Deaflympics).

In 1960, the first Paralympic Games were held directly following the Olympic Games in Rome, Italy. The event used the nearby venues and format as the

---

DID YOU KNOW?

German-born Joseph Pilates was placed in an internment camp in England in 1914. While held prisoner in the camp, he continued a life-long exploration of the rehabilitative potential of exercise by developing a workout regimen using objects readily at his disposal there, such as beer keg rings and bed springs. Unhealthy as a child, Joseph Pilates studied and explored diverse physical cultural athletic practices as a means of overcoming his skeletal and postural problems. Pilates preached his method of physical conditioning, which he would later call "contrology," to fellow detainees in the camp who suffered from a range of illnesses. After his release from the camp and a brief move to Germany, Pilates emigrated to New York and founded a contrology center. He marketed "Pilates" methods and related equipment, training hundreds of students until 1966. Pilates' New York studio put him in close proximity to a number of dance studios. Until exercise science and popular fitness cultures caught up with the Pilates exercise principles in the 1990s, it was chiefly dancers and elite athletes who kept Joseph Pilates's work alive after his death in 1967.

Olympic event and included 400 athletes from 23 countries; its purpose was partly to draw attention to the Games but also to illustrate that athletes with disabilities could compete in sports like able-bodied athletes. Also in 1960, under the organization of the World Federation for Ex-servicemen, an International Working Group on Sport for the Disabled was set up to study the problems of sports for persons with a disability. It resulted in the creation, in 1964, of an international sports federation called the International Sport Organization for the Disabled (ISOD). The ISOD offered opportunities for those athletes who could not affiliate to other sports organizations for the disabled or abled, for example, visually impaired, amputees, persons with cerebral palsy, and paraplegics. Organized sports for athletes with a disability are now generally divided into three broad disability groups: deaf people, people with physical disabilities, and people with intellectual disabilities.

Following the success of the Paralympic movement, a similar movement crystallized to promote sports for people with intellectual disabilities called the Special Olympics. In 1986, the International Sports Federation for Persons with Intellectual Disability (INAS-FID) was formed to support elite competition for athletes with intellectual disabilities. In 2006, the Extremity Games (a cousin of the X Games) was formed by the College Pak Industries for people with limb loss or limb difference to compete in extreme sports. This annual event is held in the summer in Orlando, Florida, and includes competitions in skateboarding, wakeboarding, rock climbing, mountain biking, surfing, and kayaking.

KEY EVENTS

That Paralympic movement can be traced to 1948 when Sir Ludwig Guttmann, a German-born neurosurgeon who emmigrated to England in 1939, organized an athletic competition in Stoke Mandeville for World War II veterans with spinal cord injuries. Four years earlier, at the British government's request to open Stoke Mandeville Hospital's National Spinal Injury Centre, mainly to treat wounded servicemen, Dr. Guttmann had introduced a new medical approach embracing sports as a central therapy in the total rehabilitation of paralyzed patients. What began as rehabilitative recreation evolved into athletic competition—with Guttmann emerging as the founding father of disability sports. On July 28, 1948, symbolically coinciding with the opening of the Olympic Games in London, the Stoke Mandeville Games for the Paralyzed launched the first competition for wheelchair athletes.

The Paralympic Games now take place once every four years and are held immediately after the Olympic Games in the same locations, using the same facilities. The Paralympic Winter Games are held two years after each Summer Paralympic Games—again, in the same venue and using the same facilities as the Olympic Games. As a major world sporting event involving dozens of competing nations, the Paralympic Games are now second only to the Olympic Games themselves with regard to country representation. In Athens in 2004, for example, 3,806 athletes from 136 countries competed. However, the Paralympics Games receive only a small amount of international press coverage, attract far smaller audiences than

PARALYMPIC YEARS AND SITES

Summer Paralympics

2004: Athens, Greece
2000: Sydney, Australia
1996: Atlanta, USA
1992: Barcelona, Spain
1988: Seoul, Korea
1984: Stoke Mandeville, UK & New York, USA
1980: Arnhem, The Netherlands
1976: Toronto, Canada
1972: Heidelberg, Germany
1968: Tel Aviv, Israel
1964: Tokyo, Japan
1960: Rome, Italy
1952: Stoke Mandeville, UK

Winter Paralympics

2006: Torino, Italy
2002: Salt Lake City, USA
1998: Nagano, Japan
1994: Lillehammer, Norway
1992: Tignes-Albertville, France
1988: Innsbruck, Austria
1984: Innsbruck, Austria
1980: Geilo, Norway
1976: Örnsköldsvik, Sweden

most other sporting mega-events, and their athletes receive far less accolades than Olympic athletes. Such discriminatory patterns illustrate that despite the inroads disabled athletes have made within sports culture, Westerners may still perceive medically deviant bodies as unworthy of social admiration.

Two landmark years in the twentieth century made the Paralympic Games into the international showcase they are today. In 1976, the list of disability groups that could participate in events expanded for the Games held in Toronto, Canada. In the same year, the first Paralympic Winter Games took place in Örnsköldsvik, Sweden. Then, in 1988, after the Seoul Games in South Korea, further integration between the Olympic and Paralympic Games resulted when the same venues were used for both events. Until 1988, while the Paralympic Games were held in the same city as the Olympics, they were not staged at the same venue. Critics argued that by staging the Games at separate sites a discriminatory message of "separate and unequal" surrounded the Paralympic movement.

DISABILITY SPORTS

Deaflympics

Alpine skiing
Athletics
Badminton
Basketball
Beach volleyball
Bowling
Cross-country skiing
Curling
Cycling
Football
Handball
Ice hockey
Judo
Karate
Orienteering
Shooting
Snowboarding
Swimming
Table tennis
Tae kwon do
Tennis
Volleyball
Water polo
Wrestling

Paralympics

Adapted rowing
Alpine skiing
Archery
Athletics
Boccie
Cycling
Equestrian
Football
Handcycling
Goalball
Ice sledge hockey
Judo
Nordic skiing
Powerlifting
Sailing
Shooting
Sitting volleyball
Swimming
Table tennis
Wheelchair basketball
Wheelchair curling
Wheelchair fencing
Wheelchair rugby
Wheelchair tennis

Special Olympics

Alpine skiing
Aquatics
Athletics
Badminton
Basketball
Boccie
Bowling
Cross-country skiing
Cycling
Equestrian
Figure skating
Floor hockey
Football
Golf
Gymnastics
Powerlifting
Roller skating
Sailing
Snowboarding
Snowshoeing
Softball
Speed skating
Table tennis
Team handball
Tennis
Volleyball

Other Sports

Blind cricket
Blind golf
Electric wheelchair football
Electric wheelchair hockey
Golf
Wheelchair baseball
Wheelchair hockey
Wheelchair skateboarding

The other major disability sports games, the Special Olympics, began in 1968 when Eunice Kennedy Shriver organized the First International Summer Games at Soldier Field in Chicago. The concept of a Games catering to people with cognitive impairments formed in the early 1960s when Shriver pioneered a day camp for people with intellectual disability. She saw that individuals with intellectual disability were far more capable in sports and physical activities than portrayed by athletic and medical experts. In December 1968, the Special Olympics organization was established as a nonprofit charitable organization under the laws of the District of Columbia. Since 1968, millions of children and adults with intellectual disability have participated in Special Olympics around the world. Today, Special Olympics involve more than 2.25 million athletes from over 150 countries involved in more than 200 Special Olympics programs. Rather impressively, the Special Olympics is run almost entirely by 700,000 global volunteers around the world. The Special Olympics organization itself sponsors or provides support for more than 20,000 competitions around the world each year.

The Special Olympics organization is truly unique within the world of sports for a number of reasons. First, its mission is to provide year-round sports training and athletic competition in a variety of Olympic-type sports for both children and adults. The Special Olympics group is also one that seeks to foster social bonding among disabled athletes and their families. Rather than encouraging divisiveness through intense interpersonal competition, athletes are presented with opportunities to demonstrate courage, experience joy, and participate in a sharing of gifts, skills, and friendship with their families. In this regard and others, the Special Olympics organization is one that seeks to provide a supportive lifestyle community for athletes. Indeed, Special Olympics was founded on the belief that people with intellectual disability can learn, enjoy, and benefit from participation in individual and team sports. As such, participation in Special Olympics training programs and events is open to all people with intellectual disability who are at least eight years old, regardless of the degree of their disability. Ongoing advice from coaches, mentors, support volunteers, and others are available for athletes year-round, in the effort of nurturing young participants and as a way of assisting families with economic or other social hardships. The espoused "Spirit of Special Olympics"—skill, courage, sharing, and joy—promotes a set of universal values that may seem somewhat deviant to insiders in mainstream sports worlds. Their athlete pledge—"Let me win. But if I cannot win, let me be brave in the attempt"—equally symbolizes a set of values that participants in professional and elite amateur cultures might do well to remember.

Finally, a developing, and potentially landmark, controversy in the world of disability sports is the desire among certain disabled athletes to compete in able-bodied sports contests. Through the innovation of sports technology, athletes with pronounced physical disabilities may find themselves running with and against able-bodied peers. Yet, South African Paralympic runner Oscar Pistorius lost his right to compete against able-bodied athletes because of his "over reliance" on technology. Known as the "Blade Runner," Pistorius is a double amputee world record holder in the 100-meter, 200-meter, and 400-meter Paralympic events and runs with the aid of carbon fiber transtibial artificial limbs (a commercial product named "Cheetah"). In 2007, Pistorius took part in his first international able-bodied competitions. However, his artificial lower legs, while enabling him to compete, generated claims from physiologists that he has an unfair advantage over able-bodied runners. The International Association of Athletics Federations (IAAF) agreed and amended its rules to ban the use of any technical device that incorporates springs, wheels, or any other element that provides a user with an advantage over another athlete not using such a device. Among other issues, the Pistorius case inadvertently raised another debate about the fairness of unequal access to technological advances in sports training and competition, such that critics cited the IAAF ruling as unjust and arbitrary in a world of sports where athletes from wealthy nations benefit from access to the best training and competition technology while others who come from impoverished nations are disadvantaged.

FUTURE PROSPECTS

Disability sports have grown as a global sports phenomenon. They challenge enduring cultural associations between the medically imperfect physical form and one's social worth within and outside of sports cultures. In this context, the power of sports to change social attitudes and dismantle long-standing systems of social discrimination finds powerful expression. The 2005 MTV-sponsored film *Murderball,* which showcased the exploits of the U.S. national men's wheelchair rugby team, further illustrates how disability sports have made indelible marks in contemporary popular cultures. Sports opportunities for people with disabilities continue to expand as cultural stereotypes about people with disabilities continue to erode slowly.

See also Biology and Athlete Performance; Illness; Sports for All and Fair Play Leagues.

Further Reading: Couser, G. (2007). *Recovering Bodies: Illness, Disability, and Life Writing.* Madison: University of Wisconsin Press; Foucault, M. (1977). *Discipline and Punish: The Birth of the Prison.* London: Penguin Books; Frank, A. (1991). *At the Will of the Body: Reflections on Illness.* Boston: Houghton; Howe, D. (2004). *Sport, Professionalism and Pain: Ethnographies of Injury and Risk.* London: Routledge; Howe, D. (2008). *The Cultural Politics of the Paralympic Movement.* London: Routledge; Markula, P. (2003). The Technologies of the Self: Feminism, Foucault and Sport. *Sociology of Sport Journal* 20: 87–107; Markula, P. (2006). The Dancing Body Without Organs: Deleuze, Femininity and Performing Research. *Qualitative Inquiry* 12: 3–27.

Michael Atkinson

DRAFTING AMATEUR ATHLETES

Drafting amateur athletes represents an opportunity for professional sports teams to improve their teams from the previous season. The cost of signing these amateur athletes is considerably less than signing current professional players via free agency. Thus, the amateur draft is an important process within professional sports leagues. An amateur draft is present in most North American professional sports leagues, but it is unique to North America; most European leagues do not have any sort of amateur draft. The most common format of the amateur draft is the reverse order draft described in the next section. Two contemporary issues dealing with the draft process are the age limits to become eligible for the amateur draft and tanking, when teams intentionally lose games in order to improve draft position. Both of these issues represent the current debate regarding the amateur drafting structure.

BACKGROUND

The reverse order draft is the most common amateur draft format, and the way it works is simple. The team with the worst regular season record from the previous season has the first selection in the draft. The team with the second worst record selects second, and the process continues until all teams make a selection. Subsequent rounds proceed with the same order of selection as the first round (worst team selects first, second worst selects second, etc.). The National Football League (NFL) was the first to institute an amateur draft in 1936, followed by the Basketball Association of America in 1949. The National Hockey League (NHL) began its amateur draft in 1963, and Major League Baseball (MLB) followed in 1965. The newest North American professional sports league, Major League Soccer, began its draft in 1996.

The philosophy given by North American professional sports leagues for the institution of a reverse order draft was competitive balance. *Competitive balance* is defined as "a league structure which has relatively equal playing strength between league members" (Forrest and Simmons, 2002, 229). On the surface, the reverse order draft procedure would seem to accomplish the task of making leagues more competitively balanced. Recall the worst team in the league has the top overall selection, which means the team selects the best player. Therefore, one would expect the league would increase its competitive balance. However, research has shown this is not true. Two reasons illustrate why competitive balance does not improve with the reverse order draft format.

The first reason focuses on the development time for players. Once drafted, most MLB and NHL players go into the parent franchise's minor league system. These players may stay in the system for a few years before they receive a promotion to the parent club (if the players ever do receive a promotion). Therefore, these players do not help their parent teams immediately. The NFL and the NBA do not have a minor league system, however, the impact of a single rookie player in any league is minimal because of such things as the complexities of an offensive or defensive system, adjusting to the pace of the professional game, and the physical size differential from amateur to professional sports.

The second reason competitive balance does not improve through a reverse order draft is the Coase Theorem, which was developed by Ronald Coase in 1960. Simply, the Coase Theorem states that players choose the teams who place the most value on the players. The Coase Theorem received the most testing within the free agency construct of professional sports leagues, however, it still holds true within the reverse order construct. Therefore, the rationale of reverse order drafts improving competitive balance may be false, but North American professional sports leagues still tout the competitive balance rationale for the reason behind the reverse order draft.

KEY EVENTS

Two contemporary issues emerge with drafting amateur athletes. The first issue is age limits to become eligible for the professional leagues. Currently, a potential MLB prospect can go straight from high school to the professional ranks. However, if the prospect plays college baseball, he must play at least three years in college before becoming eligible for the draft. An NFL prospect cannot become a professional until three years after high school. The NFL adopted this rule in 1990 under then commissioner Paul Tagliabue. Before the adoption of the rule, players wanting to apply for the NFL draft that did not graduate from college would apply to the NFL, and the league reviewed those applications on a case-by-case basis. An NHL prospect is eligible after age 18. Initially, any player graduating from high school was eligible for the NBA draft, but the NBA recently adjusted its rule. The rule, instituted in 2005, requires players to be at least one year removed from high school. The dialogue surrounding this rule change was interesting and worth detailing here.

Imposing age limits for the NBA draft was a hot topic in 1999. Commissioner David Stern believed imposing an age limit was the right policy decision for the NBA. The age limit might encourage kids to stay in school and not jump to the NBA. Also, the NBA may have been dealing with a diminished quality of play throughout the league due to early entrants into the NBA. Speculation was that many of these early entrants were not ready to play at the professional level and thus hurt the overall quality of the product. For example, scoring in 1999 decreased almost 10 points per game compared to scoring in 1995.

Players and coaches were split over their feelings on imposing age limits for entry into the draft. Some people believed imposing age limits was not fair. If a player had the talent to play in the NBA right after high school, no restriction should exist preventing him from playing in the NBA. Other people believed imposing age limits was a good thing for both the kids and the league. An age limit would allow a kid to mature in all aspects of their life. One idea proposed during 1999 would have given potential high draft picks a stipend paid by the NBA to stay in college to cover living expenses.

Columnist Norman Chad (*Chicago Sun-Times,* April 21, 2005) commented that imposing an age limit was a good policy for the NBA from a business perspective because "it allows the National Collegiate Athletic Association (NCAA)marketing machine to create marquee names for the league and keeps owners from signing high-risk youngsters to long-term contracts." Age limit negotiations increased between the owners and the players in the summer of 2005 during the collective bargaining negotiation. During the negotiation process, Commissioner Stern believed the age limit should be 20 years old, while the union leader opposed any age limit. One reason the union leader opposed the age limit was the limit would restrict excellent players, such as LeBron James and Kobe Bryant who were ready for the NBA right out of high school, from going directly to the NBA. Also, the union leader said the other sports leagues were not pushing for age limits, so why should the NBA adopt an age limit policy? Both sides compromised, and the new collective bargaining agreement included a provision for an age limit of 19 years old, which meant a player normally had to play one year of college basketball before being eligible for the NBA draft. The ramifications of the new policy are still unclear as the process moves from the NBA down through the NCAA basketball systems, prep schools, AAU teams, and high school basketball teams. Only time will tell the effect on each basketball system individually.

Another issue dealing with age limits occurred in 2003 and 2004 concerning Maurice Clarett. In late 2002, Ohio State Freshman Running Back Maurice Clarett contemplated challenging the NFL draft eligibility rule as early as his freshman season. Clarett decided to return to Ohio State for his sophomore season. Clarett and the Ohio State football program came under scrutiny from the NCAA regarding potential rule violations. In early September 2003, Ohio State head football coach, Jim Tressel, suspended Clarett for his sophomore season due to the investigation by the NCAA. Upon his suspension from the football program, Clarett sued the NCAA for eligibility into the 2004 draft, one year earlier than the NFL rule allows. Clarett sued the NCAA citing the draft rule violated antitrust laws.

In early February 2004, the federal judge in the case ruled in favor of Clarett, and the NFL appealed the ruling requesting a stay of the ruling. The Federal Appeals Court granted a stay of the previous ruling the week before the NFL draft took place. Clarett took his case to the United States Supreme Court for entry into the draft, and the Supreme Court upheld the stay of the appeals court's decision. Finally, in late May 2004, a Federal Appeals Court stated that the initial judge ruling was incorrect and that the NFL draft rule did not violate U.S. antitrust law.

The second contemporary issue regarding the drafting of amateur athletes is draft lotteries. A draft lottery is a relatively new format within North American professional sports leagues. The NBA first instituted the modern draft lottery for the 1985 NBA draft. The following section outlines the procedure.

The NBA draft lottery, in its earliest and least structured form, materialized in 1966. Starting in 1966, a coin flip between the two worst teams in each division determined which team received the number one pick. This draft structure was the reverse order draft format, and it stayed in place until after the 1983–1984 season. The conclusion of the 1983–1984 season led some owners and league officials to believe that teams were intentionally losing games in order gain a better draft position. The result was a new lottery format beginning with the 1985 NBA draft. The new lottery format gave all nonplayoff teams an equal chance of securing the number one overall selection (winning the lottery). NBA executives had mixed feelings regarding the lottery format. Some executives believed the lottery deterred teams from intentionally losing games, or tanking. Other executives did not believe it deterred teams from tanking. Finally, some executives were concerned with the objective of the draft and felt that the draft was in place to help bad teams get better by giving them the lower picks—the parity argument.

In 1987, the NBA made a slight modification to the process. The lottery only determined the order for the first three picks of the NBA draft. After the determination of the first three picks, the rest of the nonplayoff teams picked in inverse order of their previous season record. The rationale was the whole idea of parity; the team with the worst record has, at worst, the fourth pick in the draft (NBA.com, 2007).

In 1989, Commissioner Stern favored the lottery procedure. He believed it helped fans focus upon the future of their teams and heightened the interest that their team might win the lottery and receive the number one overall selection and, theoretically, the best player. Skeptics still existed, however, and they believed that teams just missing the playoffs the previous year should not have a chance to pick number one overall, no matter how big or small the odds were that the best nonplayoff team could win the lottery.

In 1989, the NBA believed that the league might need to alter the lottery format again in order to give the worst team a better chance of winning the lottery. A further issue for the league was expansion and how the league was going to adjust the draft procedures because of the influx of new franchises. The competition committee recommended that the league institute a weighted lottery beginning in the 1990 draft lottery. The worst team had a 16.7 percent chance of securing the number one selection while the eleventh worst team had a 1.5 percent chance. The NBA believed the weighted lottery more than likely eliminated the incentive for teams to tank because the payout for reaching the playoffs would be a bigger lure than the opportunity of winning the draft lottery.

With the adoption of the weighted lottery, the notion of teams tanking still was present in the NBA at the conclusion of the 1992 and 1993 season. Coaches and executives commented that they believed some teams were more concerned about the number of ping-pong balls they would receive rather than winning games. At the 1993 NBA draft, Mike Monroe reported on a conversation between Minnesota Timberwolves owner Harvey Ratner and Commissioner David Stern. Before the start of the 1993 draft, Ratner had posed the question to Stern about what happened if the Orlando Magic won the lottery for the second consecutive year. Stern replied, "a disaster." The Orlando Magic won the draft lottery in 1992 despite the fact that they had the best record of the nonplayoff teams and, therefore, the least chance of winning the draft lottery. Then, in 1993, the "disaster" Stern was referring to occurred when the Orlando Magic again won the draft lottery. Stern said later, "Institutionally, we have a problem with it."

As a result, the league voted to increase the chances that the team with the worst record would win the draft lottery. The adjustments are still present today and involved reworking probabilities so that the worst team now had a 25 percent chance of winning the draft lottery instead of the previous 16 percent chance of winning (NBA.com, 2007).

PATRICK EWING

Patrick Ewing of Georgetown University was the reigning college basketball player in 1985 and was deemed to be the best amateur player going into the 1985 NBA draft. This was the first draft following the adoption of the new lottery procedure in which all teams not reaching the playoffs would have an equal chance of winning the lottery (receiving the number one overall selection). Conspiracy theorists believe Commissioner David Stern "fixed" the draft by freezing the envelope of the New York Knicks. By freezing their envelope, Stern would select the "warmer" envelopes until the only envelope remaining was the "cold" envelope, which belonged to the New York Knicks, who then received the number one overall selection. Ewing went on to become one of the NBA's greatest players.

The NHL was the other professional sports league to adopt a draft lottery format, starting with the 1995 NHL draft. Conversations in the NHL surrounding the adoption of a lottery format began in the early 1980s when a rumor suggested that the Pittsburgh Penguins tanked late in the season in order to pick Mario Lemieux. In 1990, the NHL board of governors heard a proposal regarding the adoption of a lottery format similar to the NBA lottery. However, the Board of Governors rejected the proposal due to the parity argument.

In 1993, the conversation regarding the adoption of a lottery format returned due to comments made by Ottawa owner Bruce Firestone. Firestone was rumored to have told members of the media that a plan was in place for Ottawa to throw the last game of the season in order to receive the number one overall draft pick. Commissioner Gary Bettman fined the franchise $100,000 but said the commissioner's office found no evidence the team threw the game and no threat existed to the integrity of the game.

Gary Bettman commented that adopting a draft lottery format was worth considering for the NHL because the lottery is a way of dealing with the problem of teams tanking. Bettman was a member of the NBA executive office and became commissioner of the NHL in 1993, which meant Bettman was present during the adoption of the NBA draft lottery formats. In February 1994, Bettman proposed that the NHL adopt a draft lottery beginning with the 1995 NHL draft. The NHL lottery proposal included heavy weights so the best nonplayoff team had less than a one percent chance of winning the lottery. If one of the best five nonplayoff teams won the lottery, that team would not receive the first pick. Instead, that team would receive the number six overall pick because no club could move up more than four places in the draft.

Beck Taylor and Justin Trogdon (2002) investigated tanking in the NBA and confirmed that eliminated teams were more likely to lose than teams who were going to the playoffs prior to the adoption of the equal chance lottery in the 1985 NBA draft. When the NBA introduced the new format in 1985, the authors concluded that teams lose the incentive to tank when each team has an equal chance of winning the draft lottery. However, when the NBA adopted a

SPENCER HAYWOOD

Spencer Haywood was a star basketball player at a junior college in Colorado who later transferred to the University of Detroit. Haywood decided to turn pro after his sophomore season at the University of Detroit but could not because of the NBA rules saying a player had to complete four years of schooling. Haywood instead joined the Denver Rockets of the American Basketball Association (ABA) and played with the team for one season. Following that season, Haywood signed a contract to play for the Seattle Supersonics of the NBA. Haywood still was ineligible because of the age restrictions. With the threat by the NBA to disallow the contract, Haywood sued the NBA citing antitrust violation. The U.S. Supreme Court ruled in favor of Haywood and allowed recently graduated high school players to declare for the NBA Draft.

draft lottery format, Taylor and Trogdon found that the incentive to tank returned. Therefore, the playoff payout was not big enough, and the incentive to tank was still an issue for the NBA. Taylor and Trogdon's article did not investigate the final adjustment to the NBA lottery procedure, which was the increased weights.

FUTURE PROSPECTS

The contemporary issues revolving around the drafting of amateur athletes involve the draft structure and imposing age restrictions. These issues are far from resolved as leagues strive to protect the quality of their product and the integrity of the game.

See also Antitrust Violations in Professional Sports.

Further Reading: Coase, R. H. (1960). The Problem of Social Cost. *Journal of Law and Economics* 3: 1–44; Forrest, D., and Simmons, R. (2002). Outcome Uncertainty and Attendance Demand in Sport: The Case of English Soccer. *The Statistician* 51(2): 229–241; Fort, R., and Quirk, J. (1995). Cross-Subsidization, Incentives, and Outcomes in Professional Team Sports Leagues. *Journal of Economic Literature* 33(3): 1265–1299; NBA.com. (2007). Evolution of the Draft and Lottery. http://www.nba.com/history/draft_evolution.html (accessed August 12, 2007); Schmidt, M. B., and Berri, D. J. (2003). On the Evolution of Competitive Balance: The Impact of an Increasing Global Search. *Economic Inquiry* 41(4): 692–704; Taylor, B. A., and Trogdon, J. G. (2002). Losing to Win: Tournament Incentives in the National Basketball Association. *Journal of Labor Economics* 20(1): 23–41; Walton, L. (2007). How the NBA Draft Process Works. http://www.hoopsvibe.com/nba/nba-draft/nba-draft-news/how-the-nba-draft-process-works-ar43263.html (accessed August 12, 2007).

Brian P. Soebbing

E

EATING DISORDERS

Anorexia nervosa is an eating disorder that occurs primarily among girls and women. It is often characterized by a fear of gaining weight, self-starvation, and a distorted body image. The condition is usually brought on by emotional disorders that lead a person to worry excessively about the appearance of his or her body. There are generally two types of eating disorders: Anorexia is characterized by strict dieting and exercising; bulimia includes binging and purging. Binging is the act of eating abnormally large amounts of food in a short period of time, and purging is the use of vomiting or other methods, such as laxatives, to empty the stomach. Athletes in particular sports cultures are believed to be highly susceptible, or predisposed to, developing eating disorders such as anorexia and bulimia.

BACKGROUND

Anorexia nervosa, the most publicly discussed eating disorder, was first classified as a psychiatric (mental) disorder in 1980 and has since become a growing problem in North America. The number of diagnosed cases has doubled since 1970, and experts now estimate that 0.5 to 1 percent of all white females may be anorexic. About 90 percent of all anorexics are believed to be female, although the number of males with the disorder is growing. The disorder first appears most often in 14 to 18 year olds. However, anorexia nervosa may begin later in life, and some cases of the disorder have been documented in infants. Studies indicate that the disorder is increasing among women of all races and social classes in the United States.

Eating disorders like anorexia have a very high rate of mortality. In addition, they can cause some serious long-term health effects. These effects include a reduced rate of growth, chills, dental problems from repeated vomiting, dry and yellowed skin, constipation, stomach rupture, anemia, amenorrhea, loss of kidney function, growth of downy facial hair, heart problems, and osteoporosis. A combination of factors is believed to contribute to the onset of eating disorders. For example, anorexia nervosa may have a genetic component because it seems to run in some families. Women whose mothers or sisters have the disorder are more likely to develop the condition than those who do not have relatives with anorexia nervosa. Psychological risk factors include: a fear of growing up or maturing into an adult state; perceived pressure to be very thin; emotional reaction to sexual assault or abuse; a desire to remain weak and passive in the belief that men will find this attractive; a drive toward perfectionism; and response to family problems. Social factors include the overexposure and internalization of cultural ideals to be thin and to equate thinness with social success. Images of girls and women in mass media (magazines, television, and movies) have been blamed, in part, for reinforcing such stereotypes. Some girls develop eating disorders as a form of copy-cat behavior. They imitate the actions of other women whom they admire.

Eating disorders are often difficult to diagnose for a number of reasons, but especially because most people deny that they have a problem. First, a physical examination and medical history will be conducted by the physician, and other possible causes for symptoms must first be ruled out. Brain tumors, diseases of the digestive tract, and other conditions can produce symptoms similar to those of eating disorders. Blood tests, urinalysis, and other tests can be used to eliminate other possibilities. Some psychiatric conditions also produce symptoms such as those of anorexia nervosa. Doctors may use certain written tests to distinguish between these disorders and eating disorders. The Eating Attitudes Test and the Eating Disorder Inventory are two such tests. Serious cases of eating disorders may require hospital treatment. Some symptoms that may lead to hospitalization include: a weight of 40 percent or more below normal, or weight loss of 30 pounds or more over a three-month period; severely disturbed metabolism; severe binging and purging; signs of mental disorders; and severe depression or risk of suicide. According to the best estimates available, about half of all anorexics and nearly two-thirds of all bulimics make a good physical and social recovery. About three-quarters gain weight. On a long-term basis, about 10 percent of all anorexics eventually die from the disorder. The most frequent causes of death are starvation, imbalances of chemicals in the body, heart failure, or suicide.

Studies have shown that athletes are far more prone to developing eating disorders than nonathletes. In addition to all the factors outlined previously, athletes face additional pressures related to performance and, for some, aesthetic demands. For some athletes, such as distance runners, sprinters, and swimmers, low body weight is thought to confer a competitive advantage. On the other hand, competitors in sports where a subjective judging element is involved, such as gymnastics, diving, skating, and dancing, may feel that their body size will

WARNING SIGNS OF AN EATING DISORDER

1. A preoccupation with food, calories, and weight
2. Repeated expressed concerns about being or feeling fat, even when weight is average or below average
3. Increasing criticism of one's body
4. Secretly eating or stealing food
5. Eating large meals, then disappearing, or making trips to the bathroom
6. Consumption of large amounts of food not consistent with the athlete's weight
7. Bloodshot eyes, especially after trips to the bathroom
8. Swollen parotid glands at the angle of the jaw, giving a chipmunk-like appearance
9. Vomiting or odor of vomiting in the bathroom
10. Wide fluctuations in weight over short periods
11. Periods of severe calorie restriction
12. Excessive laxative use
13. Compulsive, excessive exercise that is not part of the athlete's training regimen
14. Unwillingness to eat in front of others
15. Expression of self-deprecating thoughts following eating
16. Wearing layered or baggy clothing
17. Mood swings
18. Appearing preoccupied with the eating behaviors of others

influence their score. Certain sports where weight categories are involved, such as wrestling and rowing, can lead to cycles of weight gain followed by sudden weight loss. Athletes often have heightened body awareness, making them more prone to body image concerns. Finally, perfectionism, compulsiveness, and high achievement expectations are personality traits thought to be advantageous for the competitive athlete; however, these very traits are commonly associated with the development of an eating disorder.

KEY EVENTS

Through the late 1980s and into the 1990s, psychologists of sports studied anorexia among athletes with greater frequency. Because most athletes prefer to suffer in silence, there have only been a handful of athletes who have openly discussed their battles with eating disorders. Nevertheless, anecdotal evidence from athletes suggests that the anorexic in sports is typically female (a 9:1 or 10:1 ratio to males), participates in sports emphasizing performance-related thinness ideologies or aesthetics, and is preoccupied with physical appearance. The emaciator's psychological profile is an individual with low-self esteem, an obsessive compulsion toward self-monitoring, high anxiety, a drive toward perfectionism, moodiness and negative affect state, exhibits exercise dependence, and has body dysmorphia. Athletes with emaciation-related eating disorders are not as likely to have experienced past histories of physical and sexual abuse as their nonathlete counterparts, but links between domineering or hyperauthoritarian family structures are common. The media, it is argued, promote hyper-thin images of the preferred female image, which young athletes unquestionably internalize and legitimate through sports practices. The coach–athlete dyad is often highlighted as a relationship where female athletes learn pathological patterns of eating and body ideals from trusted socializing agents.

It is suggested that other female athletes use sports and exercise merely as a weight loss strategy (and thus, a place for alleviating body image dissatisfaction) or naturally gravitate toward sports that help girls achieve culturally preferred feminine physiques (such as gymnastics, athletics, or figure skating).

The majority of research on male athletes with eating disorders (either clinically or subclinically identified cases) assigns the disorder to the pursuit of hypermuscularity in power and performance sports, such as football, wrestling, or weightlifting, and the onset of body dysmorphia among young men—often referred to as reverse anorexia, bigarexia, or megarexia (Pope, Phillips, and Olivardia, 2000). Females emaciate, then, to be excessively feminine, while males build muscle through drug consumption, overeating, and exercise addiction to be hyperbolically masculine.

In the sporadic study of male athletes who emaciate, relatively straightforward explanations are offered as to why male distance runners or other endurance athletes seek to maintain low body weight as a performance strategy, or

WHY GYMNASTICS?

Eating disorders often strike young women who try to evade the natural process of becoming adults and who use excessive measures to maintain a thin and girlish figure—the exact description of what today's female gymnast must accomplish to stay competitive at its highest levels. For these athletes, the onset of womanhood is their biggest fear because it means developing hips or breasts that might hinder their performance. Thus, starving themselves offers the most convenient solution to their problem. Gymnasts often express a greater drive for thinness, and body dissatisfaction is the subjectivity of their judging system. A tragic example of the judges' power over these athletes is an incident with gymnast Christy Henrich—a top competitor of the late 1980s who died of a multiple organ failure due to her battle with bulimia and anorexia nervosa. At a meet in Budapest, a U.S. judge commented that Henrich would have to lose weight if she wanted to make the Olympic team. Upon returning to the states, her mother recalls the first words out of her daughter's mouth: She was fat, and she would have to lose weight—that was the only way she would reach her dreams. A final reason commonly cited for the greater prevalence of eating disorders among these gymnasts is their authoritarian coaches. A large percentage of coaches are constantly instructing the girls on how to count calories, how to act, what to wear, and what to say in public. The reason so many of them even begin dieting is because their coach recommends that they lose weight. These athletes are so young and impressionable that such a recommendation may be seen as a requirement for improved performance.

how certain males dehydrate rapidly in order to make a particular weight category in sports like wrestling. Authors suggest that emaciation practices among males are not estimated or understood accurately because male emaciators are not necessarily as dissatisfied with their body images and self-identities or hold similar levels of anxiety as their female athlete counterparts. Furthermore, males in sports may engage in more episodic or otherwise subclinical forms of weight reduction as ritual practice in a full range of sports.

One of the most important clinical breakthroughs has been Sundgot-Borgen's (1999) theory of *anorexia athletica*. Sundgot-Borgen defines and identifies anorexia athletica in terms of a set of absolute criteria (which must be present) and relative criteria (which may be present) that sufferers experience. The absolute criteria are weight loss, gastrointestinal complaints, absence of medical illness or affective disorder explaining the weight reduction, excessive fear of becoming obese, and restriction of calorie intake. The relative criteria are delayed puberty, menstrual dysfunction, disturbance in body image, use of purging methods, binge eating, and compulsive exercising.

Several risk factors for the development of anorexia athletica in young people have been identified. Dieting at an early age appears to be associated with the onset of the disorder. A significant number of athletes who began dieting to improve performance reported that their coach recommended they lose weight. For young and impressionable athletes, such a recommendation may be perceived as a requirement for improved performance. The risk for anorexia athletica is increased if dieting is unsupervised. Athletes with eating disorders may not seek supervision for fear their disorder will be discovered. In addition, many athletes have little knowledge about proper weight loss methods and receive their information in haphazard ways such as from friends, from the media, and so on. Such diets are unlikely to account for the high energy requirements resulting from training or the fact that maturing females have special nutritional requirements. Unsuitable crash diets may appeal to athletes if they feel that rapid weight loss is necessary to make the team or to remain competitive. Finally, the restrictive diets and fluctuations in body weight that accompany these efforts may also increase the risk for eating disorders.

The early start of sport-specific training is also associated with anorexia athletica. An individual's natural body type usually steers the athlete to specific sports, and body type dictates in part whether the athlete will be successful. Beginning training for a specific sport before the body matures might hinder athletes from choosing a suitable sport for their adult body type. This could provoke a conflict in which the athlete struggles to prevent or counter the natural physical changes precipitated by growth and maturity. Finally, the loss of a coach occurred in some athletes with eating disorders. These athletes described their coaches as vital to their athletic careers. Other athletes reported that they developed eating disorders at the time of injury or illness, which left them unable to train at high levels. Thus, the loss of a coach, injury, or illness must be seen as traumatic events that become triggers for the onset of eating disorders.

ATHLETES WITH EATING DISORDERS

Helga Brathen—Helga, a gymnast, died from the complications of anorexia at the age of 29.

Nadia Comaneci—This famous gymnast has won 9 Olympic gold medals and is well-known for being the first gymnast to have achieved the score of a perfect 10. Despite all of this, Nadia struggled with both anorexia and bulimia.

Martina Eberl—Martina, a German golfer, struggled with bulimia. This disorder began when the golfer was about 14 years old.

Eva-Maria Fitze—A German figure skater, Eva became the youngest person to win a gold medal at the German Championships. She was 14. This young figure skater also suffered from bulimia, which interfered with her figure skating career.

Zina Garrison—Zina played tennis and successfully won two Olympic medals. Unfortunately, at the same time, she also was suffering from bulimia. She recovered from the illness, but some tennis insiders suggest her body and career were both irreparably damaged.

Heidi Guenther—Heidi was a ballet dancer who struggled with anorexia after being advised by her ballet company to lose five pounds. She died at the age of 22 because of the complications associated with her disorder.

Christy Henrich—This U.S. gymnast eventually developed anorexia and bulimia, which plagued her for several years. Eventually, multiple organ failure killed her at the age of 22; she weighed 47 pounds.

Kathy Johnson—This gymnast developed anorexia after harsh criticism about her weight from a coach.

Nancy Kerrigan—A winner of two Olympic medals for figure skating, Nancy also struggled with an eating disorder during her first Olympics.

Kelly Masey—Masey was a gymnast who suffered from anorexia, which is thought to have begun as a result of high pressure to succeed in the sport.

Christian Moser—Moser was a ski jumper, but his performance in the sport slowly declined due to an eating disorder that spanned most of his career in the sport.

Megan Neyer—Megan, a professional diver, struggled with bulimia for approximately seven years.

Laffit Pincay—Pincay, a competitive jockey, dealt with the eating disorder anorexia. Still, during his career he was named the leading jockey of the United States seven times; he also won a variety of other awards.

Bahne Rabe—This Olympic rower is a winner of eight gold medals. He also suffered from anorexia, an eating disorder that eventually killed him.

Cathy Rigby—Cathy is a gymnast, speaker, and actress. She suffered from bulimia for 12 years of her life. At the World Championships she became the first woman in the United States to win a medal in World Gymnastics.

Jamie Silverstein—After five years of struggling with anorexia, Jamie, a pairs figure skater, sought help for her disorder and is on the road to recovery.

Whitney Spannuth—This cross-country runner developed an eating disorder in an attempt to become thinner, hoping it would help in competitions. Her eating disorder, however, eventually caused her severe health complications and made her body very weak.

Mia St. John—A female boxer, Mia overcame anorexia but continued experiencing body-image issues for many years. During her career she received the title of female Lightweight Champion of the World.

Franziska van Almsick—During her swimming career, Franziska, also known as "Franzi," suffered from a variety of problems that caused performance inconsistencies across her career. In her teens, she developed anorexia, which continued for a few years.

Stefan Zund—This Swiss ski jumper dealt with an eating disorder that eventually ended his sports career. During his career, he won several victories at the World Cup.

FUTURE PROSPECTS

Leading experts agree that in order to combat the problem of anorexia in sports, prevention is the key. To address the problem of disordered eating and anorexia athletica, education is a necessary first step. Athletes, parents, coaches, athletic administrators, training staff, and doctors need to be educated about the risks and warning signals of disordered eating. It seems that without increased public awareness of the extent of the problem, multi-institutional support efforts, and more realistic body expectations many athletes will continue to suffer and die in silence.

See also Illness; Sports Doctors, Trainers, and Drugs; Women and the Apologetic.

Further Reading: Pope, H., Phillips, K., and Olivardia, R. (2000). *The Adonis Complex: The Secret Crisis of Male Body Obsession.* Boston: Free Press; Robbins, P. (1998). *Anorexia and Bulimia.* Hillside, NJ: Enslow Publishers; Sundgot-Borgen, J. (1999). Eating Disorders Among Male and Female Elite Athletes *British Journal of Sports Medicine* 33: 434.

Michael Atkinson

ENVIRONMENTAL IMPACTS OF SPORTS

Very few practices in social life have been unaffected by environmental issues, concerns, problems, and debates in the recent past. References to North America as a leader in environmental protection policy and practice would be premature, but it is safe to say that ideologies of environmentalism have penetrated the collective conscience. North Americans are more concerned than ever about the environmental or ecological "footprints" created by our social practices, and multi-institutional efforts to scrutinize our impact on the environment involve government, universities and schools, corporations, media, and families. Here, environmental impacts are conceived broadly, ranging from the chemical pollution of air, land, and water, to carbon emission levels from technological devices, to noise and light disruptions in the natural environment, to electromagnetic pollution, to the impact of human waste in ecological spaces. Most social institutions have been encouraged through cultural convention, or forced through state legislation, to initiate more environmentally friendly practices. But, as a social institution with massive global participation and resource use, sports has not been painted as a target by environmental crusaders as a site of environmental policy reform.

Ironically enough, the bulk of concern regarding the relationship between environmental destruction or climate change and sports in the past 10 years has been devoted to what clever architectural or engineering initiatives we can conjure to play sports in degraded environments, or how new social movement groups such as Surfers Against Sewage exert pressure on states and private corporations to become more environmentally friendly. For all intents and purposes, the majority of environmental battles waged within the sports sphere focus on how ski resorts, golf clubs, private beach-front hotel complexes, and other for-profit recreation spaces may be protected from (or learn how to adapt with) global warming, pollution, and ecosystem destruction. North Americans are, in a Western capitalist fashion, concerned with how to financially protect sports tourism industries in the face of environmental problems rather than examining the impacts of sports practices on the environment.

BACKGROUND

As drawn into sharp relief by former vice president of the United States Al Gore's documentary *An Inconvenient Truth* (2005), members of Western nations including the United States and Canada can simply no longer afford to ignore global pollution, climate change, and habitat loss. Yet, to turn the metaphorical tides on environmental destruction, modern forms of industrial production, distribution, and consumption require serious alteration. Changing the financial organizational foundation of Western societies is in no way a straightforward task. Critics might argue that shifting cultural ideologies about how humans understand ourselves as part of the earth's environmental community may be even more difficult to accomplish.

Human beings operate within the world and consume the natural resources around us from a specific ideological framework called the "human exceptionalism paradigm" (HEP). The HEP is comprised of a series of axioms that ostensibly justify the manners by which humans exploit the earth's resources. The HEP is predicated on the idea that humans are "masters" of the Earth and thus exempt from the ecological rules and principles that govern other species. The HEP is based on the (mis)belief that humans are the best stewards of the Earth, may use any physical material in the world to "advance" the plight of humanity, and that the Earth possesses the adequate resources (i.e., water, air, fossil fuels) to sustain social growth indefinitely.

It can be added that the HEP is an individualist rather than collectivist social mentality. It privileges individual rights and freedoms, including the right to use resources in whatever manner one wishes in the pursuit of material wealth and comfort. It is a rather minority rights approach to living, in that humans, as but one of many million species living on the planet, become the primary consumer of resources and the earth's group of chief polluters. It has been pointed out that the HEP is a present-generation and anthropocentric philosophy of life, evidencing little concern for how the actions of one generation impact many to follow.

The HEP could be replaced by a "new ecological paradigm" (NEP) if the human species wishes to move toward an environmentally sustainable and responsible style of living. While there are many emergent environmental movements and philosophies in the West that might be considered as part of the new ecological paradigm (deep green, gaia, left biocentrism, and ecofeminism theory to name a few), the NEP generally teaches that humanity, and human fate, has a very complex interdependent relationship with the physical environment that is lost in the practice of everyday, capitalist, and consumeristic life. The NEP stresses that the Earth's resources are finite, and the Earth is ill-matched with human cultures of material consumption. Advocates of the NEP believe that all social practices that potentially affect the physical environment need to be measured against a principle of common good, for all humans and nonhuman species. Spiritual wealth and global responsibility are also valued within the NEP framework, as is an ecocentric perspective. If humans resist or reject movement toward an NEP, we run the risk of permanently destroying most animal life forms and their ecosystems, oceans and freshwater systems, wetlands, forests, grasslands, the earth's climate, and all natural mineral and energy deposits.

Suggestions for change toward an NEP lifestyle are deceptively simple, but given the nature of advanced societies such as the United States, incredibly difficult to implement. The key for NEP advocates is environmental sustainability through practice, which would include the reduction of resource use, energy consumption, and waste and pollution. It would be founded on a wider cultural respect for earth, air, fire, and water and humanity's small place in the cycle of life on earth.

Where Sports Fits in to the HEP

Popular sporting practices in North America have historically jibed with the HEP. In the process of athletic play, leisure, recreation, and competition, the Earth's elements have been widely exploited with only scarce criticism. They are used to house competitions and create sports surfaces, to produce equipment and material goods used in play, as food to fuel athletes and spectators, and as technology to test and improve human performance, to name only a few. Humans have a rather antagonistic relationship with the environment in mainstream sports practices, even though many of them are intended to have people commune with nature through sports. Consider golf as a prime example.

There has been a 500 percent growth in the number of golf courses in North America since 1990. Golf courses require an enormous space and considerable resources to maintain each year, and they have noteworthy footprints on the environments in which they are situated. During the process of construction, flora and fauna are either clear cut from a space or planted where they were not before. Soil needs to be moved or reshaped, and rock and mineral deposits require extraction by energy-consuming construction equipment. Coral is often extracted from the ocean, processed into sand, and transported to courses globally. Animals are dispossessed from their homes, predators are forced to seek food elsewhere, and the natural balance and harmony of the geographic area is disrupted; including, perhaps most importantly, the loss of needed biodiversity in the area to sustain life. Because golf enthusiasts increasingly desire "pristine" or physically impressive courses, treed valleys, spaces near river ways or oceans, or sides of mountains (each with their own fragile ecosystems) are coveted as sites of course development.

Waterways are often rerouted to create a golf course, grass and sand is imported from other nations, pesticides and fertilizers are deployed to "green" the grasses, and millions and millions of gallons in water are consumed yearly to irrigate the course (even in extreme heat and drought conditions). Gas and electricity are consumed for player travel to, on, and from the course and for ongoing for course maintenance. Materials are produced all over the world to facilitate the game of golf (e.g., clubs, balls, clothing, gloves, tees, etc.) and shipped to courses for sale. Think of the production and distribution resources required just to place the goods in the club house of one golf course. Marketing the course locally, nationally, and even internationally requires computer energy, paper and other physical products, inks, dyes, personnel, and transportation resources. Tied to the development of many modern golf clubs or resorts is related economic and business development around the course, including mini-malls and retailers, housing developments or hotels, and restaurants. The list of resources needed to operate one course for a year is potentially endless, and the end result for practically every golf course on the planet in environmental terms is simple: They are a net loss.

THREATS TO THE ENVIRONMENT FROM AN URBAN SPORTS STADIUM

Consider some, but not all, of the ecological footprint created by one major sports stadium in an urban environment:

- Development on fragile or scarce land types
- Business and residential relocation
- City infrastructure development and resource use (transportation)
- Pollution from liquid spills (fuels, cleaners, solvents, etc.)
- Noise and light pollution
- Consumption of nonrenewable resources (fuel, metals, etc.)
- Consumption of natural resources (water, energy, wood, paper, etc.)
- Creation of greenhouse gases by consuming electricity and fuel
- Ozone layer depletion (from refrigerants)
- Soil/water erosion from pesticide use, during construction, and from spectators
- Waste sent to landfill, incinerator, and sewage plants
- Waste generated from signs, food services, banners, and goods
- Energy and resources used to broadcast events or report them in the media

In recognizing the impact of golf on the environment, an alliance of environmental nongovernmental organizations (NGOs), consumer groups, tourism critics, and concerned citizens in Japan formed the Global Anti-Golf Movement (GAG'M) to oppose the rapid proliferation of golf courses and golf tourism in Asia-Pacific. The group attracted public attention when it promoted the World Anti-Golf Day on April 29, 1993. The movement stirred a flurry of debate about the environmental impact of sports such as golf, skiing, snowboarding, boating, and others. The movement then spread to countries such as the United States, Canada, Brazil, and India through the mid-1990s, leading to public criticism of sports as environmentally unfriendly. Environmental designers responded by constructing "green courses" through the later years of the twentieth century. Organizations such as GAG'M and others claim, however, that such courses, including the community-resisted Silvertip golf course in the town of Canmore, Alberta, are hardly more environmentally friendly than their nongreen counterparts.

Golf is not the only environmental offender in the world of sports. Consider the resources required to operate an ice hockey rink, a ski hill, a public beach, or a swimming pool every year. It could be argued that because we see the natural environment as something to be used for sporting purposes, as part of the HEP, rarely do we examine how sports and leisure practices in the "great outdoors" cumulatively degrade our environments. Oil leaks from jet skis into lakes and oceans pollute the water and kill fish; scree and topsoil are eroded through mountain biking and hiking and can contribute to avalanches and floods; fossil fuels are wasted and carbon is emitted from racing cars around the world, further depleting the earth's chemically barraged ozone layer.

To participate in bouts of sports and leisure (from a certain perspective, nonessential human activities), participants themselves require copious amounts of resources. Consider a runner who competes recreationally but trains regularly each week, for example. That person might require 2,500–5,000 calories per day, drink 5–10 gallons (20–40 liters) of water per week, and use several hundred gallons of water for showering post-exercise. They may also consume exercise supplements (ergogenics), take painkillers, and spend 10–35 hours in training per week in sports complexes or in social spaces designed for walking or running. They may purchase several pairs of running shoes per year and clothing for running "all season," read several dozen running-related magazines per year, and participate in several running events per year (which may include from 100–40,000 participants). These are only the "surface level" resource requirements for an average runner. If we consider how these costs are multiplied by every additional runner in North America and by the hundreds of new running events held on the continent each year, the environmental impact of the sport is nothing short of massive. From an HEP perspective, however, an individual runner tends to focus on how "few" resources she or he uses in doing the sport and therefore fails to appreciate how the web of connected runners, businesses catering to running, competition organizers, and others exert influence on the environment through sports.

If our environments are as polluted and toxic as some believe, then we must also consider that through their involvement in sports, athletes are actually at a

THE GLOBAL ANTI-GOLF MOVEMENT (GAGM) MANIFESTO

1. Golf courses and golf tourism are part of a "development" package that includes infrastructure (multipurpose dams, airports, ports, roads, bridges), mass tourism, expensive housing, entertainment facilities, export-oriented agriculture (flowers, exotic fruits and vegetables), and industrial parks/zones.
2. At the heart of the golf industry is a multibillion-dollar industry involving transnational corporations, including agribusiness, construction firms, consultancies, golf equipment manufacturers, airlines, hotel chains, real estate companies, advertising and public relations firms, as well as financial institutions. The transformation of golf memberships into a saleable commodity has resulted in widespread speculation and dubious practices.
3. The bulk of the foreign exchange earned from golf courses and golf tourism does not stay in the local economy. The benefits that do remain are reaped by a few business people and their patrons.
4. Golf courses are in fact another form of monoculture, where exotic soil and grass, chemical fertilizers, pesticides, fungicides and weedicides, as well as machinery are all imported to substitute for natural ecosystems. These landscaped foreign systems create stress on local water supplies and soil, at the same time being highly vulnerable to disease and pest attacks. Just as the Green Revolution is collapsing in country after country, the Golf Green is also fraught with ecological problems. The environmental impacts include water depletion and toxic contamination of the soil, underground water, surface water, and the air. This in turn leads to health problems for local communities, populations downstream, and even golfers, caddies, and chemical sprayers in golf courses. The construction of golf courses in scenic natural sites, such as forest areas and coral islands, also results in the destruction of biodiversity.
5. In addition to environmental damage, golf course and resort development often creates skewed land use, displacing local communities or depriving them of water and other resources. In a number of countries, the victims of such projects are subject to police or military intimidation when they protest against the destruction caused by golf courses.
6. The golf industry aggressively promotes an elitist and exclusive resort lifestyle and notion of leisure. This globalization of lifestyle is also a form of exploitation, the victims being the wealthy urban population who are encouraged to spend their surplus dreams and illusions at the expense of the environment and other members of society. Golf course and golf tourism development violate human rights in every sense of the word.

For more information see www.antigolf.org.

---

greater risk of becoming ill than their nonathletic peers because they are regularly immersed in physically noxious settings. Imagine a young girl who plays soccer outdoors all summer and into the autumn. She is exposed to hotter yearly temperatures due to global warming and therefore at a risk of heat stroke and dehydration-related afflictions. Exposure to the sun's ultraviolet rays and carbon emissions from cars and factories pose risks of cancer to her skin and respiratory illness in her lungs. Even playing on a toxically treated field may cause her illness, and exposure to local traffic and noise from construction sites can cause auditory damage to her ears or her central nervous system.

From even a cursory review of the literature on the environmental impacts of sports, one quickly learns that sports insiders and outsiders know very little about the measurable ecological footprint athletes and fans create in daily practice. True to the human exceptionalism paradigm, the Earth's fields, waters, mountains, and forests are rather carelessly and unreflexively inserted into sports and leisure practices and approached as an endlessly renewable extension of an athlete's "equipment."

KEY EVENTS

In 1972, the United Nations sponsored the first global conference on environmental change in Stockholm, Sweden. Twenty years later, the UN brought over 17,000 participants from 172 nations together for the Earth Summit in Rio de Janeiro to address mushrooming problems in environmental destruction. The Earth Summit was unprecedented for a UN conference in terms of both its size and the scope of its concerns. The UN's mandate was to encourage nations to rethink economic development and find ways to halt the destruction of irreplaceable natural resources and pollution of the planet.

Speakers at the conference instructed audiences to make eco-efficiency, sustainability, and accountability guiding ideologies for everyday life. The summit culminated with the adoption of UN Agenda 21, a sweeping policy document aimed at achieving sustainable development worldwide. At its close, Maurice Strong, the conference secretary-general, called the summit a "historic moment for humanity." Although Agenda 21 has received opposition, restructuring, and ambivalence in certain nations, it and the Earth Summit more generally have altered the structure and tone of twenty-first-century social and economic development.

Prior to the Earth Summit and the full spate of economic and political summits since 1992 that have focused on environmental sustainability, the environmental impacts of sports were scarcely considered at national or international levels. Working separately and in tandem, however, private organizations and NGOs such as the Global Sports Alliance, Greenpeace, the International Olympic Committee, the UN and UNESCO, the Sports. Eco project, and Eco Flag have raised consciousness about the substantial impact sports and leisure practices have on the environment. We learned quickly that they are perhaps too expansive to catalog completely, quantify with any precision, or even estimate their long-term impact, as noted previously.

In the wake of the Earth Summit and the consciousness-raising it produced, sports leagues, teams, and corporations have experimented with green initiatives. Sports organizations have focused on five principal areas of environmental reform in sports and movement toward a new ecological paradigm: energy conservation, pollution avoidance, water conservation, protection of the natural environment, and waste management. The Olympic Games in Sydney was one of the first green sports mega-events in history. Among the green sports initiatives pioneered for the Games included: the transformation of the Games site (Sydney Olympic Park) from a rundown commercial site into a world-class sporting, residential, business, recreation, and conservation precinct; Stadium Australia in the Park has some unique environmental features including a system to collect rainwater from its arched roofs that is used to irrigate the pitch; the Athletes Village (later transformed into residential homes) is part of one of the world's largest solar-powered suburbs; recycled water used for toilet flushing at venues throughout Sydney Olympic Park reduced the consumption of drinking water by 50 percent; Games spectators used energy-efficient public transport (no paved car lots); all food and beverage packaging used on site consisted of recycled goods; and tables, bookcases, desks, and garbage bins at Games venues were made from 100 percent recycled materials and were recycled again after the Games.

Eco Flag, among others, has critiqued the "environmentalism" of the Sydney 2000 Games, however, by pointing out that while some of the materials were made from recycled goods, most were not. Sydney Olympic Park is situated on Homebush Bay, and over the course of construction, the Park disrupted and altered its ecology permanently (of further note is that the Bay itself, which was used for a series of sports in the Games, is a former toxic dump of agent orange and estimated to be one of the five most polluted bays on the planet). The 1 million people who attended the Games collectively placed immeasurable stress on Sydney's natural resources, and the ongoing cost of maintaining the Park since the Games is incommensurate with its conceivable social or cultural value.

FUTURE PROSPECTS

If sports at all levels of organization and participation is to move toward a green ethic and praxis, then small steps are required in the immediate future. To their credit, a handful of transnational sports corporations have included novel production policies in the recent past as a means of greening their products. For example, PUMA, Reebok, Nike, Timberland, Patagonia, Mizuno, and Shimano have all adopted recycling practices in the manufacturing of sports and leisure footwear in the attempt to reduce the ecological footprint made by them. Additionally, the companies have eliminated a majority of the products such as PVC, heavy metals, dyes, and plastics in their shoes. Nike developed and has championed their "Reuse-a-Shoe" program, which involves customers returning their used shoes to the company for recycling. Between 1993 and 2006, 13 million pairs of worn-out shoes were returned and reused by Nike. Three basic materials can be harvested from old shoes. Rubber from the outsole, along with factory scrap, is granulated and used to make soccer, football, and baseball fields and weight room flooring. Foam from the midsole is granulated and used in synthetic basketball courts, tennis courts, and playground surfacing tiles, and granulated fabric from the uppers is used as padding under hardwood basketball floors. These athletic surfaces are donated to communities around the world. It takes about 3,000 shoes to make a basketball court, and 100,000 go into the surface of a running track.

At an international level, the IOC has sponsored seven years of conferences on sports and environment that bring together members of the international sports community, government and business leaders, and public educators. By working in conjunction with the UN Environment Programme, the IOC developed "Agenda 21" in 2005, a policy document outlining the best practices for developing globally sustainable sports. The IOC pursued the policy further, and in 2007 published their *Guide to Sport, Environment and Sustainable Development*. The document outlines how each of the Olympic sports should be played in environmentally friendly manners.

Part of the ecolegacy of the Sydney Games is its shining example of how easily ecofriendly architecture may be woven into the development of modern sports complexes. Newly constructed stadiums in Nuremburg for the World Cup of 2006, American football stadiums such as Gillette Stadium and Ford Field, and professional rugby and football stadiums in Australia have followed the lead of the Sydney Olympic Park. These stadiums are designed to be as ecofriendly as possible. They were partially built with recycled steel and wood, include rain-catching devices on roofs for field irrigation purposes, use energy-efficient lighting and ventilation systems, contain low-flow water and plumbing systems, house their own waste and sewage treatment units, and save light energy when the buildings are not in use.

See also Adventure Racing; Equipment Manufacturing in the Third World; Parkour (Free Running); X Games.

Further Reading: Burki, R., Elassasser, H., and Abegg, B. (2003). *Climate Change and Winter Sports: Environmental and Economic Threats*. Paper presented at the 5th World Conference on Sport and Environment, Turin, 2–3 December; Curry, P. (2006). *Ecological Ethics: An Introduction*. London, UK: Routledge; Dunlap, R. (2002). "Environmental Sociology: A Personal Perspective on Its First Quarter Century." *Organization and Environment* 15: 10–29; Lenskyj, H. (2004). *Best Games Ever? The Social Impacts of Sydney 2000*. New York: SUNY Press; Suzuki, D. (2000). *The Sacred Balance: Rediscovering our Place in Nature*. Vancouver, BC: Greystone Books; Wheaton, B. (2004). *Understanding Lifestyle Sports*. London, UK: Routledge.

Michael Atkinson

EQUIPMENT MANUFACTURING IN THE THIRD WORLD

In the last two decades of the twentieth century, major Western, transnational sports equipment companies such as Nike and Adidas were exposed for their practices of outsourcing the production of sports equipment to third-world nations. While the practice of outsourcing elements of the production process to other companies in the effort of reducing a parent company's operating costs is not a crime, investigations of sports companies discovered that a series of human rights violations were occurring in the companies aiding in the production practice. Sites of production in Vietnam, Pakistan, and Indonesia in particular were found to be highly abusive and exploitive contexts of work. Debates about third-world manufacturing of sports productions for Western mega corporations shed light on the dangers of globalization processes in sports and the dangers of allowing corporations to act as their own micro societies.

BACKGROUND

Scandals related to the production of sports equipment, largely by women and children in third-world factories, emerged at a time when discussions of the impacts of globalization on sports practices were also developing. There are many ways to analyze how globalization has altered the business of sports. One of the early, and certainly most popular, ways of linking globalization to sports stems from what is called "world systems theory" (Wallerstein, 1974). A *world system* is a social conglomeration of interdependent parts that form a bound structure and operate according to a distinct set of rules. The modern world system, it is often argued, is ruled by a globally organized world economy with key nations and economic centers dominating the entire world system. The major constituents of the world system—capitalist transnational corporations and their "home" governments—work in cooperation to establish the economic, political, cultural, and social world orders.

Labor in the global world system is divided among functionally defined and geographically distinct parts arranged in a hierarchy of occupational tasks and political statuses. Core nation-states concentrate on higher-skill, capital-intensive production; they are militarily strong; and they appropriate much of the surplus of the whole world economy. Peripheral areas focus on low-skill, labor-intensive production, and extraction of raw materials; they have weak military states. In the first centuries of world-system development, Northwest Europe constituted the core and Eastern Europe and the Western hemisphere (and parts of Asia) the periphery. By the end of the twentieth century, the core comprised the wealthy industrialized countries that housed the majority of powerful transnational corporations, and poor, recently independent colonies mainly constituted the periphery. What is critical is that corporations in the core are tremendously influential in maintaining the dependency of the periphery on Western nations. Indeed, the social organization and production energies of people in the periphery are often dictated by core countries' interests.

Different forms of labor and labor control suit different types of production distributed across the world zones; historically, they included wage labor, tenant farming, servitude, and slavery. In the case of sports equipment production, Western corporations at the world-system core use production labor in the third world in a way that is not too different from historical slave labor and servitude models. Mega corporations such as Nike, Reebok, Adidas, and others extol the basic ideologies and practices of Western capitalism and Western capitalist states; they strive to find new ways of using cheap labor in global zones in order to increase their profits. Elements of the production process are outsourced to manufacturers in the third world in large part due to the availability of inexpensive wage labor, the lack of organized unions to regulate worker treatment, and the "flexible" codes of employee relations and treatment common therein. In the process of attracting sports companies, local producers will cut all costs possible in their factories (primarily wages and workers' benefits) to secure contracts from sporting transnational corporations.

A series of nongovernmental organizations (NGOs), investigating journalists, human rights advocates, and consumer trading watchdogs started to pay attention to how sports companies fit into the world-systems model in the late 1980s. Stories about worker exploitation and abuse in several nations started an avalanche of inquiry into the relationship between sports organizations and their third or developing world nation affiliates.

The results from the early reports were shocking. Researchers discovered that the liberal, "free market expansion" of Western nations into the economically developing world had drawn millions of people into conditions of unfair employment. Nike, Reebok, Puma, Umbro, Fila, Adidas, ASICS, Mizuno, Lotto, and Kappa were all found to employ people in second and third worlds under brutal physical, financial, and psychological conditions. Human rights violations in the sports equipment production were documented in Vietnam, Cambodia, Thailand, China, Turkey, Bulgaria, Indonesia, Pakistan, India, and others. In the goal of reducing the cost of production and competing in an internationally booming sports equipment market, transnational corporations found cheap, fast, flexible, and fluid (but unsecure and impermanent for workers) wage labor in economically marginal, periphery nations. Western corporations operated with mangers in outsourcing locations under a simple "don't ask, don't tell" policy.

The working conditions documented through on-site visits and interviews with factory workers were appalling. Workers were prevented from establishing trade unions through either physical violence and intimidation, and they were exposed to dangerous chemicals in factories. They were sexually assaulted and beaten if they did not produce enough, forced to work nearly 16 hours a day without break, received only pennies or a few dollars a day in wage, and fined or fired for refusing overtime work (sometimes in excess of 45 hours of overtime a week). They were hired only ever as casual or temporary employees without contracts or any rights, were not allowed to resign during peak production periods, were refused treatment for injuries incurred while on the job, were not permitted to take sick or maternity days, and were often only aged between 10 and 13 years old (Oxfam International, 2006). The reports uncovered the shocking practice of using children to hand-stitch sports equipment such as soccer balls because their small hands were efficient and effective at producing smaller and tighter stitches. Investigations also conclude that managers at the factories often paid workers to silence them, kept "double payrolls" to mask employee wage exploitation, falsified or doctored workers' time sheets, and performed one-time, factory-wide clean ups just prior to governmental inspections.

A new global social movement developed (largely with the core of the world system) to lobby governments in Western nations to enforce international labor laws and sanction the production practices of major sports companies. Nike, in particular, was targeted as the central villain in the global sports industry.

KEY EVENTS

No transnational corporation dominates the world of sports equipment like the U.S.-based Nike corporation. With revenues of $17 billion in 2007, it is a sporting colossus that employs thousands of people directly and indirectly worldwide. Starting in 1988, Nike has been criticized for contracting with factories in countries such as Vietnam, Indonesia, and Mexico. Vietnam Labor Watch, an activist group, was among the first to document that factories contracted by Nike have violated minimum wage and overtime laws in Vietnam. Through the mid-1990s the company was subject to much critical coverage of the often poor working conditions and exploitation of cheap overseas labor employed in global "free trade zones" where their goods are typically manufactured without intense regulation or scrutiny. Also in the 1990s, Nike faced damning criticism for use of child labor in Cambodia and Pakistan in factories it contracted to manufacture soccer balls. Although Nike took action to curb or at least reduce the practice of child labor, they continue, to this date, to contract their production to companies that operate in areas where inadequate regulation and monitoring make it hard to ensure that child labor is not being used.

The global exposure of Nike's third-world practices "kicked off" when an Indonesian trade union published an investigative report on a South Korea–based shoe company producing for Nike. A series of articles then appeared in Indonesian newspapers about wage protests at Nike contractors Tae Hwa and Pratama Abadi. Among other violations alleged in the reports was that most Nike shoe factories illegally paid workers wages less than the industry standard 86 cents per day (Katz, 1995). These labor rights complaints against Indonesia outsource companies were submitted to the office of U.S. Trade Representatives by the NGOs, International Labor Rights Research and Education Fund, and Human Rights Watch. By 1991, the Canadian Broadcast Company and the British Broadcast Company each ran documentaries that highlighted Nike's track record in Indonesia. That same year, the globally respected American periodical *The Economist* reported brutality and unrest at shoe factories producing for Nike. A slew of other newspapers and magazines jumped onto the anti-Nike bandwagon, conducting and reporting their own first-hand investigations of labor practices in Indonesia, including the *Los Angeles Times, Boston Globe, New York Times, Chicago Tribune, USA Today, Wall Street Journal, The International Herald Tribune, Rolling Stone,* and *Jakarta Post*. Perhaps most publicly noted was a 1996 CBS television special on child labor practices at Nike factories. Following the release of these stories, the global "Boycott Nike" campaign was launched in Germany by human rights advocate Evangelische Kirchengemeinde Duisburg-Neumuhl.

As tumultuous as the early 1990s had been for Nike in the international arena of human rights, their profits did not suffer; largely as a result of their booming basketball, tennis, and running apparel lines. Yet, in 1996, the Portland grassroots activist and antiglobalization organization "Justice, Do It Nike" began regular mass-mediated protests at Nike stores across the country. These protests sparked the American National Labor Committee to bring unprecedented national attention to the sweatshop issue and more negative

CONSIDER THE FOLLOWING ABOUT NIKE GEAR

In 1998, Nike paid the Brazilian men's national soccer team $16 million to wear their equipment. The Asian workers who made their soccer cleats and other sports gear were paid as little as 47 cents an hour to produce them. Any woman in these factories would need to work for more than a month in order to be able to pay for the goods worn by one player alone. Nike made nearly $9 billion in 1998, while workers' wages in Asia were routinely cut due for "inflationary" reasons.

---

attention Nike's way. Partly due to the burgeoning anti-Nike movement in the United States, strikes by thousands of Nike-producing workers in Vietnam were initiated in 1997. Additionally, American, Canadian, and Western European university student protests erupted against allowing Nike to link with universities. As an attempt to cool public criticism of the company, in 1998, Nike CEO Phil Knight gave a talk on Nike's Asian labor practices at the National Press Club in Washington, D.C., where he announced new initiatives such as education for workers and microenterprise loan programs. He also vowed to eliminate hazardous chemicals from shoe production plants. Knight's professed goodwill was challenged only a year later when Joseph Ha, a top adviser to Knight at Nike, sent a letter to high-ranking labor officials in Vietnam portraying "anti-sweat" activists as enemies of the Vietnamese state with an insane political agenda.

To combat increased public hostility toward the company, Nike recruited new public relations personnel to engage in a charm offensive to dismiss stories of exploitation and sow doubts about anti-sweatshop activists. At first Nike refused to acknowledge the labor question, and then they funded a series of studies by labor rights organizations to document change in their production practices. Nike funded, for example, the "Global Alliance" for $10 million to produce articles about the safety of Asian workers at their factories. Nike also employed the International Fair Labor Association (IFLA) as a quasi-stamp of approval for its labor policies even though in reality the FLA is still a nonfunctioning organization.

The Nike protest grew until the early 2000s, drawing together workers' advocacy groups around the globe to examine fair production and trade practices in sports. Included among them were Press for Change; Boycott Nike; the National Labor Committee; Global Exchange; Campaign for Labor Rights; National Organization of Women; Clean Clothes Campaign; Community Aid Abroad; The Living Wage Project; Justice, Do It Nike; and many other NGOs.

Another company to face global wrath in the emerging critique of the sports industries' role in the new, global world system was Germany-based Adidas. During the 1990s, labor watchdogs discovered that Adidas shoes and clothing were made in two Indonesian factories using child labor, forcing overtime on workers and with mangers who sexually harassed employees. Representatives of workers in the Nikomax Gemilang and Tuntex factories reported that children as young as 15 were made to work 15-hour days, were expected to work at least

70 hours a week and physically punished for refusing to do overtime, were paid less than $60 a month—rates far below the International Labour Organization's demand for a living wage—were penalized for taking leave during medical difficulties, and had illegal deductions taken from wages. In 1997, a worker from a Bangkok factory for Adidas claimed that for less than $1 per day she worked 12-hour shifts 7 days a week, producing sportswear, shoes, and replica kits for the company. She claimed conditions were poor in the Thai factory, and the management acted brutally to meet large orders within a limited time, often denying workers statutory rights such as holidays and sick pay. The accusations are similar to those made by the Indonesian workers. The woman was eventually fired in 1998 along with 23 others after they formed a union in an attempt to win more rights. Most Adidas goods are still produced in third-world countries, with orders awarded to "lowest-bidding" locally run factories. Many orders are then subcontracted at the local level, leading to claims that the parent companies have little idea of where and how their goods are produced.

On a more positive note, organizations such as Oxfam have not only raised global awareness about the dangerous links that exist between globalization, capitalism, and goods production in sports, they have helped to develop alternatives to exploitive factory production world systems. Oxfam stores now, for example, sell a series of fair-trade sports balls produced from factories in Pakistan. These balls include handmade cricket balls (which, in the past, were notoriously produced in sweatshop factories in India and Pakistan) that have been produced in line with the internationally agreed fair-trade standards and are supplied by independently certified producer organizations. Now also distributed by NGO groups such as Oxfam are fair-trade footballs, rugby balls, beach volleyballs, and basketballs. Producers of fair-trade balls established their factories in cities such as Sialkot, Pakistan, as working alternatives to the sweatshop factories in existence there. Pakistan is the world's primary exporter of sports balls, and over 40 percent of the Sialkot working population is dependent, directly or indirectly, on this industry for their livelihood.

FUTURE PROSPECTS

Altering the course of globalization in sports, the expansion of transnational sporting goods producers, the ongoing development of the capitalist world system, or the social desire for cheaper sports equipment may be unrealistic. Human rights advocates around the world contend, however, that fair employment, production, and distribution practices in the sports economy are not incongruent with market success. At a bare minimum, they argued, companies such as Nike, Adidas, and others should reform their practices and production policies to ensure that their suppliers and subcontractors: respect International Labour Organization recommendations for worker equity and protection, alter their purchasing practices and shift the "cheapest is the best" contract bidding mentality currently in place, contract in global zones respectful of fair-trade rules and laws, strictly monitor and enforce anti-exploitation production rules and provide workers with a safe means of reporting abuse, educate workers about their own employment rights, inform consumers about social and economic conditions under which the goods they purchase are produced, and work with governments to draft new working equity and protection legislation.

See also Animal Blood Sports; Antitrust Violations in Professional Sports; Environmental Impacts of Sports; Rights for Young Athletes.

Further Reading: Connor, T. (2001). *Still Waiting for Nike To Do It*. San Francisco: Global Exchange; Katz, D. (1995). *Just Do It: The Spirit of Nike in the Corporate World*. Cincinnati, OH: Adams Media Corporation; Klein, N. (2001). *No Logo*. London: Flamingo; Oxfam International. (2006). *Offside: Labour Rights and Sportswear Production in Asia*. Oxford, UK: Author; Wallerstein, I. (1974). *The Modern World-System: Capitalist Agriculture and the Origins of the European World-Economy in the Sixteenth Century*. New York: Academic Press.

Michael Atkinson

ERGOGENICS

An ergogenic aid is any external product one can consume in order to improve physical or mental performance. Ergogenic aids may directly influence the physiological capacity of a particular body system thereby improving performance, remove psychological constraints that impact performance, and increase the speed of recovery from training and competition. Ergogenic aids can be as simple as water used before and after exercising to improve hydration, painkillers to help with recovery, relaxation therapy, or something more "advanced" and illegal in sports such as anabolic steroids. Many of the current ergogenic aids used by athletes in North America and elsewhere are acceptable according to sports federation rules and standards, while others fall into grey zones of acceptability. What remains unclear is the extent to which athletes should be allowed to use ergogenics in sports, what types of ergogenics should be permitted, and how to best regulate athlete consumption of them.

BACKGROUND

More than a hundred companies in North America produce, distribute, and market ergogenic aids to consumers inside and outside of sports. The products come in the form of vitamins, minerals, amino acids, protein powders, energy bars/drinks, fat-burners, and endurance-boosting aides. Indeed, the sports supplement industry is one of the fastest growing niche markets in North America. Researchers from the U.S. Centers for Disease Control and Prevention (CDC) surveyed 12 popular health and bodybuilding magazines (one issue each) in 1999 and found ads for 89 brands and 311 products with a total of 235 unique ingredients. The American Health Foods Business index estimates that, in 2006, total commercial sales of over-the-counter ergogenic products exceeded $304 million.

The consumer appetite for ergogenic products is not unique to the present time. For well over 2,000 years, men (in particular) have extolled the virtues and benefits of high-protein diets as a principle ergogenic. The notion that massive amounts of protein are beneficial during training has evolved from the ancient Greek and Roman beliefs that great strength could be obtained by eating the raw meat of lions, tigers, or other powerful animals. Beliefs in the ergogenic power of protein were reinforced during the 1930s by American publisher Bob Hoffman, who established the first trade publications geared toward bodybuilding and muscle development. Hoffman regularly asserted that athletes have special protein needs and that protein supplements have special muscle-building and health-giving powers. Much later, as American and European scientists conducted increased research on the link between muscle development and protein consumption through the early 1990s, athletes believed even more strongly that protein was the primary ergogenic for sports.

Hoffman marketed supplement products and bodybuilding equipment through his York Barbell Company, of York, Pennsylvania. He published 2 magazines and more than 30 books on fitness and nutrition. Perhaps athletes were willing to believe Hoffman because of his athletic accomplishment first as an oarsman and then as a weightlifter; he won over 600 trophies, certificates, and awards during his athletic career. He was the Olympic weightlifting coach from 1936 to 1968 and was a founding member of the President's Council on Physical Fitness and Sports. One might argue that Hoffman is among the key figures in promoting what critics have called the modern "ethnopharmacology" in athlete cultures. Here, athletes often develop their own logics of eating and believe that certain products have special ergogenic properties despite any consistent medical substantiation or even consistent contradictory claims. Athletes are socialized in sports to eat in particular ways based on the logics of "evidence" (normally trial and error) linking ergogenics and performance that they are exposed to in sports. An ethnopharmacological culture is hard to disrupt in a sport when athletes subculturally believe that if they do not supplement in a particular way, their performance will suffer.

Indeed, it seems that companies such as York Barbell profited on the development of ethnopharmacology in the gym despite contrary scientific evidence about the effectiveness of its products. In 1960, the company was charged with misbranding its Energol Germ Oil Concentrate product because literature accompanying the oil claimed, falsely, that it could prevent or treat more than 120 diseases and conditions, including epilepsy, gallstones, and arthritis. In 1961, 15 other York Barbell products were identified as patently misbranded. Yet, despite the company's surreptitious activities, no one proposed that ergogenic products were "serious" enough of a public threat to warrant further industry monitoring, regulation, and reform.

During the 1970s, in addition to protein supplements and assorted vitamins, the main products touted commercially to athletes were wheat germ oil and bee pollen (falsely claimed to boost energy and endurance). In the early 1980s, Weider Health and Fitness introduced an "Olympians" ergogenic line said to have been developed by working closely with Olympians and nutritional researchers. Most were sustained-release vitamin concoctions that included an exotic ingredient or two such as the "newly discovered" Chinese wonder-supplement ginseng. As public interest in fitness grew (i.e., gym cultures, running cultures, aerobics cultures, surfing cultures, and many others flourished in the decade), American drug companies began falsely claiming that multivitamin or "stress" supplements were just what active people needed to stay healthy.

The publicly acclaimed, and then scientifically panned, book *Life Extension,* by Durk Pearson and Sandy Shaw, was published in 1982 and followed by appearances by the authors on hundreds of radio and television talk shows. The book erroneously claimed that certain amino acid supplements would cause the body to release hormones that would produce muscle growth and fat loss with little or no effort. The massive publicity garnered by Pearson and Shaw inspired the health-food industry to market hundreds of new products for athletes, fitness fanatics, and, perhaps most importantly, a new generation of slim-obsessed dieters. Whereas elite athletes and then recreational exercisers had been the principal population toward which supplements had been marketed through the 1950 to 1970s, a new generation of overweight or obese Americans was searching for new products designed to help slim their bodies and complement new (and dangerous) diets such as Herman Tarnower's now infamous Scarsdale Diet.

Critics of the insurgence of ergogenic supplements into sports and popular cultures have questioned whether or not scientifically engineered but largely untested products promote a certain degree of body–food detachment. Rather than promoting an eating culture that is in touch with food and its central role in regenerating the body, we have moved toward a culture where consuming specifically engineered supplements that alter the body's natural rhythms and functions is unproblematic. Equally, if sports itself is supposed to showcase the best of the human's natural abilities to run, jump, swim, throw, or climb, we must question whether or not consuming unnatural levels of foreign substances to improve on "nature" is a positive cultural ideal. In this vein, we must also question whether the world of sports has become too closely aligned with new technology and scientific industries. The ergogenic industry developed over the course of the twentieth century as technology (in the area of food production and elsewhere) and science increasingly began to dominate most forms of social life, including sports. As a result, athlete performance and success is now discussed largely in mechanical and scientific-functional terms; stated differently, athletes are often taught to "see" eating as a rational, scientific means to an end practice. In the new ethnopharmacology of high performance sports, one should eat the most scientifically engineered products on the market in order to be the best athlete possible.

Additional critiques of ergogenics focus on the question of whether or not there are any potential long-term physical or psychological side effects of the use of ergogenics such as protein powders, energy bars, or popular creatine (a muscle-builder). Given the relative newness of most of the products, and their mass use, only time will tell as to whether or not physiological side effects will manifest through long-term usage. With regard to the psychological effects, there is considerable evidence in the literature to suggest that consumption of seemingly innocuous ergogenics might lead to more patterned use of

THE RANGE OF ERGOGENICS IN SPORTS

While media often focus on and critique the use of ineffective or illegal ergogenics by athletes, there is a full spectrum of them available to athletes such as:

I. Mechanical Aids

Altitude training
Aqua (water) training
Computers (body system analysis)
Downhill running (3° to 5° slope)
Elastic cord (pulling)
Elastic cord (restraining)
Heart rate monitors
Hypoxic tents
Nasal strips
Parachutes
Sports clothing, footwear, and equipment
Timing equipment
Treadmills
Uphill running (5° to 10° slope)
Vibration training
Video recorders
Weighted vests (5% to 8% of body weight)
Weights

II. Pharmacological Aids

Amphetamine
Anabolic steroid
Androstenedione
Beta blocker
Caffeine
Carnitine
Choline
Chromium
Clenbuterol
Creatine monohydrate
Dehydroepiandrosterone (DHEA)
Gamma hydroxybutyric acid (GHB)
Hydroxymethylbutyrate (HMB)
Magnesium
Phosphatidylserine
Protein supplements
Sodium bicarbonate
Vanadyl sulphate

III. Physiological Aids

Acupuncture
Blood doping
Colostrum
Creatine
EPO
Herbal medicines
Homeopathy
Human growth hormone
Physiotherapy
Sauna
Sports massage
Ultra-violet rays

IV. Nutritional Aids

Bicarbonate of soda
Caffeine
Carbohydrate loading
Creatine
Sports drinks

V. Psychological Aids

Cheering
Hypnosis
Imagery
Music
Psychology
Relaxation
Tai Chi
Yoga

"hardcore" supplements such as anabolic steroids. As many of the popular ergogenics have been described as expensive placebos, athletes or other consumers might seek out more effective and immediate performance boosters in the form of illegal drugs. In the drug consumption academic literature this has often been described as the classic "gateway" phenomenon.

Finally, while most ergogenics are touted in trade magazines and Internet sites as sports performance enhancers, they are clearly marketed to, and are being consumed by, a wide range of people outside of sports who ostensibly do not require them or who may become psychologically and physically addicted to them through overconsumption. In the early 2000s, for example, sports performance scientists on both sides of the Atlantic begun to uncloak the relationship between caffeine consumption and physical endurance in sports. Quite soon after, caffeine was inserted into a full range of sports drinks and bars for athletes to help them endure, to improve their concentration and focus, and to provide them with quick bursts of energy. Soon after that, energy products such as the drink Red Bull were loosely marketed as workout enhancers but were then culturally adopted as a meal replacement drink, mood enhancer, cocktail mix, and simple thirst quencher by people. Few have ever questioned, then, the role of sports performance scientists and ergogenic production companies in promoting the mass consumption of drugs such as caffeine to broader cultures of people in North America.

KEY EVENTS

In addition to trends noted previously, several other key moments in the development of sports nutrition helped to establish ergogenics as staples in the diets of athletes and others. Few figures have impacted the rise in sports supplement consumption as much as bodybuilding guru Joe Weider. Weider started bodybuilding as a teenager and was 16 when he launched a newsletter called *Your Physique*. A few years later, he started a company that sold bodybuilding equipment and instructional booklets through the mail and, with his brother Ben, helped to establish Weider Nutritional International. The company is presently the dominant player in the sports-supplement marketplace with reported annual sales of $350 million. It publishes seven trade magazines, sells bodybuilding equipment, broadcasts *Muscle Magazine* on ESPN, and sponsors many athletic and aerobic events throughout the year. The magazines are *Muscle & Fitness, Shape, Flex, Living Fit, Prime Health & Fitness, Men's Fitness,* and *Senior Golfer*. The highly promoted Weider supplements include Anabolic Mega-Pak, Dynamic Life Essence, Dynamic Super Stress-End, Dynamic Power Source, Dynamic Driving Force, Dynamic Fat Burners, Dynamic Liver Concentrate Energizer, Dynamic Sustained Endurance, Dynamic Recupe, Dynamic Body Shaper, and Dynamic Muscle Builder. After years of scientific testing and controversy, none of the products appears capable of doing what their names or descriptions suggest or contain any nutrients not readily obtainable from a balanced diet.

In five court cases between 1972 and 1975, U.S. Postal Service Administrative Law Judges concluded that Weider and his companies had made false representations regarding various products. Weider later agreed not to falsely claim that these products can help build muscles or are effective substitutes for anabolic steroids. Although most of the forbidden claims no longer appear in Weider ads, similar messages appear in articles in the magazines and are implied by endorsements and pictures of muscular athletes as well as by names of the products themselves. Because very few people ever take Weider or others to task on the claims, his trade publications, like the dozens of others than now flood the sports, health, and fitness markets, feature thousands of advertisements for hundreds of products that remain relatively unchecked and unregulated.

While Weider's ergogenic empire continues to grow, it does not promote the most widely successful ergogenic supplement on the market to date. In early summer of 1965, a University of Florida assistant coach sat down with a team of university physicians and asked them to determine why so many of his football players were being affected by heat and heat-related illnesses. The researchers, Dr. Robert Cade, Dr. Dana Shires, Dr. H. James Free, and Dr. Alejandro de Quesada, soon discovered two key factors that were causing the Florida Gator football players to wilt in the sun: The fluids and electrolytes the players lost through sweat were not being replaced, and the large amounts of carbohydrates the players' bodies used for energy were not being replenished. The researchers then took their findings into the lab and scientifically formulated a new, precisely balanced carbohydrate–electrolyte beverage that would adequately replace the key components lost by Gator players through sweating and exercise: They called it Gatorade.

Soon after the researchers introduced their Gatorade formula to the team, the Gators began winning, and many on the inside of the team attributed their success to the supplement. Orders from high school, college football, and professional football programs across the country soon followed. Within two years Gatorade became the first mass-consumed sports drink in North America. Today, Gatorade can be found on the sidelines of more than 70 Division I colleges as the official sports drink of their men's and women's intercollegiate sports.

The Gatorade Sports Science Institute was founded in 1988 in Barrington, Illinois, to conduct scientific research in the areas of exercise science, hydration, and sports nutrition. Three years later, the lab would be expanded to provide advanced testing for athletes and new Gatorade products and flavors and to develop educational materials for sports health professionals around the world. Gatorade is now also the official sports drink of the National Basketball Association (NBA), Professional Golfer's Association of America (PGA), Major League Baseball (MLB), Major League Soccer (MLS), and numerous other elite and professional organizations and teams. In 2001, Gatorade launched the Gatorade Performance Series, an elite line of sports nutrition products, including Gatorade Energy Drink, Gatorade Energy Bar, and the Gatorade Nutrition Shake and Gatorade Endurance Formula Drink.

Perhaps more than any other supplement product, Gatorade helped to firmly establish the multi-institutional links between science, sports, and eating and drinking cultures among athletes. Additionally, Gatorade helped to bring "sports science" and the technology of eating for sports to wider audiences. The high-content sugar drink, unfortunately, is too often consumed by nonathletes because of its naturally sweet and pleasant taste and has been informally linked to rising obesity rates among American youth.

Recent debates about the marketing of sports supplements have also brought issues of ethics of ergogenic production and distribution to the fore. For nearly 50 years, producers of ergogenic supplements have been given a relative carte blanche to introduce new products to the market, to advertise and package them as they best see fit, and to make any number of scientific claims about their effects (Atkinson, 2007). Since 2001, clinical study after study has found that each year over-the-counter ergogenics "make it to market" containing legal and banned substances in sports that are not listed on the product's ingredients label.

In 2002, Canadian triathlete Kelly Guest paid the ultimate price for what he claims to be a colossal failure on the part of a sports supplement company to fully disclose the contents of an ergogenic product. Guest had his career in sports effectively terminated when, during the 2002 Commonwealth Games, he failed a prerace drug test. Testers found trace elements of the steroid nandrolone (1 billionth of a gram) in his system. Guest was dismissed from the Games, removed from the Canadian Triathlon Team, and sentenced to a four-year ban from the sport. Critics argued that such a minute amount of substance in his system corroborated Guest's claim that he consumed a "contaminated" legal sports supplement. He claimed that the supplement in question was approved on the World-Anti-Doping Association and Canadian Center for Ethics in Sport's lists but must have contained a banned substance not indicated on its commercial packaging. A hearing convened in Canada to review Guest's case, and it was found that in most likelihood Guest did not wittingly take a banned substance. He was allowed to compete as a professional triathlete in 2004. The Guest case highlighted the lack of regulation in the ergogenic production, distribution, and consumption industries and the need for new educational and awareness campaigns in sports to protect athletes from any unscrupulous, or at least unreliable and sloppy, sports performance corporations.

A more tragic example of ergogenic use is found in the case of ephedra. In the 1990s, sports/health supplements such as the ephedra-based Xenadrine quickly became popular as performance enhancers, stimulants, and fat loss tools. They quickly fell from grace in sports after a series of professional athletes' deaths were linked to consumption of the relatively unregulated supplements containing them. The deaths of Baltimore Orioles' rookie pitcher Steve Bechler in 2000 and National Football League (NFL) football players Corey Stringer (2001) and Rashidi Wheeler (2001) were officially attributed to heatstroke and strain. But sports insiders have argued that each were heavy consumers of ephedra as preseason aids for shedding off-season weight. Ephedra had been used until 2000 as a staple in the sport of bodybuilding as well. The case of ephedra illustrates, once more, the dangers of allowing ethnopharmacological cultures to develop in sports and the risks of not stringently testing and policing the ergogenic production and marketing industries.

FUTURE PROSPECTS

With growing consumer appetites for ergogenic supplements and the lax regulation of the industry, there appears to be little stopping the continued mushrooming of the business in the near future. In the North American culture where speed, technology, and results reign supreme, ergogenics are marketed as quick fixes to long-term problems of muscle building, weight loss, cardiovascular efficiency, mental acuity and concentration, and other "physical conditions." As long as North Americans continue to prefer easily transportable, energy-boosting, fast-food meals, sports or "health" supplements will find a niche market in the food industry. Most likely, only when more people die or become seriously ill through the long-term ingestion of ergogenics will increased attention toward and regulation of the industry occur.

See also Antidoping Rules and Policies; Biology and Athlete Performance; Erythropoietin (EPO); Gene Manipulation; Marijuana, Alcohol, and Illicit Drugs; Whistle-Blowers and Drugs.

Further Reading: Atkinson, M. (2007). Playing with Fire: Masculinity, Health and Sports Supplements. *Sociology of Sport Journal* 24:2: 165–186; Monaghan, L. (2002). Vocabularies of Motive for Illicit Steroid Use Among Bodybuilders. *Social Science & Medicine* 55: 695–708; Person, D., and Shaw, S. (1982). *Life Extension*. New York: Warner Books; Williams, M. (1999). *The Ergogenics Edge*. Champaign, IL: Human Kinetics.

Michael Atkinson

ERYTHROPOIETIN (EPO)

Performance-enhancing drugs have most likely been used since the beginning of organized sports. There is evidence that such substances were used as early as the fourth century B.C.E. in Rome and Greece, at which time there existed substances and methods to create feelings of euphoria, decrease fatigue, and increase strength among athletes. With the advent of modern organized sporting activities, dating back to the nineteenth century, has come ever-increasing interest in superior performance. The ability to accurately measure time and strength contributed to this interest, and the lure of prizes and fame led to the undertaking of sports as a profession. Notably, in recent decades there have been well-publicized increases in the use of new synthetic substances in sports including morphine, codeine, amphetamines, anabolic steroids, and corticosteroids to increase performance. There has also been a strong trend toward increased use of dietary supplements. Most recently we have seen the introduction of synthetic peptides such as erythropoietin (EPO) into elite-level endurance sports cultures; EPO is one of the first substances that researchers have documented a quantifiable and immediately perceptible impact on athletic performance, and it is very hard to detect. Since the introduction of EPO into endurance sports such as cycling and running, we have seen shocking performance increases by international athletes, as evidenced by the rate of new world records being set in sports such as swimming, cycling, and speed skating.

BACKGROUND

Erythropoietin is a hormone produced by the kidneys that promotes the formation of red blood cells in the bone marrow. It is called a glycoprotein, which is a protein with a sugar attached to it. The kidney cells that make EPO are specialized and are sensitive to low oxygen levels in the blood, releasing EPO when the oxygen level is low. The EPO then stimulates the bone marrow to produce more red cells and thereby increases the oxygen-carrying capacity of the blood. Erythropoietin is, then, the prime regulator of red blood cell production. Its major functions are to promote the differentiation and development of red blood cells and to initiate the production of hemoglobin, the molecule within red cells that transports oxygen.

Erythropoietin, athletes and scientists discovered, can be artificially produced in a laboratory and then injected into an athlete to improve his or her work abilities. Artificial EPOs are now used mainly by long-distance runners, swimmers, speed skaters, cross-country skiers, and long-distance cyclists. The drug is injected under the skin and stimulates red blood cell production in athletes—desirable because the more red blood cells in the body, the more efficient it is in carrying oxygen to the muscles. The abundance of oxygen-carrying red blood cells delays the onset of fatigue, meaning an athlete can run, cycle, or ski harder and for a longer amount of time. Tests have shown that major improvements in an athlete's performance over four weeks use of EPO would match those expected over several weeks through "natural" training methods.

Unfortunately for officials, EPO cannot be detected by most standard forms of drug testing in sports. However, new methods have been developed in countries such as France, where the results of an athlete's blood sample analysis and urine analysis are compared to look for key physiological "giveaways" regarding the presence of unnatural EPO levels. The blood test shows if there is an unusual reading of blood cells, and the urine test highlights any difference between the EPO levels produced naturally and synthetically.

Prior to the introduction of EPO into global sports (which some estimate to have occurred as far back as the 1970s) little scientific evidence existed that suggested other drugs used in the athletic community, such as amphetamines and steroids, had any measurable effect on athletes' endurance. This changed, however, with the introduction of EPO, which can enhance performance in some tests of endurance by as much as 20 percent.

A major risk, however, associated with EPO use for an athlete is cardiac arrest or even death. Injecting the drug into the body will thicken the athlete's blood by introducing more red blood cells than natural. If EPO is overused, the blood will become so thick that there is a danger of the heart stopping when the body slows down, for example, when falling asleep or merely resting. The likelihood of an athlete suffering blood clots, heart attacks, and strokes is a definitive possibility.

The sport of cycling has been especially plagued by EPO use among its elite-level competitors. Racers in two of the world's most famous cycling events, the Tour de France and the Giro d'Italia, have collectively told stories about a wide-reaching culture of EPO use in the sport. Erythropoietin is an especially attractive drug for long-distance cyclists because it helps red blood cells "recover" after damage suffered by long and grueling multiday, endurance events. The World Anti-Doping Agency (WADA) has described the use of EPO in professional cycling as an outright epidemic and claims that unless the culture of drug consumption among cyclists is changed, EPO abuse could lead to the end of the sport. Or, even more tragically, it will lead to the death of professional cyclists who use the drug over long periods.

In 2004, the world of pro cycling was shocked when two highly successful riders, John Sermon of Belgium and Marco Pantani of Italy, tragically died due to heart failure. Sermon (age 21) and Pantani (age 34) were reportedly both in good health, and their deaths signaled something everyone knew in the sport—EPO use can have tragic consequences.

Since 2003, six other professional cyclists have died suspiciously due to heart failure, including: Denis Zanette (Italy, age 32), Marco Ceriani (Italy, age 16), Fabrice Salanson (France, age 23), Marco Rusconi (Italy, age 24), Jose Maria Jimenez (Spain, age 32), and Michel Zanoli (The Netherlands, age 35). Phil Ligget, an international cycling broadcaster, argues that over 100 cyclists' deaths in the past 15 years might be attributable to the use of the drug.

Organizers of mega events in cycling have battled against the use of drugs such as EPO since the turn of the twentieth century. Allegations of doping have followed the Tour de France, in particular, since it began in 1903. For years, it seems, a major scandal related to drug use among cyclists was both feared and expected by Tour de France organizers and fans. In 1998, one of the most infamous of illegal drug-use cases in all of sports rocked the Tour and the entire sport of cycling.

KEY EVENTS

Some critics contend that the Festina scandal of 1998 is partly responsible for tarnishing the reputation of professional cycling forever. On July 8, 1998, French customs officers arrested the Festina cycling team's premiere athlete and potential tour winner Willy Voet. He was found in possession of several illegal drugs including performance-enhancing drugs as well as growth hormones and amphetamines—most notably, EPO. French police subsequently raided several other teams' hotel rooms, including the remainder of team Festina. Members of Festina and team TMV both had in their possession various amounts of EPO. Some participants in the race decried the French police's military-like tactics in raiding hotel rooms and even went so far as to boycott the race by refusing to finish. In the end, only 100 racers actually crossed the fabled Tour de France finish line in Paris. Partly in protest, the remainder of the participating riders in the Tour cycled without any deliberate effort on the last day of competition though the streets of Paris, much to the disappointment of the fans. The 1998 Tour de France is, as a result of the scandal, referred to as "The Tour of Shame."

The Festina scandal resulted in major drug policy and testing changes that continue to this day. Riders are now tested on a regular, random, and unannounced basis for illegal substances such as EPO. In addition to regulatory bodies in world cycling, WADA stepped in to police drug use in the sport with considerable force and scope. From anecdotes and stories offered by professional riders, however, these measures have not been sufficient in controlling the use of EPO among the elite cyclists. Two examples illustrate the ineffectiveness of the new rules and procedures quite well.

Just a few short years after the 1998 Tour scandal, the third-place finisher of the 2002 Tour de France was arrested on charges of doping with EPO. In 2004, members of the Cofidis pro cycling team openly admitted to using performance-enhancing drugs during competition, including EPO. Members of team Cofidis also suggested that EPO use is far more prevalent than people in charge of controlling drugs in the sport even believe, and they predicted more deaths in the sport unless the testing procedures change dramatically.

Only a handful of days prior to the start of the 2006 Tour de France, 13 riders were banned from the race due to reports stemming from a Spanish investigation into doping in sports (called Operacion Puerto). The report named nearly 100 world cyclists as suspected users of EPO and other performance-enhancing drugs. Two of the Tour favorites in 2006, Jan Ullrich of team T-Mobile and Ivan Basso of team CSC, were named in the Spanish report and immediately excluded from the 2006 Tour de France. Other notables named in the report, and who were dismissed from competition, included Francisco Mancebo (team AG2R), Oscar Sevilla (team T-Mobile), Santiago Botero (team Phonak), and Jose Gutierrez (team Phonak). Alexandre Vinoukorouv, another race favorite, was not linked to the doping scandal but was forced to withdraw when nearly half of the eligible riders on his Astana-Wurth team were suspended. Following the Spain scandal and Floyd Landis's (team Phonak's leader) failure of a drug test at the end of the Tour, the Phonak company withdrew all of their financial sponsorship from professional cycling and disbanded the team. Of note, Floyd Landis had been crowned as the outright winner of the 2006 Tour de France just before his test failure surfaced in the press.

No other cyclist, or athlete in history, has been accused of using and tested more for EPO than seven-time Tour de France winner Lance Armstrong. Armstrong, the American cyclist who returned to the sport after surviving testicular, lung, and brain cancer in 1998, has never tested positive for EPO or any other performance-enhancing substance. The most serious of recent allegations came in 2006 when the French cycling newspaper *L'Equipe* reported that a laboratory discovered trace elements of EPO in a frozen blood sample given by Armstrong during the 1999 Tour de France, his first tour victory. Armstrong responded to the allegation on his "Lance Armstrong Foundation" Web site (a foundation famous for selling yellow bracelets with the cancer-survivor motto "Livestrong" imprinted on them) claiming, "[the report] is nothing short of tabloid journalism." Armstrong went on to say, "I will simply restate what I have said many times. I have never taken performance-enhancing drugs."

Though short- and long-distance runners, like cyclists, have been targeted for EPO testing in the past decade, only a few have tested positive for the banned substance. The most famous runner caught to date is the American short- and middle-distance runner Marion Jones. Jones was found guilty of having illegal amounts of EPO in her system in 2006. Jones, a five-time world track and field champion and five-time medalist at the 2000 Sydney Olympics, had been suspected of drug use for nearly a decade. Other "caught" athletes include the Olympic bronze medalist (1,500-meter run) Bernard Lagat of Kenya; Russian runner (5,000–meter run) Olga Yegorova; American cyclist Adham Sbeih; Russian cross-country skier Natalia Baranova-Masolkin; Chinese track athletes Zheng Yongji and Li Huiquan; Moroccan runner and former 10K world record holder Asmae Leghzaoui; and French cyclist and Olympic bronze medalist Philippe Gaumont.

In 2006, members of a Chinese athletics institute, the Anshan Athletics School, were caught with illegal levels of EPO in their blood. Apparently, coaches at the institute had been injecting them with the drug and a series of other banned performance enhancers. The story came on the heels of a 2000 drug scandal in China, in which 40 members of Chinese summer Olympic team were banned from competition due to EPO use.

In reflection, the problem of EPO use in sports may well have something to do with what sociologists call the "[over] medicalization of everyday life." More pharmaceutical products than ever before are taken by people in Western cultures. Consuming pills, drugs, or medicinal remedies has become almost a normal part of our daily routines. Consuming drugs has certainly become a standard form of "nutrition" in the world of athletics. Athletes are under intense pressure to perform and to trust the advice of their doctors and trainers, and they are encouraged to use "medicine" and science to improve their bodies at any cost. To many involved in sports professionally, it is a given fact that every athlete seeks to enhance his or her performance and increasingly view his or her body as a site of "medical work." Whether they seek to improve the speed, strength, and efficiency of their body with legal products (those not on the list of forbidden substances for their sport) or whether they do it with forbidden products such as EPO, the goal of physical performance enhancement is the same.

FUTURE PROSPECTS

The drive for performance, excellence, and success has resulted in the increased use and abuse of EPO, particularly in those countries where athletes who are victorious receive considerable cultural accolades and financial compensation for winning. With drug testing procedures often years behind the development of drugs (remember, synthetic EPO was around for decades before scientists discovered how to detect it), the apprehension and punishment of users is incredibly difficult. For those who have an inside knowledge of sports cultures, one also understands how the use of performance-enhancing drugs such as EPO has what is called a "snowball effect." When one athlete or group of athletes takes illegal drugs, others feel compelled to copy them, simply to remain competitive. Clinical researchers suggest that, on average, EPO boosts an athlete's performance abilities by 10 percent. Imagine competing against someone who has the same years of training as you do but who can perform 10 percent better due to chemical intervention in the past three or four weeks. Unless drugs such as EPO are controlled "across the board" in sports and all athletes are prohibited from using them, we can reasonably expect drugs to remain part of elite athletics.

See also Cheating During Competition; Ergogenics; Gene Manipulation; Sports Doctors, Trainers, and Drugs; Steroid Use by Athletes; Whistle-Blowers and Drugs.

Further Reading: Atkinson, M., and Young, K. (2008). *Deviance and Social Control in Sport.* Champaign, IL: Human Kinetics.

Michael Atkinson

ETHNIC COACHES, MANAGERS, AND OWNERS

Sport is a social institution that is stratified by gender, social class, religion, and ethnicity. While the players who participate in many North American sports are collectively far more racially and ethnically diverse than ever before, other roles within sports organizations still tend to be underrepresented by members of visible racial and ethnic minorities. The inconsistency between the relative overrepresentation of ethnic/racial minorities in player positions in particular sports compared to their absences in power positions such as coach, manager, general manger, and owner raises a set of questions regarding whether or not there remains a pronounced color line in sports.

BACKGROUND

The color line in sports refers to the structural and cultural barriers created within sports organizations that serve to limit or block the opportunities of nonwhite people. Much has been written about the symbolic shattering of the color line by players such as Jackie Robinson and Roberto Clemente, but often forgotten in the discussion is how color lines continue to map out opportunities for people in the upper echelons of sports organizations beyond the fields of play. Any complex sports organization contains dozens or hundreds of positions that have been historically inaccessible to ethnic/racial minorities. The ethnic composition of personnel staffing of these positions represents both the historical racial balance in sports and the social distribution of power between racial groups in other social institutions.

A historical justification for limiting racial minorities' access to key power and decision-making positions in sports management and operation pertains to the centuries old "race logic," which purports that people of dark skin do not possess the requisite intellectual skills to occupy these positions. Not accidentally, socially established ruling white groups have denigrated the intellectual and moral character of nonwhites as a means of excluding them from positions of social authority in sports and elsewhere. While it is, then, completely acceptable to fill sports in the modern capitalist era with minority groups in the role of player, the ruling white elite (the dominant controllers and profiteers of modern sports) have been curiously slow in altering the racial composition of front offices, management boards, or coaching teams under their control.

For Elias and Scotson (1965), established groups tend to remain in positions of power over time because they share their power with other "likes" and pass it on generationally in both formal and informal social networks. Established social groups, such as elite white stakeholders in sports, are deeply embedded in both the base (the economy) and super-structural (government, legal system, education) segments of societies and consequently control many of its ideological state apparatuses such as the media. Established groups have greater access to, but not necessarily outright ownership of, varying institutional opportunities to shape social ideologies and practices. Conversely, outsider groups are more marginal or excluded members of a social group, less embedded in power positions and dominated on the basis of their limited statuses. While it might be tempting to view the National Football League (NFL) as a place of considerable racial equality because of its high concentration of African American players, black players' public presence on the field perhaps masks and detracts away from their outsider status in the front office, where the real power and money in sports is located. Outsiders are thus deliberately excluded from participation in socially influential power structures of a society or social organization, and their voices, ideologies, and interests are mainly silenced or invisible in popular culture.

Consider the 2005 National Basketball Association (NBA) dress code rule, which effectively took aim at the social representation of "street (African American) style" in and around the arena. Pushed forward by the established league commissioner David Stern, the code set new rules and regulations regarding what players could wear while traveling to or from a stadium. Among the targeted apparel items were gold chains, bandanas and do-rags, baggy jeans, and other "hip-hop style" fashion items. Designed and passed by a predominantly white commissioner's office to combat the "thug" image the NBA had apparently developed in the early 2000s, the new code, argued commissioner Stern, would bring back a middle-class respectability to the league and help promote the sport among new corporate sponsors. Players were overtly critical of the new rule, highlighting the way in which it seemed to target a form of black cultural expression in the league. The NBA's power play clearly shows how those in established power positions in sports deploy traditional corporate logics when plotting or altering policy therein.

The historical push toward including more visible minorities in power and decision-making positions in sports has clear links to the U.S. civil rights movement, the discourses about equity in sports stirred by Title IX, the increased ethnic minority dominance at player positions in sports including basketball and football through the 1970s and 1980s, and the development of lobbyist groups such as the Black Coaches and Administrators (BCA) association. Among the most commonly discussed issues pertaining to race and sports in the 1980s and 1990s was the many in-roads black men and women had made as athletes in sports but their relative absence in administrative power positions in sports. Critics argued that while young African American athletes are more encouraged to participate in sports than ever before, few ethnic minorities have been afforded opportunities to managerial or key decision-making positions at the organizational level.

The BCA, among others, has suggested that performance of specific players or entire teams that are primarily comprised of an ethnic minority group might be enhanced if coached by someone from their own social/ethnic background. Sports journalists have controversially noted that many of the ethnic minority hirings in sports during the 1980s and 1990s may have been "tokenistic" (such as Cito Gaston's hiring as the manager of the Toronto Blue Jays) and only thinly veiled attempts for sports organizations to appear more racially sensitive and friendly to African American fans and audiences.

Discourses and pressures in the 1980s and 1990s to hire with a greater sense of diversity at the coach and administrator positions were not the first of their kind; and certainly the visible minority coaches hired in this era did not break the color line. Fritz Pollard is generally regarded as the coach who did so, when he was hired to lead the Akron Pros of the American Professional Football League (later the NFL) in 1920. Buck O'Neil first broke the coaching color line in professional baseball in 1962 as manager of the Chicago Cubs. Four years later, Bill Russell was named the head coach of the Boston Celtics. Russell's hiring was especially path-breaking in sports because the Celtics were regarded up until this point as one of the whitest teams in U.S. sports history. It was not until

---

SUCCESS OF THE HEAD COACH

Over the dozens of championship games played in major North American sports, only 10 African American coaches have reached championship finals. A brief look at the list illustrates perhaps how underrepresented African Americans are at the coaching positions in sports.

NFL

2007: Tony Dungy, Indianapolis Colts
2007: Lovie Smith, Chicago Bears

NBA

2006: Avery Johnson, Dallas Mavericks
2002–2003: Byron Scott, New Jersey Nets
1984–1986: KC Jones, Boston Celtics
1978–1979: Lenny Wilkens, Seattle SuperSonics
1975: Al Attles, Golden State Warriors
1975: KC Jones, Washington Bullets
1968–1969: Bill Russell, Boston Celtics

MLB

2002: Dusty Baker, San Francisco Giants
1992–1993: Cito Gaston, Toronto Blue Jays

1970, when Will Robinson assumed a coaching role at Illinois State University, that an African American coach led an National Collegiate Athletic Association (NCAA) Division I basketball team. It was another nine years before Willie Jeffries broke the color barrier in NCAA Division I football, when he coached Wichita State.

In flashing forward to 2007, the data on ethnic minorities in coaching and administrative positions provides mixed messages about their status as established or outsider figures in mainstream sports. Major League Baseball (MLB) is currently represented by six ethnic minority managers (2 African American and 4 Latino), and ethnic minorities consist of 27 percent of MLB's Central Office, 23 percent of teams' senior staff, and 24 percent of teams' directors. According to MLB statistics, 33 percent of minor league affiliates to the professional clubs employ ethnic minorities in coaching positions. While coaching opportunities appear to be on the rise in the MLB, the number of African American players in the sport continues to decline. The NBA, by contrast, represents completely different figures, and the league is heralded by sports insiders as truly progressive. In 2007, the NBA employed the greatest number of ethnic minorities in U.S. sports history. Fifteen percent of its teams' vice-presidents, 79 percent of its players, 34 percent of its league office staff, 40 percent of its coaches, 41 percent of its assistant coaches, 4 percent of its teams' CEO/presidents, 8 percent of its general managers, and 26 percent of teams' senior administrator positions were ethnic minorities. Currently, Robert Johnson, who owns the Charlotte Bobcats, is the only African American team owner in men's professional sports.

In the NFL, six ethnic minority men coached professional teams in the 2007 season. The 2007 Super Bowl was historically significant because it was the first in NFL history that involved two teams coached by African Americans (the Indianapolis Colts and the Chicago Bears). Sixty-seven percent of players were African American, along with 13 team vice-presidents and 165 assistant coaches. To this day, there has never been an African American CEO/president of an NFL team.

This data indicate that the situation for ethnic minorities in established power and decision-making positions in sports is constantly in a state of flux. The NBA continues to be a leader with respect to minority hiring, while professional baseball is moving in a rather curious direction in that the number of African American players is decreasing at the same time the number of hirings beyond the playing field is increasing. The case in the NFL remains somewhat clear cut along historical lines in that while African American players still dominate by population in the league, positions of power and authority in the league remain deeply cleaved along racial lines.

KEY EVENTS

A series of high-profile coaching hires in the latter half of the twentieth century were turning points in the history of African Americans in sports. In 1975, Frank Robinson was hired as the general manager of the Cleveland Indians. Robinson had a very successful playing career in the major leagues including rookie of the year honors in 1956, league Most Valuable Player in 1961, winner of baseball's "triple crown" (league leader in batting average, home runs, and runs batted in) and World Series MVP in 1966, election to the National Baseball Hall of Fame in 1982, recipient of the Presidential Medal of Freedom in 2005, and recipient of the first (Jackie Robinson) Society Community Recognition Award in 2007. Robinson participated actively in the civil rights movement, working as a spokesperson for the NAACP in the 1960s. He became the active player manager of the Indians in 1975 until leaving in 1977. Between 1981 and 2006, Robinson managed several teams, including the San Francisco Giants, the Baltimore Orioles (where he received the manager of the year award in 1989), and the Montreal Expos/Washington Nationals. Like Robinson, when Arthur (Art) Shell was selected as the head coach for the Los Angeles Raiders in 1990, it followed an exemplary career as an athlete. Shell played as an offensive tackle for the Raiders between 1968 and 1982, where he won two Super Bowls and participated in eight Pro Bowls. Shell has been regarded as among the premier offensive linemen in the 1970s. While Fritz Pollard preceded Shell as the first African American NFL head coach, Shell's debut in 1990 at Los Angeles was heralded as a watershed moment in racial equality in the sport.

Several common features of the hires tie Robinson and Shell together as symbolic figures in sports. First, both were former players of some distinction. Second, each had experience with the organization they were hired to coach. Thus, each had exemplary credentials for a head coach position and had been familiar entities within the towns in which they first coached. Sports cynics suggest that only hall of fame caliber players could have been selected as pioneer coaches in the leagues (and situated among sports cities that knew their credentials). Other African American coaches who were not part of established sports cultures of excellence would have still been considered outsider figures and thus ineligible to coach. A potentially strong message had been sent, then, that only the very, very best of African American candidates for coaching positions would ever be considered in these professional sports.

The NBA has been, by contrast, among the historically path-breaking sports organizations (and, indeed, in business organizations in general) for African American and other ethnic minority groups. Following Bill Russell's hiring as a head coach in 1966, 54 ethnic/racial minority head coaches have been appointed in the NBA. Whereas hiring in the NFL and MLB did not rapidly adjust in the 1970s to include more diversity-sensitive practices, the NBA has carefully monitored its hirings since the early 1980s. Sports journalists, pundits, and insiders argue that the NBA brand is the most culturally popular sport for African Americans. African American players dominate by percentage in the game, and the sport draws more African American audience members than any other sport. To this end, teams have increasingly "stacked" their coaching and front office positions with African Americans. Although subject for some debate, professional basketball has developed as a definitive "black culture" sport since the 1990s.

Yet, the NBA has not ventured as far as the NFL with respect to affirmative action–based policies. Following a scathing report on minority hiring in the

NFL, the league head office instituted what is now regarded as one of the most progressive institutional policies regarding minority hiring, referred to in the NFL as "The Rooney Rule." Spearheaded by Pittsburgh Steelers owner and chair of the diversity committee, Dan Rooney, The Rooney Rule requires teams to interview at least one minority candidate for a head coach opportunity. The rule is not simply racial "window dressing" for the league. In 2003, the NFL fined the Detroit Lions $200,000 for failure to interview minority candidates for the team's vacant head coaching job. Since the Rooney Rule was established, several NFL franchises have hired minority head coaches (including the Steelers themselves, who hired Mike Tomlin before their 2007 season), although the legitimacy, legality, and effectiveness of the policy is still debated.

There are few social problems or battles within sports that have been tracked as meticulously by a research agency as that of the racial (and gender) composition of amateur and professional sports. The foremost "tracking" organization since the early 1990s has been The Institute for Diversity and Ethics in Sport (TIDES). The institute, and its published materials, serve as a comprehensive community resource for issues related to race in amateur, collegiate, and professional sports. It researches and publishes annual studies on hiring practices in coaching and sports management, student-athlete graduation rates, and racial attitudes in sports. These include the internationally acclaimed "Racial and Gender Report Card," which was first developed and published in 1992. The founder, director, and author of TIDES' annual Racial and Gender Report Card is Dr. Richard Lapchick, a professor and internationally recognized human rights activist. TIDES and other organizations were keen to point out that in 2007, the Super Bowl contest between the Indianapolis Colts and the Chicago Bears was the first in history to feature one, let alone two, African American head coaches, Tony Dungy and Lovie Smith; Dungy became the first African American coach in history to win a Super Bowl.

FUTURE PROSPECTS

The vast amount of media attention directed toward ethnic minority representation in professional and NCAA sports has drawn attention to noteworthy racial discrepancies in economically powerful positions therein. Neoconservative critics often decry the attention given to the stratification issue, claiming that in sports such as professional basketball, African American athletes are, as a group, actually overrepresented. Such arguments do little to help understand and why many ethnic/racial barriers continue to exist for minorities in most sports leagues or organizations. Without question, the battle over these highly coveted and racially segregated positions will continue.

See also Commercializing Ethnic Athletes; Cool Pose; Racial Profiling and Stacking.

Further Reading: Bass, A. (2005). *In the Game: Race, Identity and Sports in the Twentieth Century.* London: Palgrave Macmillan; Elias, N., and Scotson, J. (1965). *The Established and the Outsiders.* London: Frank Cass & Company; Miller, P. (2003). *Sport and the*

Color Line: Black Athletes and Race Relations in Twentieth Century America. London: Routledge; Powell, S. (2007). *Souled Out: How Blacks are Winning and Losing in Sports.* Champaign, IL: Human Kinetics; Rhoden, W. (2007). *Third and a Mile.* New York: ESPN; Ross, C. (2005). *Race and Sport: The Struggle for Equality on and Off the Field.* Jackson: University of Mississippi Press.

Michael Atkinson

F

FIELD INVASIONS

Field invasions, or "rushing the field" or "storming the court" as they may also be called, are rather common occurrences, although increasingly challenged, in college and professional sports. These events involve either an individual or collective act wherein fans physically transgress boundaries separating themselves and players and enter onto the field of play. Most forms of field invasion occur after a sports team wins a championship or upsets a higher-ranked team, and fans huddle around players and cheer. Thus, they arise in emotionally charged, positive social contexts of celebration. However, at other times field invasions are carried out by an individual intent to disrupt a sports event while it happens, to wage a form of political protest through sports, or to physically injury a player.

BACKGROUND

The history of professional and college sports in North America is replete with images and scenes of fans jubilantly surrounding players on the field following dramatic victories. Even though fans have been barred from entering onto the field practically since the inception of the modern sports stadium in North America, it has been generally permitted in exceptional cases such as a college bowl game victory, a World Series win, or after an unthinkable upset.

In the first instance, field invasions are most frequently collective forms of social action that might be mildly destructive but certainly tame forms of crowd contagion and expression. The most typical form of a field invasion sees fans, almost on cue, enter onto a field a play to celebrate a noteworthy victory. This phenomenon is most common in U.S. college sports, especially football. Traditionally, when fans rush the field at a football game, the goalposts are torn down by the spectators, and the sod is torn up in places. The ritual destruction of the field is mainly excused by football insiders as a form of social catharsis; fans becoming so carried away with tension and anxiety about an outcome in a game that when victory is finally achieved, they can hardly contain their joy and resort to symbolic acts of tension release. The cost of repairs and the danger to players and fans has caused many teams to employ riot police to physically prevent fans from rushing the field, a controversy in and of itself.

College basketball has a similar phenomenon, known as "storming the court." This normally happens when a team pulls off a major upset or defeats a major rival, and it is somewhat *de rigueur* on the lower levels of the sport. However, more recently some conferences have begun cracking down on excessive court invasions. For example, when University of Tennessee fans stormed the court after a major victory over number two ranked (and eventual national champion) University of Florida at the Thompson-Boling Arena in 2006, the National Collegiate Athletic Association's (NCAA) Southeastern Conference fined the Tennessee athletic department $25,000 for failure to control its fans.

These patterned cultural traditions in college sports such as football are generally tolerated, even though they are expressly deviant according to NCAA rules, which banned field invasions outright in 2004. Collective field invasions are not tolerated, however, when they take a more vitriolic and destructive tone.

One of the quintessential examples of intolerable field invasion occurred on July 12, 1979, in a professional baseball game featuring the Detroit Tigers and Chicago White Sox. In a promotion famously known as "Disco Demolition Night," fans were invited to bring disco records with them to Comiskey Park in a collective show of disgust for the music genre. The records were to be destroyed in-between games of a doubleheader. Fans became so caught up in the anti-disco

---

INNOCENT CELEBRATIONS OR DISRUPTIVE THREATS?

When Chris Chambliss hit a walk-off home run in game five of the 1976 American League Championship Series to send the New York Yankees to their first World Series in 12 seasons, fans rushed onto the field while Chambliss circled the bases. The scene was so frenetic that Chambliss himself was not even sure he touched home plate in the chaos and had to be escorted back onto the field after fans had left to step on home plate in view of the home plate umpire.

The University of Kentucky football team looked as if they would complete a historic home upset of Louisiana State University (LSU) in 2002 when they held a 30–27 lead with two seconds left in the game and LSU with the ball at their own 26-yard line. As LSU Quarterback Marcus Randall threw a last-second desperation pass downfield, fans rushed onto the edges of the field ready to celebrate Kentucky's victory. The pass was caught by LSU wide receiver Devery Henderson, who then ran into the end zone to cap a 33–30 win for LSU, leaving the fans on the field stunned. The play would come to be known as the Bluegrass Miracle.

mania that a near-riot broke out in the bleachers that eventually spilled out onto the field. The second game of the evening had to be cancelled. Such public displays of socially disintegrative crowd contagion, while common in global soccer, rugby, and even cricket cultures, remain very rare in North American sports.

Far more problematic and difficult to either predict or control with any measure of consistency is when an individual commits a solitary act of field invasion. In North America, baseball has been the main sport in which individual field invasions have occurred. Speculation holds that because of the mass audience baseball games draw, the sheer number of professional games during a year, and the amount of media coverage devoted to baseball, the sport has become a battleground for people seeking to make statements, or conduct self-promotional "stunts," on the field of play. From time to time, people enter onto the field to physically attack players or officials in either premeditated or spontaneous (and emotionally charged) acts.

One of the most prevalent forms of individual field invasion is streaking. A practice made popular in British sports in the 1970s, especially at the Wimbledon tennis tournament, streaking consists of a person shedding their clothing and running onto a field of play. In 2004, during Super Bowl XXXVIII between the New England Patriots and the Carolina Panthers, streaker Mark Roberts disrupted the game by running onto the field. The event ended in shame for Roberts, however, when Patriots linebacker Matt Chatham hit Roberts and knocked him to the ground. Despite the worldwide audience, this event was largely unnoticed due to that game's infamous halftime show wherein signer Justin Timberlake exposed Janet Jackson's breast at the conclusion of their stage performance. At the 2007 "Labor Day Classic" Canadian Football League game between the Edmonton Eskimos and the host Calgary Stampeders, seven streakers entered the field. Four of the seven were eventually caught and arrested and charged with performing an indecent exhibition in a public place. In 2002, a naked 21-year-old Tim Hurlbut jumped over the glass partition encircling the ice during a Calgary Flames National Hockey League (NHL) game. Embarrassingly for Hurlbut, he slipped as he landed, fell backwards, and was knocked unconscious. The game had to be stopped for over five minutes while medical staff attended to him. Hurlbut suffered from post-concussion syndrome and was sentenced to 35 hours of community service and fined $2,500 by a Calgary court.

At a 1993 professional boxing match between Riddick Bowe and Evander Holyfield at Caesars Palace in Las Vegas, 29-year-old James Miller decided to use the event as a stage for protesting violence in sports and society. Miller descended from the sky toward the ring in a parachute powered by a giant fan. During the descent the chute's cords became tangled in the ring lights and caught up in the ropes. Bowe's entourage attacked Miller and sent him to the hospital with multiple injuries. Only two months later, Miller extended his political crusade by repeating the feat at a National Football League (NFL) game at the Los Angeles Coliseum between the Denver Broncos and the Los Angeles Raiders. He then switched countries, making an appearance at an FA Cup match between British soccer teams Bolton and Arsenal in 1994. He "buzz bombed" the match, flying low over Bolton's Burnden Park. A month later, naked and painted green, Miller flew his parachute along Pall Mall in London, then circled Buckingham Palace three times before landing on the roof.

For some, collective and individual forms of field invasion are not grave social problems in sports, largely due to their sporadic occurrence and the minimally disruptive or injurious nature of their outcomes. While each of the aforementioned cases might seemingly support such a claim, landmark cases in North America and European sports illustrate how disruptive, and potentially deadly, patterned collective invasions and serial invaders can become.

KEY EVENTS

Whether recognized or not by sports fans, field invasions have altered the course of sports events over the past four decades, have threatened the safety of particular athletes and fans, and have contributed to what we might call the commercial "Disneyfication" of modern sports events, where the spectacle entertainment and drama on the field is far more important than the content of games themselves.

A person who almost single-handedly ushered in a new era of field invasions, and cemented a tradition of using them to make sports more commercially exciting, was Morganna "The Kissing Bandit" Roberts. From 1971 to 1995, Roberts stormed amateur and professional fields of play (predominantly baseball) to kiss players on the cheek. Morganna was only 17 when a friend dared her to run out on the field at a 1971 Cincinnati Reds game at Riverfront Stadium and kiss Pete Rose. It was the first of dozens of big-league baseball kisses and one of hundreds involving entertainers and other athletes for Morganna. She used her field invasion publicity to promote her career as a featured exotic dancer. Teams reputedly paid Morganna to "spontaneously" rush their fields and kiss high-profile athletes as part of publicity stunt campaigns. For her field invasions, she was arrested and charged with trespassing nearly 20 times. Although laughable and light-hearted to a certain degree, Morganna's antics show how field invasions can be tactically used, by individuals or teams, for strict financial gain and status enhancement.

In the final seconds of the game between Stanford University and the University of California (Berkeley) on November 20, 1982, Stanford music band members (as well as players from both teams) ran out onto the field during the last play of the game (a kickoff to University of California), thinking the game was over. University of California players amazingly lateraled the kickoff back and forth down the field and dodged through the band to eventually score a winning touchdown. "The Play" is celebrated by University of California fans, and to this day, remains one of the most famous plays in U.S. football history. The NCAA did not find as much to revere in the event and warned football teams that in the future severe penalties would be levied for similar events. Stanford players have often argued that in the absence of the chaos on the field, they might have very well stopped the play.

The college tradition of rushing the field and dismantling goal posts came to a relative end in 2005 following the tragic death of a college student in Minnesota.

On October 23, 2005, 20-year-old University of Minnesota-Morris student Richard Rose was killed when football fans pulled down a goal post at the end of the Minnesota-Morris 34–28 overtime homecoming win over state rival Crown College. Rose was a junior at Minnesota-Morris and a member of the men's basketball team. The event occurred only one year after the NCAA had instituted new rules to strictly limit any type of postevent field invasions.

Equally disturbing as the Rose case, the stabbing of tennis player Monica Seles at the 1993 German Open illustrated how lazy security efforts had become in many sports cultures. By 1993, Seles, the top-ranked women's player, had won eight grand slam titles and was poised to surpass the record of her close rival, German-born Steffi Graf. Fanatic Graf supporter Günther Parche charged from the stands onto the court during Seles's quarter-final match against Manuela Maleeva and drove a knife into her back. German police and prosecutors mishandled Parche's arrest and trial, and he was acquitted of all charges. Seles returned to tennis in 1995, but she never retained her dominant form for the remainder of her career. In light of the Seles attack, a new era of surveillance dawned on professional sports. For nearly a decade, there were no similar incidents of fans attacking players or officials. But then, in 2003, Kansas City Royals first base coach Tom Gamboa was assaulted while on the field by a father and son at Chicago's Comiskey Park. Only seven months later, first base umpire Laz Diaz was assaulted by a White Sox fan who entered the field of play during another game at Comiskey Park.

The most recent serious incident occurred during the 2004 Athens Summer Olympics when Cornelius Horan attacked Brazilian marathoner Vanderlei de Lima. With just three miles to go, leader Vanderlei de Lima of Brazil was jumped by Horan—who was dressed in a medieval costume—and pulled into the crowd of spectators lining the marathon route. De Lima recovered but eventually finished with a bronze medal. This was not the first time Horan, a defrocked priest, had invaded a sports field. In July 2003, dressed in similar garb, he ran onto the track at the British Grand Prix. Cars traveling at speeds of 200 mph were forced to swerve to avoid him. On that occasion, he was carrying a sign that read, "Read the Bible. The Bible is always right."

These events indicate the while spectators and players are told to believe that sports events are secured social zones, the harsh reality of contemporary sports is that officials can neither predict nor completely contain people from engaging in field invasions. The current climate of zero-tolerance toward security violators in North America aside, it is difficult to ignore how field invasions are patterned forms of social deviance in sports.

FUTURE PROSPECTS

Whether field invasions are attributed to the misguided collective expression of fan emotion, sports-specific subcultural traditions, the platform for self-promotion created in sports by its own mass mediation, or to the unpredictable and random acts of social "bad apples," one cannot overlook that field invasions establish dangerous battlegrounds in sports. There are definitive patterns in, and meanings attributed to, field invasions that need to be studied with more urgency and focus by agents of social control inside and outside of sports. In a post–September 11, 2001 world, there are scant grounds to claim that issues in security at sports and other mass crowd events should not figure prominently in the social planning of them.

See also Criminal Violence During Competition; Hooliganism; Missile Throwing; Parent Misconduct; Player–Fan Fighting; Postevent Riots; Publicity in Sports; Referee Abuse; Soccer Tragedies.

Further Reading: Crawford, G. (2004). *Consuming Sport: Fans, Sport and Culture*. London: Routledge; Guttmann, A. (1986). *Sports Spectators*. New York: Columbia University Press; Wann, D., Melnick, M., Russell, G., and Pease, D. (2001). *Sports Fans: The Psychological and Social Impacts of Spectators*. London: Routledge.

Michael Atkinson

FUNDING EQUALITY LEGISLATION

Women's intercollegiate athletic participation has a long history filled with triumphs and struggles. Unlike their male counterparts, these young women received little assistance from their respective academic institutions. Female athletes received no athletic scholarships and very little financial support from institutions for coaches, uniforms, travel, locker rooms, medical assistance, or athletic training. The women's facilities were typically inferior to their male counterparts, and they had little access to the athletic facilities that were reserved for the men's varsity teams. However, despite these obstacles, over 16,000 women participated on college and university varsity teams throughout the United States during the early 1970s (Carpenter and Acosta, 2008). Women's teams and organizations lobbied for years for more financial support and better facilities, only to receive little notice. When Title IX was passed by the U.S. Congress on June 23, 1972, women's intercollegiate athletics programs were changed forever.

BACKGROUND

Women's participation in sports on college campuses across the United States initially began prior to the turn of the twentieth century when physical educators sought to enhance students' health through light physical activity. Physical culture specialists trained future female physical education instructors on the appropriate forms of physical activity for young girls and women. Female

---

TITLE IX

Title IX of the Education Amendments of 1972, 20 U.S.C. Sect. 1681 (20 U.S. Code section 1681) et seq. (Title IX), is a federal statute that was created to prohibit sex discrimination in education programs that receive federal financial assistance. Nearly every educational institution is a recipient of federal funds and, thus, is required to comply with Title IX.

students were encouraged to take part in activities that enhanced and developed their physique and prepared their bodies for their future roles as wives and mothers. For example, light calisthenics and gymnastics exercises were considered ideal forms of physical activity because they helped to foster grace, elegance, and muscular endurance, all of which were required to perform daily household tasks.

Interest in physical education began to grow and foster after the turn of the twentieth century and was complimented in the growing popularity of competitive women's sports that was occurring inside and outside of academic institutions. However, competitive sports were not supported by all female physical educators. For example, in 1923, one group of influential female physical educators in the United States banded together to fight against all forms of competitive sports, which they believed threatened female athletes moral and physical well-being. The women established the Women's Division of the National Amateur Athletic Federation (WDNAAF), and their national platform was a "sport for every girl and every girl in a sport" (Cahn, 1994, 65). The WDNAAF supported physical activity for girls and women, but they emphasized that women were inherently weaker and frailer than men, and thus, sports should be modified to fit the specific capabilities and needs of girls and women. Many were concerned that competitive sports would render female athletes incapable of bearing children and would result in the masculinization of the female physique. Unmodified sports were said to endanger women's reproductive health, however, they could not find conclusive data to support this argument.

The WDNAAF also condemned competitive sports because they led to the exploitation of female athletes by athletic organizations and academic institutions. They opposed the objectification of the athlete and the increasing commercialization of male sports and argued that these trends should be resisted in women's sports. Furthermore, the WDNAAF was opposed to the corruption they witnessed within men's competitive sports and were appalled by the attitudes they witnessed in men's intercollegiate athletics. Thus, they rejected the "win at all costs" mentality. As a result, women's intercollegiate competition was banned in favor of "play days." Play days were organized in order for several colleges to come together to participate in noncompetitive activities and socialize with other college women. Participants often had no prior training or organization, and young women from the different schools in attendance were simply arranged into mixed teams in order to avoid individual institutions competing against each other. As a way to further support the noncompetitive and cooperative atmosphere, no special awards for athletic skill or achievement were awarded to the participants. The WDNAAF wanted women to participate in appropriate sports, and the only way to ensure that this occurred was for the control of women's sports to be in the hands of female physical educators and sports administrators.

While the members of the WDNAAF did not support competitive sports for girls and women, many other physical educators argued that equality was only achieved if women and men participated in the same sports at the same competitive levels. This approach to equal opportunities for women in sports was "accepted as 'commonsense' by the majority of people pioneering for improvements for women in sports" (Hargreaves, 1994, 29). Arguably, this was an accepted approach for both women and men because rather than challenge male sports, it endorsed them.

Although the WDNAAF was disbanded, the Association for Intercollegiate Athletics for Women (AIAW) was founded in 1971. The AIAW was administered by women for women's athletics and pledged to avoid the pitfalls that had plagued men's intercollegiate athletics, including athletic scholarships, recruiting gifted athletes, and a win-at-all-costs philosophy. The AIAW sponsored several national championships, beginning in 1969 with gymnastics and track and field. Volleyball and badminton championships were added in 1970, and in 1972, the AIAW sponsored their first women's basketball championships.

KEY EVENTS

During the 1960s and early 1970s, some groups of citizens openly protested against inequalities, including civil rights, women's rights, and peace movements, and demanded that the federal government take initiative and establish legislation that prohibited any form of discrimination against human beings. Liberal feminist organizations sought for reform to create opportunities for women that had previously been inaccessible. These organizations argued that the only way to achieve equity for women was "through the development and use of legal and social policies, such as Human rights and Equal Opportunity legislation" (Thompson, 2002, 109). It was believed that gender equity could be enhanced by changes in current laws, ensuring that women were provided with the same opportunities men were provided.

In 1970, U.S. Congressional Representative Edith Green chaired a series of hearings for the Special House Subcommittee on Education to assess the level of sex discrimination in education institutions across the country and found that schools overtly discriminated against female students. Green's commission set forth to draft federal legislation that stipulated, "[n]o person in the United States shall, on the basis of sex, be excluded from participation in, be denied the benefits of, or be subjected to discrimination under any education program or activity receiving Federal financial assistance" (Staurowsky, 2003, 100).

While the legislation did not mention athletics or athletics programs, Title IX brought about a revolution in women's sports. For intercollegiate athletic

KEY LOBBYISTS

Edith Starrett Green (1910–1987) was a Representative from Oregon who served as a member of the Presidential Commission on Status of Women. Green was the second woman to be elected to the House from Oregon and was only 1 of 17 women in the House at the time of her election. In 1955, her first year in the House, she proposed the Equal Pay Act, a bill that was signed into law in 1963. This bill ensured that women and men were paid equally for equal work. She served from January 3, 1955, until her resignation December 31, 1974.

programs, this meant that academic institutions that offered men's sports programs were required by law to provide opportunities for women in proportion to the number of female students at the school. Women's athletic programs were, theoretically, expected to receive the same financial support as their male counterparts. However, the enormous disparity of financial support received by women's programs made this equalization problematic. For example, in 1969, the Syracuse, New York, school board's budget for extracurricular sports allocated $90,000 for the boys' teams and $200 for the girls' teams. At the University of Washington in Seattle, the 1973–1974 budget for the men's varsity athletic program was $2,582,000, while the women's was a mere $18,000. The average expenditure on women's intercollegiate sports for the National Collegiate Athletic Association's (NCAA) Division I schools was $27,000, only 2 percent of the overall athletic budget (Guttmann, 1991).

Significant backlash ensued after the implementation of Title IX. Many were concerned that adherence to this piece of legislation would mean that men's programs would suffer because their budgets would be cut in order to finance the women's. The strongest opposition to Title IX came from the NCAA, the national governing body for intercollegiate sports. Executive director Walter Byers denounced the federal legislation and proclaimed that it would spell the "possible doom of intercollegiate sports" (Carpenter, 1993). The NCAA lobbied to Congress in 1974 to exempt athletic departments from Title IX requirements, however, their efforts were to no avail. Institutions were given until 1978 to comply or risk being fined or having their federal funding removed.

By the end of the 1970s, many within the NCAA recognized that athletic departments would have to increase their support for women's sports in order to comply with Title IX regulations. They indicated that in order to comply with its obligations under Title IX, they would sponsor women's national intercollegiate championships. During the 1981–1982 school year, the NCAA sponsored its first 10 championships for women's intercollegiate athletics. While the NCAA's sponsorship of women's intercollegiate championships did signify a new beginning for women's sports, it also marked the end of the AIAW. Unable to retain their membership, due to the interest in being part of the NCAA, the AIAW disbanded in 1983.

FUTURE PROSPECTS

The introduction of Title IX has had a significant impact on women's sports. In 1968, 16,000 female college athletes participated in varsity sports; in 2008, 9,101 varsity women's intercollegiate *teams* exist in the NCAA (Carpenter and Acosta, 2008). Currently, there are over 180,000 female athletes participating in intercollegiate sports in the United States.

While Title IX has helped to dramatically increase the number of girls and women participating in intercollegiate sports, there have also been some negatives. Prior to Title IX, women coached more than 90 percent of women's college teams, but in 2008, women held less than 43 percent of these positions. Additionally, prior to 1972, women held more than 90 percent of athletic director positions for women's intercollegiate programs. After the enactment of Title IX, schools eventually amalgamated their men's and women's athletic programs. As such, female athletic directors were either replaced by men, or their positions were eliminated. Currently, a little over 21 percent of athletic directors are women, and less than 12 percent of schools have absolutely no female athletic administrators. Some sports sociologists have argued that the increased professionalization of sports has resulted in fewer women holding positions of power in sports organizations. Ultimately, female sports administrators have traded control over sports for greater access to sporting opportunities for athletes.

See also Gender and Educational Opportunities; Gender and Game Rules; Sports for All and Fair Play Leagues; Women and the Apologetic; Women Coaches and Owners; Women Sportscasters.

Further Reading: Cahn, S. (1994). *Coming on Strong: Gender and Sexuality in Twentieth-Century Women's Sport*. Cambridge, MA: Harvard University Press; Carpenter, L. (1993). Letters Home: My Life with Title IX. In *Women in Sport: Issues and Controversies*, ed. G. Cohen. Newbury Park, CA: Sage Publications; Carpenter, L. J., and Acosta, R. V. (2008). "Women in Intercollegiate Sport: A Longitudinal, National Study Thirty One Year Update 1977–2008." http://webpages.charter.net/womeninsport/2008%20Summary%20Final.pdf; Guttmann, A. (1991). *Women's Sports: A History*. New York: Columbia University Press; Hargreaves, J. (1994). *Sporting Females: Critical Issues in the History and Sociology of Women's Sports*. London: Routledge; Mechikoff, R,, and Estes, S. (1993). *A History and Philosophy of Sport and Physical Education*. Madison, WI: Brown & Benchmark Publishing. http://ncaa.org/about/history.html; Staurowsky, E. J. (2003). "Title IX and College Sport: The Long Painful Path to Compliance and Reform," *Marquette Sports Law Review* 14: 100; Thompson, S. M. (2002). "Sport, Gender, Feminism." In *Theory, Sport & Society*, edited by Joseph Maguire and Kevin Young, 105–128. London: JAI Press.

Amanda N. Schweinbenz

G

GAMBLING

Gambling has been prevalent in sports leagues since the first ball was thrown or the first horseshoe was tossed. Gambling incidences remain alarming to fans, sports leagues, and sponsors and are a hot topic in today's sporting atmosphere. However, gambling has a positive side for sports leagues because it creates additional interest in the games. In some countries around the world (Canada and England, for example), revenues from sports gambling fund general programs for the country's citizens.

BACKGROUND

Gambling on sports has both positive and negative aspects in the view of professional sports leagues. On one side, gambling on sports matches raises the interest in the matches and increases fan interest, which is positive from a league/team standpoint. The other side of gambling, though, is serious for sports leagues: when athletes, coaches, officials, and other sports personnel gamble on a sport; leak inside information to gamblers regarding a particular match; or engage in "throwing the match." When Major League Baseball's (MLB) all-time hits leader Pete Rose received a lifetime ban for gambling on MLB games, it illustrated the negative side of gambling in professional sports. Gambling can create debt to bookmakers; when athletes cannot pay off the debts to the bookmakers, athletes become susceptible to the bookmakers demands. When this occurs, the integrity of the game is at risk within professional and amateur sports.

When the perception of uncertainty of game outcome decreases, the integrity erodes. A definition of *uncertainty of outcome* is a degree of unpredictability about a result of a sports contest. Uncertainty of match outcome is the core product of a sports league that separates sports from other entertainment options such as movies and amusement parks. Sports leagues must pay close attention to any rumors relating to athletes or other employees gambling, which could effect the perception that the uncertainty of game outcomes is threatened, and they must take swift action when necessary. The early culture of gambling within MLB highlights the conflict that professional sports leagues face when dealing with gambling because it highlighted both the challenges faced by a young league and the difficulty in balancing both sides of gambling.

The formation of MLB began in 1857 when the organizers (14 baseball clubs) chartered the National Association of Base Ball Players in response to increased popularity and the desire for baseball to become a national sport. Before the agreement, fixing games (when a match with a supposed uncertain result actually has a predetermined result) was common practice among the teams. The agreement by the new organization prohibited betting by the members. The intention was to rid the sport of gambling and fixing games. However, in examining media reports at the time, the perception of match fixing was still present within the young baseball league. For example, 10 years later in 1867, national publications stated gamblers were jeopardizing both the popularity and the game of baseball.

Professionalization first began in 1869 with the Cincinnati Red Stockings. Professionalization was important because it gave salaries to players. By providing salaries, baseball was hoping to deter players from taking money from bookmakers and other gamblers. If baseball allowed these people to control the league, the core product of the game, uncertainty of outcome, would be gone, and the integrity of the game would be lost.

The early culture of baseball provided the context to examine the biggest challenge for the young league, which was the famous "Black Sox scandal" in 1919. Eight members from the Chicago White Sox baseball club took money in exchange for fixing the 1919 World Series against the Cincinnati Reds. Major League Baseball's first commissioner, Kenesaw Mountain Landis, banned the eight Chicago White Sox players for life after allegations were made. Dan Gutman detailed the daily account of the Black Sox scandal in his book *Baseball Babylon,* and he says the eight fixed the series due to the low salaries that each player earned from White Sox owner Charles Comisky. According to Roger Abrams, the scandal was the most serious threat to the integrity and legitimacy of baseball. The punishment that Landis inflicted was two-fold. First, it was to punish the players for fixing the World Series. Second, and more important, the punishment was given to deter future MLB players from engaging in any type of match fixing activity. The punishment set a precedent for both MLB and other professional sports leagues.

KEY EVENTS

Two later events in MLB reinforced their stance on match fixing. The first event occurred in 1979 involving MLB Hall of Famer Willie Mays. In 1979, Mays signed a 10-year contract with a New Jersey casino. Upon signing of this contract, MLB Commissioner Bowie Kuhn banned Mays from associating himself with the game of baseball and with any MLB team. It was Kuhn's belief that current and former MLB players cannot and should not associate themselves with casinos or other forms of gambling. Mays did not fight the punishment inflicted by Kuhn, but he did comment that being banned from baseball stereotypes him into the crowd of the 1919 Black Sox players. Four years later, Hall of Famer Mickey Mantle also signed a contract with a New Jersey–based casino. As with Mays, Mantle had to disassociate himself with MLB due to the conflict between gambling institutions and professional sports. In 1985, Commissioner Peter Ueberroth reinstated both players to MLB.

Another event involved Pete Rose. Pete Rose is baseball's all-time career hits leader and played in the majors from 1963–1986, and he was a manager of the Cincinnati Reds from 1984–1989 with the first three seasons as a player/manager. Rumors circulated in the press regarding Pete Rose and gambling as early as 1987. Initially, reports stated Rose bet on horse racing and college basketball games, among other gambling activities (none baseball related). In spring training 1989, Commissioner Peter Ueberroth and Commissioner Elect A. Bartlett Giamatti met with Rose to discuss his gambling. An investigation later found Pete Rose bet on baseball, and Giamatti banned Pete Rose from the sport in August 1989 following constant injunctions and appeals in the U.S. court system. However, in accepting the ban, Rose never had to admit he bet on baseball.

On announcing Rose's banishment from baseball, Commissioner Giamatti stated the game of baseball would be hurt but would recover from this scandal. Ironically, Giamatti died September 1, 1989, roughly one week after announcing the banning of Rose. In 2004, Rose admitted in his autobiography that he did bet on baseball, and as of August 2008, Rose has not been reinstated and is not eligible for MLB's Hall of Fame.

More recent events with gambling and match fixing highlight the seriousness of this issue to sports leagues in conveying to their fans that matches are pure and fair. In the early 1990s, the National Basketball Association (NBA) had issues with "friendly wagers" between Charles Barkley and Mark Jackson during a game. Reports indicated that Barkley bet Jackson $1,000 that he (Barkley) would make two late-game free throws. Then, Barkley bet Jackson again that Jackson could not hit the game-tying three pointer. Both players received a $5,000 fine from the NBA. Commissioner David Stern commented that even the slightest appearance of gambling on a game is a serious matter.

A second friendly wager occurred between head coach George Karl and his Seattle Supersonics team. Karl said he would buy the whole team new computers if they won 60 games. The commissioner's office heard about the wager, and Karl subsequently had computers donated to the players.

Karl also engaged in friendly wagers with his point guard Gary Payton. The amount of the wagers was unclear, but the wagers were an additional incentive for Payton to reach performance goals. The league halted the wagers right away. Media reports said Karl and Payton engaged in some friendly wagers the previous season without the NBA either having knowledge of the wagers or taking action regarding the wagers.

In 2006, scandal rocked the Serie A soccer league (the Italian version of the English Premiership League). Luciano Moggi, the general manager of Juventus, the most popular team in Serie A, had organized match fixing. Reports surfaced of taped telephone conversations between Moggi and a league official who handed out the referee assignments for the matches. The match fixing was on two levels. First, the referees for matches involving Juventus would not give yellow cards to Juventus players for appropriate fouls, would award borderline calls to Juventus, and would disallow perfectly legit goals scored against Juventus. The second level is more complex: For games including upcoming Juventus opponents, officials booked (red carded) star opposing players so these players would be suspended for the Juventus game.

Two opposing clubs sensed that match fixing was occurring within Serie A, however, facing relegation to Serie B (the level below Serie A), these teams decided to join the match fixing instead of combating it. In the end, four Serie A teams—Juventus, AC Milan, Fiorentina, and Lazio—were investigated and charged with sports fraud. The sports fraud law in Italy was revised in 1989 following an Italian Soccer League match fixing scandal in 1980. The law punishes attempts to alter match outcomes.

The original punishments for these four teams included relegation to Serie B as well as a point penalty, the steepest being for Juventus. The point penalties almost guaranteed Juventus would not be promoted back into Serie A for a couple of seasons. The financial ramifications of being relegated into a lower division can also be steep. An appeals court, however, lessoned the penalties imposed to the four clubs as follows: Juventus received relegation to Serie B along with a 17-point penalty; Lazio was not relegated but received an 11-point penalty; Fiorentina was not relegated but received a 19-point penalty; and AC Milan was not relegated but received an 8-point penalty. Additionally, Lazio and Fiorentina were both ineligible for the Champions League and the Union of European Football Association (UEFA) Cup. Both tournaments bring additional financial streams to the participating clubs.

Tennis is a popular sport to gamble on. One of the biggest online gambling sites, Betfair, reported tennis was the fastest growing bet sport and the third largest bet sport in the world. Tennis also illustrates both sides of the gambling issue because when the gambling community recognized tennis as a viable commodity, interest in tennis increased. However, in 2007, pro tennis was threatened with its own match fixing scandal that threatened the uncertainty of match outcomes and the integrity of the league.

This scandal occurred in August 2007 between 4th-ranked Nikolay Davydenko and 87th-ranked Martin Vassallo Arguello. Davydenko won the first set, lost the second set, and then retired in the third set due to an injury. Betfair noticed an anomaly in the betting pattern, declared the bets void, and notified the International Tennis Federation (ITF). The agreement between gambling companies such as Betfair and sports leagues represents a partnership to make sure the sport is pure and uncertainty of outcome remains at its highest level.

What happened in the betting market was fascinating. Davydenko should have been the heavy favorite in the match. However, a large volume of bets was

TIM DONAGHY

Players are not the only people who can fix matches. In July 2007, NBA official Tim Donaghy faced allegations that he placed bets on NBA games, including games he officiated. The incident received media attention from all over the world. Media outlets and columnists commented that this was the worst blow for the NBA. Without the integrity of the game, columnists said, the NBA becomes a normal television show. Immediately, Commissioner David Stern assured the public that every resource was being used to investigate the threat of the allegations. Donaghy plead guilty in August of 2007 to charges of betting on games and taking part in a match-fixing scandal. As a result of the investigation, the NBA hired a person to oversee the league officials and modified its rules regarding referee gambling behavior.

placed on this obscure match, and the volume of bets was leaning heavily toward the challenger Arguello. As a result, Davydenko became a heavy underdog before the match began. After Davydenko won the first set over Arguello, the bets still were heavily favoring Arguello. After Davydenko retired in the third set with a "foot injury," Betfair voided almost $7 million in bets, and the Association of Tennis Professionals (ATP) opened an investigation.

The ATP investigation illustrated a darker side of tennis. At least 10 male players claimed they were approached and asked to fix matches. The situation constituted a dire threat to tennis in the post-1968 professional era. As of 2008, five professional tennis players have been fined and suspended for betting on tennis matches; only one person placed a bet on a match in which he was involved.

At the start of the 2008 season, the Australian Open (one of the four Grand Slam events) implemented measures to reduce the risk of match fixing. Some of these measures included setting up an anonymous hotline for people who had reason to believe a match had been fixed, closing an on-site gambling window, and banning laptop computers in the stands.

Another issue facing tennis currently is injury reports. Injury information is valuable in the gambling community and keeping information private can lead to gamblers pressuring insiders to divulge the inside information that bettors can use to make money. Currently, tennis does not have any type of injury reporting policy, and players do not want to report injuries because they don't want to give any sort of edge to their opponents. The National Football League (NFL) created its injury report rules so gamblers would not try to retrieve the inside information and risk the integrity of the game. It will be interesting to see if tennis implements an injury reporting policy in future years to provide more transparency to both the general and betting publics.

Throughout this entry, the examination has been on match fixing and friendly wagers. The final example illustrates the other side of the gambling issue. In 2006, it was reported in Australian media outlets that Cricket Australia had signed a revenue-sharing agreement with the gambling site Betfair. This agreement followed similar agreements that Betfair had entered into with other Australian professional sports leagues (Australian Rules Football and PGA Australasian Tour). The global sport of cricket has faced many match fixing scandals throughout its history, and by entering into the agreement, Cricket Australia received not only a portion of the profits from wagering on cricket but also access to betting information that could highlight a match that is not "pure," such as the information Betfair uncovered with the professional tennis match between Davydenko and Arguello. In addition to the Australian professional sports leagues, Betfair also has information agreements with other professional leagues such as UEFA, the International Tennis Federation, and the European Football Association.

The profit-sharing agreement between Betfair and Cricket Australia presented a distinct and interesting conflict within the gambling industries. For example, North American professional sports leagues such as the NBA and NFL are hesitant to be perceived as too close to the gambling industry. This is one reason why leagues have been reluctant to place a franchise in Las Vegas, Nevada. As mentioned earlier with the incident between Willie Mays and Mickey Mantle, MLB banned two Hall of Fame players from accepting public relations positions with casinos. Thus, these leagues are trying to maintain the perception of being an "arms length away" from the gambling industry with the rationale of preserving the integrity of the game.

On the other hand, this agreement represents a partnership between the gambling industry and a professional sports league. The uniqueness in this partnership gives Cricket Australia as well as the other Australian professional sports leagues a portion of the gambling profit that Betfair makes from patrons betting on the matches. This may pose a covert threat to uncertainty of match outcome due to the profit incentive that a league has due to this agreement.

FUTURE PROSPECTS

Gambling will always have a presence within professional sports. As the years go by, it will be interesting to see: whether or not more professional leagues enter into partnership agreements with the betting establishments and how the general public perceives these partnership; in more individual sports such as tennis and golf, what measures their commissioners take to preserve the integrity of the game; and finally, how the well-established sports leagues handle gambling and match fixing situations.

See also Cheating During Competition; Criminal Violence During Competition; Governments, Laws, and Gambling; Salaries of Professional Athletes.

Further Reading: Abrams, R. I. (2006). Game-Fixing in the National Game. *Florida Entertainment Law Review* 1 (1): 1–40; Berkovits, S. A. (2005). Gambling on Las Vegas: Bringing Professional Sports to Sin City. *Gaming Law Review* 9 (3): 220–231; Forrest, D., and Simmons, R. (2002). Outcome Uncertainty and Attendance Demand in Sport: The Case of English Soccer. *The Statistician* 51 (2): 229–241; Gutman, D. (1992). *Baseball Babylon: From the Black Sox to Pete Rose, the real stories behind the scandals that rocked the game*. New York: Penguin Books; Mason, D. S. (1999). What is the Sports Product and Who Buys It? The Marketing of Professional Sports Leagues. *European Journal of Marketing* 33 (3/4): 402–418.

Brian P. Soebbing

GAY GAMES

First staged in 1982, the Gay Games is an Olympic-style mega event that brings together members of the global lesbian, gay, bisexual, and transgender (LGBT) community. The brainchild of founders Dr. Tom Waddell, Matt Sprague, and Norris Pyle, the Gay Games were designed as an alternative sporting venue for men and women who felt marginalized and alienated within mainstream, heterosexual dominant sports cultures. Waddell in particular conceived of the Games as an opportunity to resist ideologies of homophobia in American (and indeed global) cultures and to promote gay pride. The Gay Games, now overseen by the Federation of Gay Games (FGG), support an ethos of inclusion rather than exclusion in sports. To this end, there are no qualifying criteria to enter the Games as an athlete. The Games bring novice and veteran athletes together from around the world to compete in over 30 sports including power-lifting, bowling, gymnastics, tennis, sailing, distance running, ice hockey, swimming, triathlon, and billiards. Seven iterations of the Games have been staged since 1982, bringing together athletes from 70 nations; including some for whom homosexual acts or relations are illegal in their countries of origin.

BACKGROUND

Sports and leisure cultures are among the last social spaces where overt homophobia is permitted, or at least socially acceptable, to varying degrees. For all intents and purposes, the Gay Games serve as the most globally recognized contexts of sporting inclusion, fairness, and pride for LGBT athletes. Nevertheless, almost since their inception, the Gay Games have been riddled with controversy and debate regarding normative definitions of sex and sexuality and their cultural representations.

First and foremost, the creation of an outsider or alternative sports context such as the Gay Games has been viewed by some members of LGBT communities as a collective cultural acceptance of their overall outsider status and the deviant nature of homosexuality itself. Rather than making or forcing in-roads in mainstream sports and fighting for human rights for LGBT individuals therein,

THE GAY GAMES TIMELINE

Name	Host City	Opening Date	Number of Athletes
Gay Games I	San Francisco	August 28, 1982	1,600
Gay Games II	San Francisco	August 9, 1986	3,500
Gay Games III	Vancouver, Canada	August 4, 1990	9,500
Gay Games IV	New York	June 18, 1994	11,000
Gay Games V	Amsterdam, NL	August 1, 1998	14,700
Gay Games VI	Sydney, Australia	November 2, 2002	12,000
Gay Games VII	Chicago	July 15, 2006	12,500

retrenchment into a Gay Games might be viewed as an act of cultural submission. Participation in a "queer" sports field only serves to underline the alternativeness/difference of LGBT identities and lifestyles and cleaves straight/gay communities even further. Even though Waddell hoped members of all social groups would compete in the Games, history has proven otherwise and the Gay Games remains a sports event predominantly attended by gay and lesbian communities.

Second, while the Games exude a spirit of competitive seriousness extolled at other sports events, organizers allow for more playful, artistic, and celebratory expressions of LGBT identities to be infused into the Games. For example, the Pink Flamingo Relay continues to be a staple cultural celebration at the Gay Games. The relay is both a quasitraditional sports event in the form of a 100-meter swimming contest and a dramatic pageant. Prior to the start of the swim, participants emerge wearing spectacular costumes and act out carefully choreographed dramatic scenes. Over the course of the relay, two participants on each team are linked together: one swims in front, pulling in a breast-stroke fashion, while the second team member holds the legs of the front swimmer and kicks. A pink flamingo is strapped to the cap of the lead swimmer, and at the 50-meter turnaround point the two participants switch caps and places in the tandem swim. The race is a playful expression of LGBT identity in sports and helps to make the Gay Games unique. While a seemingly insignificant gesture to some, events such as the Pink Flamingo Relay are offered by LGBTs as indicators that modified forms of participation in mainstream sports help to express identities that are generally not accepted elsewhere. As such, the lanes of a swimming pool become public battlegrounds wherein plastic flamingos are employed as symbolic ammunition against bigotry and as shields protecting gay pride.

Third, not everyone has been welcomed openly at the Gay Games over the past two decades. As in the context of the Olympic Games, organizers have grappled with how to classify people into gender divisions who have received sexual realignment surgery, are intersexed, and/or have received hormone/testosterone therapy. The FFG deemed it necessary in 1994 to create a policy stating that, in the interest of fair play and equity, transgendered or intersex participants have to medically prove their sexual status, prove their gender identity in accordance with their medical status (including proof of legal name), and establish that they were actively living in a gender-sex homologous lifestyle in order to compete in a particular gender category. Members of the FGG have argued that in some contact sports, safety issues are created when men who identify with a female gender role compete against women. Equally, women who have received testosterone therapy in the process of sexual realignment may hold a chemical advantage over men in particular sports. Between the 1994 and 2002 Games, lobbyists in the transgender community (people who do not strictly identify with being either male or female) such as Transgender Menace (TM) fought adamantly against the rules, arguing that they violated the ethos of inclusivity at the Games. The FGG relaxed some of its identity "proving" criteria by 2002, but medical proof of one's physical status as a man or woman is still required despite considerable opposition.

Fourth, like other mega events including the Olympic Games, there have been bidding and site controversies over where to hold the Gay Games. The 2006

Games were originally awarded to Montreal, Canada. But, in 2003, the FGG removed Montreal's 2006 mandate to host the Games, citing political–economic differences between the city's organizing committee and the FGG. The Montreal site committee believed that unless the Games were expanded and participation rates nearly doubled, the event would be a net financial loss for the city. Additionally, the Montreal site committee was questioned strenuously by the FGG regarding the amount of money requested to hold the Games and how the money would be managed in Montreal. After nearly a year of contention between the two committees, the FGG removed Montreal's mandate and considered Chicago and Los Angeles as potential host cities. Chicago was eventually awarded the 2006 Games.

As a tactical response to the FGG's decision, the Montreal organizing committee transformed itself into a rival LGBT sports federation and challenged the FGG's hegemony as the governing body of global LGBT sports. They founded the Gay and Lesbian International Sports Association in 2003 and designed a rival World Outgames to be held in Montreal in 2006 just one week before the Gay Games in Chicago. Most global participants in LGBT sports were forced to choose between attending the Gay Games and World Outgames in 2006, and both events suffered financially as a result. The Outgames drew over 12,000 participants and was the largest international sports event held in Montreal after the 1976 Winter Olympic Games. In contrast to the Gay Games, the World Outgames have aggressively recruited corporate sponsors such as Labatt brewing, Air Canada, and Bell Canada. The second World Outgames is scheduled for Copenhagen in 2009, interestingly, one year before the next Gay Games.

KEY EVENTS

There is perhaps no other event in the history of the Gay Games that illustrates the contested nature of LGBT identities in the United States as the "naming controversy" of 1982. Tom Waddell originally called and promoted the Games as the Gay Olympics. Waddell sought to draw on the spirit of global togetherness and inclusion promoted during the global "Olympic Truce" between nations to articulate how sports could be used as a vehicle for combating homophobia and promoting self-esteem among traditionally shunned or closeted members of the community. Waddell perhaps naively believed that the Gay Olympics could be a great social equalizer such that the public showcasing of LGBT excellence through athletics could effectively alter mainstream ideologies of homophobia within and outside of sports.

Just seven weeks before the opening ceremonies, and amid a new moral panic in the United States concerning the spread of what was called GRIDS (Gay-Related-Immuno-Deficiency Syndrome) and then AIDS (after 1983) among the gay population, the U.S. Olympic Committee (USOC) told Waddell to alter the name of the event because it infringed on the Olympic trademark. Even though the term *Olympics* had been used in a variety of sporting contexts without reprisal, such as the Special Olympics, the Police Olympics, the Animal Olympics, the Diaper Olympics, the Xerox Olympics, and even in

WADDELL AND OLYMPIC PROTEST

Tom Waddell was no stranger to either Olympic sports culture or controversy prior to the 1982 Gay Games naming scandal. Waddell qualified for and competed in the 1968 Olympic Games in Mexico as a decathlete and placed a respectable sixth overall in the event. At the Games, Waddell spoke out publicly against the racism experienced by African American members of the track and field team, Tommy Smith and John Carlos. Smith and Carlos were excused from the U.S. Olympic team after raising their fists in protest with a Black Power salute during the meal ceremonies for the men's 200-meter dash. Waddell publicly criticized their removal as a racist response by the USOC, leading some to speculate that the 1982 injunction against the use of the term *Gay Olympics* served as the retribution.

modified form for a 1977–1979 Hanna-Barbera cartoon on ABC called the Laff-A-Lympics, the USOC pursued the matter and obtained a court injunction prohibiting Waddell's use of the term. Every piece of Games paraphernalia and publicly distributed promotional material had to be altered or scrapped entirely, costing the event's organizing committee (which had been operating on a miniscule budget) thousands of dollars. Waddell even had a lien placed against his home to recover costs, and Gay Games organizers faced legal harassment through the mid-1980s. Political maneuverings by the USOC cast a shroud of anxiety and controversy over the first Gay Games.

Waddell continued his battle with the USOC over the name until his death in 1987 from AIDS-related physical complications. The Supreme Court of the United States ruled later that year that the USOC had an absolute right to police the use of the term *Olympics* within the United States under corporate trademark law and declared that Gay Games organizers were not victims of homophobic discrimination or civil rights violation. Gay Games organizers are to this day prohibited from even mentioning the term *Olympic* or using any symbolic referent to the Olympic Games (such as the five-colored Olympic rings) during any Gay Games events.

FUTURE PROSPECTS

If participation rates are reliable indicators, the Gay Games is becoming one of the most significant cultural sites for the expression of gay pride and the public contestation of homophobia. The Games might have imploded due to legal, cultural, and scientific controversy in the past decade, but they have remarkably overcome obstacle after obstacle. In many ways, the struggle of and for the Games in the 1980s and 1990s well represents LGBT members' ongoing battle for cultural freedom, the power of self-definition, and social inclusion in the United States and abroad.

See also Biology and Athlete Performance; Homophobia; LGBT Sports Leagues; Openly Gay Athletes; Transsexual Athletes.

Further Reading: Coe, R. (1988). *A Sense of Pride: The Story of Gay Games II*. San Francisco: Pride Publications; Griffin, P. (1998). *Strong Women, Deep Closets: Lesbians and*

Homophobia in Sport. Champaign, IL: Human Kinetics; Pronger, B. (1990). *The Arena of Masculinity: Sports, Homosexuality and the Meaning of Sex.* Toronto: University of Toronto Press; Symons, C., and Hemphill, D. (2006). Transgendering Sex and Sport in the Gay Games. In *Sport, Sexualities and Queer/Theory,* edited by J. Cauldwell, 109–128. London: Routledge; Waddell, T., and Schapp D. (1996). *Gay Olympian: The Life and Death of Tom Waddell.* New York: Alfred A. Knopf.

Michael Atkinson

GENDER AND EDUCATIONAL OPPORTUNITIES

On June 23, 1972, U.S. President Richard Nixon signed into law Title IX of the Higher Education Act. The law reads: "No person in the United States shall, on the basis of sex, be excluded from participation in, be denied the benefits of, or be subjected to discrimination under any education program or activity receiving federal financial assistance." The wording of the law follows the format of Title VI of the Civil Rights Act of 1964, as does Section 504 of the Rehabilitation Act of 1973 for those with disabilities, and the 1975 Age Discrimination Act. Thus, federal court decisions on any one of these laws impact every one of them. The purpose of the law was to open previously closed doors of opportunity for women in educational endeavors. In regard to many areas of primary, secondary, and most importantly higher education, the law fostered considerable change in a short time span. Due in large part to gender restrictive admissions policies, in 1971, women earned only 1 percent of dental degrees, 9 percent of medical degrees, 7 percent of law degrees, and 14 percent of doctoral degrees. By 2005, those numbers had grown to 45 percent of dental degrees, 49 percent of medical degrees, 48 percent of law degrees, and 49 percent of doctoral degrees (U.S. Department of Education, 2007). Yet, these impressive educational gains for women have not been the focus of debates surrounding Title IX. Rather, the impact of Title IX on scholastic athletics has dominated public discourse since the passage of the law—so much so that Title IX is often thought of, and referred to incorrectly, as a sports law.

BACKGROUND

Acosta and Carpenter (2004, 2008) have been tracking women's sports participation since the passage of Title IX, and in 2004, they published *Title IX,* which clearly outlines the policy and scope of the law as well as the cases that have shaped it over time. Currently, the Office for Civil Rights (OCR) of the Department of Education (DOE) oversees Title IX regulation—including enforcement and interpretation. (The Department of Education, formerly the Health, Education and Welfare [HEW] Department, was formed in 1980. All Title IX regulations before 1980 were handled by HEW.) Title IX policy covers three overarching requirement areas in regards to scholastic athletics that were developed throughout the 1970s, finalized in 1979, clarified in 1996, and supported by the most recent OCR review of policy in 2002. The three areas are financial assistance; effective accommodation of students' interests and abilities; and benefits, opportunities, and treatments.

In regards to debates over Title IX, "effective accommodations" is the area that gets the most attention. In order to demonstrate "effective accommodations of student interests and abilities" a three-part test is outlined in Title IX policy. Compliance with Title IX in this area is achieved if *one* of the following three criteria is met: (1) opportunities for male and female athletes are substantially proportionate to their respective undergraduate enrollments; (2) where one sex has been underrepresented, there is a history and continuing practice of program expansion responsive to the interests and abilities of that sex; (3) where one sex is underrepresented, and a history of continuing program expansion cannot be shown, an institution must demonstrate that the present program fully and effectively accommodates the interests and abilities of that sex. While schools can demonstrate compliance by selecting any one of these criteria, the area of substantial proportionality has become synonymous with public understandings of Title IX and remains the focus of debate.

During 1972, the year Title IX quietly slipped through Capitol Hill, the women's liberation movement was in full force, and women seemed determined to explore every avenue previously closed to them. Witness: female firsts as a naval admiral, as a pilot at American Airlines, and as a U.S. forest ranger. While some women tested their endurance by officially running the 26.2 miles of the Boston marathon, other women tested their strength and agility, donning their shoulder pads for a fledgling professional football league, and still others tested membership privileges at upscale athletic clubs. Women entered the inner sanctums in the world of sports in such previously all-male sports occupations as athletic training and facilities maintenance. Meanwhile, the very heart of Americana sports, professional baseball, hired its first woman umpire, Bernice Gera. While clearly impressive, this list remains an unfulfilled promise—a hint at "progress" that never followed.

"Firsts" imply an opened door of opportunity with many women standing on the shoulders of their foremothers in a move toward cultural equality. Instead, as the debate in the 1970s over the passage of the Equal Rights Amendment reflects, as well as the furor over Title IX and athletics that quickly ensued, the issue of gender equality even now is far from settled. As one journalist commented on the Equal Right Amendment, "It's going to be a long and bruising battle, dominated much of the time by emotions, not logic. The senate must decide, in effect, if modern society has made obsolete those intriguing differences between male and female which have enriched the human experience in the past" (Edwards, 1972, p. 26). Clearly, the firsts of the 1970s reflect fields still primarily dominated by men today.

Given current debates over Title IX pitting men's minor sports against women's sports for apparently scarce resources, it is interesting to note the financial issues faced by collegiate athletics even before the passage of Title IX. Yet, as soon as athletics were mentioned within the same breath as Title IX, male football coaches and athletic directors made repeated attempts to exclude football and men's basketball from consideration of equality in educational opportunities between males and females through sports. Then president of the National Collegiate Athletic Association (NCAA) John Fuzak exclaimed that Title IX applied to athletics " 'borders on insanity' that threatens to destroy many university athletic programs." Darrell Royal, then coach and athletic director at the University of Texas, complained that "the end result could very well be that we'd have to give up all athletic programs. Eventually, we can see a dying process for all athletics for both men and women." Needless to say, his worries have not come to fruition as collegiate sports has exploded into a multibillion dollar industry.

KEY EVENTS

While the 1960s and 1970s marked great strides in civil rights and government intervention in gaining institutional access for those who had been marginalized for centuries—women, racial and ethnic minorities, and those with disabilities—in 1980, the political landscape of the United States shifted significantly with the election of Ronald Reagan as President. Although Reagan publicly supported civil rights, the early 1980s are marked by administration attempts to curtail the scope of Title IX and all civil rights legislation. Education Secretary Bell wrote, "Since I had heard Ronald Reagan speak out convincingly against all forms of discrimination, I felt my own dedication to enforcement of civil rights laws as they applied to education would have the full support of the President" (Williams, 1987, p. A16). Yet, that was not to be the case. Eventually Bell resigned in frustration shortly after Reagan's re-election in 1984.

The lack of funding that came with the Reagan administrations' low priority on civil rights had a detrimental impact on the Departments of Education and Justice to carry out investigations and enforcement. Specifically for Title IX, two major events impacted the law in the 1980s. The first was the *Grove City College v. Bell* Supreme Court decision in 1984, which relieved educational institutions from their Title IX obligations in areas that did not directly receive federal funding, including nearly all athletic departments. The second was the Civil Rights Restoration Act of 1988, which passed through the legislature over the veto of President Reagan, restoring the broad meaning of Title IX and other civil rights laws after a four-year struggle in the legislative bodies.

The Reagan administration carefully chose and fostered a legal case in *Grove City College v. Bell* that would effectively change the face of most civil rights laws for the decade to come. Once the Supreme Court sided with the federal interpretation of the narrowed scope of Title IX and other civil rights laws written similarly, thousands of discrimination cases were dropped or narrowed across the country. The expanded power of the executive branch became abundantly clear from the Reagan administration's influence on the Supreme Court to its ties and loyalty within the Senate as legislation set to reverse the *Grove City* decision was continually stymied. As one newspaper columnist wrote: "There's more than one way to kill a cat. If you're a bit on the devious side, you can smother the poor thing to death while murmuring 'nice kitty.' I don't want to accuse Sen. Orrin G. Hatch of deviousness, but his approach to the Civil Rights Restoration Act has the distinct overtones of 'nice kitty' " (Raspberry, 1985, p. A17).

The bond between the New Right and the Religious Right became stronger as the rhetoric of the Reagan administration gave lip service to antidiscrimination even as it was dismantling it legally—all on the platform of religious freedom and individual rights. By enmeshing the Civil Rights Restoration Act within arguments over abortion, the New Right was able to rally the cries of the Religious Right thereby symbolically pitting the civil rights of women, racial minorities, disabled, and elderly against the religious freedoms of those opposed to abortion. Despite the fact that the Civil Rights Act had majority support in both the Senate and House, this strategy kept the issue from coming to a vote for four years.

Since the 1990s, the debate has been framed as an either/or division of resources between men's "minor" sports and women's athletics, with Title IX as the crux of the argument. According to those who view Title IX as a threat to men's minor sports, the rise in participation numbers in women's sports not only correlates to a decrease in men's minor sports participation numbers but is also the cause of that decrease. In response, women's sports advocates argue that the relationship between men's minor sports and women's sports is a spurious one with the confounding factor being the development of a big business sports model within collegiate programs. This model is reflected in the escalating costs of men's football and basketball along with an "arms" race for bigger and more elaborate facilities. They argue that skewed spending within athletic departments has not only contributed to decreases in opportunities in men's minor sports but is also the reason that women continue to receive less than their full share of the athletic pie.

Title IX has also been considered in terms of "unintended consequences," such as the loss of women in positions of power in coaching and administration. Some scholars have examined media representations of wrestling and Title IX, the narratives surrounding the 2002–2003 U.S. Department of Education Commission on Opportunities in Athletics, and the cultural history of the law. Susan Ware (2007) offers a very brief history along with some primary and secondary source documents related to Title IX history from the 1970s, 1990s, and early 2000s. Similarly, editors O'Reilly and Cahn (2007) include a chapter on Title IX in their documentary reader. Hogshead-Makar and Zimbalist (2007) also offer many primary and secondary sources as part of their anthology. Furthermore, Mitchell and Ennis (2007) devote half of their encyclopedia to appendices of Title IX policy, regulation, and interpretation.

There is considerable debate among these writers as to what exactly the "equal opportunity" guaranteed by the law should mean. A look at women's scholastic sports history reveals an ongoing ambivalence toward women playing those sports traditionally understood as men's sports (i.e., wrestling, football) or organizing sports in men's ways (i.e., win-at-all-costs, business-oriented spectator sports). Most support the notion that women's and men's participation does not need to be in the same sports or in the same way for there to be equality. Some even argue that the traditionally women's sports model, with a focus on participation over competition, offers an alternative sports model for both men and women. In contrast, Walton (2003c) notes that one girls' and women's wrestling advocate, Kent Bailo, argues for "equal" to mean the same—the same sports and the same benefits. Thus, if men are afforded the opportunity to play football with

85 scholarships, then women should receive the same. Title IX policy remains flexible in how individual institutions choose to create equity. The main concern of the law, and the courts, remains equal educational opportunities in relation to gender.

In regards to debates since the 1990s about the losses of some men's sports in relation to Title IX, Walton and Helstein (in press), among others, demonstrate that numbers are used selectively to support the notion that the gains in women's sports have come at the cost of men's minor sports. For example, in examining NCAA participation statistics for men's wrestling and women's gymnastics they find that:

> While the number of Division I wrestling programs dropped from 117 in 1981–2 to 86 in 2003–4 (a 25% loss), and in all divisions from 363 to 223 in the same time period (a 39% loss); women's gymnastics teams dropped from 99 Division I programs in 1981–2 to 64 in 2003–4 (a 35% loss), and from 179 to 86 in all divisions (a 52% loss) in the same time period. (Walton and Helstein, in press)

So, while some men's sports and some women's sports have faced considerable losses since the passage of Title IX, men's losses are understood as *caused by* Title IX, while women's sports opportunity losses are not explained. Instead, cuts in particular men's sports are compared to overall gains in women's participation numbers.

More recently, McDonagh and Pappano (2007) argue that rather than promoting women's equal opportunity, gender segregated sports actually hold women back. In keeping with other critiques of Title IX as an example of liberal legislation, they argue that Title IX policy and enforcement fundamentally reinforce the underlying ideology that women are inherently athletically inferior to men. They find that not only is this ideology supported by Title IX, but the use of Title IX to construct separate, and unequal, sporting realms for boys and girls/men and women systematically ensures that women will continue to be understood and socialized as athletically inferior.

There have also been some works produced by politically conservative writers who argue that rather than construct women as athletically inferior, scholastic sports and current uneven participation numbers are actually reflective of essential differences between men and women. This is also a perspective shared by radical feminists. According to this view, women are inherently different from men, and those essential differences lead to different interests. For example, in *The War Against Boys* Christina Hoff Sommers (1994) argues that attempts to feminize boys by making them more caring and less aggressive is unnatural and harmful. She criticizes progressive legislation like Title IX for creating quota systems that essentially hand women opportunities in which they are not even interested and therefore deny them to boys. An example of this perspective specifically targeting Title IX is Jessica Gavora's (2002) *Tilting the Playing Field*. In relation to Title IX, Gavora and others argue that women and men are essentially and naturally different and that women are therefore less interested in sports. This argument holds that men are consequently punished when overall participation rates between men and women are compared to undergraduate enrollment and used to determine compliance with the effective accommodations aspect of Title IX policy. Many anthologies on Title IX include these viewpoints. Politically conservative organizations such as the Independent Women's Forum and the College Sports Council also work to advance these views.

At the same time, many academics and interest groups with a focus on U.S. collegiate athletics have called for reform. Of these, some argue that Title IX could be a spark for a structural reform of college sports. In regards to the way university athletics are structured, Suggs (2005), among others, notes that the hostile takeover by the NCAA of the Association for Intercollegiate Athletics for Women in the early 1980s destroyed an alternate model of athletic governance based on a participatory educational model. "These observers suggest that articulations over Title IX could be a catalyst for understanding the confluence of concerns over men's minor sports, women's rights for equal educational opportunities afforded by Title IX (including those made available through athletics), and also the systematic exploitation of particular collegiate athletes" (Walton and Helstein, in press). Indeed, according to Francis (2001), "efforts to remedy discrimination against women and minorities in university athletics thus take place against a background of at best mixed [ethical] support for the enterprise generally" (p. 252).

In particular, these groups and researchers share concerns about the ethics of running a nonprofit educational endeavor (collegiate athletics) within a business model, with unpaid labor. For example, economist Andrew Zimbalist (1999, 2005, 2007) systematically examines both collegiate sports participation and economic statistics to expose some of the myths surrounding university athletics more generally and Title IX specifically. For example, he exposes the myth that college football programs create enough revenue to support entire athletic departments and instead shows that a large majority of football programs do not make as much as they spend.

FUTURE PROSPECTS

The prominent themes over the last 30 years of mediated debate about Title IX and athletics—the interruption of male sporting space by women, the impact of the law on women's positions of power within athletics, the understanding of what women's increase in resources means for men's minor sports, and the legal issues—have each had material consequences for women within sporting spaces. Further, these debates carry significance far beyond determining allocations of resources between men and women within athletic departments. Mediated and scholarly debates of Title IX offer a window into current and historical articulations of appropriate gender roles given the ways those roles intertwine with understandings of class, ethnicity, and sexuality within the scholastic sporting arena. From the question of "do women belong in sports?" in the 1970s, to questions of deregulation and burdensome government interference in the 1980s, and to the question of "is women's sports killing men's minor sports?" in the 1990s and 2000s, the underlying assumption of sports as male space "invaded" by women is clear, and this drives the ongoing public debates and, as we have seen, the ongoing academic work on Title IX. While Title IX continues to open educational doors for women, athletics remains the popular focus of controversy. As a public and traditional domain of masculinity building that serves to maintain the gender hierarchy, sports remain an important cultural site for understanding shifting power relations.

See also Funding Equality Legislation; Rights for Young Athletes; Women Coaches and Owners; Women in Men's Sports; Women Sportscasters.

Further Reading: Acosta, R. V., and Carpenter, L. J. (2008). Women in Intercollegiate Sport: A Longitudinal, National Study—Thirty-One Year Update. Retrieved March 27, 2008, from http://www.acostacarpenter.org; Carpenter, L. J., and Acosta, R. V. (2004). *Title IX.* Champaign, IL: Human Kinetics; Edwards, W. (1972, Feb. 17). Senate Faces Women's Rights Class. *Chicago Tribune,* sec. 1, p. 26; End of College Sport Forecast: Coaches Opposed to Equal Funding. (1975, June 18). *Los Angeles Times,* III: 1; Francis, L. P. (2001). Title IX: Equality for Women's Sports? In *Ethics in Sport,* edited by W. J. Morgan, K. V. Meier, and A. J. Schneider, 247–266. Champaign, IL: Human Kinetics; Fuzak Urges Review of Title IX Issue. (1975, Sept. 17). *Chicago Tribune,* 6: 3; Gavora, J. (2002). *Tilting the Playing Field: Schools, Sports, Sex and Title IX.* San Francisco, CA: Encounter Books; Hogshead-Makar, N., and Zimbalist, A. (Eds.). (2007). *Equal Play: Title IX and Social Change.* Philadelphia: Temple University Press; McDonagh, E., and Papano, L. (2008). *Playing with the Boys: Why Separate is Not Equal in Sports.* Don Mills, ON: Oxford University Press; Mitchell, N., and Ennis, L. A. (2007). *Encyclopedia of Title IX and Sports.* Westport, CT: Greenwood Press; O'Reilly, J., and Cahn, S. K. (Eds.). (2007). *Women and Sports in the United States: A Documentary Reader.* Boston: Northeastern University Press; Raspberry, W. (1985, April 5). Smothering a Civil Rights Bill. *Washington Post,* p. A17; Suggs, W. (2005). *A Place on the Team: The Triumph and Tragedy of Title IX.* Princeton, NJ: Princeton University Press; U.S. Department of Education, Institute of Educational Sciences. (2007, June). Table 270: First-Professional Degrees Conferred by Degree-Granting Institutions, by Sex of Student, Control of Institution, and Field of Study: Selected Years, 1985–86 Through 2005–06. *Digest of Education Statistics.* Retrieved from http://nces.ed.gov/programs/digest/d07/tables/dt07_270.asp; Walton, T., and Helstein, M. (In press). Triumph of Backlash: Wrestling Community and the 'Problem' of Title IX. *Sociology of Sport Journal* 25 (3); Ware, S. (Ed.). (2007). *Title IX: A Brief History with Documents.* Boston: Bedford/St. Martin's; Williams, L. (1987, Oct 21). Racist Jokes in White House Reported in a Book. *New York Times,* p. A16; Zimbalist, A. (1999). *Unpaid Professionals: Commercialism and Conflict in Big-Time College Sports.* Princeton, NJ: Princeton University Press; Zimbalist, A. (2005). What to Do About Title IX. In *Title IX 30 Years Later: Sporting Equality,* edited by Rita Simon, 71–76. New Brunswick, NJ: Transaction Publishers; Zimbalist, A. (2007). Title IX by the Numbers. In *Equal Play: Title IX and Social Change,* edited by N. Hogshead-Makar and A. Zimbalist, 302–305. Philadelphia: Temple University Press.

Theresa Walton

GENDER AND GAME RULES

Sports is a social place where gendered statuses and identities matter when it comes to determining how games are organized and played. In principal, sports has been used in Western countries such as Canada and the United States as a primary site for confirming young boys' and men's masculinities. While sports has been and continues to be a relative masculine-identity-proving terrain, it has not been a place where a range of femininities have been celebrated. The very structures and cultures of most mainstream sports in North America have been exclusionary along gender lines, and women struggled through the latter half of the twentieth century just to find their own spaces in sports worlds. Even when women do compete in sports, it is often under very different circumstances and social conditions than men. There continues to be two separate and unequal "rules of the game" in many sports; where men play by one set of rules and women by another.

BACKGROUND

Many North American sports, such as baseball, football, ice hockey, tennis, basketball, track and field, and others, operate under a separate and unequal policy with regard to female participation. There are both subtle and overt ways that the rules of participation assert that women are lesser competitors than men. In some instances, the rules seek to underline that women are atypical athletes, or not as strong, fast, able-bodied, or intelligent as their male counterparts. In others instances, behind-the-scenes or seemingly innocuous forms of discrimination serve to undermine women's statuses as legitimate athletes.

The very language of sports is replete with unequal references to women's sports. Linguists have argued that most modern English terms and phrases are essentially male-oriented, in that seemingly neutral terms such as *mankind* refer to all but have a decisively male base. Stated differently, the masculine is taken as the base category in speech. To this end, sports organizations such as the National Hockey League (NHL), the Professional Golfer's Association of America (PGA), and the National Basketball Association (NBA) are the neutral terms for the respective sports of golf and basketball; but each refer to the men's versions of the games. By contrast, women's sports are treated as the *other* version, labeling their professional leagues with an extra prefix, "W" or "L," signifying difference. The acronyms LPGA (Ladies Professional Golf Association) and WNBA (Women's National Basketball Association) all highlight how women's sports tend to be defined after the men's versions, or as a derivative of them.

At the college/university sports level in both the United States and Canada, women's teams are also given different nicknames, by university rule, than the standard men's nicknames (the latter which are adopted by all students in the university). In 2007, as many as 63 four-year colleges and universities at all levels of competition in the United States still included the word "Lady" when labeling at least one women's team. And that list does not include Centenary College of Louisiana and Kenyon College in Ohio, where Ladies stands alone as a nickname (alongside Gents and Lords, respectively). Nor does it include suffix-saddled schools such as Kentucky State, where men are known as the Thorobreds and women as the Thorobrettes, or those employing alternative adjectives. Central Arkansas, for example, is home to both the Bears and the "Sugar" Bears. Female student-athletes at both Delta State and William Penn carry the oxymoronic moniker "Lady Statesmen." Gender-specific nicknames are often used to differentiate men's and women's programs. Critics argue that in keeping these naming traditions, schools either purposefully or unintentionally demean the women's games and leagues. Nicknames that clearly articulate the separate but (un)equal ideology in sports include the Cowboys and Cowgirls of Hardin-Simmons University, McNeese State, Oklahoma State, and University of Wyoming, the Minutemen and Minutewomen of the University of Massachusetts, and the Peacocks and Peahens (St. Peter's College). The University of Southern California calls its men the Trojans and its women the Women of Troy.

The naming of teams provides only one instance of how patriarchal ideologies are inscribed into the rules of sports. Consider for example the use of alternative rule structures for women's versions of men's sports. At the yearly Wimbledon tennis championship in England, women compete in the best 2 out of 3 set matches, while men compete in the best 3 out of 5 set matches. In international ice hockey, according to the International Ice Hockey Federation (IIHF) rules, women are not allowed to bodycheck. Bodychecking is not only a staple of the men's game, it is one of the most exciting and significant aspects of the sport for spectators. After the 1990 Women's World Championship, the IIHF ostensibly eliminated bodychecking from the women's game because organizing officials believed that women from countries outside of North America did not have the size and mass to compete with North American players at the World Championships or the Olympic Games. There are many who feel that the relative lack of physical play is a detriment to its popularity among the mainstream hockey public. After nearly 20 years of equality in the sport of National Collegiate Athletic Association (NCAA) basketball with regard to the distance of the three-point shooting line, the men's line was extended by an additional foot to 20′9″ in 2008 while the women's remained at 19′9″. At the professional level, the NBA three-point line is 3′3″ further from the net than the line in the WNBA. In Canadian Triathlon sponsored events, elite women often start in different "waves" (always following) then the men.

A less overt form of gender-based discrimination in sports is league payment/salary rule structures (which are not regularly publicized). In most sports, men earn considerably more money than their female counterparts. Economists might argue that this is not shocking, nor discriminatory, because men's sporting events typically garner more media exposure, higher attendance, and greater amounts of sponsorship dollars. Still, a comparison of the huge differences in gendered player salaries suggests that there is a veritable glass ceiling for women in sports.

In professional basketball, Sue Bird of the WNBA's Seattle Storm (first round draft pick in 2002 and former Olympic gold medalist) earns the league maximum, $87,000 per year. The current average salary in the NBA is $5 million. That means the men made, on average, around 45 times more than the top-ranking women players such as Bird. A few WNBA players earn more than

WNBA ATTENDANCE FIGURES

Critics of the pay structure in the WNBA have long argued that due to poor or inconsistent media exposure, teams have difficulty in developing a loyal fan base of paying spectators. Consider the average team attendance figures for 2007.

Chicago Sky: 3,710
Connecticut Sun: 7,970
Detroit Shock: 9,749
Houston Comets: 8,166
Indiana Fever: 7,227
Los Angeles Sparks: 8,695
Minnesota Lynx: 6,971
New York Liberty: 8,698
Phoenix Mercury: 7,711
Sacramento Monarchs: 8,413
San Antonio Silver Stars: 7,569
Seattle Storm: 7,974
Washington Mystics: 7,788

$100,000 a year, but that is only because they have side jobs, such as playing in other leagues, receive bonuses for winning playoff games, or helping with WNBA marketing efforts.

Professional golfer Annika Sorenstam won her third U.S. Open title in 2006, a year in which she won $1.9 million in prize money. That same year, Tiger Woods earned over $12 million in prize money. The total purse at the 2006 Open was $3.1 million, making it the most lucrative event on the ladies' tour. However, the U.S. Golf Association (USGA) gave more than twice that amount ($6.8 million) to the men's U.S. Open. David Fay, the agency's executive director, told the Associated Press (AP) that the men's tournament has a higher payout because it has more audience members, entries, and press coverage. Golf critics once again suggest that these figures simply suggest a separate and unequal ethos in the sport. For example, in 2007, the LPGA paid out $54 million in total prize money; the largest amount in the tour's history. Tiger Woods grossed over $75 million in endorsements alone that same year.

While some are amazed to learn the Women's Professional Football League (WPFL) actually exists, they may be even more stunned by the players' salaries. The average player in the WPFL, including 2006 WPFL player of the year, Stacy Agee, earns $100 per game (less than a National Football League [NFL] cheerleader). The average player salary in NFL football in 2006 was $1.4 million. Of interest is that the sport with the narrowest difference between men and women's salaries in 2007 was professional bowling, where women earned 70 cents for every dollar men earned in the sport.

Women's sports also tend to be marginalized through the "rules" of mass mediation in North America. When media outlets (television, print, and virtual) are considered separately and together, women's sports receive around 4.5 to 5.5 percent of all media devoted to sports. Rarely is women's sports, or high-profile female athletes, showcased in media coverage, critics argue, in a serious or professional manner (i.e., without being sexualized or trivialized). Media channels have arisen, however, to exclusively highlight women's sports, such as the Canadian sports channel WTSN, which operated from 2001–2003 but collapsed due to poor revenue generation for sponsors and advertisers.

Ethnic minority women also face a series of obstacles and ideological barriers to participation both within sports cultures and based on their own faith-based practices. For example, Muslim women who wear traditional clothing and believe in modest (and no co-ed) forms of sports participation have been ritually excluded from physical education classes across North America when they either refuse to wear an institutionally approved standard gym uniform or exercise among men. Starting in early 2008, Harvard University provided Muslim women on the campus (much to the dismay of many students), a special "women's only" gym space and time. A seemingly simple concession on the part of the University grew into a heated debate about not only women's only classes but also ethnic minority women's expressions in sports.

KEY EVENTS

The creation of the All-American Girls Professional Baseball League in 1943 stands as one of the watershed moments in the contestation of gender-based rules in sports. With so many young American men serving in the armed forces during World War II, the major and minor baseball leagues in America struggled to earn profits. During the early months of 1943, Chicago Cubs owner Phillip Wrigley proposed an idea to establish a professional women's softball league. His plan was to play in large cities such as Philadelphia, Chicago, and St Louis using the existing major league ballparks. Owners rejected the idea because they felt that crowds would not support women's sports. Undeterred, Wrigley then decided to scale back and create a league in wartime industrial centers in the midwestern states. The All-American Girls Softball League launched play in 1943, with four teams playing eight games a week respectively. The Kenosha Comets and Racine Belles were located in Wisconsin, the Rockford Peaches in Illinois, and the South Bend Blue Sox in Indiana. The traditional softball rules were modified to make the game more like baseball. By midseason, Wrigley changed the name to the All-American Girls Professional Baseball League. Spurred by initial success, the league expanded with a new team in 1944 (the Milwaukee Chicks) and another in 1945 (the Fort Wayne Daisies). Many people feared the league would fold after the men returned from World War II and the major leagues were revitalized, but in 1946, the league added two new teams, Muskegon Lassies (Michigan) and Peoria Red Wings (Illinois). The league disbanded in 1954 when it was no longer profitable for team owners.

THE AAGPBL CODE OF PRACTICE

The All-American Girls Professional Baseball League (AAGPBL) practiced a policy whereby all payers in the league had to attend a "charm school" to learn proper feminine behavior in sports. As part of the charm school manual, players were provided with the following beauty routine:

Suggested Beauty Routine

"After the Game"

Remember, the All American girl is subjected to greater exposure through her activities on the diamond, through exertion in greater body warmth and perspiration, through exposure to dirt, grime and dust and through vigorous play to scratches, cuts, abrasions and sprains. This means extra precaution to assure all the niceties of toilette and personality. Especially after the game, the All American girl should take time to observe the necessary beauty ritual, to protect both her health and appearance. Here are a few simple rules that should prove helpful and healthful after the game.

1. Shower well and soap the skin.
2. Dry thoroughly to avoid chapping or chafing.
3. Apply cleansing cream to face and remove with tissue.
4. Wash face with soap and water.
5. Apply skin astringent.
6. Apply rouge moderately but carefully.
7. Apply lipstick with moderate taste.
8. Apply eye makeup if considered desirable.
9. Apply powder.
10. Check all cuts, abrasions or minor injuries.

If you suffer any skin abrasion or injury, or if you discern any aches or pains that do not appear to be normal, report them at once to your coach or chaperone or the person responsible for treatment and first aid. Don't laugh off slight ailments as trivialities because they can often develop into serious infection or troublesome conditions that can handicap your play and cause personal inconvenience. See that your injuries, however slight, receive immediate attention. Guard your health and welfare.

After the 1950s, nearly every decade produced a set of landmark events that challenged men's outright dominance in sports and the many gendered rules that exist in sports worlds. Among the most consequent of the challenges was Title IX, The Amendment of the Education Act of 1972. Title IX is a 37-word federal law that states: "No person in the United States shall, on the basis of sex, be excluded from participation in, be denied the benefits of, or be subjected to discrimination under any education program or activity receiving Federal financial assistance." Title IX, as it is commonly known, was enacted on June 23, 1972, and was designed to, among other things, eliminate forms of gender-based discrimination in practices such as the funding of school-based sports programs. Congresswoman Patsy Mink wrote the law as an outgrowth of adversities she faced in obtaining her college degrees at the University of Hawai'i, University of Nebraska, and University of Chicago. However, the American Association of University Women has consistently argued that while the ideas behind Title IX were fundamentally important, the U.S. government has not effectively instituted or policed this amendment.

Title IX has created controversy with some groups who claim that it has caused some schools to actually spend more money on women's sports programs and less money on men's sports programs such as wrestling or, in some cases, to end some traditional male sports programs all together. On the other hand, supporters of Title IX point to national statistics that indicate that male collegiate sports participation has actually increased since the inception of Title IX and that so-called nonrevenue sports were being eliminated frequently even before Title IX. Nonetheless, Title IX has been instrumental in the development of women's sports, and it can be said that it helped the public prepare for the development of women's professional sports such as the WNBA and Women's United Soccer Association.

A long list of trailblazer women athletes in sports dominated by men provides evidence of the collective quest to level the playing field in women's sports. Especially noteworthy are several women who have sought to rewrite the gender rules in sports by competing against men in men's sports leagues.

In 1965, Shirley Muldowney earned the license to drive a gasoline-powered dragster in the largest sanctioning body, the National Hot Rod Association (NHRA). She was the first woman to do so in an NHRA professional category. She then spent the better part of the next four years on the drag racing match race circuit in the East and Midwest. On June 15, 1975, she became the first woman to advance to the finals in the Top Fuel racing circuit, losing the last round of racing to Marvin Graham at the NHRA Spring Nationals. Two months later on August 24, she became the first woman to break the five-second barrier. Muldowney entered the history books early in 1977, becoming the second person to run over 250 mph at a race in Arizona on January 17 posting a speed of 250.69 mph and then going 252 mph during qualifying. From 1977–1980, she became the first racer ever to win three consecutive NHRA national events back to back. Today, in over four decades of drag racing, she is still the only woman ever to win an NHRA Top Fuel points championship. So monumental were her achievements, in 1977 the U.S. House of Representatives bestowed on Shirley an "Outstanding Achievement Award." Muldowney raced in, and dominated, a variety of drag racing formats until 2003. Shirley Muldowney remains the single most accomplished woman to compete in professional motorsports and, most certainly, a woman who helped to crack ideologies of exclusion in sports.

Others who would follow Muldowney's lead included Manon Rheaume and Hayley Wickenheiser. Rheaume gained notoriety in 1992 and 1993 when she became the first woman to play in the National Hockey League. Rheaume, a goaltender, played three exhibition games for the Tampa Bay Lighting. In 2003, Wickenheiser became the first woman to suit up in a men's professional hockey league at a position other than goalie when she played for HC Salamat in Finland. During this season, she also became the first woman to score a goal playing in a men's professional league. Her transition to the league did not proceed smoothly, though. Wickenheiser was initially signed to play in Italy, until the Italian Winter Sports Federation ruled that women were ineligible to play in a men's league. She also turned down an offer from Phil Esposito to play for the Cincinnati Cyclones of the ECHL. However, Finland's Hockey Federation unanimously supported letting women play in a men's league, allowing her to debut with Salamat on January 10, 2003. That same year, golfing phenom Annika Sorenstam played on the PGA tour at the Colonial Open. While Babe Zaharias had already broken the gender line in gold by playing at the 1954 Los Angeles Open, Sorenstam's involvement at the Colonial Open became a flashpoint of debate about gender segregation in sports. So hotly contested was her involvement in the tournament that high-profile players including Vijay Singh stated that she did not belong on the men's tour and that if she was paired with him in the first round of play he would withdraw from the tournament.

Finally, after decades of defending their prerogative to reward men with a bigger paycheck than women, Wimbledon officials reversed course and announced that, as of 2008, they will award equal prize money to the men's and women's tournament champions. The policy change, which had been advocated by the Women's Tennis Association, a host of former champions, and even British Prime Minister Tony Blair, brought the tournament in line with the other majors that comprise the tennis Grand Slam. The U.S. and Australian opens have offered equal prize money to men and women through all rounds for years, and the French Open pays its respective champions equal prize money. Three-time Wimbledon champion Venus Williams drew the controversy to a head in 2007 by writing a stinging commentary against Wimbledon's pay inequity in the *London Times*. Bowing to public pressure, Wimbledon officials had narrowed the pay gap in recent years yet defended the disparity by arguing that the effort men's and women's players offered warranted the pay structure given that men played best-of-five matches and women played best-of-three. Further, they argued that women stood to make more money at Wimbledon because so many opted to play doubles, in addition to singles, while the rigor of the men's format made it almost impossible for men to do the same. Advocates for equal pay have long attacked such arguments on both literal and symbolic grounds.

FUTURE PROSPECTS

There are both formal and informal rules that govern sports practices. These rules are embedded with codes about how men and women should play, and be represented in, sports. Over the past six decades, women athletes have struggled to change gender-based "rules" in sports that effectively situate them as inferior or generally unequal to men. Formal rules in particular sports cultures such as golf and basketball may be changing slowly toward egalitarianism, but cultures and structures of inequality between the genders in sports continue to exist.

See also Gender and Educational Opportunities; Men in Women's Sports; Salaries of Professional Athletes; Women and the Apologetic; Women Coaches and Owners; Women in Men's Sports; Women Sportscasters.

Further Reading: McDonagh, E., and Papano, L. (2008). *Playing with the Boys: Why Separate is Not Equal in Sports.* Don Mills, ON: Oxford University Press; Messner, M. (2007). *Out of Play: Critical Essays on Gender in Sport.* Albany, NY: SUNY Press; O'Reilly, J., and Cahn, S. (2007). *Women and Sports in the United States.* Boston, MA: Northeastern University Press; Sokolove, M. (2008). *Warrior Girls: Lifted Spirits and Broken Bodies in the Wake of Title IX.* New York: Simon and Schuster.

Michael Atkinson

GENE MANIPULATION

The use of genetic technology and genetic manipulation (GM) to enhance sports performance or capabilities has been the subject of increasing ethical discussion in recent years. Genetic modification involves the manipulation of genes to enhance sports performance and was introduced to the World Anti-Doping Code as a banned method of performance enhancement in 2004; the Code describes gene doping (or cell doping) as "the non-therapeutic use of genes, genetic elements and/or cells that have the capacity to enhance athletic performance" (p. 6). Although banned, there are currently no tests available to detect for genetic enhancement in athletes. Also, the only direct method of testing for gene doping would involve a muscle biopsy, which would not be ethical to carry out on elite athletes in advance of an important competition due to the invasiveness of the procedure. In any case, the focus on gene doping has been exclusively limited to modifications to individuals, and yet, it will be necessary to consider how the rules of sports might apply should genetic modification be applied to future generations as well.

Genetic modification itself is still in the early stages of development with very few therapeutic interventions proving successful. As such, the application of this science to the enhancement of athletic capabilities meets with fierce opposition. While some of these debates are confined to the world of sports, their broader implications for society often permit their discussion in nonsporting institutions. For example, in 2003, the U.S. President's Council on Bioethics heard two sessions on the use of gene doping, which later informed its key advisory document published the same year. Within this wider world, questions arising from gene technology have been central to the discipline known as bioethics since the completion of the human genome. However, the spectre of gene doping is also invoked via broader biological modifications, such as interventions on the embryo, stem cell research, or cloning.

In this entry we explain how the use of genetic modification in sports has emerged and its prospect as an imminent means of performance enhancement for athletes. We also outline current ethical and legal debates concerning its application to international sports.

BACKGROUND

In June 2001, the International Olympic Committee (IOC) Medical Commission discussed the implications of genetics for sports. In the same year, the World Anti-Doping Agency (WADA) placed genetic modification on its agenda in its fight against doping with a meeting scheduled for mid-September. Since then, such organizations as the U.S. President's Council on Bioethics, the Australian Law Reform Commission, and various governments worldwide have undertaken work to discuss the relationship between genetic science and sports. The second landmark WADA meeting on gene doping took place in December 2005, at which forms of detection were discussed along with a new moral stance against the use of genetic testing in sports that stated:

> 7. The use of genetic information to select for or discriminate against athletes should be strongly discouraged. This principle does not apply to legitimate medical screening or research. (WADA, 2005)

This meeting was shortly followed by suggestions that the substance repoxygen (a type of gene therapy that induces controlled release of erythropoietin [EPO] in response to low oxygen concentration) might have been in use during the Torino 2006 Olympic Winter Games. In June 2008, WADA's third symposium on gene doping took place. To this extent, the prospect of gene doping is more real than it has ever been, and the policy work surrounding this verifies the imminence of this particular form of performance enhancement within elite sports.

What are the legitimate uses of science and medicine? What should athletes be allowed to use as a method of performance enhancement? These questions apply equally to gene doping as they have for other forms of doping. As such, our task in considering this new technology is whether it presents any new issues for how we read the current situation of antidoping or whether there are new degrees of concern that should alarm us. Perhaps more than any other form of doping, gene doping has engaged the interests of ethicists outside of sports, particularly within bioethics, and an important reason for this is that the concerns about this application occur at a time when genetic science is approaching maturation. As such, a number of genetic researchers who have spent decades working on techniques to no avail now find themselves subject to public scrutiny on the basis of a mythical concern that the first designer baby is imminent. To this extent, the scientific professions are actively concerned about protecting themselves against speculative propositions that might diminish the seriousness of their work. The application of this work to the genetic enhancement of athletes is one such application.

Perhaps one of the most notable genetic scientists to bridge medical research and sports enhancements is Lee Sweeney. Sweeney's work is interested in muscle wasting diseases but has found itself closely linked to elite sports because the same science of boosting muscle mass could be utilized by athletes seeking a performance boost. In this sense, a novelty of gene doping is the fact that it emerges within a unique set of biopolitical conditions.

Gene doping is also distinct in that it promises a form of performance enhancement that is absent of side effects. One of the major problems with substances such as steroids is that they are synthetic, which means that their side effects are often unknown, multiple, and serious. The possibility of genetic enhancement that utilizes the athlete's own physiology and biochemistry to develop tailor-made modifiers provides the opportunity to create safer forms of performance enhancement.

A further distinguishing factor of gene doping—and genetic science more generally—is the degree to which it shapes the distribution of social goods. For many years, considerable amounts of funding have been poured into genetic science, with very few results. To this extent, some scholars have questioned the legitimacy of such an investment that might have been better used in other approaches to addressing health problems. If one extends this argument to sports, then one might argue that this constitutes an unreasonable redistribution of resources toward a practice that is less valuable than the attempt to relieve the suffering that arises from genetic illnesses. However, there are various responses to this view, one of which argues that the pursuit of enhancement could have a resultant positive effect for our knowledge of how to treat disease. In this sense, the dichotomy between pursuing therapy or enhancement might be false.

On this basis, sports may offer a rich context through which to research the potential of genetic technology for broader therapeutic medical purposes. Indeed, perhaps the broader issue that informs this debate is the realization that the pursuit of health—through genetic science or otherwise—necessarily commits us to the pursuit of *enhanced* health. For instance, consider how Sweeney's work might be applied to people as they grow old and begin to suffer from the natural ageing process of muscle depletion. In these circumstances—as we do already—there will be considerable interest to enable greater mobility in elderly people, even if its aim is to counteract this natural ageing process. To this extent, genetic science could then be used to enhance people even if this enhancement is really a mechanism to allow individuals to enjoy a reasonable quality of life. In this sense, much of the discussion about gene doping differs from other forms of doping in that it raises specific questions about the impact of biotechnologies in a much broader medical sense. In other words, it is concerned with the end goals of science and the application of genetic modification per se, not just for the use of genetic technologies among athletes.

KEY EVENTS

Debates *within* sports have tended to focus on genetic technology in terms of what is permissible specifically in terms of sports ethics. Discussions have focused on such concerns as fairness and cheating: Does the use of genetic enhancement constitute an unethical form of performance enhancement? One of the major difficulties in this discussion is establishing what system of fairness should apply to sports. This is made more complex by the fact that the relevance of genetic variation among athletes is contested and largely unknown. So, if one athlete were to claim that they were genetically disadvantaged—as might be said of someone who was shorter than another athlete where height assisted competitive advantage—then it does not follow necessarily that this is a reasonable appeal to unfairness. While we might grant that there is a performance advantage from being tall, we might point out that the athlete who pursued a sport that involves advantage through height has voluntarily accepted the conditions of that disadvantage when entering the sport. To this extent, the acceptance of these conditions removes the ethical concern that the disadvantage suffered should be corrected. The difficulty is that genetic variations are not all like height. For instance, it is still unknown whether there is, say, a genetic predisposition for endurance activities, though if there was, then it is much harder to claim that athletes accept this disadvantage when entering the sport because they will not know whether they are genetically enabled or not. This raises the ethical debate about whether genetic tests should be utilized to determine performance capacity, which we will attend to later.

A further concern about gene doping is its capacity to corrupt some celebration of natural endeavor that is often associated with elite sports. While this concern has been applied to other forms of doping, genetic enhancement invokes the possibility of "Playing God," which marks it out against other methods of performance enhancement. As noted, the categorization of gene therapy as a performance enhancement is rooted in the belief that genetic therapy would threaten what is natural in elite sports, yet, this may be misguided given that the context of elite sports is itself highly artificial. This concern is connected to the need to keep elite sports in line with fair competition. However, despite popular myth, genetic engineering, much like any other performance enhancer, would not determine that an individual had the capabilities to perform at an elite level. In this sense, genetic modification would not diminish the merit of sporting achievement. Rather, genetic engineering would provide *the potential* for an athlete to achieve elite status, but it is still up to the athlete to accomplish this through the usual methods of training, nutritional specification, psychological readiness, good coaching, and so on. In this sense, genetic modification does not reduce the need for considerable investment on behalf of the athlete. This further complicates discussions as to whether genetic enhancement even contravenes the ethics of sports and whether GM athletes would be considered cheats. While a number of organizations have warned against the use of genetic enhancement, others suggest that the realization of genetic enhancement presents a complex ethical and moral challenge that is not comparable to other forms of doping.

A further concern about gene doping is whether it would lead to the creation of super-athletes, thus representing a new era of posthumanity where all expectations of what is biologically normal are transformed. Indeed, a great deal of reporting on these technologies conveys this possibility, and it is widely regarded that genetic science in particular has suffered significantly from such wild speculation. Reports on GM in the popular press are often accompanied by futuristic images of grotesque superhuman athletes. Such imagery perpetuates the fear of genetic modification that has long plagued this technology. However, genetic science is still in relative infancy, and it would be difficult to conceive of legitimate forms of enhancement that could either have the potential to alter the body in such drastic ways or be accepted within sports and society. However, genetic enhancement that does little to significantly alter the surface of the body may be a more imminent reality though, in this sense, GM athletes would not resemble grotesque monsters.

Some consider that gene doping is inevitable and may be impossible to avoid. If it does not appear first in sports, it is likely to find application to improve the health conditions of citizens generally, and this will likely affect the willingness of sports to embrace such enhancements. It has been suggested that the sports community would be better served by permitting the use of genetic modification in sports on the grounds that it has a stronger chance of providing safer methods of performance enhancement compared with synthetic drugs. Given the science and resources required to genetically modify one's body, it might also be a technology that athletes are required to use effectively and safely.

The imminent realization of GM athletes has brought about the prospects of its use for changing significant features of sports. Some have asked whether being genetically less gifted than another athlete would warrant gene doping to level the playing field. For example, recent deliberations have considered whether it is possible to induce a more equal gender order in sports and society via the use of athletic enhancement and genetic modification. It has been argued that biological differences between men and women may be a result of cultural inequalities impacting upon the evolution process, most notably the increased capacity for muscle mass in men. On this basis, he argues that the use of GM might be a legitimate means through which to reduce the gender gap in particular activities. Whilst this is a particularly complex and lengthy discussion, the reliance on GM to address social differences places the burden change with women themselves; it is women who would have to undergo genetic modification, to manipulate their bodies, and develop their bodies in ways that may run counter to wider social construct. Surveillance techniques are *already* institutionalized in sports, many of which have prevented women from developing physical capacity. For instance, bodybuilding tries to limit the achievement of women's physicality by adding "femininity" to the list of aesthetic categories that they are expected to fulfill. In these contexts, explicitly gendered ideologies are inherent within the structures of sports that limit the capacity for women to develop their muscularity. There is an explicit drive toward trying to determine the extent to which women can develop their muscularity without losing what it is to be feminine. Given this, it is difficult to image how bioamazons would exist in these structures.

The second related issue concerns the use of genetic information and its relationship with genetic tests to predict for the performance of an athlete. Genetic tests rest on the idea that specific genes determine specific kinds of predispositions that affect athletic ability and performance. Although the scientific literature does not yet support such a view, a genetic test called the ACTN3 genetic test for performance came on the market in 2004. The test emerges from collaborative research between various universities and the Australian Institute for Sport. Its producer, Genetic Technologies (Australia), claims that it can "identify whether you may be naturally geared toward sprint/power events or towards endurance sporting ability" (Genetic Technologies Limited, 2004). Moreover, publicity for the test states that, "Regardless of whether you are an accomplished athlete, or a beginner, your ACTN3 Sports Performance Test result could assist you in optimising your training to make the most of your natural ability within a wide range of sports." Within the brochure for the test, this text is accompanied by an image of young children (male and female, approximately age 10) crossing the finishing tape in a race. Later on in the brochure, Genetic Technologies provides more advanced details on the scientific basis of the test, including reassurances that the test is completely painless and that it should not be a sole measure for aptitude. Finally, they include the bibliographic details of two scientific references. This tests remain controversial because the research claiming to identify "performance genes" derives from studies that rely on small sample sizes and, as such, are limited in their capacity to firmly indicate genetic predisposition for specific kinds of performance.

The future availability and use of genetic tests brings forth a range of questions about legitimate use of this information. For instance, could the results of performance tests on adults be accessed by coaches or team selectors? Should this information be used to make decisions about funding of athletes? The World Anti-Doping Agency (2005) argues against discrimination against athletes on the basis of genetic information, thus preventing its use as a preselective mechanism within elite sports.

This matter is further complicated by the possible range of genetic enhancements, their specific and often unique implications, and their relationship to wider public use. While there is not scope to address all these variations, one might, for example, note the distinction between pre- and postbirth enhancements. In addition to concerns about the scientific credibility of these tests, ethical issues arise from the application of genetic tests on embryos or children. Parents or coaches may be interest in selecting the right sport for children based on genetic tests and thus use genetic tests to positively select for specific kinds of abilities. This may severely limit the openness of a child's or athlete's future who may be encouraged into a particular event or sport purely on this basis. Using genetic tests to select which children receive investment and what sports they should focus on is unjustified on this basis.

Perhaps more seriously, genetic testing for performance might become a future selection possibility for those seeking to select the "best" embryo. It has been argued that it is possible to make an initial distinction between the kinds of performance enhancement that we have discussed here and prebirth engineering where the enhancement is made to the germ-line of the individual (the hereditary cells). The enhancement is something that is done to an individual or potential life on the authority of a legal guardian rather than being something that is chosen by the individual who is receiving the enhancement. This information could lead to decisions being made about whether a potential life is given value on the basis of such characteristics.

FUTURE PROSPECTS

Genetic enhancements present new challenges for sports philosophers, bioethicists, and sporting bodies to consider and to decide upon their acceptability, though it is also a matter for society generally to consider. Gene doping differs from other performance enhancement concerns in that its implications are not confined solely to the contexts of sports but extend to broader aspects of medicine, human enhancement, and the legitimate application of biotechnologies. The controversial moral and legal status of these prospects has warranted great attention from a range of agencies who have sought to provide ethical guidance on these issues.

See also Antidoping Rules and Policies; Biology and Athlete Performance; Sports Doctors, Trainers, and Drugs; Virtual Sports.

Further Reading: Genetic Technologies Limited. (2004). *Your Genetic Sports Advantage*™, Version 1A. Available online at: http://www.genetictechnologies.com.au (accessed February 24, 2006); Lee, S., Barton, E., Sweeney, H., and Farrar, R. (2004). Viral Expression of Insulin-Like Growth Factor-I Enhances Muscle Hypertrophy in Resistance-Trained Rats. *Journal of Applied Physiology* 96: 1097–1104; Lopez, E. (2004). *Genetic Modification and Egalitarianism: Distinguish and Distribute*. UCSC Center for Biomolecular Science and Engineering. http://www.cbse.ucsc.edu/pdf_library/GeneModifEgal_Lopez061604.pdf; MacArthur, D., and North, K. (2004). A Gene for Speed? The Evolution and Function of Alphaactinin-3. *BioEssays* 26: 786–795; Miah, A. (2004). *Genetically Modified Athletes*. London: Routledge; Miah, A., and Rich, E. (2006). "Genetic Tests for Ability? Talent Identification and the Value of an Open Future. *Sport, Education and Society* 11: 259–273; Savulescu, J., and Foddy, B. (2005). Comment: Genetic Test Available for Sports Performance. *British Journal of Sports Medicine* 39: 472; Tamburinni, C., and Tännsjö, T. (2005). *Genetic Technology and Sport: Ethical Questions*. London: Routledge; van Hilvoorde, I., Vos, R., and de Wert, G. (2006). Flopping, Klapping and Gene Doping: Dichotomies Between "Natural" and "Artificial" in Elite Sport. *Social Studies of Science* 37: 173–200; World Anti-Doping Agency. (2004). *The 2004 Prohibited List International Standard*. Lausanne: Author; World Anti Doping Agency. (2005). *The Stockholm Declaration*. http://www.wadaama.org/en/dynamic.ch2?pageCategory.id=530; Yang, N., MacArthur, D. G., et al. (2003). "ACTN3 Genotype is Associated With Human Elite Athletic Performance." *American Journal of Human Genetics* 73: 627–631.

Emma Rich and Andy Miah

GOVERNMENTS, LAWS, AND GAMBLING

The relationship between governments and gambling in sports is multilayered. U.S. and Canadian law either prohibits sports-related gambling outright or, in specific states and provinces, strictly limits how wagering on sports may be undertaken. Yet, by and large, until gambling mega-scandals are reported in the mass media, rarely are sports gambling enthusiasts actively prosecuted by police or other agents of social control. Moreover, governments at national and local levels have endeavored to profit from sports betting by legalizing it within situated contexts in order to tax it heavily. Organized gambling on North American sports contests is almost as old as the games themselves, and recent developments with online gaming have made sports betting more accessible than ever.

BACKGROUND

Betting on sports is a multibillion-dollar industry in contemporary North America. In 2005 alone, the 150 legal "sports books" (bookies) alone reported $2 billion in betting handled through their offices. In 2007, ESPN experts estimated that at least one-quarter of the American population bets on at least one sporting event yearly, with 15 percent betting regularly. How the sports gambling habits of all of these people remain unfettered, by and large, is a fascinating social phenomenon. Two points of consideration regarding the role of sports and sports betting provide a preliminary answer to the question.

In most societies, certain groups exist that may be categorized as all-encompassing, esoteric, or otherwise insular organizations. Groups such as the military, religious sects, psychiatric hospitals, or private schools are all examples of social settings that often act within their own rules and codes, occasionally appearing as if they exist above and beyond the law. In his landmark text *Asylums,* Goffman (1961) describes such institutions in the following way:

> Every institution captures something of the time and interest of its members and provides something of a world for them; in brief, every institution has encompassing tendencies. When we review the different institutions in our Western society, we find some that are encompassing to a degree discontinuously greater than the ones next in line. Their encompassing or total character is symbolized by the barrier to social intercourse with the outside and to departure that is often built right into the physical plant, such as locked doors, high walls, barbed wire, cliffs, water, forests, or moors. These establishments I am calling *total institutions.* (p. 15)

Goffman identifies five conceptual types of total institutions in his classification: (1) those established to care for incapable and "harmless" persons (e.g., an orphanage); (2) those established to care for incapable but dangerous persons (e.g., psychiatric institutions); (3) those organized to protect the community against what are felt to be intentional dangers to it (e.g., prisons); (4) those established to pursue some work-like tasks and justifying themselves only on these instrumental grounds (e.g., the military); and (5) those established as retreats from the world (e.g., monasteries). Although Goffman intended his fifth category to represent an ascetically oriented refuge such as a monastery, it might be argued that sports, and associated sports gambling, allow for a certain type of retreat from the banality of modern life.

Related to this, Robert Stebbins describes certain types of total institution, sports-related behavior as tolerable deviance. Tolerable deviance is that which is prohibited either by law or cultural convention but does not receive widespread public scorn or tangible official prosecution. Tolerable deviance is regarded as a victimless social offense or breach of a rule that is unreflective of contemporary sensibilities. From a tolerable difference perspective, gambling is an ideal-type example in a wide array of social contexts. Of course, gambling on sports is not tolerated by everyone, and contemporary battles about what instances of sports gambling are permissible by governments and other authority figures is an ongoing source of debate.

Early forms of tolerable gambling in North American sports involved people betting on frontier horse races, cockfights, dog fights, coursing contests, and bare-knuckle boxing. Horse racing saw the most widespread popularity among the upper classes throughout the nineteenth century and into the early twentieth century.

Many enterprising bookmakers innovated "auctions pools" during the era, which involved auctioning off bets for each horse in a race. They would quickly shift their emphasis to the standard odds-making scenario common in racing today. By the 1920s, racing had reached its peak, and there were more than 300 racetracks in the United States in addition to thousands of off-track betting facilities, which were connected to the tracks by telegraph wires. Horse racing retained its place as the most popular form of betting until professional sports leagues began forming and capturing the attention of the nation's gamblers.

In the late 1800s, professional baseball began to gain popularity and, consequently, so did betting on the sport. But the fixing scandal involving the 1919 Chicago White (Black) Sox threatened the fragile state of play in the baseball gambling world.

Sports bettors and betting organizers were linked to the Chicago and New York mafia through the scandal. The police and baseball authorities intervened and cracked down on the gambling on the sport. An association between organized crime and betting in baseball still lingers to this day.

From the 1920s to the 1950s, college football and basketball, boxing, and other sports developed their own gambling cultures. The implementation of the now massively popular point-spread system in sports gambling, along with the widespread emergence of television in the 1950s, are two factors that perpetuated the massive growth of sports betting. More games were offered by bookies, and people could actually watch the contests they bet on their TV at home or at their local tavern.

During the boom in sports gambling, moral reformers inside and outside sports sought to alter the extant laws and seriously curtail gambling practices. Senator Royal S. Copeland of New York introduced the federal Anti-Racketeering Act in 1934, which partially took aim at organized crime activities; an act that was rarely, until the early 1950s, applied to sports gambling activities. In 1952, Senator Estes Kefauver held the first nationally televised hearings on organized gambling, which eventually led to the creation of new federal laws (such as those outlined in the Johnson Act), which further limited sports betting possibilities in the country. Attorney General Robert Kennedy spearheaded the Wire Act, which established the interstate transportation of wagering paraphernalia across state lines or the discussing of wagering across telephone lines as federal crimes. The Organized Crime Control Act of 1970 deepened anti–sports gambling laws in the country by making any violation of a state antigambling law a federal crime.

But of all the laws enacted to date, none has been as controversial as Senator Bill Bradley's Professional and Amateur Sports Protection Act (PASPA) of 1992. The act effectively outlawed sports betting nationwide, excluding a few states such as Nevada, Oregon, and Delaware. The PASPA makes it unlawful for "a governmental entity to sponsor, operate, advertise, promote, license or authorize by law or compact a lottery, sweepstakes or other betting, gambling, or wagering scheme based, directly or indirectly … on one or more competitive games in which amateur or professional athletes participate … or on one or more performances of such athletes in such games." What often escapes public scrutiny with regard to the law is that the PASPA apparently, by claiming federal jurisdiction over sports gambling, potentially violates the constitutional rights of sovereign states to police this issue within each of their boundaries.

Economists of sports might point to a more consequential issue for those in the business of gambling. The PASPA law restricts state access to the estimated $80 billion to $380 billion bet on sporting events in the United States every year. One is hard pressed to find another example of a mass economy that is only accessible, legally, to entrepreneurs in three states. Due to the 1992 PASPA law, financially desperate states are locked out of a potentially lucrative sports gambling market. Without the ban, they could follow the example of Oregon, which has run its Sports Action game through the state lottery since 1989. Sports Action, which takes bets up to $20 per ticket on National Football League (NFL) games, has raised more than $28 million for state universities over the past decade.

KEY EVENTS

The foundation of modern sports gambling in the United States arguably crystallized when gambling was legalized in Nevada in 1931. While sports betting would not take hold in the state until many years later when Nevada became the epicenter of gambling in the United States, it altered the manners by which people approached the gambling process. Casino gambling on games of chance was deemed legal in 1931; sports betting was still illegal (to some historians, an artifact of the White Sox 1919 scandal) until a regulation was passed by the U.S. Congress in 1951. The new regulations allowed for the professional bookmaking industry to develop and paved the way for casinos to pioneer the first betting lounges in the country.

The first legal sports booking agents, called "turf clubs," were independent businesses. The sports betting industry remained relatively small in Nevada until the 1970s because federal law placed a 10 percent tax on all sports bets made within booking agent shops or in casinos. The federal government reduced the tax to 2 percent in 1974, and sports betting became a staple of the modern casino. In 1975, sports gambling revolutionary Sam Rosenthal, who operated gaming at the Stardust casino in the 1970s and had organized crime affiliations, exploited the new laws to industry advantage. His sports gaming lounge featured televisions with live broadcasts of a range of sports and high-tech betting methods all set within a plush, upscale, and relaxed environment. Today, nearly every large casino in the state emulates Rosenthal's sports lounge model.

From time to time, major scandals in college and professional sports remind North Americans as to why gambling on sports by athletes is federally prohibited but still considered as part of the total institution of sports. Cases involving the

1919 White Sox and Pete Rose are most cited, but many significant others fill sports history book pages. For example, in 1952, the University of Kentucky had its basketball program suspended for the 1952–1953 season after a point-shaving scandal where players would deliberately miss shots or score points in order to cover particular "spreads" predicted by bookmakers. In 1963, Green Bay Packer halfback Paul Hornung and Detroit Lions defensive tackle Alex Karras were suspended for one year by NFL commissioner Pete Rozelle for betting on their own games. Rick Kuhn, a former basketball player at Boston College, and four others were found guilty of conspiring to shave points to fix basketball games in the 1978–1979 season. Kuhn was later sentenced to 10 years in prison. In 1997, former Arizona State basketball players Stevin Smith and Isaac Burton, Jr. plead guilty to charges of conspiracy to commit sports bribery in a point-shaving scheme that fixed four Sun Devils' games. Less than two decades after the Boston College basketball scandal, 13 Boston College football players were suspended in 1997 for betting on college football, professional football, and major league baseball games. In 2006, Phoenix Coyotes assistant coach Rick Tocchet was accused of financing a nationwide gambling ring in which a half-dozen National Hockey League (NHL) players bet on professional and college sports, mostly football and basketball. These cases and literally dozens of others illustrate that even with the increased regulation of sports gambling, sports insiders appear to develop total institutional cultures of gambling that promote the activity as a form of tolerable deviance.

The advent of Internet sports gambling has once more turned the world of betting, and its legal status, upside down. Whereas only a few dozen Internet sites existed in the late 1990s that facilitated sports gambling in the United States, there are nearly 2,000 today generating over $3 billion in revenue. Among the problems associated with Internet gambling are underage patterned gambling, credit card fraud and abuse, gambling addiction, and athletes anonymously betting on sports through pseudonyms. Internet gambling is, of course, illegal in the continental United States but filtered into and run through the country via Canadian, Caribbean, or Latin American countries. Ed Looney, director of the New Jersey Council on Compulsive Gambling, has recently argued that the number one form of problem gambling for college students is Internet betting on sports. The subject attracted national attention when ex–Florida State quarterback Adrian McPherson pleaded no-contest to misdemeanor charges of betting on college and professional sports, including his own games, on the Costa Rica-based site SBG Global. Industry insiders once more balked at the regulation of Internet gambling, arguing that Congress could generate millions in revenue (as is done in Canada, the UK, and elsewhere) by licensing and taxing sports betting online and elsewhere.

In Canada, the provincial and federal governments have considered public appeals to use revenue from online sports gambling in innovative ways. Assembled in 1997 to examine the benefit of increased public support of professional sports teams in Canada, the House of Commons–sponsored Mills Committee reported that if Canadian sports teams were to survive over the long term, at least a temporary solution to their financial crises was required. The Committee submitted its "Mills Report" to the House of Commons in 1998. None of their suggested funding initiatives were incorporated into either federal or provincial budget strategies. While the Mills Report recommendations were being rejected by the government, the House of Commons, at the request of NHL team owners in Canada, considered a proposal to use national and provincial lottery or sports gambling money to provide financial assistance to struggling NHL franchises. In part the request was motivated by a fear that several teams in financial crisis (Edmonton, Calgary, and Ottawa) could not compete financially (as smaller market teams) with their U.S. counterparts. Two Canadian teams, the Quebec Nordiques and the Winnipeg Jets, had already been relocated to U.S. cities (Denver and Phoenix, respectively), and league insiders worried that without State intervention, other Canadian teams would either collapse or suffer a similar fate. Media reports of the suggested financial brokering and salvaging of Canadian teams met with immediate, and predominantly negative, public response. Sentiment held that Canadian team owners were simply seeking to extract unneeded money from the federal government that should be devoted to the Canadian "social safety net" or that multimillion dollar salaried players were to blame for the financial crisis. Thus, in Canada, the debate centered around nothing to do with the illegality or immorality of sports betting but rather who should own access to the tax money generated from the legal sports gambling industry.

In 1998, one year before the proposed revenue issue, sports lottery companies generated over $172 million in profit in Canada. In return for the new revenue, the NHL offered to allow the provincial lotteries to use league and team logos to promote lottery sales. The NHL also promised to keep the six Canadian teams in place for at least five years and continue its revenue sharing to help support the Canadian teams (the NHL helped fund them between 1995–1999 with over $42 million). The issue of using tax money from sports gambling and lotteries to support teams raised the public ire, and the provinces with NHL teams (British Columbia, Alberta, Ontario, and Quebec) each refused to divert tax money made from sports betting away from social assistance and welfare programs.

The National Collegiate Athletic Association (NCAA) has been particularly concerned with online gambling in college sports since the late 1990s and with good reason. NCAA offices have surveyed over 30,000 college athletes on gambling issues since the mid-1990s. In 1998, a University of Michigan study found 35 percent of 758 student-athletes surveyed had gambled on sports and that 5 percent of the male athletes had either provided inside information for gambling purposes, bet on their own games, or accepted money to play poorly. In 2000, a University of Cincinnati study found 26 percent of the 648 Division I basketball and football players surveyed had gambled on college sports events, 4 percent on their own games, and 1 percent had accepted money to play poorly or shave points.

FUTURE PROSPECTS

If sports is a total institution with its own sense of morality and tolerable social practices, then gambling certainly has been a part of organized sports' "total culture" for well over 100 years. If legislators wish to eliminate gambling from sports then new legal initiatives and codes must attempt to alter socialization processes within athlete, coach, audience, and gaming groups so that their penchants for, and roles in, sports betting are not culturally transmitted across generations. With ambiguities, impracticalities, and apparent irrationalities/hypocrisy in the extant laws that prevent sports gambling, there is every reason to believe that it shall be more widely tolerated within North American sports insiders than it shall be shunned.

See also Academic Misconduct Among Athletes; Gambling; Salaries of Professional Athletes; Ticket Distribution and Scalping.

Further Reading: Cantelon, H. (2003). Sport and Politics. In *Canadian Sport Sociology,* edited by J. Crossman. Toronto: Nelson; Goffman, E. (1961). *Asylums.* New York: Anchor; Stebbins, R. (1996). *Tolerable Differences: Living with Deviance.* Whitby, ON: McGraw-Hill; Zimbalist, A. (2001). *Unpaid Professionals.* Princeton, NJ: Princeton University Press.

Michael Atkinson

GOVERNMENT SPONSORSHIP OF TEAMS

Since the late 1950s, both the U.S. and Canadian governments have diverted federal and state/provincial tax money to the maintenance of sports programs, leagues, and teams. A government's interest in financially supporting all levels of sports is complex and multilayered. There are clear public health and wellness reasons as to why sports programs should be made widely available to citizens, collective identity and status reasons as to why nations would seek to fund sporting excellence, and economic reasons as to why college and professional sports should remain staples of the entertainment industries. But the use of "public money" to support particular kinds of sports programs or teams is not always met with mass public support. At a historical period when social welfare programs are heavily underfunded, cities' social services are overstretched, and other social problems abound (crime, unemployment, disease, etc.), the use of tax money to support sports and leisure has never been more contested.

BACKGROUND

In any discussion of the modern nation-state, issues and questions relating to how governments should spend publicly generated tax money are prevalent. From a rather simplistic perspective, Western federal/national governments express the ideology that whenever possible, the distribution of tax dollars into spending programs should and must meet national interests. Of course, the notion of what a is national interest is complicated within very pluralist and multicultural societies such as Canada and the United States. At a bare minimum, the spending of national tax dollars is intended to assist in the protection of citizens, their social and cultural growth and development, and the development of national economies. Where sports fits into this schematic is open to debate and contestation. Progressively, it has been asked, does the funding of sports through national, public tax money fit in with a country's national interests? On one side of the debate, people argue that sports is a voluntary cultural pursuit and, thus, a matter for "civil society" to sort; therefore, funding for sports must come from/by those directly involved. On the other side of the debate, people argue that sports is a "state society" matter because athletics are vital in developing healthy populations, economies, and international reputations; thus, public money should be allocated to assist the development of amateur and professional sports.

Sports funding programs in Canada and the United States developed rather similarly. Until mid-century, governmental officials believed sports to be almost wholly a matter of civil society. Elite and professional athletes were viewed to be privileged, white males whose athletic interests had little, if anything, to do with national interests. However, after World War II, with Cold War tensions running high and increased Soviet and Eastern European presence (and success) at international sporting competitions such as the Olympics, U.S. and Canadian governments increasingly viewed sporting contests as key ideological/political battlegrounds. Viewed from such a perspective, international wins and losses of athletes and teams transformed into matters of national interest; funding of sports became justified, then, as a matter of promoting Western political economic lifestyles and cultures. Stated differently, sports became recognized in Canada and the United States as a matter of *public policy* because the international cultural reputation and status garnered through sports mattered greatly in a world of political and economic axes and allies. At the same time, the general zeitgeist of excitement, vibrancy, and strength of the postwar generation translated into growing social requests and demand for sports and leisure programs and facilities (especially for youth).

In Canada, for example, new bills and funding programs were quickly established (such as Bill C-131, "An Act to Encourage Fitness and Amateur Sport") to promote and fund amateur sports. The bill firmly established the federal governments' role in providing ongoing financial assistance to sports. The bill was subsequently followed by the Report of the Task Force on Sport (1969), the origin of Sport Canada (1971), and the Toward a National Policy on Fitness and Recreation (1979), A National Policy on Amateur Sport (1981) and Amateur Sport: Future Challenges (1990) documents among others.

Over the course of three decades, public policy related to the funding of amateur (and school-based) sports in Canada, like the United States, operated under the premise that the government possessed a moral, social duty to nurture athletic development among citizens to help facilitate cultural pride and physical wellness through sports. But underwritten across the separate policy documents outlining governmental positions on the state funding of sports was an important set of "hidden" principles.

Again, in the case of Canada, the government wrote into sports policy a belief that the funding of school, community, and amateur sports was, up to a point of development, strictly a civil matter. Public funds would only be directed to elite development programs or to athletes already identified as excellent in their sports. Second, and in a related way, the design, implementation, and stewarding of sports programs for youth should operate on the basis of volunteerism (at least up until elite sports levels, where government agencies would assume control over athlete/team development). Finally, because, as of the early 1960s, the state has funded between 75–90 percent of elite amateur sports programs, it assumed hegemony over how they are to be run; including what sports should be funded, where elite training facilities should be located, the number of programs to receive funding, and the level of excellence an athlete requires for funding consideration. As a consequence, agencies such as Sport Canada hold tremendous power in determining what sports are played by Canadians and how they are represented internationally at sports contests.

Clearly, while public tax dollars have been progressively funneled into particular sports environments, the number or range of funding initiatives has perhaps decreased in the recent past. Since the mid-1990s, more sports organizations at the grassroots, amateur, and professional levels have lobbied for greater funding.

KEY EVENTS

North American sports organizations, recreational clubs, and professional teams alike seek funding from governmental sources to sustain their operation and expansion over the long term. Most teams or leagues simply cannot run, at

ORGANIZED YOUTH PROGRAMS AND THEIR SPONSORS

For the most part, publicly funded organizations such as the YMCA or Boys and Girls Club of America who provide predominantly free sporting opportunities for youth are few and far between. With no surprise, perhaps, the following major types of youth sports organizations are cleaved not only along lines of socioeconomic status but ethnic/racial and religious as well. In essence, they represent as a social microcosm patterns of inequality and stratification existing at a broader societal level.

- *Publicly funded youth leagues:* Waning in number, these leagues (generally operated out of public parks) provide free organized sports for youth. They are inclusive for all youth but are unfortunately among the first to be "chopped" in times of economic crisis within a region.
- *Publicly funded youth sports facilities:* Like the YMCA, these are facilities that provide a range of sports, leisure, and educational opportunities for youth. These sites are increasingly funded by commercial organizations.
- *Private, nonprofit sports leagues:* These leagues operate in conjunction with national sports federations, leagues, and organizations (such as the Little League program) and charge participation fees for all members. These leagues are the garden variety form of organized youth sports in North America.
- *Private, commercial clubs:* These are incredibly exclusive youth sports organizations (such as a golf club or equestrian school) that often require exorbitant annual/ongoing fees from parents.

all levels of sports, without reliable and sufficient funding. But with the privatization of youth sports in the second half of the twentieth century and the wide-scale withdrawal of public funds from youth sports, opportunities for many to participate in athletics declined considerably. Until the 1960s, most elite amateur (including college/university) and professional sports ventures in North America were funded principally by private rather than public funds. This practice has changed only marginally over time. Youth sports programs in school or in local communities (such as Little League baseball) were similarly funded by private money but also somewhat subsidized through local government funding. Through the 1960s and 1970s, as youth sports became more popular, organized, institutional, and competitive, public funds dried up and were replaced by private funding sources. Local businesses and the parents of players became the chief sponsors of the games. Coakley (2004) has argued that with the rise of dual income households in the 1970s and 1980s parents were financially able to support their children's interest in youth sports but also required them as a key child-minding service and as inoculants against problems of juvenile delinquency. Increased public demand for government tax dollars and budget crises across North America in the mid-1980s resulted in funding for many of the remaining public sports programs in North America to be cut. With the rise of increasingly expensive and privately funded sports cultures, many families in the working classes were simply unable to support their children's interests in sports.

At the national and international levels, while people in the United States and Canada highlight the successes of their Olympic athletes as symbols of their social power or status, public funds are disappearing or simply do not match the cultural emphasis placed on Olympic sports success. We often forget that elite amateur athletes devote their lives to training and competition and simply do not have the time to fund their own involvement through paid labor outside of sports. Unless they come from privileged socioeconomic backgrounds (which many do), their long-term sporting aspirations are regularly cut short. Established in 1981, Sport Canada's government-funded initiative (which had been recommended as early as 1969), the Athlete Assistance Program (AAP), is a multimillion dollar reservoir of money to be allocated, in part, to athletes to help subsidize their participation. However, critics might point out that only athletes who are recognized to have special Olympic or Paralympic potential (i.e., the ability to place in the top 10) and are "carded" athletes (internationally ranked at high level) are generally given significant funding (ranging from C$3,500 to $18,000—income figures hovering around the national poverty line in Canada). Other promising or developing athletes may receive only a few hundred dollars a month, or year, to fund their involvement in sports. Considering the massive costs of sports (think of yearly equipment costs, travel costs, gym and coaching fees, etc.) many young athletes or their families cannot, even with the highest amounts offered under the AAP, afford to purse high caliber sports. It is ironic that while nation-states such as Canada are quick to highlight their Olympic athletes as national heroes, they are deemed, while they develop, not worthy of considerable national funding.

In the United States, athletes may be eligible for funding under the U.S. Olympic Committee's (USOC) range of Athlete Support Programs. Yet, while certain athletes may receive up to $25,000 under this scheme, there are inherent biases in the range of funding possibilities available to elites. First, the programs tend to favor sponsorship in the forms of tuition grants or educational scholarships, which have inherent biases toward athletes who have the requisite grades and opportunities to be in post-secondary institutes. Second, as in the case of Canada, the USOC tends to fund athletes who finish consistently high in national and international tournaments (i.e., through its Operation Gold or Direct Athlete Support funding schemes). Finally, the USOC also provides opportunities through its Olympic Job Opportunities Program for athletes; in this instance, the USOC works with sports and nonsports organizations to find part-time jobs for its (not yet highly ranked) athletes. In conjunction with these publicly and privately funded opportunities, U.S. athletes have been more successful historically in securing sponsorship money from private organizations and commercial businesses.

Elite amateurs are not the only athletes to seek more public dollars in the current era. For nearly four decades, proponents of increased subsidization of (especially professional) sports teams argue that the public monies allocated to them should be considered by the government as tactical investments in local economies rather than grants. These arguments are especially punctuated within conversations about the building or refurbishment of new stadiums. In the United States, professional sports teams have been incredibly successful in convincing municipal and state governments to bankroll the (re)construction of sports stadiums in the belief that by doing so jobs are created or maintained, new corporate investors will be drawn to the team, and the entertainment culture facilitated by the stadium will generate millions in local revenue. While such arguments are a matter of ongoing economic debate and contestation, taxpayer money in the United States funded $5.5 billion worth of professional sports stadium (re)constructions in the 1990s alone. Public money, it turned out, paid for 64 percent of the total cost of the work. In a review of the subsidies of the 110 professional sports teams in the 1990s, U.S. teams receive on average $50 million in governmental subsidies to help develop their physical infrastructures. By contrast, only 8 percent of stadium builds or rebuilds in Canada were funded through tax money.

The House of Commons in Canada, at the request of National Hockey League (NHL) team owners in Canada, considered a proposal to use national and provincial lottery money to provide financial assistance to struggling NHL franchises. In part the request was motivated by a fear that several teams in financial crisis (Edmonton, Calgary, and Ottawa) could not compete financially (as smaller market teams) with their U.S. counterparts. Two Canadian teams, the Quebec Nordiques and the Winnipeg Jets, had already been relocated to U.S. cities (Denver and Phoenix, respectively), and league insiders worried that without State intervention, other Canadian teams would either collapse or suffer a similar fate. Media reports of the suggested financial brokering and salvaging of Canadian teams met with immediate, and predominantly negative, public response. Sentiment held that Canadian team owners were simply seeking to extract unneeded money from the federal government that should be devoted to the Canadian "social safety net" or that multimillion dollar salaried players were to blame for the financial crisis.

What emerged in relocation and financial assistance discourses is that Canadian-based NHL teams were being gouged by governments by heavy taxation unlike their U.S. counterparts. Among the other taxes Canadian teams faced were staggering property taxes for their stadiums in each of their respective municipalities. The Montreal Canadiens, for example, paid more in property tax in 1998 than all of the U.S. teams combined. The six Canadian teams paid $24 million in property taxes in 1999. That year, the Ottawa Senators spent more of their budget on taxes than player salaries. Further still, massive capital gains taxes and income taxes were crippling Canadian teams' abilities to attract star players or foreign investors in the teams.

Driven by concern that cities housing NHL franchises would suffer economic loss from the movement of a team—estimates suggest that a franchise generates anywhere from $100–$150 million for a local economy—team owners such as Rod Bryden of the Ottawa Senators and government officials such as John Manley proposed to reduce the "entertainment taxes" in provinces such as Ontario (i.e., Toronto and Ottawa pay millions every year in the province because the government views sports teams as non-Canadian entertainment) to help struggling teams and to use sports lottery/gambling money generated from legal betting industries in the country such as ProLine. Proponents contended that because hockey is an essential part of Canadian culture, the government should step in to keep the six teams in Canada. Opponents argued that the lottery revenue should continue to be used for health care, charities, and social services, not for millionaire players and owners.

FUTURE PROSPECTS

Governments find merit in funding sports as a means of providing for the health and welfare of its citizens and as a method of fostering patriotism and civic pride. Whereas critics of a government's involvement in the funding of sports point out that the tax money allocated to sports initiatives is perhaps allocated toward the solution of pressing medical and social problems among people (employment, health, subsistence, etc.), others believe that sports plays a vital role in the maintenance of integrated social communities.

See also Funding Equality Legislation; Governments, Laws, and Gambling; Private vs. Public Sports Spaces; Sports for All and Fair Play Leagues.

Further Reading: Cantelon, H. (2003). Sport and Politics. In *Canadian Sport Sociology*, 1st edition, edited by J. Crossman. Toronto: Nelson; Coakley, J. (2004). *Sports and Society: Issues and Controversies.* New York: McGraw-Hill Ryerson.

Michael Atkinson

H

HAZING

Hazing is most commonly practiced in university fraternities and sports teams, but it also has a long history in the military, police forces, rescue services, and even some social service clubs in North America. *Hazing* may be defined as a coercive, and often physically dangerous, initiation activity that someone joining a sports team experiences. Hazing activities are designed and overseen by veteran members of a sports team and generally carried out in front of an entire team as part of an "initiation night." Hazing rituals are intended to humiliate, degrade, and abuse young or new members of a team. On many sports teams at the university or college level, a young player is not socially recognized as a legitimate player on the team until he or she has passed through one or several hazing rituals.

BACKGROUND

Knowledge of the history and contemporary pervasiveness of hazing in sports is limited. Hazing practices, because they are banned in most universities or professional sports teams, have become rather esoteric practices and thus tightly guarded by participants. From anecdotal evidence gathered in the last third of the twentieth century, hazing has been until quite recently found in male, team sports at the high school, university/college, or semiprofessional levels. Hazing rituals are common in contact sports such as ice hockey, rugby, wrestling, and football. The rituals, either conducted in one evening (known as a "Rookie Night" or "Rookie Show") or throughout an initiation week, frequently involve nudity, binge drinking, eating disgusting substances, shaving body hair, and certain levels of violence.

Despite the fact that most North American high schools, colleges, and semi-professional and professional teams have banned hazing outright, hazing cultures continue to flourish in sports. Teams with young participants (high school and college) tend to be the most vicious and unapologetic about their hazing rituals. At the professional sports level, hazing is still present, but it may take on a less dangerous and publicly humiliating tone. For example, first-year members of a professional team will often be forced to pick up the bill after the team goes out to an expensive restaurant. In professional baseball, a rookie player is often forced to dress in women's clothing after a game and field questions from reporters. In September 2004, a member of the Cleveland Indians was dressed as a cheerleader on the team bus on the way to the airport in Kansas City. In 2000, San Diego Chargers veterans tied a rookie to a pole in the downtown area of San Diego and threw eggs at him while onlookers laughed.

EXAMPLES OF HAZING RITUALS

The list of hazing rituals practiced on North American teams is lengthy. Here are a few typical hazing rituals practiced.

- "Running the gauntlet": The athlete is forced to run naked while being hit with a paddle.
- "Red rover": Two males are stripped, and one end of a rope is tied to each male's penis. They are then instructed to perform a tug-of-war.
- "Marshmallow races": Nude participants are made to pick up marshmallows with their buttocks, and then run a designated distance competing with other rookies. The last person across the finish line is forced to eat their marshmallow.
- "The elephant walk": Nude participants bend over and walk in a straight line, taking turns tugging at each other's genitalia.
- "Kangaroo court": Athletes are stripped and blindfolded and then accused of various "crimes." They are then forced to consume heavy amounts of alcohol within a short timeframe.
- "The Holocaust": Rookies are stripped and blindfolded and driven to a remote location during the night. Their clothes are soaked, balled up, taped together, and thrown into a ditch. The rookies are then let off the bus and told to find their clothes, untangle them, and find their way back to town.
- "Scavenger hunt": Rookies dress in flamboyant and outdated clothing and are sent to a public location (such as a bar or gymnasium) with a list of "items" to find and bring back (rarely any of which are actually present at the location). For any item the rookie does not recover, s/he is required to drink a predetermined amount of alcohol.

Regardless of the level of sport, or the seriousness of the outcome, the main point of hazing rituals is clear. The acts are classic social degradation ceremonies that symbolize a young player's willingness to respect his or her elders' statuses on a team. Hazing rituals are intended to lower the person's status in the group and publicly illustrate this low status to others. The hazing ritual reinforces the idea that, as a group, a sports team is defined in part by a rigid social hierarchy. At the same time, rookies receive great kudos from veteran players for undergoing the rituals. For this reason, athletes on the inside of sports and hazing rituals often value them as key team bonding ceremonies. When challenged about the appropriateness of hazing by outsiders, team members often aggressively defend their rights to haze and claim that people outside of sports cannot understand "what it takes" to be a member of a sports team.

Not all athletes respect, want, or celebrate hazing practices. From the mid-1980s onward, more players and their parents have been willing to come forward and challenge the legitimacy of hazing rituals in sports. These players have often been outcast by their teammates and ostracized by coaches. Universities and agents of social control have not, however, ignored player complaints. Players and coaches responsible for the structure and culture of hazing rituals in high school and college sports have been fined, dismissed, sentenced to community service, or ordered to participate in psychological counseling as a result. Still, a chilly climate exists for players who choose to violate the code of silence about hazing in sports.

KEY EVENTS

A series of media-amplified cases of hazing in the United States during the early 1990s brought new light on the issue and danger of hazing in sports cultures. Each of the cases showed, on the one hand, that schools and local police forces would not tolerate hazing as it had been in the past. But on the other hand, each case illustrated that the increased punishment of hazing by schools and other agents of society had only minimal deterrence effects. Other critics of hazing in North American sports suggested that the increased media exposure of the practices would not help to eliminate them and would only force them further underground. Two (in)famous cases of sports-related hazing show these points quite clearly.

In 2005, the Ontario Hockey League (OHL) levied fines totaling C$35,000 against the Windsor Spitfires and suspended the team's coach and general manager, Moe Mantha, for 40 games. The fines followed an investigation by the OHL into a hazing incident on September 9, 2005, that occurred on the team bus when the Spitfires were returning from an exhibition game in London, Ontario, against the London Knights. Four players were told to strip and stand in the washroom (designed to fit one person) at the back of the bus. The ritual is known in the league as the "hot box" and is common within the sport's culture. The players were told to enter the washroom at the beginning of the two-hour trip and remain there for the duration. News of the incident was leaked by an unnamed source to the OHL, and the league initiated the investigation. It is not

NOTORIOUS HAZING CASES IN THE UNITED STATES

1980, University of Michigan, Hockey

Freshman J. T. Todd reportedly was given large quantities of alcohol in a player's off-campus house in an annual initiation ritual. He allegedly was stripped, shaved, and covered with jam, eggs, and cologne and left outside in near-freezing weather for 90 minutes.

1988, Lyndhurst High School, New Jersey, Football

At a football camp, one sophomore was allegedly forced to insert his finger into the anus of another sophomore while 20 to 30 other teammates looked on. Two upperclassmen were dismissed from the team, and two others were demoted on the squad as a result of a school inquiry into the matter. No coaches were disciplined.

1990, Western Illinois University, Lacrosse

Nicholas Haben, a member of the school's lacrosse club, died in a dormitory after being carried back to school following a drinking initiation near campus. Twelve veteran participants were given community service.

1992, Sunnyside High School, Washington, Wrestling

In the school's wrestling room, a 15-year-old boy was allegedly sodomized with a mop handle while teammates held him down and dozens of others watched. The attack sent the boy, bleeding and traumatized, to the hospital for a week. He suffered internal injuries. Richard Melendrez, 18, pleaded guilty to second-degree reckless endangerment and was given 60 days in a work-release program.

1996, Alexander High School, Ohio, Football

Travis Hawk, a team captain, pleaded no contest to a misdemeanor charge of hazing involving several freshman teammates in the locker room showers. Parents of the victims contended their sons were sodomized with shampoo bottles after practice and suffered from mental anguish and continued harassment in school. Hawk was given a suspended sentence and $50 fine, plus community service requirement.

1998, New Orleans Saints, National Football League

In a hazing similar to a gang "jump-in" ritual, rookie Cam Cleeland suffered an eye injury when bashed with a bag of coins, and rookie Jeff Danish was sent through a window and hospitalized for stitches. Danish sued the Saints, teammate Andre Royal, an assistant coach, and five other players, seeking damages from the team of more than $650,000.

1999, North Branch High School, Michigan, Basketball

One player was expelled and six players were suspended for a series of hazing acts at a summer camp. One freshman was allegedly hit in the genitals with a wooden coat hanger, another was sprayed with urine from a shampoo bottle, and a third had his face forced onto another player's buttocks. Two coaches lost their jobs for failing to provide adequate supervision.

clear if the decision to suspend Mantha had any impact on the culture of hazing in the sport.

The case of hazing at McGill University in Montreal, Canada, in 2005, drew attention to one of sports most victimizing hazing traditions. In this case, the player who received a socially and physically cruel ritual came forward to complain. An 18-year-old member of the university's "Redmen" football team reported being sodomized by other members of the team as part of a hazing ritual. The player was taken to a darkened squash court on the last day of training camp in late August and told to remove his pants. The player allegedly refused several times but was reportedly coerced in compliance by fellow teammates. The player was then brought to his hands and knees, and other players prodded his rectum with a broomstick that team members subculturally refer to as "Dr. Broom."

McGill University launched an investigation and found that despite its antihazing policies, despite the fact that all of its football players signed commitments that they would not engage in hazing, and despite warnings from the coach that inappropriate behavior would not be tolerated, the hazing ritual was planned and carried out in clear violation of the rules. Cases of hazing in sports that so flagrantly violate league rules have been cited as prime examples of what sociologists call athlete hubris; athletes have a pride-driven arrogance because they are socially "special" populations. As a result of the football team's hazing, McGill University canceled the remainder of the varsity football season, took disciplinary action against several individuals on the team (university suspensions), forced players to engage in community service, reviewed and renewed its policies and procedures regarding hazing, and launched a series of alternative educational and team-building initiatives. In addition, the University further challenged other sports programs, leagues, and federations to adopt several of their "new" rules, including: to immediately suspend anyone for an entire season who engages in hazing; to revoke the athletic awards of any student who engages in hazing; to appoint special monitors of teams to police hazing/initiation week practices; and to broaden the definition of hazing to not only include physical acts but also emotionally and psychologically damaging acts such as verbal abuse.

What these cases illustrate is that even in an era of widespread criticism and control of hazing, the practices continue within a cultural insularity often cherished on sports teams. Especially in the case of the McGill Redmen football team, what is troubling is that the players engaged in hazing despite having institutionally promised they would not. These cases similarly point to the problem of policing the practice of hazing with harsh punishment but not addressing the culture of hazing in sports and its role therein. Without recognizing why hazing occurs, critics argue, no new policy aimed at punishment will be effective.

FUTURE PROSPECTS

Hazing might only disappear if subcultural traditions, and cultures of hubris, within sports are challenged and changed. At present, the culture/practice is under threat from the outside, but it needs to be changed from within. A promising step, argues hazing critic Jay Johnson, is to replace physically dangerous and psychologically damaging hazing rituals with other more pro-social and positive experiences. Week-long retreats at wilderness camps, participation in "Outward Bound" or adventure sports events, and involvement in collective public service programs such as Habitat for Humanity have all been recommended as group cohesion–building exercises for athletes. Standing in the way of these innovative ideas is a generational "payback" mentality among athletes, in which they find comfort in the idea that they can haze other players in ways they experienced in the past, or coaches who feel as if hazing, as long as it remains unseen and private, serves a critical function in team sports.

See also Academic Misconduct Among Athletes; Homophobia; Sports for All.

Further Reading: Johnson, J. (2004). *Making the Team: Inside the World of Sports Initiations and Hazing.* Halifax, NS: Canadian Scholars' Press; Nuwer, H. (2002). *Wrongs of Passage.* Bloomington: Indiana University Press; Nuwer, H. (2004). *The Hazing Reader.* Bloomington: Indiana University Press.

Michael Atkinson

HOMOPHOBIA

German psychologist Karoly Maria Benkert coined the term *homosexuality* in the late nineteenth century However, the term was discussed in Plato's *Symposium* in 360 B.C.E. *Homophobia* (from the Latin translation *homo:* man or human; *phobia:* fear, phobia) implies fear, hatred, discrimination, intolerance, or aversion to homosexuals. An interesting definition of homophobia comes from Audrey Lorde: "the fear of feelings of love for members of one's own sex and therefore the hatred of those feelings in others" (Lenskyj, 2003). Examples of homophobia can be found in sports for both male and female athletes.

BACKGROUND

Homophobia has been compared to racism, anti-Semitism, and other forms of bigotry that dehumanize large groups of people and deny their humanity, dignity, and personhood. In order to discuss homophobia, there are some important terms and definitions that should be outlined:

Bisexual—an individual whose emotional and sexual attractions and connections are with persons of both sexes.
Coming out, or being out of the closet, or being out—the process of accepting one's own homosexuality and telling others about it.
Gay—an individual whose primary emotional and sexual attractions and connections are with persons of the same sex (also homosexual).
Gender dysphoria—the intense and continuous discomfort a person feels when their physical sex and gender identity are not aligned.

Gender identity—a person's internal sense of themselves as male, female, or a combination of both.

Heterosexism—the assumption that everyone is or should be heterosexual and that heterosexuality is the only normal or natural expression of sexuality.

In the closet—keeping one's sexual orientation secret. People can be in the closet to varying degrees: for example, while they might be "out" in their personal life, they might remain "heterosexual" with their families, work colleagues, or sports team.

Lesbian—a more specific term to describe a homosexual female.

LGBT, or LGBTQ—an acronym for lesbian, gay, bisexual, transgender (queer or questioning). Increasingly, this general acronym is used to describe a broader community of sexually diverse minorities.

Questioning—a term used to describe individuals who are unsure of their sexual orientation.

Sexual orientation—the direction of one's sexual attraction toward the same sex (homosexual), the opposite sex (heterosexual), or both sexes (bisexual). Sexual orientation occurs along a continuum.

Straight, or heterosexual—an individual whose primary emotional and sexual attractions and connections are with persons of the opposite sex.

Transgendered—an umbrella term used to describe a wide array of persons whose gender identity does not conform to stereotypical gender norms of male or female.

Transitioned—a person experiencing gender dysphoria who chooses to align their gender role and gender identity. Transitioned individuals undergo hormonal treatment, surgery, and possibly other body modifications so that they may live their lives physically, psychologically, and emotionally as either a woman or a man.

Heterosexism is a central concept in the analysis of homophobia and refers to the privileging of heterosexuality over homosexuality. It may be expressed in terms of prejudice, discrimination, harassment, and violence toward those identified to be homosexual. In the sports environment, gay men and lesbians in the past were not accepted, homophobia was widespread, and the topic of homosexuality was avoided for fear that the two-category gender classification system (heterosexual or homosexual) might dissolve if people acknowledged and talked about it. The silence surrounding homosexuality and bisexuality in sports is deafening. People know that gender variant individuals play sports, but discussions that acknowledge such are usually avoided. Exceptions to this silence exist among openly gay men and lesbians who play and watch sports, as well as among women and men who play on teams and in programs that have developed an open and inclusive culture in which lesbian and gay coaches and teammates are accepted. The irony of the silence about sexuality and sports is that sports is a highly sexualized arena, even though it is presented in cultural mythology as asexual or nonsexual; the sexuality of sports is often denied because homophobia does not allow it to be recognized. We are afraid of homosocial contexts and ignore the idea of homoeroticism. Locker rooms are separate on the basis of sex because of the fear of creating potentially erotic situations. However, there is little concern or acknowledgement of the potential of arousal in an all male locker room, for example.

One of the most influential historians of sexuality, Michel Foucault, argued that sex has become the pivot for the organization and control of life in the modern world. In his view, people tend to take their sexuality very seriously as a primary source of identity, insight, and self-realization that determines their acceptability as human beings and their cultural status. In the nineteenth century, sexuality was centered on the extended, patriarchal, and heterosexually extended family. This dominant social organization of desire formed a disciplined social order that contributed to the larger political and economic aspects of society where homosexuality was not accepted and deemed to be wrong.

The stereotype of the lesbian woman was apparent following World War II, when female athleticism represented heterosexual failure. Controversy over women's participation in athletics involved two central concerns: fear that strenuous physical activity would damage women's reproductive organs and that it would interfere with their heterosexual sexuality. A common derogatory term for women athletes was "Muscle Moll"; the word *moll* referred to either the female lovers of male gangsters or to prostitutes. Both imply heterosexually deviant womanhood. In the wake of wartime, there was a need to reestablish the social order, and a "homosexual panic" occurred that resulted in the persecution of homosexuals. After World War II, the sports media focused on women athletes' sexual achievements at the expense of their athleticism and sporting success. In the late 1930s, psychologists were invited to speak to women and physical educators about the "problems" of sexual adjustment. The belief was that the all-female environments hindered heterosexual development. Other derogatory names such as "tomboy" and "dyke" were used to ridicule women and girls who did not fit the stereotypical ideal heterosexual woman. Likewise, males were referred to as "pussy," "fag," and "homo" if they did not represent the stereotypical ideal heterosexual male.

While advances in inclusive media coverage have been made in recent years, homosexuality was ignored in nearly all media coverage in the past, while heterosexuality was acknowledged directly and indirectly among men and women in sports. Lesbian images are still often carefully erased from coverage, even though the partners of players and coaches are usually known and visible among spectators. Men's physical connections with each other are noted when they hold hands in a huddle or pat one another on the buttocks, but similar connections among women athletes are typically ignored for fear that lesbian images might offend traditional media audiences. Lesbian athletes in golf, tennis, and basketball are rarely profiled in ways that acknowledge partners or certain aspects of their lifestyles—those parts of their personal stories are not told, whereas women athletes' children and husbands are frequently acknowledged if present. In media-constructed sports reality, lesbians and gay men in sports generally are invisible unless they make it a point to present themselves as "out," and even then, they often receive marginalized coverage. Homosexuality doesn't sell. Many myths surround homophobia and include the following: lesbian and gay people are sexual predators; lesbians and gays are unwanted on the team or in the locker room; gay athletes prefer artistic sports to contact sports; lesbians prefer softball or hockey to other sports; and girls who excel at sports must be lesbians. Double standards are also frequent: gay men have less aptitude for sports and, conversely, lesbian women have greater aptitude for sports than their straight counterparts. Men and women are also perceived using different standards: Older women involved in sports who do not appear to have husbands are presumed to be lesbians, while no such presumptions are made about older men's sexuality.

KEY EVENTS

Homophobia is a powerful cultural factor that has discouraged many girls and women from playing sports or making sports an important part of their lives. There is ample evidence of the chilly climate confronting lesbians in the sports contexts. Incidents of sexual harassment and overt discrimination against lesbians have been documented in school and university sports contexts as well as in community recreational sports. Therefore, many lesbian coaches, administrators, physical educators, and athletes attempt to hide their sexual orientation from their peers and employers. Homophobia may cause parents to steer their daughters away from sports they believe attract lesbians (rugby, football, ice hockey, handball, and soccer) and away from teams or programs where lesbians are believed to play or coach. When women fear the label of *lesbians* or fear being associated with lesbians, they may avoid certain sports or limit their commitment to playing sports. These fears may be grounded in personal homophobia among others and how others express their own sexuality. These fears influence both heterosexual women and lesbians. Many women athletes go out of their way to emphasize traditional feminine attributes and even say in interviews that being an athlete is not nearly as important as eventually getting married, settling down, having children, or becoming a nurturing homemaker in order to combat or prevent accusations of lesbianism. Homophobia affects all women, lesbian and heterosexual alike; it creates fears, it pressures women to conform to traditional gender roles, and it silences and makes invisible the lesbians who manage, coach, and play sports.

Pat Griffin's important research provides clear evidence that sports and lesbians have always gone together. She notes that this evidence has been ignored and that widespread homophobia has led to the creation of many myths about lesbians. Myths about lesbians have a range of consequences in sports. They have created among lesbian athletes a sense of loneliness and isolation combined with fears about being outed. Furthermore, they have created a situation in which lesbians must carefully choose and use one of the following six identity-management strategies: (1) completely closeted, (2) passing as heterosexual, (3) covering lesbian identity, (4) being "out" by not covering identity in all situations, (5) being "out" by revealing identity only to trusted others, (6) or being an open lesbian in sports. In general, women's sports are characterized

PEOPLE

When tennis start Martina Navratilova publicly revealed her lesbian identity, she faced various forms of hostility and lost many millions of dollars in endorsements, according to most estimates. Over the course of her career, she netted 18 grand slam singles titles, and she holds the record for both males and females for single match victories. By 1985, she had accumulated $8.5 million in winnings, which was more than any other player in the history of the sport. In 1988, American late-night television host Arsenio Hall inappropriately joked: "if we can put a man on the moon, why can't we put one on Martina Navratilova?" Despite holding the all-time record for tournament victories, male or female, she consistently received fewer endorsement contracts than her female counterparts. During the 2002 Australian Open, Damir Dokic, father of Australian player Jelena Dokic, told a Serbian newspaper that he would commit suicide if he found out that his daughter was a lesbian. Navratilova had the last word, "It's a good thing that I'm not his daughter … [then again] … maybe it's too bad I'm not" (Lenskyj, 2003).

Sheryl Swoopes, a Women's National Basketball Association (WNBA) player, became pregnant during the inaugural season of 1997. Some believe that she became the favored most valuable player because she had a baby and six weeks later was back on the court. The league's image seemed to become more acceptable if the women were viewed as heterosexual. In 1998, Swoopes divorced her husband and seven years later announced publicly that she is a lesbian. Despite the story being "big news" because she is one of the only high-profile athletes in team sports to come out, it was important to see that Swoopes, unlike Navratilova, kept her major sponsorship contracts with Olivia and Nike. She was the first women's basketball player to have a Nike shoe named after her, "Air Swoopes."

by a "don't ask, don't tell" atmosphere. Many heterosexuals are uncomfortable dealing with the idea and reality of lesbians in sports, and many lesbians in turn choose a "don't rock the boat" strategy, which enables them to play the sports they love to play without being harassed. However, such an approach has its costs, and it does not encourage changes that might decrease or even eliminate homophobia in sports.

Men's sports have always been key sites for reproducing dominant forms of masculinity. Playing sports is a rite of passage for boys to become men, and many people define male athletes in contact and power sports as the epitome of what it means to be a heterosexual man in society. Therefore, there is much at stake in maintaining the silence about gay men in sports and in discouraging gay male athletes from revealing their true identities. Often, gay men are perceived as "letting the team down" by sabotaging the masculinity norms and ideals that sports typically celebrates. The message to boys and men in sports is loud and clear: "Don't be a fag, and don't play like a girl." The message to gay men of all ages is also clear: "Don't challenge the working system." Heterosexual men have developed threatening antigay locker room discourse in the forms of verbal gay bashing that would keep gay men in the closet forever and

PEOPLE

Stories about gay male athletes have been nearly nonexistent. Canadian gay athletes, such as Mark Tewksbury (Olympic gold medalist in swimming), often wait until their competitive careers are over before "coming out." Tewksbury publicly announced he was gay in 1998. As a result, he lost a six-figure contract as a motivational speaker because he was "too openly gay." Prior to 1998, Tewksbury's agent arranged for him to have "fake" female girlfriends in order to ensure sponsorship and athletic success. A founder and leader of the Outgames and proponent of human rights in sports, Tewksbury also published a book, *Inside Out: Straight Talk from a Gay Jock*.

In 2007, John Amaechi, a former English National Basketball Association (NBA) player, came out four years after his retirement and published a book, *Man in the Middle*. He is known as the first NBA player to speak publicly about being gay. Many former NBA players voiced their concern after Amaechi's outing. For example, Tim Hardaway voiced outright homophobic comments during a media radio interview. Hardaway believes that there is no place for gay men in the NBA.

heterosexual men silent about homosexuality and fearful of doing anything that could be labeled "gay."

Sports is an expression of the myth of orthodox masculinity. The most masculine sports tend to be the most violent. Less masculine sports are those in which struggle rather than violence is a dominant characteristic; the athlete struggles with his opponents and or himself without creating violence. The least masculine sports are those where success is determined by the combination of skill and aesthetic expression: figure skating, diving, and dance. These aesthetic sports are generally considered the least masculine because they involve the lowest degree of aggression. A boy or man who plays a sport like football is not only capable of performing masculine moves, but he is also understood because his sports participation is entirely masculine. He is aggressive, rough, tackles other players, and represents the ideal heterosexual male. The silence creates a context in which boys and men feel ashamed about feelings of masculinity to avoid being accused of being "fags." The stereotype that real men play with pain and injuries; they do not admit they are afraid; and they do not confide affectionately in other men, even the teammates who they care very much about, continues to linger.

FUTURE PROSPECTS

Gay athletic clubs can be found in major cities in Europe, Australia, New Zealand, North America, and parts of South America and Africa and constitute an important part of gay community life. There are also many gay sports governing bodies. For instance, the North American Gay Amateur Athletic Alliance is a nonprofit organization dedicated to promoting amateur softball for all people, but with special emphasis for gays.

The Gay Games, a prestigious international festival that celebrates athletic competition and the arts, was launched in 1982 and is held quadrennially as a celebration of the international gay community. The Gay Games were founded by former decathlete Tom Waddel in 1981 and continue to be organized by volunteers. The purpose of the Gay Games is to foster and increase the self-respect of lesbians and gay men and to augment understanding from the nongay world. The Gay Games are open to participants who are gay, lesbian, bisexual, transgendered, queer, and heterosexual. For many, the Games represent a reaction to homophobia in mainstream sports; significant numbers of participants had little sporting involvement prior to participation but are attracted to the mission of inclusion and the community that the Games offer. The original Games were called the Gay Olympics, but after a four-year unsuccessful court battle in the United Sates from 1982 to 1986, the Games reluctantly agreed to change the name to The Gay Games to satisfy the International Olympic Committee (IOC). The Gay Games' winners are recognized, medals are awarded, and records kept. The Gay Games allow highly trained athletes whose careers had been challenged by homophobia to have their own "Olympics." The Outgames also celebrate diversity, however, in a less competitive context. The Outgames included an *International Conference on LGBT Human Rights* that was held in conjunction to the first games in Montreal in 2006.

In 2006, the Canadian Association for the Advancement of Women in Sport (CAAWS) released a position paper on homophobia, "Seeing the Invisible, Speaking about the Unspoken." The release of the paper was timed to celebrate May 17, the International Day against Homophobia, and the purpose was to initiate discussions on homophobia and to increase all athletes' enjoyment and participation in sports. The Canadian Commonwealth Games Association of Canada created a positive space program for the 2006 Games in Melbourne, Australia. They attempted to ensure that the host city was a safe place for LGBTQ team members and included information of interest to the LGBTQ members in the "Guide to Melbourne" handbook.

"Getting Over It: Homophobia, Sports and University Education" was published in 2006 in Australia by the School of Human Movement, Recreation and Performance at Victoria University. The purpose of the booklet is to improve professional practice among those involved in sports and exercise-related fields, such as coaching, teaching, therapy and rehabilitation, counseling, and management. Guidelines on creating safe climates and inclusive spaces are outlined and intermixed with direct quotes from gay Australian athletes. Documents like this one help to decrease myths about homosexuality and homophobia and increase knowledge and respect.

The Women's Sport Foundation in the United Sates initiated an educational program "It Takes a Team: Making Athletics Safe for Lesbian and Gay Athletes and Coaches" with the intention of ending homophobia in sports. The director of the program is Pat Griffin, former coach, athlete, and a leading researcher on sexuality and sports. Programs like this one help to eliminate discrimination in sports and provide practical information for athletes, coaches, administrators, and the general public. Addressing homophobia in sports helps create a supportive environment for lesbian and gay youth who are at greater risk of isolation and harmful behaviors than their heterosexual counterparts.

See also Gay Games; LGBT Sports Leagues; Marketing Female Athlete Sexuality; Openly Gay Athletes.

Further Reading: Cahn, S. (Summer 1993). From the "Muscle Moll" to the "Butch" Ballplayer: Mannishness, Lesbianism, and Homophobia in U.S. Women's Sports. *Feminists Studies:* 19 (2) 343–368; Cahn, S. (1994). *Coming on Strong: Gender and Sexuality in Twentieth-Century Women's Sport.* New York: Free Press; Griffin, P. (1998). *Strong Women, Deep Closets: Lesbians and Homophobia in Sport.* Champaign, IL: Human Kinetics; Lenskyj, H. (2003). *Out on the Field: Gender, Sport and Sexualities.* Toronto: Women's Press; Palzkill, B. (1990). Between Gymshoes and High-Heels: the Development of a Lesbian Identity and Existence in Top Class Sport. *International Review for the Sociology of Sport* 25: 221–234; Pronger, B. (1990). Gay Jocks: A Phenomenology of Gay Men in Athletics. In *Sport, Men, and the Gender Order Critical Feminist Perspectives,* ed. M. Messner and D. Sabo, 141–152. Champaign, IL: Human Kinetics; Pronger, B. (1992). *The Arena of Masculinity: Sports, Homosexuality and the Meaning of Sex.* Toronto: University of Toronto Press; Theberge, Nancy. (2000). *Higher Goals: Women's Ice Hockey and the Politics of Gender.* Albany: State University of New York Press.

Charlene Weaving

HOOLIGANISM

Hooliganism, predominantly associated with world soccer, is a term first used in the media to describe the organized, riotous, violent, and destructive lifestyles of sports fanatics who over-identify with a specific (normally local) team. Hooliganism, at least in its most dramatic form, predominantly flares up between groups of rival team supporters (often called "firms" or "crews") in and around high-profile matches. While English soccer fans have been globally positioned as the main contributors to hooliganism in sports, there is evidence that hooliganism occurs not only throughout soccer fans, but throughout the sporting world.

BACKGROUND

Riotous fan behavior in sports is nearly as old as organized sports itself. But the patterned social organization of riotous behavior among sports fans is a trend of modern sports cultures. From the 1960s to the early 1990s, hooliganism in and around the sport of soccer became the most globally referenced type of organized sports crowd disorder. In particular, British hooligan cultures were mass mediated as the leading offenders. One social historian argues that in the UK, soccer hooliganism grew to become one of the nation's leading social problems. His review of major soccer hooligan incidents from 1908–1990 indicated, however, that countries including Argentina, France, Brazil, USSR, Chile, Italy, India, Ireland, Hungary, Canada, Spain, and Germany (to name only a few) each experienced regular bouts of hooliganism.

Dunning and others provide evidence that reveals how soccer hooliganism in England and other countries dates back to, at a minimum, the 1880s. Early forms of organized hooligan behaviors (i.e., fist fighting, property destruction, petty acts of vandalism, arson) most common at especially significant matches that pitted close geographic rivals against one another. A staple of soccer culture at the time was showcase matches between two local teams, known as "derbies." British newspapers described how working-class, male fans, then called *roughs,* caused considerable public nuisance at the London derbies. An enduring roughs subculture emerged by the end of the nineteenth century, with participants traveling to away fixtures in groups to create "a bother" (cause violence) at rivals' stadiums.

During the interim period between the World War I and World War II, roughs culture dissipated to a large extent but resurfaced at the onset of the 1960s. British soccer matches started to feature regular fights among fans from rival cities in England, Wales, and Scotland and saw the emergence of more organized hooliganism. The ascendance in popularity of the sport in the postwar era and the mass mediation of the game created a new level of excitement and significance for fans who increasingly tied portions of their collective identities to the successes and failures of their teams. Fans started to form hooligan groups, mostly drawn from local working-class areas. They tended to all stand together on the "terraces" (bleachers) in stadiums, sang aggressive and derogatory chants to other fans, threw missiles onto the field, consumed large portions of alcohol, and generally regarded the soccer fields as their own tribal territory to be defended from outsiders. It has been suggested that the segmenting of stadium seating into separate "ends" for the fans particularly fostered a camplike or warlike mentality among rival fans. With the growth of fans traveling to watch their local club play away matches, gangs of marauding fans became described in the press as hooligan "firms," and during matches they focused their attentions on intimidating opposing fans.

During the 1970s, organized hooligan firms emerged in pathological support of clubs such as Birmingham City (Zulus), Chelsea (Headhunters), Leeds United A.F.C. (Leeds Service Crew), Manchester United (Red Army), Millwall (F-Troop), Tottenham Hotspur (Yid Army), and West Ham United (Inter City Firm). To a lesser extent, lower league clubs also had firms, such as Blackpool's (Rammy Arms Crew). As a result of two major incidents between rival crews in 1973 (i.e., when Manchester United were regulated to the Second Division, and when a Bolton Wanderers crew members stabbed a rival from Blackpool), the separate leagues collectively introduced new crowd segregation and fencing at soccer codes around stadiums in England. Yet, incidents involving English hooligans dramatically spiked in the 1980s, leading Parliament to introduce new laws and policies to monitor fans and control crowds within stadiums.

Soccer violence within British stadiums declined after the introduction of the "Football Spectators Act" in 1989, but during the 1990s, English fans were targeted and heavily surveilled by international police organizations such as INTERPOL during international tournaments. The 1990s witnessed a sharp incline in hooligan incidents involving English national team supporters. British police, FIFA, and INTERPOL worked together to monitor English hooligan crews, at times even preventing them from leaving England during international tournaments. By the early 2000s, hooligan crews that had managed to slip through the widening net of social control engaged in riotous behavior with rivals far away from stadiums. At the Euro 2000 Cup tournament, for example, England's national team was threatened with expulsion from the tournament after English hooligan crews fought with rival fans at nearby pubs and parks. Since Euro 2000, however, social control efforts appear to be functioning because only a handful of incidents involving English hooligans have been documented at international tournaments.

Explaining why hooligan crews develop or behave in flamboyantly violent manners is another matter entirely. Five major explanations of hooliganism continue to be debated. The first, and perhaps most simplistic, is that riotous behavior results when fans consume excessive alcohol at matches. Inhibitions among them are subsequently lowered, and when provoked by rivals, they engage in violence. Second, and only moderately more elaborate than the first explanation, is that frustration, aggression, and then violence among fans results because of poor or biased officiating. Acts of violence between rival fans are displaced forms of aggression that are, in essence, symbolically directed at officials. Third, because hooligan crews are, historically, predominantly but not exclusively working class, mainstay sentiment in England is that in times of economic spiral or crisis, hooligan violence escalates among "slum people" supporting a "slum game." Violence between fans on the terraces is a metaphor for economic class angst and frustration. The fourth and fifth explanations are related and stand in direct contrast to the third. Critics of soccer culture in the UK have suggested that the postwar era, and its immediate affluence and permissiveness, created a culture of entitlement and bravado within the English. These attitudes were subsequently carried over into sports cultures.

KEY EVENTS

After a spike in social concern about hooligan crews in the UK during the early 1970s, English hooliganism appeared to dissipate until 1985. But 1985 would be considered one of the most important times, and horrifically dramatic perhaps, during the unfolding of organized crowd disorder in English soccer. In March 1985, a Millwall hooligan crew viciously rioted with Luton fans during an FA Cup match. The events received international media attention as the "rebirth" of the hooligan cultures in England. Then Prime Minister Margaret Thatcher appointed a governmental committee, dubbed the "War Cabinet," to explore the resurgence of hooliganism. Only two months later, in May of 1985, a 15-year-old boy died when a wall collapsed at St. Andrews stadium. Rival hooligans rioted during a match between Birmingham City and Leeds United and attempted to tear down a makeshift wall separating them. When riot police entered the stadium to quell the hostilities, it only served to incense the fans who would (1,200 strong) eventually tear down the wall. Local magistrate Justice Popplewell later described the confrontation as resembling "the Battle of Agincourt [rather] than a football match."

Only three weeks following the tragedy at St. Andrews, as a result of riotous behavior by Liverpool fans during a European Cup final match held in Brussels (at Heysel stadium) between Liverpool and Juventus, 39 Juventus fans lost their lives. A wall separating the rival groups collapsed and crushed them after Liverpool fans scaled it, shook it, and dislodged it from its bearings. Despite the escalating tragedies, it would not be until 1989, after that year's Hillsborough disaster involving fans of Liverpool and Nottingham Forest (in which 94 Liverpool fans lost their lives after being crushed against a steel fence within the stadium), that the FA or the British government would take action. British Parliament hurriedly enacted the "Football Spectators Act" in late 1989, which at once developed policies to monitor the identities of hooligans and to change the structural conditions of sports stadiums to control them. That same year, Lord Taylor of Gosforth was commissioned to conduct an investigation into Hillsborough (published as the *Taylor Report* in 1990). His conclusions altered the ways in which fans/hooligans were managed within and on the terraces. In some ways most consequentially for English fans, however, was that in the wake of Hillsborough (and other events) all English professional clubs were banned from international competition for 5 years, and Liverpool FC itself banned for 10 years (later reduced to 6).

In the aftermath of the bans, a general air of international persecution developed among English fans. With the proliferation of international tournaments, English fans carried their form and style of hooliganism abroad, creating havoc at World Cup and other national team tournaments and contests (Italy 1990, 1997; France 1998, 2000; Slovakia 2002; Germany 2006). English hooligans were further vilified in global soccer culture for their riotous behaviors, and important global rivals developed between crews representing their nations (i.e., English hooligans developed intense rivalries with German, French, Dutch, and Italian fans, in particular).

Among the most notorious soccer hooligan crews in English history are Millwall's firm, the Bushwackers. Originating in the 1930s as F-Troop, the Bushwackers lay claim to the most patterned, and destructive, legacy of hooliganism in the country. Reaching the apex of its membership and destructiveness in the 1980s (pre-Hillsborough), the Millwall Bushwacker name became synonymous in England with hooliganism. The parent club Millwall, and even Millwall police, has historically supported the firm; despite the teams' ground being temporarily closed or its organization being fined by the FA for the actions of the crew. The Bushwackers were the subject of a BBC documentary in early 1972, drawing the social problem of hooliganism in England into sharp relief. Millwall's enduring rivals are West Ham United, and firms representing these two teams have clashed in some of the most vitriolic fights in soccer's history. In 2002, then owner of Millwall, Theo Paphitis, instituted a new membership scheme in the club to prevent known hooligans from having access to season tickets. The move followed one of the most violent hooligan incidents in the country, wherein the Bushwackers clashed with rivals from Birmingham City outside of New Den Stadium.

The FIFA World Cup of 1998 (held in France) signaled in a new style of hooliganism and its policing in soccer. With the advent and mass proliferation of the Internet through Western Europe and English fans' decade-long resentment of the techniques of international soccer policing following Hillsborough, hooligans from England and other countries actually met "virtually" in the weeks before the tournament and scheduled clashes with one another in the quest to determine which country contained the "best" hooligans in Europe. The policing operation at the 1998 World Cup in France thus evolved into one of the most elaborate in sports history to date. It involved collaboration with a dozen European countries but, in particular, between English, German, and French police forces. This consultation was specifically so that French police would be aware of which known hooligans would attempt to enter France and where English hooligans stayed, met, and scheduled clashes in France. The particular problem with security at France 1998 was, of course, the relative ease by which hooligans could cross French borders. Sharing borders with England and Germany proved troublesome and demanding of new initiatives to tightly control fan migration into the country. Troublingly, security efforts at the border were hampered in France 1998 as a result of a new agreement between Western European nations, "the Schengen Agreement," which prohibited people from being turned away at a national border without significant cause. As a result, English fans routinely rioted in Marseilles, and German fans severely injured rivals and even police in Lens and Paris. The 1998 World Cup was further evidence that hooligan cultures were still alive and kicking in international soccer and that authorities had not yet devised efficient schemes to combat hooliganism.

One of the most dramatic, non-English cases of soccer hooliganism occurred in Colombia in 1994 following the World Cup in the United States. Andres Escobar, a defender for the Colombian national team, was shot and killed after making a critical mistake during a game against the United States. Stretching to cut out across into his own penalty area, Escobar accidentally kicked the ball into his own goal, placing the U.S. team in the lead (one that they did not relinquish). In Medellin, Colombia, 10 days later, Escobar was shot 12 times by a gunman after leaving a nightclub. Pretournament rumor and speculation held that organized hooligans in Colombia had intimidated and harassed players and coaches, threatening that if the team failed to win, violence would result.

FUTURE PROSPECTS

Despite governmental, media, and academic claims that soccer hooliganism has experienced a roller-coaster cycle of appearance and disappearance over the twentieth century, global data on hooliganism suggests that the social practice has never really gone away, nor come back; it has always been present in varying degrees. Despite a century of social control efforts, we still know very little about how hooligan crews emerge and why they persist, or why agents of authority appear ill-equipped to manage hooliganism on a broad social scale. Hundreds of deaths, thousands of injuries, and hundreds of millions of dollars in property damage later, none of the long-term "scores" have been settled between rival crews, and hooligan subcultures thrive just beneath the outer facades of "squeaky-clean" professional soccer.

See also Field Invasions; Missile Throwing; Postevent Riots; Soccer Tragedies.

Further Reading: Armstrong, G. (1998). *Football Hooligans: Knowing the Score.* Oxford: Berg; Dunning, E. (1999). *Sport Matters.* London: Routledge; Kerr, J. (1994). *Understanding Soccer Hooliganism.* Buckingham: Open University Press; Marsh, P. (1978). *Aggro: The Illusion of Violence.* London: Dent.

Michael Atkinson

ILLNESS

Once a person's body is diagnosed as ill, they are considered medically unique. They are deviations from a healthy norm. Once the body is designated as a medical problem, it is also marked socially. And, just as an ill body is a problem for the individual, it is also a symbol of life's harshest reality: death. If the diseased body is individually stigmatizing and socially disruptive in mainstream cultures, it is perhaps doubly deviant in sports cultures, where images of virile, dominating, and perfect bodies are valued. Athletes from a variety of sports, social backgrounds, and global cultures are embarrassed to be ill in front of peers, coaches, and fans. Illness or injury may be viewed as a marker of an inability to perform athletically, a failed athletic self, an end of a career, a lack of masculinity or femininity, or even a sexual or an ethnic deficiency. Illness in sports is essentially unwanted because it symbolizes weakness, frailty, and failure. For many athletes, becoming ill violates the rule of body law established by medicine and by conventional norms of embodiment in perfection- and performance-oriented sports cultures.

BACKGROUND

The conventional medical and broader cultural approach to illness and ill people is often challenged within sports cultures. Some athletes who experience injury or disease are viewed as weak and are encouraged to come back as a display of personal fortitude and grit. Other athletes seek to challenge medical and traditional sports world distinctions between ill bodies and athleticism and to challenge the very construction of illness as a form of social deviance. These athletes reject the accepted simple opposition between health and illness and deliberately insert the discussion and representation of illness into sports.

In particular, "comebacks" from illness by athletes have become very valued cultural stories in North America. They are used to publicly testify about the strength of the human spirit and the will to succeed through dedication and hard work. As it has been long believed that participation in sports builds personal character, we often place pressure on ill athletes to "comeback" from disease to reaffirm this cultural idea. Therefore, the comeback story in sports is meaningful because it documents an athlete's successful return and because it reaffirms body codes associated with the athlete social identity.

Increasingly, the comeback story in sports has been linked with disease awareness and fundraising campaigns; especially in the sport of distance running. The growing number of cause-related athletic events held each year in North America

---

RECENT COMEBACKS

Ludmila Engquist, a former Olympic and world champion in the 110-meter hurdles, underwent surgery for breast cancer in the months leading up to the 1999 IAAF World Athletics Championships in Seville, Spain. Doctors gave her a bleak prognosis for a return to sports and suggested that recovering before the Seville competition was not possible. However, Engquist managed to regain her fitness and won a bronze medal.

Mario Lemieux, a Canadian ice hockey all-star, was diagnosed with Hodgkin's disease in 1993. He missed 23 games during the season while receiving aggressive radiation treatment. Incredibly, Lemieux returned to play during the same season and won the National Hockey League's (NHL) scoring title. He rested for the entire 1994–1995 season, but he returned to the sport to win two Art Ross trophies (as the NHL points champion) and a Hart Trophy (as the NHL most valuable player) before announcing his retirement in 1997. In 2000, Lemieux shocked the sports world once more by returning to the ice.

Bethany Hamilton, a 13-year-old amateur surfboarder, was attacked by a 15-foot shark in waters off the coast of Kauai's north shore in Hawai'i on October 31, 2003. The shark bit off her left arm just below her shoulder, leaving Hamilton with an open wound 16 inches long and 8 inches wide. Hamilton paddled to shore, losing nearly 70 percent of her blood. She miraculously survived, and only 4 months after the attack, found herself back on a surfboard and performing competitively. She placed fifth in the 2004 U.S. National Surfing Championships and earned a place on the U.S. National Surfing Team that year. She won an ESPY Award for Best Comeback Athlete in 2004.

Teddy Bruschi, a player in the National Football League, was taken to a hospital after a mild stroke on February 16, 2005. Doctors discovered that he suffered from a congenital heart defect. After several months of rehabilitation, on October 16, 2005, Bruschi was medically cleared to resume playing football, and he rejoined the team on the practice field three days later. The New England Patriots officially activated him on October 29, and he played the following night against the Buffalo Bills. He was named ESPN's 2005 Comeback Player of the Year.

illustrates how people use sports as a site of collective battle against illness. In many cases, the events are held annually or even more frequently. The Canadian Imperial Bank of Commerce (CIBC) and Canadian Breast Cancer Foundation have been co-organizers of an annual Run for the Cure since 1992. The annual run and walk, branded by a pink ribbon, raises awareness about breast cancer, honors the memories of family members and friends lost to cancer, and collects funds for breast cancer research. The first event saw 1,500 runners take part in Toronto. By 2007, more than 50 communities in Canada hosted Run for the Cure events involving more than 170,000 participants. Run for the Cure races have even migrated to the United Kingdom, the United States, Australia, and Japan. In the United Kingdom, the British United Provident Association (BUPA) sponsored Great North Run is the largest half marathon in the world. More than 50,000 runners participate, and the event helps to raise awareness about and funds for children living with leukemia. Acknowledging the importance of talking about illness, the Great North Run Web site (http://gnr.realbuzz.com) also includes space for participants to write their own stories about the race and experiences with illness.

KEY EVENTS

Lance Armstrong's comeback is perhaps the most globally told story of its kind in modern sports. Armstrong's Tour de France victory in 1999 occurred just 3 years after doctors predicted that he would die from cancer. At the age of 25, just as his professional cycling career had blossomed, Armstrong received notification on October 2, 1996, that he had stage III testicular cancer. The cancer had spread to his abdomen, lungs, and brain. Armstrong received aggressive chemotherapy in 1997 and returned to professional cycling later that same year. The upstart U.S. Postal cycling team signed Armstrong in 1998, and from 1999 to 2004 he captained the team in six straight Tour de France races. Incredibly, Armstrong won the overall Tour title in each race. In 2005, Armstrong led a new team, the Discovery Channel team, to a seventh straight Tour championship. His unprecedented and record-smashing seven consecutive tour victories—each plagued by unsubstantiated allegations of illegal doping—in one of the world's most grueling sports competitions became symbols of hope to millions of cancer patients.

Armstrong's comeback narrative does not end, however, with his tour victories or the many biographies and autobiographies chronicling his life. Armstrong publicly argues that stories about his comeback take their most important form through the Lance Armstrong Foundation (LAF). Established in 1997, the foundation is a fund-raising, research, interactive outreach, sports organizing, and personal counseling service designed to support people surviving cancer. The LAF raised millions of dollars in cancer research funding and founded counseling programs in U.S. hospitals from 1997 to 2003. Concomitant with Armstrong's ascending global popularity, the LAF launched the Livestrong Web site to promote cancer awareness and mediate survivor stories. In 2004, the LAF worked with Nike in order to create and disseminate the Livestrong wristband. The LAF and its yellow wristband campaign are now among the most recognized support resources for people living with or affected by cancer. Throughout the early 2000s, the LAF also worked globally to establish international fund-raising, propose and script national policy plans for increased government funding of cancer research, establish "Survivor Days" themed sports events, create children's survivorship days, promote cancer education programs, and endow young innovator awards to help fight the physical, social, and emotional outcomes of cancer.

Among the pioneering initiatives of the LAF is the use of the Livestrong Web site as a narrative resource center for people and families who have survived cancer. The Livestrong site includes space for people to read and share survivor narratives and to join the symbolic LAF survivor peloton (a peloton is group of cyclists riding together in a tight and cooperative cluster). The stories of survival, loss, doubt, hope, and the future are shared through diary entries and personal testimonies. Armstrong's vision for the Livestrong space is clear: It is designed to inspire frontline dialogue about cancer and its effects on people. As the LAF motto states, "We believe in focus: getting smart and living strong. Unity is strength, knowledge is power. Attitude is everything."

The LAF's showcase of survival narratives certainly fits into—but also breaks new paths within—public talk about illness and recovery in countries such as the United States. The Livestrong Survivorship Center of Excellence Network and SurvivorCare program, for example, promotes the idea of *winning* against cancer by narrating a survivalist mentality among patients. Illness stories showcased through the LAF advocate personal empowerment and recovery through grassroots *battles* against disease. Patients are discouraged from being passive victims of disease.

Terry Fox was born on the Canadian prairies and raised on Canada's west coast. An active teenager involved in many sports such as rugby, baseball, and basketball, Terry was only 18 years old when diagnosed with osteogenic sarcoma (a form of cancer that makes bones turn soft). As a result, doctors amputated his right leg 6 inches (15 centimeters) above the knee in 1977. Fox was then fitted with an artificial leg. While in the hospital, Terry was so overcome by the experiences of other cancer patients and the inspirational story of Dick Traum—a man who ran the New York City Marathon with a prosthetic leg—that he decided to run across Canada to raise money for cancer research. Fox would eventually call his journey the *Marathon of Hope*. Before undertaking the run, he joined the basketball team of the Canadian Wheelchair Sports Association in British Columbia in 1977, and he played in three national championships with the team. Despite pain produced by a poorly fitted prosthesis, Fox completed his first marathon in Prince George, British Columbia, in 1979.

In turning his attention full time to the Marathon of Hope, Fox aimed to raise C$1 of research money for every member of the Canadian population by running a marathon a day across Canada. At the outset, Fox solicited dozens of public and private companies for funding support, but only a few responded—the Ford Motor Company donated a van, Adidas provided several pairs of shoes, and the Safeway grocery store chain provided food vouchers. After 18 months and more than 3,107 miles (5,000 kilometers) run in preparation, Terry started his marathon in St. John's, Newfoundland, on April 12, 1980, with only a little fanfare and media attention. Public enthusiasm and awe of Fox's venture grew quickly as he ran through the Atlantic provinces, and the money he collected along his route began to mount. He ran 26 miles (42 kilometers)—and on many occasions more than 30 miles (48 kilometers)—a day through Canada's Atlantic provinces, through Quebec, and into Ontario. By the time Fox reached the Ontario border, the nation had embraced him as a public hero. Canadian dignitaries, charities, and local celebrities donated huge sums of money to Fox's marathon, and international media picked up his incredible story.

In the early morning of August 31, 1980, Fox woke up just outside of Thunder Bay in Ontario in his Ford marathon van complaining of a cold. Persistent coughing and lung pain during the run that day forced him to consult a doctor, who delivered a chilling diagnosis. On September 1, after 143 days and 3,339 miles (5,374 kilometers) of running, Terry was forced to stop because cancer had appeared in his lungs. Laying prostate on a hospital gurney outside of an ambulance, Fox announced to the nation that his marathon would have to end. During the interview, Fox stated to the world, "How many people do something they really believe in? I just wish people would realize that anything is possible if you just try. Dreams are made if people try."

A massive outpouring of support followed in Canada, with telethons and other charity events showcasing Terry's situation. Through his stay in the hospital and his treatment for lung cancer, Fox wore his Marathon of Hope T-shirt. The Governor General of Canada, Edward Schreyer, awarded Fox as a Companion of the Order of Canada. Even while in the hospital, Fox volunteered to appear in educational films produced by the Canadian Cancer Society.

But 1981 did not usher in better health news for Fox. He received notification in early January that his cancer had spread into his abdomen, but he nevertheless continued to hope. Terry Fox passed away on June 28, 1981, at age 22. He had achieved his dream—he had raised more than C$24 million for cancer research, precisely matching the number of people living in Canada at that time. Now, 26 years after his death, more than C$400 million has been raised worldwide for cancer research in Terry's name through the annual Terry Fox Run held across Canada and around the world. In 2005, Fox was named among the CBC Top 10 Greatest Canadians, and he is fondly remembered as one of Canada's greatest heroes.

At the age of 43, Jane Tomlinson of Leeds, England, lost her life to cancer. She was first diagnosed with breast cancer and mastectomized in 1990, at the age of 26. Determined to wage her own war with cancer on her own terms and to help others with similar experiences, she changed career paths and enrolled at Leeds General Infirmary to train as a pediatric radiographer. Doctors discovered lumps in her remaining breast in 1996, and after rounds of chemotherapy and radiotherapy, they performed a second mastectomy. In 2000, doctors delivered even more bad news—the cancer had metastasized, spreading to her bones and lungs. Jane was told at the time that she had merely 12 months to live.

The personal agony that Tomlinson, like so many others, faced through illness could have led her to retreat into herself and die passively. Instead, Tomlinson decided to author her own exit narrative of hope and inspiration. She embarked on a series of athletic challenges to raise money for cancer research and for charitable organizations that help the families of people with chronic illness. Tomlinson started conservatively on her athletic ventures, competing in running events such as the 5K Race for Life and the 5K Leeds Abbey Dash in 2001. But by 2002, Tomlinson's determination to push her body amplified, and she competed in both the London Marathon and the New York Marathon. Later that year, she presented the Jubilee Baton to the Queen of England at a festival in Leeds commemorating the Queen's 50th anniversary as the monarch. Later still, she completed the London Triathlon, the first athlete with an incurable illness to do so.

Undeterred by her failing body, Tomlinson went on to complete a staggering number of grueling physical challenges that even the most seasoned of athletes would be proud to list: She finished the Hawai'i Ironman (she was the only person with a terminal illness to do so), cycled 1,060 miles (1,700 kilometers) across England and 2,000 miles (3,200 kilometers) across Europe (stopping along the way to climb Mont Ventoux in France), cycled 4,200 miles (6,800 kilometers) across the United States and 3,100 miles (5,000 kilometers) across Africa, raised nearly £2 million for charities, ran countless local races of varying lengths in support of cancer research, wrote two books about her experiences with cancer

ATHLETES WITH HIV/AIDS

A series of high-profile cases of athletes with HIV/AIDS in the 1980s and the 1990s—such as Earvin "Magic" Johnson, Arthur Ashe, Greg Louganis, and Tommy Morrison—created controversy, concern, and disorder in the world of sports. Questions about whether HIV-positive athletes should be allowed to compete in sports against others and how to ensure the health and safety of all athletes involved in sports almost immediately followed these cases. Specifically, following ex-diver Greg Louganis's 1995 admission that he competed with an open head wound at the 1988 Olympic Games in Seoul while he was HIV positive, and then in 1996 when boxer Tommy Morrison tested positive for HIV, debates raged regarding whether athletes in all sports should be required to be tested. Of course, an array of ethical and legal issues surrounds such a suggestion. Currently, most leagues and professional organizations do not require mandatory testing. However, boxers in the United States are tested when they apply for a license to fight. Given that the risk of contracting HIV in sports is virtually zero, antitesting advocates argue that leagues should not have the right to test or prohibit HIV-positive athletes from participation. Questions about with whom information about one's HIV status would be shared have also been raised, as have concerns about the legality of any sports organization to force athletes to disclose their medical histories. Because, according to American law, a person with HIV is legally defined as disabled, the relative persecution of them violates the Rehabilitation Act of 1973 and the Americans with Disabilities Act (ADA) of 1990. Currently, there are no clear legal precedents governing the participation of HIV-positive athletes. What do you think, should all athletes be tested for HIV? Why or why not?

and sports, and helped organize a 10K charity run: the Run For All. Along the way, she periodically received bouts of chemotherapy to treat her cancer and eventually developed chronic heart disease as a result. For her efforts, Tomlinson received a wide range of accolades, including the BBC Sports Personality of the Year in 2002, the Helen Rollason Award in 2002, and the Pride of Britain Award in 2005. She was made a Member of the Order of the British Empire in 2003 and then a Commander of the Order of the British Empire in late 2007 (only 3 weeks before she died).

Tomlinson's heroic and inspirational efforts, like those of Lance Armstrong and Terry Fox, certainly defy medical knowledge about how an ill body should perform and be represented. Despite discouragement and sporadic public criticism—incredible claims were often made in British tabloids about Tomlinson faking her illness, and she repeatedly faced threatening and accusatory phone calls and e-mails from enraged skeptics—athletes who are ill often choose to face illness with optimism, joy, and concern for the well-being of others even in the face of death. While neither Fox nor Tomlinson chose to have cancer, they chose to exit life on their own terms as supporters of the common good. Their battles with illness in sports were other-directed rather than self-directed, empathic and selfless at a time when each had every reason to be selfish, angry, and closed to the world. In a classic sports metaphor, Fox and Tomlinson went down swinging for others facing similar crises.

FUTURE PROSPECTS

Recent trends suggest people who have experienced traumatic illness might increasingly seek out physically grueling activities for catharsis or, simply, the release of emotions stirred through illness. If this is the case, we might expect more and more athlete's future stories about sports to be filled with intense emotional language. As a bigger culture, then, we might find cause to be more attentive to how and why people experience intense physicality through sports as a way of reconnecting their minds, bodies, and feelings in the illness process. We might then encourage, rather than discourage, people who have been diagnosed with HIV, cancer, stroke, or many other critical illnesses to explore sports activities as a way of healing emotionally. Individuals seem to be telling stories that say they do not want to distance themselves from catharsis in sports; rather, they place their bodies in the middle of the rituals. We might understand grimacing in pain, breathing heavily, screaming, or crying in athletic competition—each relatively normal in power and performance sports because they often symbolize commitment to competition—as catharsis for people who have been coached to keep illness-related emotions in check.

See also Disability Sports; Eating Disorders; Ultraendurance Running; Yoga and Alternative Fitness.

Further Reading: Armstrong, L. (2000). *It's Not About the Bike: My Journey Back to Life*. New York: Berkley Trade; King, S. (2001). An All-Consuming Cause: Breast Cancer, Corporate Philanthropy, and the Market for Generosity. *Social Text* 19: 115–143; Seale,

C. (2001). Sporting Cancer: Struggle Language in News Reports of People with Cancer. *Sociology of Health and Illness* 23: 308–329.

Michael Atkinson

INTERNATIONAL OLYMPIC COMMITTEE (IOC)

The International Olympic Committee (IOC) is an international, nongovernmental, nonprofit corporation based in Lausanne, Switzerland, owning all rights to the Olympic Games worldwide. The organization was founded in 1894 through the efforts of a French aristocrat and educator, Baron Pierre de Coubertin, and became a Swiss corporation for tax purposes in 1981. The IOC is governed by the "Olympic Charter," which it created and revised over the decades. The most recent edition of the Olympic Charter was revised on July 7, 2007, during the 119th IOC session held in Guatemala. This charter is the codified fundamental principles of *Olympism*, with the rules and bylaws adopted by the IOC. The charter governs the organization, action, and operation of the *Olympic Movement* and sets forth the conditions for the celebration of the Olympic Games. The Olympic Charter serves three main purposes: (1) It sets forth and recalls the "Fundamental Principles" and essential values of *Olympism*; (2) It serves as the governing statutes for the IOC; and (3) It defines the main reciprocal rights and obligations of the three main constituents of the Olympic Movement: (1) the International Olympic Committee, (2) the International Sports Federations, and (3) the National Olympic Committees. It also governs the rights and obligations of the organizing committees for the Olympic Games, which are responsible for actually hosting and conducting the Games themselves.

BACKGROUND

The Olympic Games were originally the athletic portion of a religious festival in ancient Greece that honored the mythical god Zeus at a sanctuary in western Greece known as Olympia. The ancient Elians were the hosts and keepers of the festival that was held every four years for over a thousand years. The origins of these ancient Olympic Games are unknown, but several theories and myths have been expressed in both ancient Greek and Roman literature. Evidence indicates that the origins may date back as early as the twelfth century B.C.E., but even the ancient Greeks themselves did not know when the Olympic Games began. Various ancient writers and historians tried to create "victor lists," and from these works the date 776 B.C.E. is the first year there was a known, recorded winner in an Olympic running race. Hence, the written records begin with the year 776 B.C.E., and it was known to the ancient Greeks as the Games of the 1st Olympiad. An Olympiad is a four-year period of time, and the Greeks used this as a common calendar throughout their history.

Eventually, the Romans conquered the Greek city states and by the fourth century C.E. the Romans had accepted the new religion of Christianity. Roman emperor Theodosius I issued an edict that banned all pagan religious festivals, and this led to the end of the Olympic Games that honored the Greek god Zeus. The Romans sent an army to Olympia to physically destroy the religious sanctuary, the statue of Zeus was removed to Constantinople, and both Greek and Roman pagan sanctuaries were turned into Christian churches. Over the next few centuries, the sanctuary at Olympia was further damaged from earthquakes and floods from two nearby rivers. The site became forgotten and covered in layers of soil and was buried until it was rediscovered in the 1700s. In 1829, a French expedition uncovered some artworks and removed them to the Louvre in Paris. In the 1870s, a German expedition began a lengthy excavation under the direction of Ernst Curtius, and a large portion of the ancient site was uncovered and studied. Interest in classical civilization boomed in the nineteenth century. The expeditions at Olympia, under German supervision, have continued to this day except for interruptions caused by World War I and World War II.

Pierre de Coubertin was born in Paris in 1863 to an aristocratic French family. He became an educator working for the French Education Ministry. He was only 8 years old when the Prussians crushed the French in the Franco-Prussian War (1870–1871) resulting in the creation of a united Germany under Otto von Bismarck. As a young man working for the French Education ministry his mission was to find ways to better educate the youth of France who were deemed to be physically weaker than their neighbors—and enemies. Traveling to England and the United States in the 1880s he was exposed to different systems of education and physical culture, as well as at least two Olympic revival attempts— the Wenlock Olympian Games in Great Britain, started by Dr. William Penny Brookes in 1850, and the Zappas Olympic Games in Greece, started by Evangelis Zappas in 1859. He traveled to the United States and visited universities on the East Coast as well as in Chicago and California. He was influenced greatly by the British sport of rugby and the U.S. college system of athletics where the students competed against other university students in sports such as rowing. He was also influenced by the work of Brookes and Zappas and the academics in archeology and classical history.

Coubertin was a vigorous promoter of physical culture in France and was himself an athlete and founder of sports organizations. Working for the French Education Ministry he was determined to change physical education in the schools of France. In 1892, Coubertin hosted an athletic conference in the Sorbonne University in Paris where he pitched his idea of reviving the ancient Olympic Games, but his effort failed. He tried again at a second Sorbonne conference in 1894 where his idea was enthusiastically received by the 79 delegates from 13 nations. The International Olympic Committee was formed during that conference on June 23, 1894. The first Olympic Games were originally supposed to be in Paris in 1900, but the Greek representative, Demetrius Vikelas, made a passionate plea for the Games to be in Athens in May, 1896. The result was that the first Olympic Games were scheduled for Athens in 1896 and the second Olympic Games were scheduled for Paris in 1900.

In accordance with Coubertin's plan to have the president of the IOC coming from the host city or country of the Olympic Games—Vikelas was elected President of the IOC and served in that capacity until 1896. With the 1900 Games planned for Paris, Coubertin was elected President for the next four years. However, he was re-elected repeatedly for extended terms and served as President of the IOC until 1925.

The IOC was very small in its early years and was primarily run by de Coubertin through annual meetings with his fellow committee members, most of whom were also aristocrats or educators. The headquarters of the IOC were located in Paris, Coubertin's home town. When World War I erupted in Europe, Coubertin moved his residence and the IOC offices to Lausanne, Switzerland. In 1968, the IOC relocated to new offices in the Chateau de Vidy in Lausanne where it remains to this day. Additional offices exist in Lausanne as well as a new library and museum that was opened in 1993. From a small group of idealistic aristocrats, the IOC has grown into an internationally powerful and wealthy organization that controls all aspects of the world's most popular sporting event, the Olympic Games.

KEY EVENTS

Sports in the late nineteenth century were primarily local events. International travel was expensive and difficult with horse and buggy, trains, and passenger ships as the only means of travel. The IOC in the late nineteenth century did not in any way resemble the IOC of today. The first IOC members, numbering 13 individuals, were chosen on June 23, 1894, and included Pierre de Coubertin (France), Charles Herbert (Great Britain), William Milligan Sloane (USA), Demetrius Vikelas (Greece), Ernest Callot (France), Mario Lucchesi-Palli (Italy), Alexei de Butowski (Russia), Jiri Guth-Jarovsky (Bohemia/Czechoslovakia), Viktor Balck (Sweden), Leonard A. Cuff (New Zealand), Jose Zubiaur (Argentina), Arthur Russell, 2nd Baron Ampthill (Great Britain), and Ferenc Kemeny (Hungary).

In the beginning, the IOC members were simply hand-picked by Coubertin. He also produced the first publications of the IOC known as the *Bulletin*. Produced in newspaper format, it was the only source of information for several years. Published irregularly, it evolved into the *Olympic Revue*. For many years this publication was a smaller booklet, but in the 1960s and 1970s it grew into a more professional publication with a "perfect" binding instead of staples. Today it is a large, glossy magazine format that includes sponsor advertisements, reflecting the change that has taken place over the past century with the growth of the Olympic Movement.

The IOC was originally a small body of elite members—self sustaining and beholden to no one. By World War I (1914), there were 48 members; by 1939, there were 73 members. Following a bribery scandal over the bidding process for the winter Olympic Games of 2002, the IOC changed its own rules and instituted several major reforms and limited its membership to 115. Over the century, the IOC has changed from an elitist group of aristocrats and educators to a more transparent business-like board of directors who are influenced by the money paid by the major sponsors who keep the Olympic Movement financially alive with their sponsorship or "rights" fees.

Aside from the original influence and power of Pierre de Coubertin, other individuals have had significant influence on the direction of the IOC. Each IOC president has been involved in a controversial issue.

After Coubertin came Count Henri de Baillet-Latour of Belgium. He was president during the era when women were first emerging as participants in the Olympic Games. He wanted less women in the track and field program because he thought they were too weak for strenuous activities, but he was outvoted by the other members of the IOC, and in 1932, Babe Didrickson proved him wrong when she excelled and won two golds and a silver medal at the Los Angeles Olympic Games. Baillet-Latour was also the President during the difficult period of the 1936 Berlin Summer and Garmisch-Partenkirchen Winter Olympic Games, hosted by Germany after Adolf Hitler came to power. In spite of strong boycott efforts, these politically controversial Games were celebrated and were followed by World War II and the cancellation of both the 1940 and 1944 Olympic Games. Baillet-Latour died in 1942.

He was followed by the Swedish industrialist J. Sigfried Edstrom, who was the leader of the Olympic Movement during the Cold War and saw the Soviet Union return to the Olympics in 1952 as well as two German teams, from West Germany and East Germany, competing under different flags.

Politics became intense during this era: the Cold War, the two Germanys, Red China and Taiwan, India and Pakistan, the end of colonial rule in Africa and the emergence of African nations, and the case of racism in Rhodesia and South Africa—a major source of international tension because of a national policy on apartheid. Athletes worldwide ostracized the two countries, and both Rhodesians and South Africans were eventually banned from participating in the Olympic Games. Avery Brundage, a U.S. sportsman/millionaire who diligently enforced the code of "amateurism" during his reign as President, followed Edstrom in 1952 and reigned for 20 years. A dominant force in world sports during this era, Brundage dealt with these numerous controversial issues during his 20-year leadership with the banishment of Rhodesia and South Africa near the top of this list. However, he is probably remembered today mainly because of his staunch stand that "the Games must go on" following the murder of Israeli Olympians during the Munich Olympic Games.

Michael Morris Lord Killanin followed Brundage, and the Olympic Movement changed direction quickly. Lord Killanin had a more diplomatic and neutral approach to controversy, welcomed by many as a change from Brundage's more authoritarian and conservative administration. But Killanin was immersed in some of the great controversies of Olympic history, including the boycott of African nations to the 1976 Montreal Olympic Games over South African apartheid. He also oversaw the easing of the rules concerning amateurism, which Brundage had so rigidly enforced. The IOC was financially in danger in the late 1970s as the Montreal Games cost over $1 billion. Those Games also involved corruption within the city of Montreal over the stadium construction and caused concern worldwide about hosting the Olympics. By 1984, no city wanted the Olympic Games, and only Los Angeles bid for them.

In 1980, Juan Antonio Samaranch of Spain followed Killanin as president. He managed through the 1984 Olympics with the Soviet Union boycott and led the IOC in new directions. He had a major influence in making the IOC a wealthy corporation through corporate sponsorships and huge television rights deals. During his 21-year presidency, which ended in 2001, he saw the rules for amateurism fade and the admission of professional athletes into the Olympic Games, and now hundreds of millions of dollars flow into the IOC from the sale of Olympic "rights" for everything from water bottles to fast food. However, along with this money came greed, corruption, scandals, and overcommercialization of the Olympic Games. Following the bribery scandal of Salt Lake City's 2002 bid where bribes were given to IOC members, the IOC kicked out 10 of its own members, which had never been done before. It then revised its own charter and rules for membership.

In 2001, Jacques Rogge of Belgium became president and has taken a more personal hand in IOC affairs by staying in Olympic Villages during the Games and endorsing the hosting of the Olympic Games in developing nations. One of the major concerns at this time in the Olympic Movement concerns the use of drugs and doping, which continues to fill sports headlines every month with new allegations against numerous previous medalists. Some have had their medals revoked.

The IOC itself does not control any sport—that is left to international sports federations. The IOC, however, can make a demand or create a rule for the Olympic Games that can heavily influence the rules in sports such as boxing, gymnastics, or ice skating, where judges use their opinions to grade events.

The IOC does not control any National Olympic Committees (NOCs), but it approves or rejects NOCs that apply from their country. For instance, even though there is no country of Palestine, there is a Palestinian NOC as well as an Israeli NOC. Even though Puerto Rico is a territory of the United States, it has its own NOC and does not send its athletes as part of the U.S. Olympic team. There are many similar examples.

FUTURE PROSPECTS

The IOC started as a small group of elite men with idealistic dreams of reviving the ancient Olympic Games. Although it is still self-sustaining, it has evolved into a much larger and more democratic institution by including more members from a wider variety of social, economic, and political strata than a hundred years ago.

Future issues will be over the influence of sponsorship money in establishing the schedule of the Games. Because U.S. television money is a major source of IOC income—it bends to the will of television executives over the timing of events. Doping of athletes has become a serious problem with more athletes cheating and getting caught. Politics has always been and will continue to be an issue because it is nearly impossible to get past bitterness and hatred between or among groups in spite of the mightiest efforts of idealists such as Coubertin and Brundage. The size of the Games, the cost of hosting, and the sports that are on the schedule are all issues that will be sources of concern in the future. It is hard to imagine that the modern Games will last as long as the ancient Games.

See also Gay Games; Media Broadcasting Rights; Militarism and the Olympics; Steroid Use by Athletes; Terrorism and the Olympics; X Games.

Further Reading: Findling, J. E., and Pelle, K. D. (1996). *Historical Dictionary of the Modern Olympic Movement.* Westport, CT: Greenwood Press; Guttman, A. (1992). *The Olympics: A History of the Modern Games.* Urbana: University of Illinois Press; Lucas, J. (1980). *The Modern Olympic Games.* South Brunswick, NJ: A. S. Barnes; Lucas, J. A. (1992). *Future of the Olympic Games.* Champaign, IL: Human Kinetics; MacAloon, J. J. (1981). *This Great Symbol: Pierre de Coubertin and the Origins of the Modern Olympic Games.* Chicago: University of Chicago Press.

Harvey Abrams

LABOR MIGRATION

Labor migration is an established feature of the sporting "global village." This migration centrally involves athletes but also includes coaches, officials, administrators, and sports scientists. This movement of "workers" occurs both within and between nations and continents on a worldwide basis. This phenomenon has been studied with attention focusing on several sports including ice hockey, cricket, baseball, basketball, and perhaps most notably, soccer. Consideration has been given to tracing the patterns in sports migration, how and why these patterns occur, and what meaning and significance this migration has for those involved—either as hosts or migrants. Although migrant labor has been a feature of the sports process for some time, it is also correct to observe that its frequency and extent has grown in complexity and intensity over recent decades. It is also possible, in some circumstances, to view such migration as a form of child and/or human trafficking or involving refugees or asylum seekers.

BACKGROUND

Several issues can be explored in making sense of sports labor migration. First, which sports are most involved, why have they been so affected, and what structural or cultural changes have thus occurred in those sports? Second, what are the patterns of global movement, and how and why have they developed in this manner? Third, what is the impact on host and donor countries? Fourth, why do professional athletes become labor migrants, and what do they experience along their journey? Fifth, in what ways does such migration reflect the movement of highly skilled workers more generally? Lastly, what implications are there for sports, domestic, and foreign policies of nation-states?

EXAMPLES OF SPORTS LABOR MIGRATION

The list of sports labor migration examples is lengthy, but here is a typical range of examples:

Intra-continental movement takes various forms and includes:

- the involvement of athletes from the Dominican Republic in U.S. baseball teams.
- the movement within Western Europe and between the European Union and Eastern Europe in sports such as soccer, ice hockey, basketball, and track and field.
- following the "people's revolutions" of 1989 and the subsequent "opening up" of Eastern Europe, Hungarians, Czechs, Slovakians, and Romanians moved west.
- the western movement of Bosnian and Croatian athletes during the civil wars in the former Yugoslavia. The further enlargement of the EU eastward accelerated these processes even more.
- the flight of Cubans to the United States seeking both asylum and professional sporting opportunities for their talent.

Inter-continental movement takes various forms and includes:

- movement of labor in sports such as U.S. football, baseball, basketball, and soccer between North America, Europe, South America, and Asia. By the mid-1990s, for example, over 400 Americans were playing in Europe's professional men's basketball leagues, with again the higher caliber of players residing in Italy and Spain. Over 15 percent of the National Basketball Association roster in the most recent season was non-American and came from five continents.
- Canadians migrate in significant numbers and use their ice hockey skills in Britain, Germany, France, and Switzerland. There is also a flow of sports labor in the opposite direction. North American ice hockey clubs recruit Scandinavian and Eastern European players.
- U.S. universities have also actively recruited European men and women in sports such as track and field, football, rugby, basketball, and swimming.
- African track and field talent is also part of the U.S. university scholarship program.
- Australian, Afro-Caribbean, South Asian, and South African players also figure prominently in English cricket and have done so for many decades. With the recent development of 20/20 cricket in India, players from England, Australia, New Zealand, and South Africa are now attracted to the Indian subcontinent.

From the available evidence it is clear that the migration of athletes and others involved in the sports industry occurs at three levels: within nations, between nations located within the same continent, and between nations located in different continents and hemispheres. In focusing on athletes it has been established that there are discernible national patterns evident in the recruitment and subsequent retention of people in sports such as U.S. football, basketball, cricket, ice hockey, track and field, and soccer.

KEY EVENTS

In specific sports, such as cricket and rugby, migration has a seasonal pattern, with the northern and southern hemispheres offering two seasons of play. As such, one consequence is that the natural rhythm of the traditional sporting calendar has thus diminished in importance. Other sports stars experience an even more transitory form of migration because their workplace is constantly shifting. Take, for example, the experience of European, American, and African athletes on the European track and field Grand Prix circuit or European and American skiers on the World Cup alpine skiing circuit. Other examples include cycling and motor racing ranging from Formula One to motorcycling. In team sports, labor tends to be hired by a specific club or organization, and individuals reside in the host country for a limited period. However, some athletes stay on and make the host country their home. This occurs either through marriage to a citizen of that country or by having stayed attached to a specific country for a sufficient length of time to qualify for nationality status. Sometimes, such as in European basketball, individuals begin to play for the country in which they have become resident and for whom they subsequently claim nationality. In this connection, and with the hosting of the 2012 Olympic Games in mind, the British Olympic Association and the British government have been involved in the active identification and recruitment of qualified migrants for the Great Britain Olympic basketball team: The pool of available indigenous talent is simply not enough.

There are other dimensions that need consideration. Sometimes, seasonal and transitory migration patterns interweave, as with golf and tennis players. Tennis stars cross the globe in search of world-ranking points and grand slam titles. These migratory forays tend to last no more then eight days at each tournament venue. In this respect, tennis players, along with golfers, are arguably the nomads of the sports migration process with constantly shifting workplaces and places of residence. It also needs to be understood that men and women have their own global circuits in these sports and others such as skiing. Not only do women tend to earn less then their male counterparts, but the enabling and constraining features that characterize their experiences may well be markedly different.

Migrants in general have to do sports work in various locations and, as a group, experience degrees of exploitation, dislocation, and cultural adjustment. Although women are traveling more frequently and in greater numbers, the trend of men moving more freely and in greater numbers over time and across space remains. This trend is based on a social structure that ensures that it is usually women who perform domestic and reproductive labor, whether in the company of their traveling partners or waiting at home. Gender relations are then one dimension that plays a crucial part in contouring a migrant's life. Yet, so too does national identity and ethnic affiliation—a migrant's life is patterned along the same fault lines that characterize other global flows and sports and broader cultural practices.

Migrants are often sports pioneers and possess a passion and zeal in promoting the virtues of their sport. Their words and actions can be seen as a form of proselytizing by which they seek to convert local people to new sports culture. In European soccer, migrants of this kind can be traced back to around the turn of the nineteenth century. The movement of British citizens and anglophiles returning from a visit to the birthplace of soccer, and developing the game in places where clubs such as Athletic Bilbao, Zurich Grasshoppers, and Djurgarden (Stockholm) have subsequently developed, is a good example of pioneer activity. In sports such as ice hockey a similar role is perceived to be currently played by some Canadian migrants in Britain.

Some migrants can be identified as settlers who subsequently stay and settle in the society where they perform their labor. Other migrants can be viewed as mercenaries who are motivated more by short-term gains and who use agents to secure lucrative deals with several clubs. These migrants have little or no attachment to the local, to a sense of place where they currently reside or play their sport. In contrast, some migrants are nomads who are more motivated by a cosmopolitan engagement with migration. They use their sports career to travel, experience other cultures, and enjoy being the outsider, the stranger. Yet, some cosmopolitans, along with pioneers, mercenaries, and even long-term settlers, act as returnees in the European process. The motivation of migrants, then, is complex and multifaceted. So what is it about playing in, or for, a foreign land that is so appealing?

A series of questions that can also be used to consider the motivation of sports stars more generally include: Are such moves considered as a developmental stage in the personal lives of the players? Do players see migration as a rite of passage that will enhance their playing development? Are their motives tied to financial lure or imperative? And finally, is migration part of the desire to be the best they can be, to perform on a global stage, and to play for a nation irrespective of their own sense of national identity?

FUTURE PROSPECTS

As with global processes more broadly it would appear that an economic analysis is a necessary but not sufficient explanation. Rather, a complex and shifting set of interdependencies contour the migrant trails of world sports. These interdependencies are multilayered and incorporate not only economic but also political, historical, geographical, social, and cultural factors. Thus, in seeking to explain global labor migration, a broad approach must be taken involving an examination of wider societal processes—not merely focusing on the economic aspects of the sports industry. Questions concerning power relations, talent pipelines, stereotyping, and the ascribing of qualities to athletes from different countries and ethnic groups are also part of the decision-making process.

Sports migration is bound up in a complex political economy that is itself embedded in a series of power struggles that characterize the global sports system. Migration is marked by a series of political, cultural, economic, and geographical issues and pressures of which in the process of migration owners, administrators, agents, officials, and media personnel play a prominent part in structuring the migrant's life. These issues and pressures vary between sports played in different continents—they interweave in a fashion where no one factor dominates.

In studying sports migration, beyond the question of why athletes move or the reasons why they are recruited, there is a series of issues that deserve more attention and that will become more prominent with the intensification of global sports processes. Here, attention is given to several of the more important.

First, the labor and human rights enjoyed by sports migrants, and indeed indigenous sports workers, vary considerably between sports and across continents. The employment rights achieved by players in team sports such as soccer are minimal compared to the freedoms gained by athletes in individual sports, particularly in tennis and golf. Not all participants in individual sports enjoy the advantages of tennis players or golfers, of course. Within team sports, employment rights also vary across sports played in different continents. Although North American athletes in sports such as football, ice hockey, basketball, and baseball are unionized and conduct negotiations with owners based on collective bargaining they have not been that successful in gaining the same employment rights as other workers.

College athletes are still drafted or assigned to specific professional football and basketball teams. In comparison, the free movement of labor is now part of EU law. Individuals are free to perform and work where they wish within the EU. Employment protection legislation also applies to migrant labor. The European Court action brought by Jean-Marc Bosman against the Union of European Football Association (UEFA) effectively secured the rights of EU sports stars to work in any country of the community without restriction. Yet, the rights that the Bosman case established are not applicable to all players. Individuals from countries outside the EU are subject to a selection procedure. Sports migrants have to prove international status in their respective sports. Further, as with migrants more generally, exploitative labor practices also take place. Questions concerning the recruitment and retention process and whether African and East European soccer players receive comparable wages and conditions to their EU counterparts needs to form part of further research. Question of child and human trafficking also arise in this context.

Secondly, large scale and prolonged migration of athletic labor can amount, in specific instances, to the de-skilling of donor countries. Latin and Central American countries, for example, regularly experience the loss of baseball stars and football players to the United States and Europe. Less developed countries invest in the production of athletic talent, but once this talent reaches maturity, more economically developed leagues, such as Major League Baseball, recruit the best available talent. Not only is the local audience denied direct access to the talent nurtured and developed in their country, but in some instances, such as with African national soccer teams, sports lose some of their quality performers when the demands of European clubs clash with international matches. Questions concerning national identity, underdevelopment and dependent development need to be addressed as part of the wider debate concerning sports migration.

Thirdly, the reaction of sports labor migrants to the host culture also requires consideration. The constant moving back and forth between different cultures requires that particular types of migrants develop new types of flexible personal controls, dispositions, and means of orientation. In developing this new kind of conduct migrants such as tennis players and golfers face problems of intercultural communication. Major global sports festivals and tournaments involve a multi-layered form of cultural communication involving interaction with fellow players, coaches, officials, the crowd, and media personnel. While some sports migrants may find the move from one culture to another relatively free of culture shock, this may not always be the case. There may be specific features of these processes that reflect broader gender inequalities that differentially hamper and constrain women: The gendered nature of these processes requires consideration.

Apart from leading to problems of adjustment, sports migration can also engender hostility in the host country. Sports labor unions, such as in soccer, have sought to protect indigenous workers (players) by arguing for quotas and qualification thresholds to be applied to potential migrants. The common themes that run through the cases of basketball, cricket, ice hockey, and football concern questions regarding the perceived threat to national team performances and the underdevelopment of indigenous talent. These issues will continue to bedevil global sports in the future.

See also Drafting Amateur Athletes; Environmental Impacts of Sports; Snowboarding; Yoga and Alternative Fitness.

Further Reading: Bale, J., and Maguire, J. (Eds.). (1994). *The Global Sports Arena: Athletic Talent Migration in an Interdependent World*. Cass: London; Klein, A. (1991). *Sugarball: The American Game, the Dominican Dream*. New Haven, CT: Yale University Press; Maguire, J., Jarvie, G., Mansfield, L., and Bradley, J. (2002). *Sport Worlds: A Sociological Perspective* Champaign, IL: Human Kinetics.

Joseph Maguire

LGBT SPORTS LEAGUES

Lesbian, gay, bisexual, transgender/transsexual (LGBT) organized sports leagues are typically "open" leagues that encourage inclusive participation by people from a full range of social backgrounds and abilities. With social roots dating back to the late 1960s and early 1970s, LGBT leagues have been organized for softball, tennis, curling, badminton, hockey, basketball, soccer, running, rugby, rodeo, gymnastics, sailing, snowboarding, track and field, swimming, and a range of other sports. These LGBT sports leagues not only challenge the deployment of sports as a site for reaffirming heterosexuality as socially "natural," they also serve as stark reminders that the dominant social structure of organized sports systematically labels and excludes large populations of athletes as unsuitable.

BACKGROUND

The post–civil rights era in the United States witnessed the emergence and spread of a wide range of political movements such as the gay and lesbian movement. These movements have tactically engaged with dominant cultures that oppress them through a program of identity politics. *Identity politics* refer to the practices socially marginalized or oppressed groups engage in in order to subvert, challenge, or redefine the dominant ways they are categorized and characterized within a culture. Sport has been, and continues to be, a central site of identity politics work for LGBT groups.

One might argue that conceptual struggles over group identity have been more pronounced in the lesbian and gay liberation movement and, as it is commonly referred to, through "queer politics." Queer political struggles involve, among other things, the right to be freely sexual beings under the law, the right to marry, rights in the workplace, freedom from harassment and hate crime, and the right to self-define through collective celebrations and affirmations of identity. Queer identity politics, in general, work to trouble the taken-for-granted conceptual definitions of *gay* and *lesbian* in a given culture (and challenge the basis of their common stigmatization) and its conceptual cousin, *straight* or *heterosexual*. Queer theorists point out that the homosexual/heterosexual dichotomy is not only mutually linked but also hierarchical (heterosexuality is superior, normal, and healthy, while homosexuality is inferior and deviant). The task of gay and lesbian "identity politics" is to constantly denaturalize and deconstruct the identities in question with a political goal of their subversion rather than their accommodation. In particular, heteronormative constructions of identity in institutions (such as sports) are targeted for deconstruction.

One can point out that *heteronormativity* is a set of practices that enforce heterosexual relations and related gender roles in social groups. Sports has been described as a heteronormative "deep closet" for the ways in which gay and lesbian athletes have been culturally and structurally ostracized for nearly 200 years. By interrogating how gay, lesbian, and transgender identities and symbols of representation have been historically denigrated in sports worlds, others have revealed how Western sports remain some of the last bastions of overt and socially tolerated homophobia. *Queer* identities and sexual preferences were, until relatively recently, blatantly denied, excluded, and even aggressively marginalized in the masculine-hetero world of sports. Even today, gay and lesbian identities are among the least publicly acknowledged and celebrated within the sports media.

Collective expressions of queer politics in sports, including those of visionary and activist Tom Wadell (creator of the Gay Games in 1982), signal resistance to heteronormativity politics in sports. Public and media awareness campaigns and the formation of gay, lesbian, and transgender sports leagues in Canada also identify how gay men and women are not only common and active in sports but that the absence of homoerotic desire and expression in sports is more myth than cultural reality. "Queer activists" in sports worlds endeavor to disrupt the essentializing constructions of sexuality in sports, the exclusionary white and heterosexual norms underpinning most sports practices, and the cultural tendency to deny sports space as a site of multiple sexual experiences and possibilities. McDonald (2007) presses for a further examination of how gay and lesbian experiences in sports may in fact encourage a larger critique of the (white) hetero–homo, normative–deviant binary lines of identity construction. Theorists such as McDonald encourage innovative reconceptualizations of how identity is constructed along sexual lines, suggesting a complete destabilization of the ways in which we assign and hierarchize identity to athletes.

The LGBT sports leagues in North America are socially significant as cultural battlegrounds in a number of important ways. First, the colonization and institutionalization of sports spaces by LGBT groups destabilizes the historically entrenched heterosexist ethos of mainstream sports. In this regard, active and athletic LGBT bodies help dislodge historical constructions of the gay/lesbian body as inherently docile, weak, abhorrent, or ill. Second, the creation and survival of organized LGBT sports leagues signals a refusal of ongoing cultural pressures for LGBT groups to be silenced or relegated to the back regions of social life. Third, LGBT leagues serve as points of connections for gays, lesbians, bisexuals, and transgendered people that help to form rights activism across the country. Fourth, organized leagues help bring to the public consciousness the sheer presence of gays and lesbians in urban spaces and the need to appreciate their civil liberties, rights, and freedoms.

KEY EVENTS

First staged in 1982, the Gay Games is an Olympic-style mega-event that brings together members of the global LGBT community. The brainchild of founders Dr. Tom Waddell, Matt Sprague, and Norris Pyle, the Gay Games were designed as an alternative sporting venue for men and women who felt marginalized and alienated within mainstream, heterosexual dominant sports cultures. Waddell in particular conceived of the Games as an opportunity to resist ideologies of homophobia in American (and indeed global) cultures and to promote gay pride. The Gay Games, now overseen by the Federation of Gay Games, support an ethos of inclusion rather than exclusion in sports. To this end, there are no qualifying criteria to enter the Games as an athlete. The Games bring novice and veteran athletes together from around the world to compete in over 30 sports including power-lifting, bowling, gymnastics, tennis, sailing, distance running, ice hockey, swimming, triathlon, and billiards. Seven iterations of the Gay Games have been staged since 1982, bringing together athletes from 70 nations; including some for whom homosexual acts or relations are illegal in their countries of origin.

Despite their description as *the* organized movement that altered the course of LGBT sports access and participation, organized gay softball leagues in San Francisco predated the Gay Games by nearly a decade. In the spring of 1974, the Gay Community Softball League, the first of its kind in the world, was formed in San Francisco under the direction and through the vision of Jack "Irene" McGowan and Peter Switzer (who became the league's first two commissioners). The name was ultimately changed to the Community Softball League (CSL). The sexual climate in San Francisco, while the most liberal perhaps in all of the United States, did not yet allow for, some worried, public displays of gay sexuality in sports. Some of the early participants feared being outed, stigmatized, and discriminated against as a result of their membership in the organization. Mid-1970s U.S. culture, even in its more liberal contexts, questioned anyone who participated with known gays and lesbians in public spaces.

The tall order of raising operating revenue for the fledging league fell onto Jack McGowan's shoulders. Wearing a sandwich board that advertised for softball players and sponsors, McGowan canvassed the city streets of San Francisco asking for anything people could spare. The main obstacle faced in establishing a gay league was the opposition of most municipal park and recreational field managers to allowing gays the use of public playing fields. Operators of the Collingwood facilities in the heart of the burgeoning gay community, the Castro district, seemed particularly opposed to the league and its cultural meaning. Early practices and games drew negative attention from local residents around the parks, often resulting in homophobic comments from other park visitors and, from time-to-time, physical confrontations between players and protestors of the league. The League sought further counsel with park and recreation representatives, staff from Mayor Joseph Allioto's office, and State Senator Willie Brown (an avid supporter of gay rights) to determine the CSL's right to use public parks and recreation spaces. Members of the Park and Recreation Department were forced to acquiesce because it was determined that the refusal to allow CSL players to stage games on public fields violated their civil liberties. The first worldwide gay softball tournament was held at San Francisco's Rolph Field in November 1975. The first teams involved were the local San Francisco squads: The Pendulum, Sutter's Mill, Twin Peaks, The Mint, Purple Pickle, Kokpit, Missouri Mule, and The Mistake. Together and separately, these events provided the groundwork for the development of most LGBT sports leagues in the United States.

Also in 1974, Jack Baker and Gardner Pond, with the help of a free newspaper called *Lavender U,* started a gay running club in San Francisco. They would later call their group the Lavender U Joggers. Baker and Pond organized the group through the newspaper as a social/community networking club and as an outdoor pursuit divorced from typical gay leisure hangouts (i.e., bars) in the city where other gay sports clubs (such as the teams in the CSL) congregated. In most accounts of the club's origins, it is mentioned that the club did not keep a formal membership list, and club members often used first names only to avoid any potential social persecution. By 1978, membership in the club grew, and their name was altered to FrontRunners. By 1980, FrontRunners sponsored its first gay 5K and 10K runs. Later that year a FrontRunners chapter was started in New York; soon after, new chapters popped up across the United States and in Canada. Today, FrontRunner clubs exist in 15 countries with over 80 chapters in the United States and over 40 worldwide. From its humble beginnings and first members reluctance to identify themselves within the club (or as being affiliated with the club), FrontRunners is an international leader in promoting LGBT pride in global sports cultures.

Clearly, the critical groundswell in the organization of softball and running leagues (and others such as bowling, swimming, and tennis) for LGBT communities in the United States during the 1970s illustrated the necessity for larger organizing sports bodies to help bring LGBTs together in a unified sports community. Created in 1977, the North American Gay Amateur Athletic Alliance (NAGAAA) established itself as a nonprofit international sports organization that comprised men and women dedicated to the promotion of organized softball competition for the gay and lesbian community.

Currently, 56 gay and lesbian softball leagues in 35 North American cities make up the 12,000 members of NAGAAA. Teams representing these leagues participate in the NAGAAA Gay Softball World Series (GSWS) hosted each year in a different member city. The NAGAAA has two divisions of competitive play—the Open and Women's Divisions. The Women's Division consists of exclusively women, while the Open Division teams consist of co-ed teams or exclusively male teams. In addition to hosting the Gay Softball World Series each year, NAGAAA helps to organize local events and awareness campaigns in each of its member cities. Almost unthinkable only a decade early, the establishment of the NAGAAA and its ascendance through the 1980s as a political and social force shifted the sporting landscape for gays and lesbians in North America.

A member of NAGAAA, The Big Apple Softball League (BASL), New York City's gay and lesbian softball league, has accomplished more than any other

LGBT SPORTS ORGANIZATIONS

Listed below are only a few of the national and international sports organizations for LGBT athletes that have developed in the past 30 years.

All Sports: Gay and Lesbian Athletes Association (GLAA); European Gay and Lesbian Sports Federation (EGLSF)
Aquatics: International Gay and Lesbian Acquatics (IGLA)
Athletics: Gay and Lesbian Athletics Foundation (GLAF); North American Gay Amateur Athletic Alliance (NAGAAA)
Basketball: International Gay Men's Basketball
Bowling: International Gay Bowling Organization (IGBO)
Field Hockey: International Gay and Lesbian Field Hockey Federation (IGLFHF)
Figure Skating: International Figure Skating Union (IGFSU)
Gymnastics: International Gay Lesbian Gymnastics Union (IGLGU)
Martial Arts: International Association of Gay and Lesbian Martial Artists (IAGLMA)
Rodeo: International Gay Rodeo Association (IGRA)
Rowing: Gay and Lesbian Rowing Federation (GLRF)
Rugby: International Gay Rugby and Board (IGRAB)
Sailing: Gay and Lesbian Organization for Racing and Yachting (GLORY)
Snowboarding: Outboard—Gay and Lesbian Snowboarders
Snowsports: International Gay Lesbian Snowsports Association (IGLSA) / Gayskiers
Soccer: Gay Football Supporters Network (GFSN) UK; International Gay and Lesbian Football Association (IGLFA)
Tennis: Gay and Lesbian Tennis Alliance (GLTA)

softball league in raising consciousness about the need for inclusive and prejudice free sports zones. The BASL was born in Greenwich Village in 1977 and was a major player in founding NAGAAA. The League is open to all persons regardless of age, race, religion, gender, sexual orientation, or playing ability. The BASL not only provides very competitive and recreational divisions for people over 18 years old, it is also a nonprofit organization that sponsors New York rights groups such as Equity Fights Aids and Life Beat. The BASL is among the most diverse sports leagues in the nation with representatives from gay, lesbian, straight, transgender, transsexual, bisexual, and ethnic/religious minority communities. Thus, the BASL prides itself in providing a positive softball environment for not only gays and lesbians but also straight men and women, as well as players identified as seniors (i.e., over 55 years old). Impressively, the BASL invests in the local Greenwich community by channeling its nonoperating capital back to help support its cultural and financial infrastructure. Greenwich Village businesses that sponsor teams, such as Cowgirl Hall of Fame, Ty's, Village Apothecary, Dugout Bar, Stonewall Bar, Bluemoon Café, Manatus, and Little Ricky Productions, are in turn supported by the players who frequent their businesses.

Between 1980 and 2001, LGBT sports leagues cropped up across the continent. They received overt, homophobic discrimination in many cities, but have gradually become parts of the sports and leisure landscapes in many urban zones. In 2002, the first gay flag football tournament was held in Los Angeles and touted as the Gay Super Bowl (now called Gay Bowl) by organizers Jim Buzinski and Cyd Zeigler. Staged as a two-day tournament involving teams from San Francisco, Boston, and Los Angeles, the first Gay Bowl and the national media attention it received paved the way for the development of gay football leagues throughout the United States. In 2007 teams from across the nation participated in Gay Bowl VI. The Gay Bowl is now the annual championship tournament of the National Gay Flag Football League (NGFFL).

With striking similarities to the form and content of other LGBT sports organizations, the Toronto Gay Hockey Association (TGHA) is a noncontact, social, ice hockey league for LGBT and heterosexual men and women over the age of 18 in the Toronto (Canada) region. Founded in 1994, the TGHA began as a group of like-minded people who got together to play hockey in a friendly environment free from the aggressive and intolerant atmosphere of mainstream leagues. The sport of ice hockey is historically renowned as a hypermasculinity and homophobic environment, and in this cultural context, the development of the TGHA was as much a benchmark moment in Canadian sports because its participants faced some risk of recrimination. The TGHA strives to provide an environment free from all forms of harassment and discrimination and encourages fair play, openness, and friendship in a sports world that is characteristically divisive, hierarchal, and stratified.

When reviewing and critically reflecting on the struggle for basic social rights to freedom and inclusion waged by members of the North American LGBT community, the creation of sports leagues may seem, on their surface, insignificant. Yet, we must remember to contextualize the formation of the leagues and organizations against the overarching territorial exclusion of LGBT groups of people from sports over nearly 100 years of organized sports history on the continent. The social organization, performance, and representation of sports has traditionally excluded LGBT social needs and identities because they have violated the hypermasculine, heteronormative codes underpinning organized sports. While the creation of leagues for LGBT athletes across the social landscape is by no means an indicator of equality or diffuse social tolerance toward sexual differences between people in the North American mainstream, it does suggest that spaces are being seized by heretofore marginalized communities for the purposes of bringing people together and doing collective identity politics through athletics.

FUTURE PROSPECTS

Progress in the realm of identity politics is often measured by how groups who are struggling to redefine their collective roles, statuses, and social opportunities are able to create institutional change. The organization and ongoing proliferation of LGBT sports leagues in North America should be recognized and lauded a major identity politics victory for gays, lesbians, and others. Heteronormative codes in sports worlds do continue to buttress a majority of athletic institutions and practices, but the ascendance of LGBT leagues has opened a cultural space in sports for alternative definitions of athletes, athleticism, and sports itself. Gay and lesbian leagues provide, in many instances, truly unique and attractive contexts of athletic competition for people and continue to expose discriminatory social codes underpinning the social organization of mainstream (sports) cultures.

See also Gay Games; Homophobia; Openly Gay Athletes; Sports for All; Transsexual Athletes.

Further Reading: Anderson, E. (2005). *In the Game: Gay Athletes and the Cult of Masculinity*. Albany: SUNY Press; Cauldwell, J. (2007). *Sport, Sexualities and Queer Theory*. London: Routledge; Eng, H. (2007). Queer Athletes and Queering in Sport. In *Sport, Sexualities and Queer Theory*, edited by J. Cauldwell. London: Routledge; Griffin, R. (1998). *Sports in the Lives of Children and Adolescents*. London: Praeger; Lenskyj, H. (2003). *Out on the Field: Gender, Sport and Sexualities*. Toronto: Women's Press of Canada; McDonald, M. (2007). Beyond the Pale: The Whiteness of Sports Studies and Queer Scholarship. In *Sport, Sexualities and Queer Theory*, edited by J. Cauldwell. London: Routledge; Pronger, B. (1990). *The Arena of Masculinity: Sports, Homosexuality, and the Meaning of Sex*. New York: St. Martin's Press.

Michael Atkinson

M

MARIJUANA, ALCOHOL, AND ILLICIT DRUGS

The consumption and distribution of performance-enhancing drugs in sports is a noted problem in contemporary sports cultures, but athletes' consumption of mood-altering and not necessarily performance-enhancing drugs is far too infrequently critically analyzed. The consumption of illicit drugs—those either banned by criminal law or prohibited within sports cultures on predominantly moral ground—by players occurs across sports cultures with considerable frequency. Despite codes of conduct implemented by school-level, elite amateur, and professional sports cultures, athletes continue to experiment with, and in many cases abuse, illicit drugs. Questions arise regarding how to effectively police drug consumption in sports, whether or not certain drugs should be simply permitted within sports cultures, and what actually constitutes a "bad" drug within sports worlds.

BACKGROUND

The modern era of drug prohibition in sports followed the development of the World Anti-Doping Agency (WADA) and the production of its annual list of banned substances in sports. A substance finds its way onto the list if it is a chemical or otherwise unnatural performance enhancer, if it poses serious danger to an athlete, or if it contravenes the spirit of competitive sports (i.e., fairness, morality, justice). As more sports leagues and federations at all levels of play have voluntarily adopted WADA's banned substance list and created testing procedures to monitor what their athletes are consuming, fierce arguments are waged regarding what drugs or substances should or not should not fall on the list.

Yet, following WADA's banned substance list as a moral compass for understanding what sports cultures will not tolerate is problematic. A strong argument can be made, for example, that illicit drug consumption has been a part of competitive sports for over 100 years. The consumption of alcohol, note some sports historians, has been long associated with most sports and their cultures. Whether alcohol consumption is part of masculine bonding on teams, hazing rituals, team celebrations, sports spectating, or sports team/league sponsorship, there is an enduring cultural link between athletics and this mood-altering substance.

Facts about alcohol's historical and contemporary prevalence in sports cultures certainly does not fit in with the dominant cultural argument in the United States and Canada that athletes are "special populations" that embody particular virtues and moral characteristics. Both statistical and anecdotal evidence gathered in National Collegiate Athletic Association (NCAA) sports over the past 20 years has consistently shown that college athletes are not only regular binge drinkers but also that they view over-drinking as congruent with their statuses and role expectations as athletes.

Part of WADA's rationale for banning a huge swath of drugs from professional sports cultures is the image it sends to young people who idolize athlete role models. Data collected on high school males over the past 30 years in the United Sates indicates that they look up to athletes more than any other social group/profession.

Even more problematic for sports organizations, teams, and leagues is when their names are associated with illegal or illicit drugs in sports. With the mass commercialization of sports and the ownership of teams controlled by megacorporations such as Disney, Viacom, Anheuser-Busch, and Gillette, the financial backers in the industry scarcely wish to have their corporations linked to drug cultures. Team policies and programs designed to monitor for drugs, then, are not only developed to ensure fair play in sports and protect the "character" building potential of sports but also to protect corporate sponsors from being stigmatized by player actions.

Explanations of player's consumption of drugs tend to be oversimplistic and normally anecdotal rather than based on carefully collated evidence. Some illegal drugs such as cocaine are reputedly taken for their performance-enhancing benefits in training and competition. Others such as alcohol are ascribed to the cultures of extreme masculinity and bravado common in contact sports such as rugby, football, and ice hockey. Further explanations revolve around the idea that some athletes possess great amounts of hubris and believe they can consume any substance they wish in a lifestyle of excess, without fear of reprisal. While certain forms of drug consumption in sports might be explained by these ideas, they clearly do not capture the full spectrum of why athletes choose to violate rule structures in their respective sports that patently forbid drug consumption.

One controversial idea is that athletes' drug consumption in the modern era is part and parcel of a "science culture" in sports that views athletes' bodies as "things" to be manipulated through ergogenic supplements. From this perspective, athletes learn very early in their respective careers to view their bodies as entities to be experimented upon with a variety of chemical "drinks." Included among such drinks are, of course, heavily laden caffeine concoctions that are designed to improve focus and endurance in athletes. Rarely is athletes' consumption of high volumes of caffeine (as part of training) treated as problematic, apart from WADA rules regulating how much caffeine an athlete may have in her or his system while competing. Furthermore, athletes' use of chewing tobacco in sports such as baseball is rarely an issue, even with a collective understanding of the addictive properties of nicotine and the ostensible links between tobacco chewing and a variety of cancers.

Confusion, contestation, and contradictions in sports cultures remains as to why players are not allowed to consume illicit, non–performance-enhancing drugs. The number of drugs falling onto the WADA banned substances list increases every year, and sports insiders why and if, given other more surreptitious and sports-related drugs that need stern policing, illicit drugs have a legitimate place on such lists.

KEY EVENTS

The consumption of beer, wine, and spirits is routinely defined as problematic in the world of sports but predominantly when it is tied to felonious behaviors among players or sports insiders, such as assault and sexual abuse, vandalism among fans, or drinking among underage athletes. Indeed, organizations such as WADA show little interest in arguably the most patterned and prevalent form of drug consumption among athletes. Few moral panics have ever developed around the culture of drinking that exists in many sports cultures. The April 2007 edition of *Runner's World* magazine, for instance, published research suggesting that distance runners drink twice as much alcohol as the average American.

The abuse of alcohol by isolated players does become, from time to time, mass mediated as a problem in sports. Here, binge drinking or alcoholism is socially written off as an unfortunate and uncontrollable feature of organized sports. It is common for sporting celebrities to struggle with alcoholism, and teams are often encouraged to bond by drinking together. Indeed, many major sports teams and leagues are branded with Budweiser or Molson's beer logos or manufacturers of other alcoholic drinks. From hooliganism to commerce, from advertising and sponsorship to health and fitness, if there is one thing that brings athletes, fans, and financial backers together it is alcohol. Despite certain prohibitions in amateur federations and leagues and the acknowledgement of alcohol's deleterious effects in sports training processes, the association between sports and alcohol remains culturally entrenched. The problems with letting sports cultures maintain a largely laissez-faire attitude toward alcohol consumption, however, is emphasized when we examine the sheer number of cases in North America of players who have been charged with driving while under the influence.

CASES OF DUI AMONG PROFESSIONAL ATHLETES IN 2007

- Richie Williams, NCAA, San Diego State (college basketball)
- Charles Oakley, retired NBA player
- Britney Lohman, NCAA, University of Montana (basketball)
- Herb Pope, NCAA, New Mexico State (basketball)
- Warren Moon, retired Candian Football League (CFL) and NFL player
- Jim Leyritz, retired MLBA player
- Tony La Russa, MLBA baseball coach
- Darrell Hackney, NFL, Denver Broncos
- John LeClair, NHL, Pittsburgh Penguins
- Jerramy Stevens, NFL, Tampa Bay Buccaneers
- David Boston, NFL, Tampa Bay Buccaneers
- Chris Chambers, NFL, Miami Dolphins
- Jared Allen, NFL, Kansa City Chiefs

It has often been suggested, and criticized, that athletes are given a relative legal "pass" when it comes to drinking and driving. Even when they are arrested, sentences are predominantly light due to their celebrity statuses. On September 29, 2003, Dany Heatley of the National Hockey League's (NHL) Atlanta Thrashers crashed his Ferrari into a wall (at a speed of 82 mph [132 km/h] in a 35 mph [55 km/h] zone), splitting the car in half and ejecting Heatley and his passenger, teammate Dan Snyder, from the vehicle. Heatley suffered a series of minor injuries to his upper body and tore three ligaments in his right knee. Snyder was critically injured with a skull fracture, fell into a coma, and died six days later. Despite forgiveness from Dan Snyder's family, Heatley was charged with vehicular homicide. He pleaded guilty to second-degree vehicular homicide, driving too fast for conditions, failure to maintain a lane, and speeding. At the time, his blood-alcohol content was at the maximum legal limit; doctors testified it was enough to seriously impair his driving and was likely a chief contributor to the accident. Heatley was sentenced to three years probation and forced to make 150 community speeches about vehicular safety. The maximum sentence Heatley could have received was 20 years in jail. A case like this suggests that professional athletes often have a different set of rules when it comes to legal matters pertaining to illicit drugs. The judge presiding in the Heatley case said that for his sentencing he took into consideration the possibility of ruining Heatley's hockey career and that he did so on the advice of Dan Snyder's father, who did not want Heatley's career to be ruined.

Alcohol consumption may generally fly under the social problems radar for the majority of the time, but since the late 1980s, marijuana consumption has been an explosive topic in the sports world. One of the first public punishments for marijuana consumption occurred in 1998 when Canadian snowboarder Ross Rebagliati's gold medal was stripped. Though Rebagliati appealed the

"MAMA, DON'T LET YOUR BABIES GROW UP TO BE COWBOYS"

In 1997, Michael Irvin of the Dallas Cowboys was convicted and sentenced to four years probation following a no-contest plea to cocaine possession. His teammate Erik Williams had just finished a probation sentence for a drunken-driving charge and had also paid an out-of-court settlement to a 17-year-old exotic dancer to avoid her pressing charges of sexual assault. Seven members of the Cowboys accounted for the majority of the 13 drug suspensions levied by the NFL in 2007. The NFL barred Irvin from the season's first five games after the no-contest plea. Among the other Cowboys suspended by the league included defensive lineman Leon Lett, the NFL's premier run-stopper. Lett was suspended for a year for multiple violations of the league's drug policy. At Nate Newton's hearing for his drug possession and use, he rationalized some players renting a party house for drug/alcohol consumption near the team's headquarters by saying it was "just [a place] to run some whores in." The Cowboys franchise has a legacy of drug abuse among its players; ex-Cowboys Lance Rentzel, Thomas Henderson, and Rafael Septien each had highly publicized incidents involving drugs in the 1960s, 1970s, and 1980s.

International Olympic Committee's (IOC) move and won his case, the event signaled to the Olympic sports world that marijuana was clearly unwanted in those cultures. Arguments have been raised that the new Olympic sport of snowboarding served as an example because the sport itself, like it's water counterpart surfing, has long been associated with a fringe drug culture.

Athletes and sports insiders protest that WADA's claims that marijuana has performance-enhancing effects are scientifically unfounded; they claim precisely opposite. Rather than a performance enhancer for athletes, marijuana is a social drug and not something for WADA to be concerned with in its policing process. The NCAA collected data between 1987–1991 that suggested that athletes take the drug to relax in part due to the rigors of their lifestyles and as a socialization mechanism with other athletes. Bans on the drug in sports say more about leagues' and teams' wishes for their athletes to be socially clean rather than physically on the same biological playing field.

The problem of actually policing marijuana use in sports has been a pronounced issue in North American sports cultures as far back as the late 1970s. Players from the National Basketball Association (NBA) and the National Football League (NFL) have respectively described their sports as replete with marijuana use, and poll after poll in North American college/universities charts a steady increase of the drug's use among athletes even in an era of heightened prohibition. And, because the consumption of marijuana by athletes in a majority of sports is often ignored by sports insiders, mixed messages are sent to them regarding its acceptability. Due to these arguments and others, the Canadian Center for Ethics in Sport announced in 2007 that it would consider removing marijuana from its banned substance list; especially because the country has moved to decriminalize the drug in its federal legal statutes. Their counterparts in the UK and The Netherlands athletics followed suit shortly thereafter.

PROBLEMS WITH DRUGS IN THE NATIONAL HOCKEY LEAGUE

The NHL is not atypical with respect to drug consumption among players. Consider the following cases:

1978: Don Murdoch of the New York Rangers was suspended for the 1978–1979 season after his arrest for possession of cocaine.

1983: Ric Nattress of the Montreal Canadiens was suspended for the 1983–1984 season for possession of marijuana and hashish.

1986: Borje Salming of the Toronto Maple Leafs was suspended for the 1986–1987 season for admitting previous use of cocaine in a newspaper article.

1989: Bob Probert, winger for the Detroit Red Wings, was suspended for life for smuggling cocaine into the United States from Canada. He was later reinstated.

1990: Grant Fuhr of the Edmonton Oilers was suspended for one year for admitting prior substance use.

1994: Bob Probert, winger for the Chicago Blackhawks, was suspended indefinitely without pay and immediately ordered into a league-supervised treatment center in California. It is believed to be the first time the league has assisted in a player's rehabilitation. Probert was reinstated, again, in April 28, 1995.

1997: Ken Daneyko, defenseman for the New Jersey Devils, became the first player to publicly announce his voluntary participation in the NHL's new substance abuse program.

2000: Kevin Stevens of the New York Rangers was arrested in a suburban St. Louis motel for felony drug possession of crack cocaine and was admitted to the NHL's treatment program.

2000: Ed Belfour of the Dallas Stars was arrested for assault and resisting arrest after a fight at a Dallas hotel. He pleaded guilty to a misdemeanor charge of resisting arrest and was enrolled in the NHL's substance abuse program.

2002: Jere Karalahti of the Nashville Predators was suspended for six months without pay by the NHL for a third violation of the league's substance abuse policy.

Unlike alcohol and marijuana—whose users will frequently confess to their consumption practices—one of the most complicated illicit drugs to document in professional sports is cocaine. The substance is a legitimate target for antiperformance drug crusaders in sports because it has immediate (and dangerous) performance-enhancing effects and has been linked to player deaths. The tragic cocaine-related deaths of NBA basketball player Len Bias and NFL footballer Don Rogers in 1993 sent shockwaves through the sports community. One must question the long-term impact of the deaths, though, because only 7 years later professional football player Dave Wymer died of a cocaine overdose. A selection of other players to be arrested for cocaine use, or who tested positive for cocaine in their sports' drug tests, include MLBA players Dwight Gooden, Darryl Strawberry, Butch Hobson, and Ken Caminitti; NFL players Jamal Lewis and Hollywood Henderson; wheelchair athlete Jeff Adams; equestrian rider Eric

Lamaze; and pro tennis players Mats Wilander, Lourdes Dominguez, and Martina Hingis.

One of the most poignant illustrations of the effects of cocaine on a player's career is Derek Sanderson. Sanderson literally went from the penthouse to a park bench. A highly touted player, Sanderson scored 24 goals and added 25 assists in his first season with the Boston Bruins in 1967–1968. Once named one of the sexiest men in America by *Cosmopolitan,* Sanderson lived a life of decadence. In 1972, he briefly became the highest-paid athlete in the world when he signed a $2.6 million contract with the Philadelphia Blazers of the World Hockey Association (WHA). But the partying eventually caught up to him. Sanderson lost millions through alcohol, bad investments, and cocaine abuse. By the end of the 1970s he was out of the NHL and eventually found himself sleeping on a park bench in New York City.

Illicit drug consumption in sports is no less, and perhaps even more, problematic to control and police than consumption outside of sports cultures. Professional athletes live and work in a physical cultural environment saturated with the consumption of legal, illegal, and illicit drugs. Subcultural traditions of use are evident in amateur and professional sports. It is a major problem when we actually encourage the consumption of certain drugs such as alcohol and turn a blind eye toward or tolerate others such as marijuana; policing the use of more dangerous drugs such as cocaine becomes somewhat unrealistic.

FUTURE PROSPECTS

The consumption of drugs will most likely remain one of the flashpoint issues in North American social discourse for years to come. As sports federations and leagues have become hyperconcerned with performance-enhancing drug consumption, the global "drug police" of sports, such as WADA, have also targeted drugs that are not, perhaps, in their mandate to police. It seems that WADA and its affiliates have assumed a moral directorship of global sports cultures in this regard, seeking to "clean up" (particularly amateur) athlete cultures. Without contestation and resistance from sovereign sports organizations, teams, and players, the specter of control should only widen and deepen in the future.

See also Ergogenics; Erythropoietin (EPO); Sports Doctors, Trainers, and Drugs; Steroid Use by Athletes; Whistle-Blowers and Drugs.

Further Reading: Collins, T., and Vamphew, C. (2002). *Mud, Sweat and Beers.* Oxford, UK: Berg; Waddington, I. (2002). *Sport, Health and Drugs: A Critical Sociological Perspective.* London: Taylor and Francis.

Michael Atkinson

MARKETING FEMALE ATHLETE SEXUALITY

The contemporary world of sports is a commercial zone rife with capitalist beliefs and practices. At the same time, it is a social space wherein gender codes influence how sports are played by athletes and interpreted by audiences. Where the matter of gender is concerned, part of the selling of modern sports rests on its producers' abilities to market athletes as appropriately masculine and feminine. As part of selling women's sports in particular, North American team and league owners tend to reproduce practices of discrimination and objectification of women by using female athletes' sex appeal to market women's sports.

BACKGROUND

Selling the sexuality of female athletes as a means of marketing women's sports in general is a deeply patterned trend. Few would contest the idea that many female athletes such as Maria Sharapova or Danica Patrick are pop cultural sex icons of the twenty-first century. The tendency to sexualize female athletes for sporting audiences has been a part of sports for several decades, but women's historical involvement in sports has not always involved their objectification.

Called the "Golden Age of Women's Sports," the period immediately following World War I witnessed a mushrooming of women's sports. Women's opportunities for playing sports such as basketball in the United States and ice hockey in Canada had emerged through the war as women's teams often "stood in" for men in organized leagues, but team sports such as basketball, ice hockey, and softball became organized for women in the postwar period. By the late 1920s, to draw further attention to women in sports, major newspapers and national magazines across the country started to run columns on them. In a social world still cleaved by gender logics casting women as inferior to males in most social institutions, such a groundbreaking into sports could not be considered as anything other than ideologically progressive.

But conservative critics of women's venture into predominantly masculine terrain would not be silenced for long. The 1930s witnessed a growing condemnation of women's involvement in team sports and their involvement in the Olympics. It was believed and feared that involvement in rigorous physical training could, in the first instance, foster "manly" bodies and behaviors in women. The involvement of women in sports would also confuse participants about their ascribed social positions and roles, instilling in them qualities such as leadership, confidence, authority, and resolve, which were deemed unnecessary for female "homemakers." Rule changes were instituted in games such as basketball and hockey to eliminate even quasiaggressive forms of play, and rules were altered in sports such as tennis to ensure women would not be portrayed as serious competitive athletes like males.

A widespread cultural preoccupation settled in by the 1950s for channeling young female athletes into sports that emphasized stereotypical feminine qualities of grace, beauty, and refinement. Sports such as figure skating, synchronized swimming, skiing, tennis, badminton, and golf were deemed acceptable in the socialization of young women because they posed less of a social threat to the established gender order. In Canada, figure skater Barbara Ann Scott (dubbed Canada's Sweetheart) was one of the best-known female athletes in the 1950s because she almost perfectly symbolized how a prototypical female athlete should look, act, and think. Through the 1960s, female athletes were not so much sexually objectified, then, as molded into social figures, which neither represented strong and powerful people embodied with special virtue (such as male athletes) nor challenged the social order of sports. Nevertheless, the cultural gender rules underpinning sports still marginalized their involvement in athletics as decisively separate and unequal to men's.

Popular female athletes of the 1970s and 1980s hardly shattered the mold established for women's sports representation decades earlier. Playing their sport in a post–Title IX but still masculinist sports world, athletes such as figure skater Dorothy Hamill, tennis player Chris Evert-Lloyd, gymnast Mary Lou Retton, and track and field star Florence Griffith-Joyner became the most successful female athletes in their sports, but they were also heavily marketed and mass-mediated as traditional women in a number of important ways. Hamill, for instance, was well-known for her Olympic success in 1976 and as a technical innovator in her sport, but she was equally recognized by men and women for her signature "bob" haircut. These women, separately and collectively, were media "darlings" because their images, personas, and physical styles were easily reconcilable with lingering stereotypes about women and femininity. Equally, they were marketable within their sports because they did not look, in rather homophobic discourses at the time, overly "butch" or lesbian, a criticism many female athletes faced during this time period.

There are many ways to decode the significance of women's treatment as veritable second-class citizens in the world of sports. Italian theorist Antonio Gramsci's theory of hegemony is one of the most direct and poignant, however. *Hegemony* refers to a process of rule by consent rather than coercion and reflects Gramsci's premise that social power does not stem from outright force over others. According to Gramsci, a ruling group forms and maintains its hegemony in civil society by creating cultural and political consensus around their core ideologies through social and cultural practices within institutions. For example, young athletes are taught to believe a set of core ideas that reaffirm and exaggerate codes about what it means to be a "real" man in society, what it is to be white, the value of particular class-based work ideologies, and other beliefs that maintain the social status quo. Gramsci maintains that any organization, such as sports, serves as a vehicle for disseminating ideologies that serve and sustain the ruling groups (such as men in a patriarchal society) who organize and operate them. Over time, the ideologies underpinning the organizations become taken-for-granted as natural or culturally true; thus, they tend to be simply accepted by participants as legitimate. The media, in particular, play a central role in the extension and maintenance of hegemony across social institutions because they serve to send out images of, for example, standards of masculinity and femininity that others should strive to achieve.

The mass mediation of female athletes since the 1950s has been part of masculine hegemony work in North America. The showcasing of selected women, and selected women's sports cultures, tends to replicate enduring stereotypes of women and femininity. Up until the late 1970s, the dominant ideological image framing female athletes in their media representation was grounded in traditional images of femininity. But in the 1980s, the mass-mediation and marketing of female athletes shifted decisively toward the hypersexualization and objectification of them. Organizers of sports leagues or organizations with female athletes, sports apparel, and equipment producers, along with women athletes themselves, discovered that more money could be made by hyperbolizing and sexualizing (in hegemonic, patriarchal ways) the "diva athlete" as a modern symbol of femininity.

KEY EVENTS

Actress and political activist Jane Fonda revolutionized the health and exercise industry in the early 1980s by patenting and promoting a unique aerobic workout first sold on video (VHS) as "Jane Fonda's Workout" in 1982. Fonda marketed the video to women seeking to lose weight, develop strength, and generally improve their health. In the video, Fonda and others appeared in fashionable leotards, headbands, and legwarmers (perhaps worn by Fonda as a result of her ballet background), a style that quickly became incorporated into popular cultural fashion. The image of a former model/actress dressed in a leotard doing exercise clearly appealed to North American men and women. The Fonda workout videos (from 1982–1995) at once both called women to the gym to work out and participate in feminine aerobic (versus masculine weight training) exercise and provided "pretty" and mass-marketable images of women working out. Either intentionally or unintentionally, the Fonda workouts and their associated hegemonic images of femininity launched a new era of feminine athletic-fashion styles at a time when more women were seeking to engage in physical fitness programs. Fonda's programs were cleverly marketed because they tapped into cultural stereotypes about how a woman should act and look in the context of working out. Physical fitness became a process of feeling better and being healthier but also looking fashionable as a woman.

Sports Illustrated's *(SI)* annual swimsuit issue set another precedent in the objectification of women through sports and sports media. First released in 1964, the issue remains the single most popular edition of the magazine yearly. For corporate investors and advertisers in *SI*, its cultural popularity leads them to invest nearly $40 million in the issue yearly. The edition typically contains models and supermodels in exotic locations, dressed in bikinis, and posed suggestively. Critics have long argued that the edition has absolutely nothing to do with sports and all to do with the crass sexualization of females for male consumption. Because *SI* is regarded as one of if not *the* most authoritarian sports periodicals in North America, one has to question what hegemonic message is sent out about women in sports, when the issue containing the greatest representation/volume of them on its pages is the swimsuit edition.

While it might not seem tremendously consequential that these athletes appeared in bikinis in the magazine, one has to ask whether or not elite or male athletes would be asked to sexualize themselves in this manner.

With the enduring success of the *SI* swimsuit issue, legions of copycat magazines have exploited the swimsuit-style format as regular (and not merely one-off yearly) editions. College, Olympic, and professional female athletes have

THE HISTORY OF THE JANE FONDA WORKOUT

Jane Fonda's exercise videos have sold millions of copies worldwide. Her first video sold 17 million copies and is still the number one selling exercise video of all time. Media scholars often suggest the VCR "craze" in North America during the early 1980s was partially fuelled by Fonda's first exercise videos. Listed chronologically, here are the Fonda videos:

1982: Jane Fonda's Workout (aka Workout Starring Jane Fonda)
1983: Jane Fonda's Pregnancy, Birth and Recovery Workout
1983: Jane Fonda's Workout Challenge
1984: Jane Fonda's Prime Time Workout (re-released as Jane Fonda's Easy Going Workout)
1985: Jane Fonda's New Workout
1986: Jane Fonda's Low Impact Aerobic Workout
1987: Jane Fonda's Start Up (aka Start Up with Jane Fonda)
1987: Jane Fonda's Sports Aid
1987: Jane Fonda's Workout with Weights (re-released as Jane Fonda's Toning and Shaping)
1988: Jane Fonda's Complete Workout
1989: Jane Fonda's Light Aerobics and Stress Reduction Program (re-released as Jane Fonda's Stress Reduction Program)
1990: Jane Fonda's Lean Routine Workout
1990: Jane Fonda's Workout Presents Fun House Fitness: The Swamp Stomp
1990: Jane Fonda's Workout Presents Fun House Fitness: The Fun House Funk
1991: Jane Fonda's Lower Body Solution
1992: Jane Fonda's Step Aerobic and Abdominal Workout
1993: Jane Fonda's Favorite Fat Burners
1993: Jane Fonda's Yoga Exercise Workout
1994: Jane Fonda's Step and Stretch Workout
1995: Jane Fonda's Personal Trainer Series: Low Impact Aerobics & Stretch
1995: Jane Fonda's Personal Trainer Series: Total Body Sculpting
1995: Jane Fonda's Personal Trainer Series: Abs, Buns & Thighs

---

been featured on the pages of these magazines in bikinis or even half or fully nude. Magazines such as *Maxim, Loaded, Gear, FHM,* and even *Playboy* have created a new sports sex icon: the athlete-as-pin-up-girl. Five members of the U.S. Olympic Team, for example, appeared on the cover of *FHM* magazine's 2004 "Sexy Olympic Special." Since then, *FHM* has been an industry leader in showcasing female athletes in highly sexualized ways. The list of U.S., Canadian, and Western European athletes who have posed for the magazine or one of its rivals is considerable: including Sue Bird, Jamie Sale, Ashley Force, Sasha Cohen, Danica Patrick, Missy Gibson, Natalie Gulbis, Niki Gudex, Kristi Leskinen, Heather Mitts, Lokelani McMichael, and Daniela Hantuchoca. Going

ATHLETES APPEARING AS MODELS IN THE "SWIMSUIT ISSUE"

Over the years, athletes have been asked to participate as models in *Sports Illustrated*'s swimsuit issue. While the sexual representation of models in the issue has been accepted, the use of women athletes as models is only a trend of the past decade. Here are a few of the female athletes to appear in the issue as models:

- Steffi Graf
- Serena Williams
- Ekaterina Gordeeva
- Anna Kournikova
- Amanda Beard
- Jennie Finch
- Jenny Thompson
- Lauren Jackson
- Venus Williams
- Maria Sharapova
- Danica Patrick

even further toward hypersexualization, high jumper Amy Acuff appeared in Playboy in 2004, six years after figure skater Katarina Witt shattered that social boundary. Volleyball icon Gabrielle Reece also appeared in *Playboy* in 2001, as did 1500m runner Katie Vermeuleun in 2004 and Amanda Beard in 2007.

Feminist scholars point out that one of the main motivations for women to appear as models in these magazines boils down to the sheer economics of participation. Given that the majority of women's sports are funded, sponsored, or invested in by people in a tiny fraction compared to men's sports, even elites can earn greater money posing topless than they can as amateurs or professionals within their sports. College and female athletes in particular are vulnerable because they are not heavily sought after to sponsor commercial products. In many sports, a female athlete is not financially successful until she is able to secure money through self-objectification away from the playing field.

There is perhaps no greater example of how sexualizing oneself as a female athlete can create profit than that of former professional tennis player Anna Kournikova. At the apex of her tennis career (reaching a world ranking of eighth), Kournikova was the highest female income earner in all of professional sports despite the fact that as a singles player she had never won a singles tournament on a professional tour. Since the young age of 15, Kournikova has been portrayed as a highly sexualized tennis player within a sport desperate to attract new (male) audiences. By 2000, the tennis and sports sex phenomenon was the number one searched sports figure through the Google Web site. This was reaffirmed in a 2000 advertisement campaign for Berlei's sports bras that featured her wearing only a bra and skirt under the caption "Only the Ball Should Bounce." Between 2000–2006, Kournikova appeared as a scantily clad model in print ads, feature magazine spreads, and in music videos. ESPN, however, rated her among the biggest flops in sports history and the number one overrated/overmediated athlete on the planet. Critics of Kournikova's overt objectification have argued that her own willingness to sexualize her athletic body and the public's insatiable interest in her as a sports sex icon almost single-handedly erased 50 years of women's progress toward equality in sports worlds.

Kournikova was not the first hypersexualized athlete in the 1990s. When U.S. soccer player Brandi Chastain of the national team ripped off her jersey after scoring the final penalty kick at the 1999 World Cup championship game, she drew an incredible amount of media attention, not for her skill as an athlete, but for her tanned, muscular, sexy body. Quickly after the game her commercial value as a product endorser increased exponentially. The photo of her shirtless, kneeling on the ground with arms raised circulated the globe. Only a day after the World Cup, the majority of Americans had not seen the game (or even knew the tournament had been played on American soil), but they had seen Chastain posed seminude on the field. Later that year, in a *Gear* advertisement for Nike, Chastain posed nude (except for her Nike cleats), only covering her breasts and genitals with soccer balls. She argued that the pictures did not diminish her status as an athlete, but rather drew critical public attention to women's sports and muscular female bodies. A year later, Canadian water polo player Waneek Horn-Miller posed nude on the cover of *Time* magazine, expressing a similar justification as Chastain. Horn-Miller, a Native Canadian of Mohawk descent, used the photo to draw attention to First Nations struggles in the province of Quebec. Jenny Thompson, heralded by many as the greatest female swimmer ever, posed topless for *Sports Illustrated* in the summer of 2000. She strategically covered her breasts with two clenched fists, and declared that the purpose of the photo was to show off her muscles rather than to promote any kind of sex appeal. Like Chastain and Horn-Miller, Thompson described her photograph as one about strength, fitness, and the beauty of muscles, not about sex. From a hegemony theoretical perspective, however, what is interesting to note is how and why female athletes feel as if the best way of raising political consciousness and debate is through sexualizing their female bodies. From Gramsci's (1971) perspective, by portraying the body in overtly stereotypical ways, the importance of their political messages disintegrates.

Partly in a marketing attempt to negate cultural stereotypes between women's golf and lesbian lifestyles (or, to reaffirm the standard of the hegemonically straight, docile, sexual woman in sports), the Ladies Professional Golf Association (LPGA) engaged in a "fashion campaign" during the late 1990s to sell the sport to a wider male audience. The LPGA worked in conjunction with high-end fashion designers such as Armani, Prada, Tommy Hilfiger, Burberry, Ralph Lauren, and Escada to outfit young, attractive players with sexually suggestive clothing to be worn at events. In 2002, *Sports Illustrated* profiled Natalie Gulbis, who, in her first year on the tour, showed up to major events in short skirts resembling those worn by figure skaters. That same year, Swedish golfer Catrin Nilsmark, outfitted by high-end designer Johan Lindeberg, sparked considerable debate in sports circles when she routinely arrived to competitions in tight shorts. Ty Votaw, the commissioner of the LPGA, had suggested in 2002 that the status of the sport could be elevated in North America if players would consider looking more attractive and fashion forward. Similar requests, and sometimes demands, have been made in sports such as beach volleyball and tennis. It is ironic that at most North American private golf clubs women are prohibited from wearing suggestive shorts or shirts that are both collarless and sleeveless.

FUTURE PROSPECTS

There has probably never been a period in the history of women's sports in North America where the objectification of women has been so pronounced. In an ironic but predictable twist of fate, as women's sports have grown and developed, and as women have made considerable inroads into professional sports worlds, the sexualization of women athletes reminds us that not all is yet level on the playing field. Women are still encouraged to behave in hegemonically defined ways, showcasing their feminine sex appeal (and lesser social status as athletes). While the strategy of selling sexuality to sports audiences is a lucrative venture for sports insiders, the act of (self)sexualization in sports teaches us that two very different sets of gender codes are applied to membership in the sports world.

See also Eating Disorders; Funding Equality Legislation; Gender and Game Rules; Homophobia; Media Coverage of Women's Sports; Ubersexuality; Women and the Apologetic; Women Coaches and Owners; Women in Men's Sports.

Further Reading: Davis, L. (1997). *The Swimsuit Issue and Sport: Hegemonic Masculinity and Sports Illustrated.* Albany: SUNY Press; Gramsci, A. (1971). *Selections from the Prison Notebooks.* London: Lawrence and Wishart; Heywood, L., Dworkin, S., and Foudy, J. (2003). *Built to Win: The Female Athlete as Cultural Icon.* Minneapolis: University of Minnesota Press; Messner, M. (2002). *Taking the Field: Women, Men and Sports.* Minneapolis: University of Minnesota Press; Sandoz, J. (1999). *Whatever it Takes: Women on Women's Sport.* New York: Farrar, Straus and Giroux; Smith, L. (1998). *Nike is a Goddess: The History of Women in Sport.* Cornwall, UK: Atlantic Press.

Michael Atkinson

MASCOTS

In the past 20 years, sports critics have questioned the role of "mascots" in both amateur and professional sports. A mascot is a symbolic figure, usually an animal or human character dressed up in a costume, representing a group such as a sports team. North American university and lower school sports teams are often recognized socially by their mascot alone. Professional sports teams, like their college or amateur counterparts, normally place a mascot in the stands at home games in order to help cheer on the team and stimulate crowd excitement. Also, much of a professional sports teams' merchandise will carry the mascot. While people publicly recognize and appreciate the role of a mascot in generating crowd enthusiasm during games, providing people with a common symbol to identify with, and as an important marker of collective expression, some American sports mascots have been called either racist or sexually exploitive in expression.

BACKGROUND

A practice that started at Princeton University in the 1880s (and then flourished at colleges nationally soon after), cheerleading has been frequently debated as merely the practice of keeping "female mascots" around the sporting field for male fans. In North America, nearly 90 percent of all cheerleaders are female. In the context of professional sports team cheerleading, participants are often dressed in highly sexual and revealing outfits. Although the Baltimore Colts National Football League (NFL) football team in the 1960s is believed to have started the first pro sports cheerleading squad, the Dallas Cowboys' cheerleaders set the proverbial "bar" for the dance-style cheerleading that now predominates in professional sports. The Cowboys' cheerleaders ascended to national and international fame due to their revealing outfits and sophisticated dance moves. Up until this point, cheerleaders at the university and college levels had been viewed as legitimate athletes, skilled in gymnastics and other athletic disciplines. The NFL teams in the 1970s, however, saw more of a potential fan "attraction" to cheerleading coming from the sexual overtones of scantily clad, pom-pom waving women rather than leaping and flipping gymnasts. The Cowboys' cheerleaders debuted in the 1972–1973 season and attained a cultural icon status following their televised showcasing during Super Bowl X in 1976.

Arguably, the advent of the Dallas cheerleading squad altered the sports image of cheerleaders forever. Even though a strong subculture of competitive gymnastics-style cheerleading exists to this day in the United States, Canada, and the United Kingdom, common cultural associations between cheerleading and sports often revolve around the sexualized cheerleader-mascot image. Since the 1990s, NFL, National Hockey League (NHL), Major League Baseball (MLB), and National Basketball Association (NBA) teams have developed their own troops of cheerleaders. Many of the women involved resemble fitness models and dancers more than gymnasts who perform risky feats of tumbling. These groups of cheerleaders might be, then, best described as mascot "dance teams" rather than groups of athletes. Most do not encourage crowd chanting or noise nor do groups entertain crowds with cheerleading routines underpinned by athleticism.

Feminist scholars suggest that professional sports cheerleaders not only objectify women in sexual ways, but they further a long-standing cultural stereotype that women should be spectators or cheerleaders in sports rather participants. By claiming that the role of the modern cheerleader in professional sports is to sexually stimulate male audience members, critics argue that pom-pom waving and body gyrations have nothing to do with the spirit of encouragement among spectators nor action in the contests. Further still, they draw our attention to how female sports leagues never showcase male models or dancers in stadiums as professional cheerleaders.

Finally, the very role of mascots in sports has been questioned by a series of high-profile cases of "mascot madness" or, simply, notorious cases of mascots "taking over" the playing field.

Without question, the most notorious of all American mascots is the San Diego Chicken, now known as The Famous Chicken. The chicken was partly the brainchild of Canadian-born Ted Giannoulas. In March of 1974 on the campus of San Diego State, a representative from a rock 'n' roll radio station (KGB in San Diego) searched for a volunteer to wear a rented chicken suit for a promotional stunt. It was just a one-week, temporary job offering to visit the local zoo and give away candy Easter eggs. Ted Giannoulas agreed, and KGB paid him $2 an hour for the job. After his stint at the zoo was completed, Giannoulas saw an opportunity and volunteered to attend San Diego Padres baseball games dressed in costume as the station's sports ambassador. From that day forward, The Chicken became a regular fixture at sports events across the United States. The Chicken's infamy was partially established by the way he would taunt players and fans, pull practical jokes on spectators, and occasionally offend umpires.

The radio station fired Giannoulas in May of 1979 and sought to legally block his right to work in a chicken costume or refer to himself as the San Diego Chicken. The California Supreme Court went on to rule in Ted's favor and allowed him to continue with his "pranking" of audiences at sports and music events as The Chicken. Only a few years later, The Chicken would be in court again after grabbing a Chicago Bulls Cheerleader and rolling around on the court with her. She sued him, and a U.S. court awarded her over $300,000 in 1991. The Chicken has become a cultural icon since his debut in the 1970s and through his legal battles. In May 2001, The Chicken was asked by President Bush to perform at the celebrated first T-ball game at the White House broadcast live on C-Span and hosted by Bob Costas. Years earlier, both President Reagan and President Ford had The Chicken help introduce them at public events from the podium. The Chicken has performed at more than 8,500 games and never missed one due to injury or illness. To date, he has made more than 17,000 total event appearances when parades, trade shows, banquets, conventions, and TV and radio dates are factored into his mascot work. He has been featured in television commercials and programs, endorsed sporting equipment and food products, and made cameo appearances in movies such as *Attack of the Killer Tomatoes*.

The Philadelphia Phillies' baseball team mascot, the Philly Phanatic, is one of the most loved and hated mascots in professional sports. The Phanatic, otherwise known as Tom Burgoyne, had a long history of taunting opposing team players and managers, but he became nationally known in August of 1988 as a "mad" mascot when he and Los Angeles Dodger manager Tommy Lasorda got into a fist-fight during a game. The Phanatic had used a doll of Lasorda as a punching bag during the game, and Lasorda eventually protested the taunting by punching the mascot. In 1994, baseball fan Charles Donoghue sued the Phanatic after the mascot grabbed him with such force that Donoghue's back was injured. Donoghue was later awarded over $2.5 million in damages. Since then, the Phanatic has scaled back his antics and has even been inducted to the MLB Hall of Fame.

NOTABLE CASES OF "MASCOT MADNESS"

- September 1989: Miami's Sebastian the Ibis led the Hurricanes onto the field for their annual clash with Florida State carrying a fire extinguisher, intending to douse the Seminoles' famous flaming spear. Five police officers surrounded the mascot and emptied his extinguisher.
- October 1992: A fight between mascots broke out during Northeast Louisiana University's homecoming game against Northwestern State, with Northwestern's Vic the Demon landing a series of punches after Chief Brave Spirit ripped off his mascot head.
- August 1994: Colorado Rockies radio announcer Jeff Kingery shoved and cursed out Dinger the Dinosaur after the team mascot fell down a step and bumped into the broadcaster during the game.
- October 1994: At an exhibition game in Puerto Rico, the Miami Heat's Burnie pulled a female spectator onto the court by her legs. The woman, wife of a local Supreme Court justice, was not amused. Burnie was convicted of aggravated assault and later sued for $1 million.
- February 1995: Don Jackson, coach of the International Hockey League's Cincinnati Cyclones, was suspended 10 games and fined $1,000 for climbing over the glass and attacking Atlanta Knights mascot Sir Slapshot, who had hit the glass while Jackson was leaning on it.
- October 1995: Cal State offensive tackle Tarik Glenn struck Benny Beaver on his way into the locker room after the Oregon mascot (a 5'9", 135-pound woman) tapped the 330-pounder on the shoulder with an inflatable hammer. Later that season, Arizona's 305-pound Frank Middleton punched Benny in the head.
- April 1995: Denver Nuggets mascot, "Rocky the Mountain Lion," challenged Phoenix Suns' player Charles Barkley to a friendly boxing match, only to get hit in the face.
- July 2000: Florida's Billy the Marlin accidentally hit an elderly man in the eye with a tightly wadded T-shirt launched out of a pressurized gun and temporarily knocked him unconscious.
- January 2001: The Miami Hurricanes suffered a 15-yard penalty during their Sugar Bowl game against University of Florida when Sebastian the Ibis ran onto the field and taunted the Gators after a Miami touchdown.
- January 2003: Edmonton Oilers' head coach Craig MacTavish, fed up with Calgary mascot Harvey the Hound dangling over his team's bench, ripped the dog's fabric tongue out of his mouth and tossed it into the stands.
- March 2003: A scuffle ensued between the Oregon Duck and Utah's Swoop during halftime of a first-round NCAA basketball tournament game when Swoop accidentally ripped off the Oregon mascot's head. The two were sent to a room beneath the stands to reconcile and later hugged at center court to a standing ovation.
- July 2003: Pittsburgh Pirates baseball player Randall Simon was arrested and fined $432 for hitting one of the Milwaukee Brewers' Italian Sausage mascots with a bat during their seventh inning "human sausage race." The woman in the Italian sausage costume was knocked to the ground but not seriously injured.

KEY EVENTS

Debates about the representation of Native Americans, in particular, have emerged since the late 1970s in the United States. For well over a hundred years, little league, school, amateur, and professional sports teams have used images of native peoples as team logos or as mascots, including so-called traditional native peoples adorned with headdresses, feathers, war paint, and loin cloths. Such teams have been given native sounding names such as the Warriors, Braves, Chiefs, Tribe, Redmen, Savages, Redskins, or in some cases even Squaws. Although largely unchallenged for many decades, the use of Native American icons and mascots in sports came under intense scrutiny in the last three decades of the twentieth century as native activists across the United States increasingly protested "we are people, not mascots."

In the 1990s, the Indian mascot controversy came to a boiling point in both university and professional sports. Notwithstanding the efforts of native rights lobbyists, one might argue that the issue of Native American representation through professional sports mascots came to the cultural forefront because of two main factors. First, the popularity of the *Major League* Hollywood movies—based on the fictional exploits of the Cleveland Indians baseball team—brought international attention to the team mascot, Chief Wahoo, the reference to the teams and their fans as "the tribe," and the informal naming of the Indians' outfield bleachers at Cleveland Municipal Stadium as "the reservation."

Supposedly, the Cleveland Indian's team name was intended to honor the first native professional baseball player, Louis Sockalexis, who played for Cleveland from 1897–1899. By 1928, the team symbolized the name on the uniform by placing a red-faced mascot logo on the sleeve of the players' jerseys. Around 1940, the team started to refer to the mascot as "Chief Wahoo," and quickly following, fans of the team adopted the image as a source of collective identification, entertainment, and amusement. By 1951, Chief Wahoo's symbol was placed on the players' hats. Although the picture of Chief Wahoo used on the uniforms has changed slightly over time, his image remains that of a grinning, red-faced, young native man wearing an eagle feather in his hair. Since the 1950s, every version of the Cleveland uniform has contained a representation of the Chief Wahoo mascot. For decades, Cleveland Indian fans have personified the smiling native mascot by often showing up to games with their faces painted, dressed in fake deerskin costumes, shouting made-up war chants, and beating traditional Indian drums.

Second, the success of the Atlanta Braves (a team with its professional roots in Boston and then Milwaukee) baseball team through the 1990s placed the fans' practice of the "tomahawk chop" (holding one arm out straight and bending it up and down from the elbow) to intimidate opposing players and their ritual "native chanting" in the stands under serious criticism. These displays and practices can be traced back to at least the 1940s. For example, the Boston Braves organization used Chief Wildhorse as their mascot starting in the mid-1940s. The Chief rode around the field atop his horse during the games in the initial period of his introduction. At different points in the team's history, personnel responsible for the organization's publicity and promotion used "Take Me Out to the Wigwam" as a ticket sales slogan. When the team found its home in Milwaukee, they changed the mascot's name to Chief Noc-A-Homa. Owners erected a makeshift tepee in the bleachers near the field so that each time a Braves player hit a homerun, the chief came out of the structure and danced ritually for the crowd. Only in the 1980s did the Atlanta Braves end the use of Chief Noc-A-Homa as their official mascot due to mass public pressure.

In addition to the cases of the Cleveland and Atlanta baseball teams, concerns regarding the racist undertones of native mascots and imagery surfaced in other professional sports. Included in the debate about Native American mascots and team names were the NFL's Washington Redskins and Kansas City Chiefs, the NHL's Chicago Blackhawks, and the NBA's Golden State Warriors. As a response to the criticism, professional sports teams consistently claim that they, as private organizations, are free to represent themselves in any manner of their choosing under the principle of free speech in the United States. Furthermore, they claim their intention in using Native American references with mascots or team names is done out of respect and admiration for native peoples.

While professional sports teams have been successful in defending their legal or cultural use of Native American mascots, U.S. colleges and universities have proven to be an intense battleground of controversy and change. Beginning in 1971, some U.S. colleges and universities discontinued the use of native mascots and team names. For example, the University of Oklahoma discontinued the use of the Little Red mascot; Marquette University stopped using their Willie Wampum mascot; Syracuse University terminated its use of the Saltine Warrior mascot; and, the University of Tennessee discontinued the Chief Moccanooga mascot.

Not all colleges or universities in the United States have been as accommodating to mascot or team name change requests. Some schools are feverishly against retiring their mascots, claiming that team mascots and names are school traditions and deep symbols of the colleges or universities. Most visible among the resisters is Florida State University with its Seminoles team name and Osceola as their mascot. As perennial favorites or contenders in National Collegiate Athletic Association (NCAA) football and other sports, the Seminoles are considerable targets of antimascot groups in the United States. For these reasons and others, the Seminole name and mascot has become a sort of "line in the sand" for people on either side of the debate in the United States. Equally controversial is the University of Illinois's mascot Chief Illiniwek. Chief Illiniwek—almost always a white student dressed up in mock Native American clothing—entertains basketball and football fans with dancing and gymnastics during half-time presentations.

After three decades of attempts to retire Chief Illiniwek, and even an NCAA labeling of the mascot as "offensive" in 2005, the Chief was officially "retired" on February 21, 2007. At the University of Illinois, nearly a dozen academic departments lobbied for the official retirement of the symbol. Organizations including the National Association for the Advancement of Colored People, the National Education Association, Amnesty International, the Modern Language Association, and the Society for the Study of the Indigenous Languages of the Americas protested the continued use of the symbol. In the face of such pressure and eventual change, though, pro-Illiniwek groups such as the Honor the Chief Society and the Chief Illiniwek Educational Foundation remain dedicated supporters of the mascot and team logo. An informal nonstudent vote on the status of Chief Illiniwek as a university mascot in 2004 revealed that 69 percent of those voting were in support of keeping him as a representative of the school.

FUTURE PROSPECTS

The landmark decision at the University of Illinois to cease and desist with its use of Chief Illiniwek is perhaps indicative of the growing intolerance audiences have for mascoting. At best, it seems, audiences will tolerate mascots if they are harmless, cartoonish, and generally inoffensive characters. However, with more complex dance teams, audio visual systems, and other means to emotionally "rev up" crowds, it would not be surprising if the twenty-first century witnessed the general demise of the mascot in most mainstream sports cultures.

See also Collective Protests and Social Movements; Commercializing Ethnic Athletes; Racial Profiling and Stacking.

Further Reading: Davis, L. (1999). Protest Against the Use of Native American Mascots: A Challenge to Traditional American Identity. *Journal of Sport and Social Issues* 17: 9–22; Wolburg, J. (2006). The Demise of Native American Mascots: It's Time to Do the Right Thing. *Journal of Consumer Marketing* 23: 4–5.

Michael Atkinson

MEDIA BROADCASTING RIGHTS

Today's sporting battles are equally as likely to be waged in the corporate boardroom, in the commercial marketplace, or through the popular media universe. The convergent forces and relations shaping contemporary sports are exemplified by what has been described as the "unholy trinity" linking sports, commerce, and the media—a tryst whose complexities and preoccupations are graphically illustrated in the issue of sports media broadcasting rights. The selling of media broadcasting rights contracts has become among the most highly visible, and indeed influential, practices shaping the structure, delivery, and ultimately the experience of the contemporary sports economy. Just as the relentless rise and expansion of the commercial media in the post–World War II era had a profound influence on reshaping culture and society, so the media-industrial complex has come to dominate sports. The selling of broadcast rights has become the single most important source of revenue generation for many prominent sports franchises, leagues, and events and has played a large part in the spiraling wages paid to professional athletes over the past few decades.

BACKGROUND

Although the sports media rights scramble has become a routinized aspect of the sporting cycle (joining other secondary elements such as league player drafts and the awarding of major games and events, that is, aspects not directly related to sporting performances but vital to the staging and delivery of such performances), it is important not to overlook the core reasons for the commercial media's willingness to invest such large sums in securing the broadcast rights to particular sporting properties. In short, the commercial media have no inherent interest in sports; rather, they are motivated by its broad-based popular appeal and thereby potential to generate profit. In other words, while public service broadcasters may engage sports programming as part of their remit to service the needs of the general public, commercial broadcasters are doing so purely to generate audience figures. The economics of free-to-air commercial television are simple. They are centered on the need to generate audiences, which are, in effect, the product sold to media advertisers and sponsors: The larger the audience, the higher the price levied for advertising time and sponsorship relationships and, hence, the greater the profits generated by the broadcaster. Of course, increased advertising revenue is not the only perceived benefit of televising popular sports spectacles. They also represent a priceless opportunity for promoting a network's other programming (particularly new shows) to otherwise unreachable percentages of the national populace. This point of entry into audience consciousness can have important effects on establishing the popularity (and hence longevity) of new programming thereby affecting the profitability of entire networks.

One also has to consider why sports should be viewed so favorably by viewing audiences and, thereby, the communications industry alike. Sports can be considered a unique form of mass entertainment for a number of reasons: First, it incorporates a blend of performative physicality; second, it is prefigured on a narrative and excitement-inducing competitive structure; third, it both benefits from and nurtures deep-rooted personal identifications and loyalties. This popularity of televised sports programming is evident when examining the rankings of highest-rated television broadcasts over a given period. For instance, within the U.S. context, sports programming (specifically coverage of the Super Bowl) occupies every spot in the top 10 rankings of network telecasts during the period 2000–2008.

While the fragmenting commercial media universe has resulted in a noted decline in the audience share for some sports broadcasts, figures for the Super Bowl and Olympic Games have remained robust. These are the major sporting spectacles to which the American public, at least, continues to frequent en masse. Therefore, they are the sports programs for which the broadcast companies are able to levy the highest advertising rates: $2.7 million for 30-second advertising spots during the 2008 Super Bowl and $700,000 for a prime-time spot during NBC's coverage of the 2004 Athens Olympics. In addition to attracting significant audiences in terms of sheer *quantity* to high-profile sports broadcasts, more routine sports programming also possesses the ability to attract a high-*quality* audience. For instance, within the U.S. context, sports programming regularly attracts high concentrations of 18- to 34-year-old males; the disposable income–heavy, consumer demographic prized by corporate advertisers. Given the concentration of this demographic among sports' viewership, it is clear to see why the following corporations should invest so heavily in their annual sports-related advertising spending (these are figures for 2007): Anheuser-Busch ($218 million); Chevrolet Motor Division ($174 million); AT&T Mobility ($171 million); Ford Motor ($140 million); and Verizon Communications ($139 million). Furthermore, it should be noted that Anheuser-Busch dedicated 83.8 percent of its total advertising spending to sports programming.

Clearly, sports represents a relatively scarce, and thereby highly desirous, form of popular media content and one that possesses the potential to generate profitable audiences, in terms of the key measures of quantity and quality. Major sporting bodies are thus in an advantageous position simply because the clamor for sporting content provides the occasion for intense, and often hyperinflationary, media broadcast rights battles. For instance, the National Football League (NFL) was able to negotiate a combined $21.4 billion for broadcast contracts with CBS, ESPN, Fox, NBC, and the NFL Network beginning in 2006. Equally astoundingly, NBC paid the International Olympic Committee (IOC) $820 million for the 2010 Winter Olympics and $1.18 billion for the 2012 London Summer Olympics. This level of investment renders NBC something more than a broadcaster of the Olympic Games; since 1988, and having contributed more than $4.7 billion, NBC has become a key financial partner within the Olympic movement as a whole, and a major factor in the $10 billion in television broadcast revenues realized by the IOC since 1984. Indeed, such is the reliance of the IOC on television rights fees—with approximately 50 percent of the movement's revenue now deriving from this source—that it is unfeasible to imagine the continuation of the games

NOTABLE EXAMPLES OF MEDIA BROADCAST RIGHTS CONTRACTS

1982: National Football League. NBC, CBS, and ABC purchased combined television rights for $3 billion over 5 years.

1984: Los Angeles Summer Olympic Games. ABC purchased television rights for 180 hours of coverage for $225 million.

1992: English Premier League. BSkyB purchased television rights for £304 million over 5 years.

1993: National Football League/National Football Conference. Fox television purchased television rights for $1.58 billion over four years.

2006: National Football League. CBS, ESPN, Fox, NBC, and the NFL Network purchased combined television rights for $21.4 billion over 6 years.

2007: English Premier League. Sky and Setanta Sports purchased combined television rights for £1.7 billion over three years.

2008: Indian Premier League. Sony/World Sport Group consortium purchased television rights for $1.026 billion over 10 years.

2008: Beijing Summer Olympic Games. NBC television purchased rights for as yet unconfirmed hours of coverage for $894 million.

2012: London Summer Olympic Games. NBC purchased television rights for as yet unconfirmed hours of coverage for $1.18 billion.

without television's financial input. Equally, other entities within the crowded sporting landscape are reliant on broadcast relationships for their financial stability, and perhaps even their continued existence.

KEY EVENTS

The Rupert Murdoch figure-headed News Corporation has arguably been the most aggressive and influential player within the global sports media economy over the past 15 years or so. This is particularly true with regard to the acquisition of sports media broadcasting rights, which is perhaps the core component of News Corporation's global strategizing. In order to diversify into the television industry, and to transform into a truly global entity, this onetime Australian-based newspaper corporation has utilized sporting content as a means of engaging the new markets it sought to penetrate and the new media platforms it sought to advance.

Despite Murdoch's reported ambivalence for sports, he clearly recognized its popular appeal among viewing audiences. He also recognized the particularity of national sporting cultures, which demanded that News Corporation's global media strategizing was attuned to, and looked to engage, local sporting preferences. Thus, within each national television market it expanded into, News Corporation (in the guise of its localized media brand, Fox, Sky, etc.) looked to purchase the broadcasting rights for the sporting entity most prized by the local populace. Such an acquisition would provide News Corporation with an instantaneous public profile, it being one of the networks—if not the only—to which the populace would need to turn for their sporting fix. This was particularly important in media markets where News Corporation was introducing fee-based satellite systems. The rationale being that sports would facilitate the migration of viewers from free-to-air platforms.

Given the centrality of sports programming to its expansionist ambitions, it is clear to see why News Corporation has been willing to pay broadcasting rights fees that are far beyond market rates. Indeed, it would be true to say that News Corporation has been largely responsible for the hyperinflationary growth of sports broadcast rights fees, with some rival broadcasters no longer willing, or indeed able, to compete in this sports media marketplace. Although News Corporation's initial forays into sporting and televisual dominance came within the Australian context, the paradigmatic example of this design can be gleaned from Sky Sport's virtual cooption of soccer beginning in the early 1990s. In seeking to establish fee-based satellite television within the British context, in 1992, BSkyB (50% of which was owned by News Corporation) secured a five-year exclusive broadcast rights deal with the newly established English Premier League for £304 million—a figure that represented a staggering 600 percent increase on the previous broadcast rights contract. Such a mammoth investment was soon vindicated as Sky's subscribers doubled to approximately 3 million within a year of the contract thereby helping to establish what had been a floundering new media platform. From this point on, Sky's success within the British media market has been closely tied to its relationship with the English Premier League, resulting in it being equally aggressive in subsequent contract renewals: spending

£670 million for four seasons beginning in 1997; £1.1 billion for three seasons beginning in 2001; and, £1.024 billion for three seasons beginning in 2004. Indeed, such was its dominance of the soccer media marketplace that, in 2006, the European Commission outlawed Sky's exclusive hold over live game coverage, forcing Sky to share live game broadcasts with Setanta Sports for a combined broadcast rights fee of £1.7 billion for three seasons beginning in 2007.

The English Premier League scenario is instructive because it illustrates how the control of sports media broadcast rights has both revolutionized the broadcast media landscape (satellite television was floundering before this relationship was forged) and resuscitated an entire sport (soccer has been transformed by the influx of Sky money). News Corporation, this time through its Fox television armature, has also contributed to the financial advancement of the NFL in the United States. In order to establish its recently constituted Fox television network, in December 1993, News Corporation paid $1.58 billion for a four-year contract to broadcast National Football Conference (NFC) games, which, as well as high-profile Thanksgiving Day and playoff games, included a much vaunted slot in the broadcast rotation of the NFL Super Bowl. Fox's investment provided significant opportunities for magnifying the fledgling network's national visibility, elevating direct advertising revenues and enhancing opportunities for network programming promotions. As a result, Fox's relationship with the NFC proved hugely influential in establishing and defining its network identity within the American popular consciousness and underscoring the importance of NFL football within both terrestrial and satellite television economies.

News Corporation has certainly contributed to the restructuring of the global sports media landscape through its aggressive courting of sports broadcast rights contracts. However, the monopolistic tendencies of the sports media marketplace have spawned some interesting, if perhaps unexpected, outcomes. For those media corporations unwilling, or more likely unable, to compete for certain major sports broadcast rights contracts, an alternative has been to devise and present their own sporting competitions and spectacles. Hence, in the United States, the short-lived XFL football league (funded and televised in part by NBC) and the X Games (owned and televised by ESPN/ABC) are both examples of media-driven sporting initiatives that have circumvented the broadcast rights fee morass. An almost reverse aspect of this trend has been the sporting establishment's willingness to modify sports forms in order to create more television-friendly sports spectacles that would appeal to viewers and advertisers alike and thereby be of interest to potential broadcasters. The recent establishment and advancement of Twenty20 cricket certainly speaks to this trend, particularly in its most sophisticated iteration: the Indian Premier League (IPL) competition initiated in 2008 by the Board of Control for Cricket in India (BCCI). Here is an accelerated and intensified version of an established sport, devised in order to appeal to the lifestyle and sensibilities of the contemporary media consumer, in order that it can be sold as such to the highest broadcast bidder, which, in the case of the IPL's Indian broadcast rights, proved to be the Sony/World Sport Group consortium for a fee of $1.026 billion over 10 years.

FUTURE PROSPECTS

There is little doubt that sports is presently in the midst of an inflationary bubble, propelled largely by the staggering increases in broadcast rights fees over recent years. As such, there are some worrying corollaries in this regard, not least of which is the degree to which sporting bodies have fueled their own inflationary economy based on the influx of media broadcast monies. This financial lifeline is not guaranteed in perpetuity, and the media industry is by no means guaranteed to continue the same scale of sporting investment in the future. Thus, the future of sports becomes largely tied to the whims and dictates of a once subsidiary industry, which has now assumed primacy: perhaps an instance of the media tail coming to wag the sporting dog. Furthermore, even if this bleak projection is never realized, the future of sports in a commercial media–dominated environment is far from healthy because the populist rationalities of the commercial media will doubtless privilege the most popular sports practices, leaving those less media-friendly practices to adapt accordingly or struggle for their very existence.

See also Commercializing Ethnic Athletes; Corporate Branding; Corporate Stadiums; Salaries of Professional Athletes.

Further Reading: Andrews, D. L. (2003). Speaking the "Universal Language of Entertainment": News Corporation, Culture and the Global Sport Media Economy. In *Critical Readings: Sport, Culture and the Media,* edited by D. Rowe, 99–128. Berkshire, England: Open University Press; Bellamy, R. V. (1998). The Evolving Television Sports Marketplace. In *Mediasport,* edited by L. A. Wenner, 73–87. London: Routledge; Bellamy, R. V. (2006). Sports Media: A Modern Institution. In *Handbook of Sports and Media,* edited by A. A. Raney and J. Bryant, 63–75. London: Lawrence Erlbaum Associates; McChesney, R. W. (1989). Media Made Sport: A History of Sports Coverage in the United States. In *Media, Sports, and Society,* edited by L. A. Wenner, 49–69. Newbury Park, CA: Sage; Rowe, D. (1999). *Sport, Culture and the Media: The Unruly Trinity.* Buckingham: Open University Press; Sage, G. H. (1998). *Power and Ideology in American Sport: A Critical Perspective* (2nd ed.). Champaign, IL: Human Kinetics; Williams, J. (1994). The Local and the Global in English Soccer and the Rise of Satellite Television. *Sociology of Sport Journal* 11 (4): 376–397.

David Andrews

MEDIA COVERAGE OF WOMEN'S SPORTS

The media coverage of women's sports has been a subject of controversy for over 40 years. As elite sportswomen rose to prominence in the late 1960s and early 1970s, athletes and academics began to criticize the coverage of women's sports for its very small amount within total sports coverage and for the stereotypes perpetuated within the writing and broadcast commentary. Since then, debates about the media coverage of women's sports have focused both on the amount of coverage devoted to women's sports and the ways that the media covers women's sports as well as about the things said and written and the effort put into producing high-quality coverage.

BACKGROUND

Since analysis of the media coverage of women's sports began in the early 1970s, there has been a consistent finding that women's sports make up a very small part of the total coverage devoted to sports on an everyday basis. This is consistent across broadcast mediums (television, radio, newspapers, magazines, and now the Internet) and around the world, including the United States, Canada, Australia, the United Kingdom, and various other European and Asian countries. While there have been improvements over time, the total media coverage given to women's sports during regular sports coverage remains quite small. For example, from 1989–2004, the coverage of women's sports on major U.S. television networks varied from 6–11 percent of the total sports coverage and did not increase significantly over time.

Sportswriters, editors, and others involved in producing sports coverage often argue audience interest as a determining factor in the amount of coverage devoted to women's sports. The typical audience for sports media, be it broadcast or print, is made up of males aged 18–40. This is the demographic group that advertisers seek to reach and count on through sports coverage. It is assumed that this audience would have a much greater interest in professional and elite-level men's sports and little in women's sports. Furthermore, even many women who consume sports media indicate a preference for watching men's sports.

Critics counter that much of audience interest is generated by the quality of the coverage devoted to a particular sports event and the media's own build-up to it. Compared to coverage of men's sports, women's sports often receive much less in terms of "production values"—the quality of the writing and photographs of print media and, in the case of television, the "add-ons," such as statistics, slow motion replay, and sideline interviews. In newspapers, articles and photographs of women's sports appear more frequently in less prominent places and on "off-days" when there are fewer total events and thus more space to fill. The argument is that if the coverage is less prominent and less well produced, as often seems the case for women's sports, then it is no wonder why even audiences who are interested in a particular sport might not consume media coverage of it. Added to this, for women's sports, the media engages in much less intentional audience building—advance promotion of events, creation of and focus on identifiable stars, and general hype around events and people, so again less interest is built.

Both sides of this question of interest could point to the coverage of women's sports at major international events as supporting its views. When it comes to the media coverage of major international multisports events such as the Olympic Games or Commonwealth Games, the balance between the amount of coverage devoted to men's and women's sports becomes much more equitable. Recent studies find that the coverage of women's sports during a major multisports event usually comes out to at least match with the participation rates of women, and for some media outlets, the coverage comes to nearly 50 percent. It could be argued that during an event such as this, the public takes much more interest in women's sports due to concerns related to nationalism and medal counts, and thus, the media follows that interest. Conversely, it could be argued that interest in women's sports is generated by the increased production value and intentional audience building that occurs during the coverage of a major multisports event. Either way, it can be stated that the coverage of women's sports at a major multisports event is generally much greater than during regular, everyday sports coverage.

A further factor in the general lack of coverage of women's sports on a regular basis is the structure of sports news gathering agencies and the typical work routines of sports journalists. Sports departments, especially at newspapers, must cover a large spectrum of sports with fairly limited resources. The time or space devoted to sports, known as the "newshole," is known in advance because advertising is put in place first with news structured around it. To fill the newshole, agencies have developed systems of reporting and writing with established work routines. In newspapers, for instance, there is a "beat reporting" system where one of the few full-time writers is assigned to the beat of a particular team or league. They become responsible for this sport, filling a set space each day with results, news, and information. In part driven by notions of interest and in part by ease of access to information on highly commercialized sports, most beats are focused on elite-level or professional men's sports. As such, the need to fill the newshole and the structure of news gathering mitigate against covering very many women's sports because the resources to do so have already been assigned.

Added to this is a structural aspect of the sporting world itself. Highly commercialized sports make access to information quite easy for news agencies through press releases, press conferences, and promotional personnel because it provides promotional value for them. With scarce resources for information collecting, news agencies naturally rely on this information quite heavily. Given that most highly commercialized sports are men's sports, ironically in part because the media's coverage of women's sports means they do not often achieve the same level of commercialization and public interest, most of the readily available information will not be about women's sports.

KEY EVENTS

Even if the coverage of female athletes approaches numerical equity as it does during major events, there may still be issues with the content of that coverage. More coverage of women's sports may not necessarily be a positive thing if the nature of that coverage is less than positive. Much criticism has been made of the way that the media covers women's sports, in terms of the narratives and images and the way they frame sportswomen.

Much of the small amount of media coverage of women's sports tends to focus on very few sports. The media mainly covers women's sports that would be stereotypically considered "gender appropriate," that is, they have an emphasis on aesthetics or grace or are individual sports that do not typically require power, strength, and body contact. Women's sports that receive the majority of coverage include tennis and golf in everyday reporting and sports such as gymnastics and figure skating at major events. It might be maintained that these are the sports in which women achieve the highest success and level of competition, so this is what the public wants. Critics point out that such selective coverage could impact the image of sportswomen in general by making it seem that they can only be successful or deserve interest in sports that match with commonly held notions of feminine behavior and physical attractiveness.

Early studies found stereotyping and overt sexualization of sportswomen across different types of sports media. Such coverage stressed feminine traits and downplayed the power of female athletes by taking the focus away from their athleticism. Recent coverage has moved away from overt stereotyping and sexualization, although there are significant examples where female sexuality is still the focus, such as the annual *Sports Illustrated* swimsuit issue. It appears the media have made very conscious efforts to avoid making sportswomen sexual objects. However, this still appears in subtle, probably unconscious ways. For instance, female athletes will appear much more often than men in inactive photographs where they are in street clothes, away from the sporting environment, with the focus on their appearance rather than athletic performance.

Some female athletes are complicit in the media's tendency toward sexually oriented content, themselves working to project an image of sexuality and physical attractiveness and in some cases posing seminude or completely nude for magazines and calendars. This could, as in the case of tennis player Anna Kournikova, serve as a technique to enhance their marketability to sponsors and advertisers. Some athletes and supporters argue that this helps present a positive image of strong, powerful women who can still feel confident and sexy. Critics argue that it takes away from the athleticism of women's sports and feeds into an overall tendency toward women's sports not being taken as seriously as men's sports.

Many typical sports media practices highlight the supposedly natural sexual differences of women from men. When compared to male athletes, sportswomen tend to be framed as having less emotional control and less natural talent and ability. The successes and failures of sporting men and women tend to

THE *SPORTS ILLUSTRATED* SWIMSUIT ISSUE

Each year, the major U.S. magazine *Sports Illustrated* releases a special swimsuit issue that features female swimsuit models in evocative poses in exotic locations. Critics charge that this issue, in a magazine that normally offers very little coverage of women's sports, suggests that women are not to be taken seriously as athletes and only have a major role in sports as athletic supporters and the prizes for victory. Furthermore, the swimsuit issue mostly highlights the bodies of models, not sportswomen, thereby perpetuating unrealistic body images as sexy to the general public and further stigmatizing the female athletic body. Regardless of the controversy, the swimsuit issue proves very popular, selling over 10 times the newsstand sales of any other issue of the already hugely popular magazine.

be attributed to different things. Men tend to be construed as succeeding due to their own efforts and hard work and failing due to circumstances beyond their control such as weather conditions. Women are more liable to be constructed as being dependent on coaches and significant others for their success and as failing due to things such as their own lack of emotional control or preparation. Photographs in magazines and newspapers are frequently pointed to as naturalizing sexual differences in a powerful way because the nature of photographs masks the selections and decisions of photographers and editors. Photographs of female athletes are much more likely to feature them in inactive poses and with downward camera angles, making the athlete subordinate to the camera/viewer. All of these practices naturalize common understandings of the physical and psychological differences between men and women, even though men and women exhibit a range of body types and traits that overlap rather than have sharp divisions. In this naturalization of sexual difference, women tend to come out to being "less than" men.

Similarly, men's sports are often held up as a comparative standard for women's sports. One very subtle way this occurs has been called the "hierarchy of naming." In this, women's sports are called "women's sports," whereas men's sports are not marked by gender. There is the National Collegiate Athletic Association (NCAA) Final Four and the "Women's" NCAA Final Four. This very subtle difference suggests that the men's event is the "real" event, while the women's event is "other than" that or is a lesser event. This practice is very common across mediums, and while some conscious effort has been made to address it by gender marking both men's and women's events, it is still quite prevalent.

There are a number of other common practices in the coverage of women's sports that serve to diffuse the physical power of sportswomen and thereby diffuse the threat that such women make to culturally held notions of physical difference and gender relationships. Sports journalists and commentators often seem to have a general ambivalence about women in sports, as if sometimes they are not really sure what to make of them. On the one hand, they will discuss skill, strength, and determination, while on the other they will stress the athletes' femininity, focus on their appearance, and make them seem less intimidating. Women are described as being both pretty and powerful. This may be an unconscious practice of the media or may sometimes be built in to make women's sports more attractive to a public that may not be entirely comfortable with strong, powerful women.

Other "strategies of containment" that symbolically contain the threat that strong women with hard bodies offer to established notions of gender and sexual difference include infantization, frequent use of first names, and stressing the heterosexuality of female athletes. *Infantization* is the use of descriptors that make grown athletes seem more child-like and cuddly and the stressing of the youth or inexperience of female athletes. Media commentators tend to use the first name of female athletes much more than they do with male athletes. This suggests a familiarity with athletes for media consumers, making athletes seem less intimidating. Heterosexuality is reinforced by making references to families, husbands, and partners and to how women athletes operate within typical supportive female roles in these relationships. This not only stresses the femininity of female athletes, but, in a society that generally looks on homosexuality as less than positive, ensures consumers that these athletes are "safe" in their gender roles. It almost goes without saying that these concerns are not raised for male athletes who match with presumptions that athleticism, power, and aggression are masculine traits.

One of the possible factors in the amount and nature of media coverage of women's sports may be the very low number of women working in the field of sports journalism, particularly in positions of power such as editor and columnist. Women make up only about 12 percent of people in newspaper sports departments in the United States, and this is the area of sports journalism in which they have the highest representation.

Liberal feminists argue that increasing the number of women in sports journalism will naturally improve the amount and quality of coverage devoted to women by the sports media. More radical feminists argue that simply increasing the number of women will not be enough. They point out that the values held by the field of sports journalism mirror those held in sports itself—determination, aggression, individualism, competitiveness—and that these masculine values are part of the reason that women's sports are left out. Having more women in the field who have been socialized within the normal masculine-oriented value system will make little difference, they argue, and more radical changes in the values stressed in sports and sports journalism are needed.

Ultimately, much of the concern for the media coverage of women's sports relates to the potential impact on the sports themselves and effects on consumers. Sports and sports teams that receive more media attention are able to attract more revenue from sponsorship, marketing, and merchandising. As such, the lack of media attention to women's sports can impact on the development of women's sports and the competitive opportunities for female athletes. This may even set up a cycle where lack of media attention means less elite-level women's sports, leading to less media attention.

DID YOU KNOW?

A 2006 study looked at the racial and gender makeup of sports department at over 300 Associated Press newspapers. It found that:

- Women make up only 12.6 percent of total staff in sports newsrooms and 8.4 percent of reporters.
- Women make up 24 percent of the support staff/clerk positions, double their number in any other position.
- Women and people of color combined to make up only 16.4 percent of columnists.
- There were only 15 female sports editors (the most important job), and all of them were Caucasian.

This study and others demonstrate that there are very few women in sports journalism, especially in influential positions, and clear connections to racial issues.

The effect of media coverage on viewers or consumers is a topic of much debate. Research on media in general, beyond just sports, is notoriously contradictory, sometimes showing how media messages directly effect people's attitudes and behaviors, and other times not showing a tangible effect. Part of this is because media consumers are not simply passive, but they actively interpret the media presented to them. Having said this, a number of reasonable assertions can be made in regard to the influence on consumers of the media's coverage of women's sports. The overall lack of attention to women's sports suggests that they are less important then men's sports. The focus on particular sports and particular types of athletic female bodies suggest the most appropriate sports for women to participate in, which may impact on the activity choices of girls and women and the opportunities for participation created in the first place. Certainly, the media coverage of women's sports has the potential to influence commonly held notions of gender, femininity, and sexual difference. The sports media is, and could continue to be, a place where traditional gender norms could be broken in highlighting the performance of strong, powerful, athletic women. Unfortunately, the sports media is, and will likely continue to be, a place where traditional norms are instead reinforced, circulated, and perpetuated through the common practices that occur in the coverage of women's sports.

FUTURE PROSPECTS

Over the past 35 years or so, improvements have been noted in the media coverage of women's sports, both in terms of the basic amount of that coverage and in such elements as stereotyping and blatant sexualization of women athletes. These are trends that should continue. However, the amount of coverage of women's sports in the regular media is still quite tiny and only meets or exceeds participation rates of women in sports for major multisports events such as the Olympic Games. Furthermore, there are still many common practices in the media coverage of women's sports that highlight sexual differences, diffuse the power of sportswomen, and bring their bodies into line with traditional notions of gender and femininity. These are also trends that will probably continue unless fundamental changes happen in the structures of the world of sports and in the values and practices of sports journalism.

See also Funding Equality Legislation; Media Broadcasting Rights; Ubersexuality; Women and the Apologetic.

Further Reading: Davis, L. (1997). *The Swimsuit Issue and Sport: Hegemonic Masculinity in Sports Illustrated.* Albany: SUNY; Duncan, M. C., and Messner, M. (1998). The Media Image of Sport and Gender. In *MediaSport,* edited by L. A. Wenner, 170–185. New York: Routledge; Duncan, M. C., and Messner, M. (2005). *Gender in Televised News and Sports Highlight Programs, 1989–2004.* Los Angeles: AAFLA; Hardin, M., and Shain, S. (2005). Strength in Numbers? The Experiences and Attitudes of Women in Sports Media Careers. *Journalism & Mass Communication Quarterly* 82: 804–819; Lapchick, L., Brenden, J., and Wright, B. (2006). *The 2006 Racial and Gender Report Card of the Associated Press Sports Editors.* Orlando: University of Central Florida.

Fred Mason

MEN IN WOMEN'S SPORTS

The desire to exclude women from men's sports is an ancient one, and the all-naked performances at the original Greek Olympic Games certainly performed this function. The reverse of this—keeping men out of women's sports—appears comparatively modern; systematic sex testing at international sporting events was introduced only in the 1960s—although at first it did consist of naked parades, mirroring the situation in the Greek arena. Genetic and chromosomal testing was rapidly introduced, and all this was done apparently to stop male competitors from "cheating" by participating in women's events. Male physiology often confers advantages in competitive sports, even when compared weight-for-weight and height-for-height with female physiology, so the principle behind sex testing to keep men out of women's events appears, at first glance, to be sound.

In the twentieth century, there has only been one recorded case of a man pretending to be a woman for the sake of sporting glory. Instead, as athletes and human rights advocates have argued, sex testing actually became a form of discrimination against people with genetic and physical abnormalities and was based on sexist assumptions about what men's and women's bodies could do. Not only do the critics of sex testing claim that it was unfair, but they also point out that there are no tests for other physiological advantages (genetic predisposition to strength or height, for example). Most international sports organizations abandoned sex testing in the late twentieth century in part because of the enormous controversy that surrounded the often unsatisfactory tests. Many organizations also argued that body-hugging sports fashion (and the drug test requirement for athletes to pass urine in front of officials) made it practically impossible for any man to compete in a woman's event.

BACKGROUND

Two rather obvious conditions have to be satisfied before we can expect widespread concern about men competing in women's sports. First, sports must be

---

SEX TESTS

Sports organizations have generally used three types of tests for sex. First is the visual or manual examination of athletes, which is a test for phenotypic sex—in other words the visual and physical appearance of primary and secondary sexual features.

Second there are chromosomal tests: Chromosomal sex is defined by one pair of chromosomes, XX for women and XY for men. The second X chromosome in women becomes deactivated in most cells and forms a dense body of chromatin (the Barr Body), which can be fairly easily stained and observed with a microscope. In the 1980s, some sports organizations also tested for the presence of the Y chromosome as well as for the absence of the Barr Body.

Finally, there are genetic tests. The most commonly used of these is a test for a small region on the Y chromosome known as the Sex Determining Region, or SDR. Presence of the SDR indicates maleness and the absence of femaleness.

divided along gender lines, but second, there must be motives for the men to deny their masculinity and compete as women. It is the second condition that provides a stark division between men in women's sports in the twentieth and twenty-first centuries and at any other point in history. Women's competitive sports are as old as men's sports; while the Grecian male athletes competed at the Olympic Games, female athletes competed at the Heraea Games from about the sixth century B.C.E. Likewise, female-only events have been recorded in many cultures, particularly those where sex-segregation is enforced across most activities. In these situations, female sports is still subordinate to male sports; male participation in these events would presumably be more for the sake of illicitly enjoying the company of women than to achieve success in the sport itself.

So, it was not until the twentieth century that women's sports began to gain enough prestige to make gaining a medal an impressive enough achievement to warrant competing as a woman instead of a man. Even then, the only alleged case of this occurring involves a high jumper doing it "for the glory of his country" rather than for his own glory. It is a perverse indicator of the rising status of women's sporting activity that we are willing to consider the possibility of men cheating by coming first in a women's event rather than, say, fourth or fifth in the equivalent men's competition. Ostensibly, the reason for introducing testing was to prevent cheating or unfair competition. The presumption is that women are physiologically disadvantaged when it comes to competitions involving physical strength, speed, or stamina. While there is some biomedical evidence to support this notion, it is not necessarily the case across all sports; women may have advantages in some events, including endurance and ultraendurance competitions.

The assumption that women are weaker athletes is more than just a medical or biological convention, it is also a function of social assumptions about what is appropriate for men and women. Women's sports, at least in Europe and the English-speaking world, were regarded with some anxiety in the early twentieth century. Fears were expressed that sports would masculinize women, that it would interfere with their fertility, make them aggressive and competitive, and even that it could encourage homosexuality. Women's restrictive clothing made sports difficult and uncomfortable, and athletes wearing skimpy outfits were regularly regarded with shock and disapproval. International sports organizations often brought in restrictions and rules to protect what they considered to be the fragile female body—a clear example would be the absence of a women's marathon from the Olympic roster until as late as 1984.

This paternalistic attitude extended into the justification for sex testing; it was there to protect women not only from unfair competition but also from accusations in the press and gossip in the changing room about their gender. Female athletes themselves noted that this attitude was based on sexist assumptions about the physical capacity of women. Female participation in international sports had broadened in the interwar years, and performances improved—almost incredibly so after World War II with the infamous success of female athletes from the Soviet Union and German Democratic Republic. In an atmosphere of mistrust fostered by the Cold War, audiences were incredulous that such records could be set by women and suggested that these women must surely be men in disguise.

So histories of sex testing tend to concentrate on the tests introduced in the 1960s in response to the success of women athletes from Communist countries. There is no doubt that the introduction of sex testing was caused by the heightened atmosphere of competition during the Cold War, where sports itself was used as a demonstration of the superiority of one political system over another. That said, while the introduction of testing may be due to increased fears of cheats (drug tests were introduced at the same time), the fact that sex was tested is the result of more longstanding tensions between femininity and physical activity. Could someone really be that good at sports and still be a "proper" woman?

Because of this tension, sex testing started long before the sex scandals of the 1960s. Accusations of gender fraud date at least from the 1930s, when many sports organizations (national and international) began to require proof of femininity from would-be competitors in women's events. A further complication is that there is a clear difference between sex fraud, where a man takes part in a woman's event, and the participation of ambiguously or divergently sexed athletes. All but one of the athletes caught cheating and banned from women's sports in the twentieth century were people who had been brought up as women and who believed themselves to be female; there is little evidence that any of these athletes were deliberately committing gender fraud.

KEY EVENTS

The confidentiality of medical records, athletes' own embarrassment, and even the political sensitivity of an accusation of cheating means that it is all but impossible to come up with an accurate list of gender frauds, even at an elite international level. Most histories cite around half a dozen notable cases: Stella Walsh (U.S./Poland runner in the 1930s and 1940s), Hermann/Dora Ratjen (German high jumper, 1930s), Zdenka Koubkova (Czechoslovakian 800m runner, 1930s), Lea Caurla and Claire Bressolles (both French runners, 1940s), and Eric(a) Schinegger (Austrian downhill skier, 1960s). These are usually cited as "men" in women's sports—all had sex-change operations and lived as men, with the exception of Ratjen who claimed to have been a man all along, and Walsh, whose story is more complicated and tragic and is discussed later on.

In fact, this list misses the first transgender athlete. In late 1935 or 1936, the British shot putter and javelin thrower Mary Louise Edith Weston (known as the Devonshire Wonder) had a series of sex-reassignment operations in Charing Cross Hospital. Having won the British women's javelin championship in 1927 and the world championship in shot-putting in 1934, Weston retired from sports and became a *male* masseur—known to the world as Mark Weston. The tabloids covered the story broadly and sympathetically, especially when (in 1938) he married his long-term friend Alberta Bray, a woman he described to the *Daily Mirror* as his "girl in a million."

Weston's change was half the reason (the other half being Koubkova) that a conference on the so-called Man–Woman problem was held at the Berlin Olympiad in 1936. Britain and Czechoslovakia were cochairs because it was their sportswomen who appeared to be setting a bad example; the U.S. Olympic team coach Avery Brundage justified his demands for sex testing by citing the cases of Weston and the Polish competitor Koubkova (who had also undergone sex reassignment surgery and been legally recognized as a man). Testing was planned to be brought in for the 1940 Games, which were canceled with the outbreak of war. At the next Olympiad, in London 1948, female competitors had to bring medical certificates attesting their femininity (in accordance with the rules of the International Amateur Athletics Federation, which had quickly adopted a rule demanding proof of sex).

Brundage may have been particularly sensitive to the problem of men in women's sports because one of his own athletes had been accused of being just such a fraud. The U.S. runner Helen Stephens (the Fulton Flash) won gold at the 1936 Olympics in the 100m race, beating reigning champion Stella Walsh. Spectators accused Stephens of being a man; the German authorities intervened, performing an unspecified test on Stephens before declaring her a woman. This is probably the first outright accusation of sex fraud and the first sex test performed at a major international sporting event.

The irony of this accusation, when in later years it was Walsh who was revealed to have ambiguous sexual characteristics, has perhaps led commentators to pay too much attention to Walsh's unusual case. Stella Walsh competed as a woman for the whole of her sporting life until her retirement in 1951. She immigrated to the United States in 1947 when she married the boxer Neil Olsen, and she did much charity work for Polish sporting groups there. In 1980, she was shot, an innocent bystander in an armed store robbery; her autopsy showed unusual sexual physiology. Of course, Walsh's sexual identity is completely irrelevant to the story of sex testing or to the story of men in women's sports until 1980. No one responsible for introducing formal, at-event, sex testing in the 1960s knew that Walsh might fail such tests; her case was irrelevant for the early debates in the 1960s and 1970s about the ethics of the test, and yet, Walsh is regularly cited as a poster girl for sex fraud. This is probably because, as an Eastern European competitor, she fulfils our prejudices about the sorts of competitors likely to *be* sex frauds—the gender conflict between Walsh and the all-American Helen Stephens reinforces the point.

If Walsh is, however unfairly, the poster girl, then Hermann Ratjen is the poster boy. "Dora" Ratjen took a rather unremarkable fourth place in the high jump at the 1936 Berlin Olympiad; she improved on this performance by setting a world record a few years later, but she was disqualified in 1938 at the European Championships for having ambiguous sexual features (possibly being a hermaphrodite). In the late 1950s, Hermann Ratjen revealed himself as a man, claiming that the Hitler Youth had made him bind his genitals and compete as a woman to increase the German medal tally.

Ratjen's confession, and the increased competition in international sports caused by the Cold War, did influence the introduction of sex testing in international sports in the 1960s. Women competitors were already required (at least by 1948) to produce certificates proving their femininity—usually signed by their family or team doctors. But the suspicion surrounding dope cheats as well as sex cheats meant that self-certification was no longer acceptable by the

FALSE NEGATIVES AND FALSE POSITIVES

All medical tests are subject to some errors, and most can be categorized as false negatives (where a negative result is given instead of the true positive result) and false positives (vice versa). In the case of sports sex testing, this is made more common by the fact that the test may be for chromosomal or genetic sex when the test is actually intended to distinguish between people with phenotypical sex advantages.

Many chromosomal and genetic conditions could cause athletes to fail sex tests but not give them any sporting advantage. For example, Androgen Insensitivity Syndrome (also known as Androgen Resistance, or AIS) is a genetic condition where a developing XY fetus does not respond fully to hormone signals that should lead to typical male development. This leads to a range of different symptoms, but in the case of Complete AIS, the fetus would develop into someone who appeared phenotypically female (with primary and secondary female sexual features) and who would not have any proven sporting advantage over other XX females. Such an athlete would, however, fail all the chromosomal and genetic tests used so far in sports.

1960s. The first at-event testing took place in 1966 at the European Athletics Championships (Budapest) where would-be female competitors were asked to parade naked before three female doctors. At the 1966 Commonwealth Games in Jamaica a manual examination was added—much to the distress of several athletes. The first failure to come from these new testing regimes was Ewa Klobukowska, a Polish sprinter who passed in Budapest in 1966 but for some reason failed the exam at the European Cup in Kiev (1967); Klobukowska's medals and titles were stripped from her. Perhaps European Cup officials were left pondering the evidence when she gave birth to her first child in 1968!

The objections to manual and visual inspection, from athletes and also from interested commentators, led the International Olympic Committee (IOC) to seriously consider alternatives. The IOC introduced a test for chromosomal sex in 1967, trying it out at the Winter Games in Grenoble (disqualifying the Austrian skier Schinegger) and then using it as an official practice at the Mexico Games in 1968. At the Montreal Olympics in 1972, 1,800 female athletes were tested, and none failed; in the LA Games of 1984, 2,500 tests were conducted with no failures. The IOC considered this a success, but athletes and their representatives continued to complain and campaign against disqualification. Perhaps the most famous case was that of Spanish hurdler Maria Martinez-Patino, who fought a three-year battle for reinstatement after disqualification at the World University Games in Japan in 1985. Human rights activists joined Martinez-Patino's campaign, arguing that her specific genetic condition (Androgen Insensitivity Syndrome) meant that although she failed the chromosomal sex test, she had no physiological advantage over other women and was being unfairly excluded from women's sports.

International sports organizations began to reconsider the effectiveness of the sex test; the first to remove it was the International Amateur Athletic Federation

(IAAF), which switched in 1988 from genetic or chromosomal tests to health checks by team doctors; they removed the requirement for sex testing completely in 1992. In the same year, the IOC introduced a genetic test; this test proved no more satisfactory. Some geneticists and sports doctors refused to conduct the tests, and some nations (including Norway) declared sex testing in sports illegal under human rights legislation. In 1996, at the Olympic Games in Atlanta, 3,387 tests were given, but all 8 of the women who failed were allowed to compete as women after further medical investigation. The IOC's own World Conference on Women in Sport, also in 1996, urged the IOC to dispense with sex testing; it had never caught a man and was merely discriminating against women with chromosomal or genetic abnormalities. In 1999, the IOC's Athletes' Commission joined the chorus advising that sex testing should be abandoned as useless and unfair: This time the IOC agreed, and the millennial Games in Sydney were the first in 42 years with no sex testing.

FUTURE PROSPECTS

Sex testing has not been entirely abandoned—competitors might be asked to take tests if they are accused of being a man. Testing has been made more complicated by the recent acceptance by most international sports organiziations that male-to-female transsexuals should (legally) be recognized as women—the reverse of the challenge posed back in the 1930s by Mary/Mark Weston. However much sports organizations might want there to be just two sexes who have different sporting skills and need to compete in segregated events, biology, society, law, and medicine say the situation is more complicated than that.

Those responsible for sex testing have always claimed that the main reason for testing is to make sporting competitions fair. Men have a (genetic) physiological advantage over women and, therefore, should not be allowed to compete in women's events. But this logic is undermined by the fact that there are many other genetic variations that give people a sporting advantage, and we do not test for any of them. Most notable is height—this is strongly genetically determined and plays a significant role in sporting success. Of course, human beings do not come in just two height forms—tall and short—but many, which makes setting boundaries difficult. But then, although it can appear that human beings come in just two sexual forms, genetics tells us we come in many variations of sex and gender. What of other advantages—stronger bones, more powerful muscles, better hand–eye coordination? If we test for sex advantages because it is "fair," then why not nonsex advantages?

We test for sex because we think that the category *sex* is important, while a category such as *bone density* is not. There is, however, no good reason why sports should be used to confirm social prejudices about gender any more than prejudices about nationality, sexuality, or ethnicity. Ironically, the abolition of compulsory sex testing could make gender prejudice in sports worse. Only athletes who are accused will be tested, and only those who are suspect will be accused. Inevitably athletes who appear unfeminine or who are taking part in masculine sports will be under more suspicion than those who conform to social stereotypes about womanly behavior and appearance. If tests are only done on unfeminine athletes, then only unfeminine athletes will ever fail sex tests!

The problem is not really men in women's sports but rather the man-woman in woman's sports, which is as much to do with what society thinks is appropriate for women as it is about fairness or sporting achievement. After all, there have never been tests for maleness in modern sports, yet it is quite possible that some competitors may be genetically or chromosomally female and therefore eligible to take part in women's events. Such competitors are heavily disadvantaged by having to compete against men, and yet the fairness of women having to compete in men's sports is rarely considered.

See also Biology and Athlete Performance; Gender and Game Rules; LGBT Sports Leagues; Transsexual Athletes; Women in Men's Sports.

Further Reading: De la Chapelle, A. (1986). The Use and Misuse of Sex Chromatin Screening for "Gender Verification" of Female Athletes. *Journal of the American Medical Association* 256: 1920–1923; Ferguson-Smith, M. A. (1998). 3.3.2 Gender Verification. In *Oxford Textbook of Sports Medicine,* edited by Harries et al., 329–336. Oxford: Oxford University Press; Olsen-Acre, H. K. (2006–2007). The Use of Drug Testing to Police Sex and Gender in the Olympic Games. *Michigan Journal of Gender and Law* 13: 207–236; Ritchie, I. E. (May 2003). Sex Tested, Gender Verified: Controlling Female Sexuality in the Age of Containment. *Sports History Review* 34: 80–98; Wackwitz, L. (2003). Verifying the Myth: Olympic Sex Testing and the Category "Woman." *Women's Studies International Forum* 26: 553–560.

Vanessa Heggie

MILITARISM AND THE OLYMPICS

Militarism refers to a political orientation that leaders of a nation or government adopt and is based on the idea that strong displays of aggressive force by an army are the foundation of society's overall security. For well over a century, the Olympic Games have been affected by displays and acts of militarism between participating nations at the Olympics. Because many nations are involved in the modern Games, it has been difficult to keep the Games safe from political hostilities between participating nations or from intense military displays. Perhaps because the Games are broadcast around the world, include such a diverse group of people, and overtly contain warlike competitions between (sometimes warring) nations, military display and outright acts of militarism have accompanied them since 1896.

KEY EVENTS

A cornerstone philosophy of the modern Olympic movement is the concept of the "Olympic truce." Based on the ancient Olympic Greek custom of *Ekecheiria,* the modern version of the Olympic Games is designed to be a place wherein nations cease all hostilities toward one another and come together through sports in order to develop lines of communication between people, foster a spirit of global togetherness and justice, and to encourage peace among nations. Pierre de Coubertin, a French educator who pioneered the reinvention of the Olympics in 1896, believed the Games could provide people on earth with a safe context for friendly competition. Since 1896, the Games have evolved into one of the most popular social events on the planet. By 1992, the International Olympic Committee (IOC) challenged all nations on earth to observe its Olympic truce. By 1993, the United Nations (UN) General Assembly followed suit by encouraging all members of the UN to observe the Olympic truce.

Yet the very first Games of the Modern Olympic era, in Greece in 1896, represented a stage for militarism between the host nation and Turkey. In 1896, a group of militant Greeks traveled to Crete to stage a military campaign against the Turkish government. At the same time, another Greek army led by the Greek Prince Constantine invaded the Turkish province of Ioannina. A Turkish military force from Monastir eventually pushed the Greek army back to Thessaly, where it routed a Greek counterattack and advanced to the Gulf of Volo. The Turks subsequently withdrew in exchange for monetary compensation from Western nations.

During the 1908 Summer Games in London, military tensions between English Protestants and Irish Catholics again threatened the peace at the Games. Organizers hoped that growing hostility toward the English in Ireland would not spill over into the Olympic venues. While very few Irish nationalists actually participated in the 1908 Games, worry spread throughout England over an impending Irish terrorist paramilitary attack in London. With ardent support for Irish nationalism from the Irish American contingent at the Games, members of British parliament and the British Olympic Organizing Committee feared violence among spectators at Olympic facilities. The strategic lowering of the American flag to half-mast during the opening ceremonies of the Games and recurrent cries of biased British officiating during Olympic events exacerbated the anxieties of local authorities in London. While the events themselves unfolded without disruption, the 1908 Games foreshadowed how the Olympics would become increasingly inserted into the politics of militarism over the course of the century that followed.

The 1936 Berlin Games, often referred to as the Nazi Games, heightened international concerns about military conflict in high-profile sports spheres. Because the Aryan Nazi philosophy in Berlin at the time rejected the Olympic theme of equality and cultural inclusion, members of the IOC, led by the American Avery Brundage, rallied to secure Germany's peaceful involvement in the Games and its promise that the Olympic truce would not be compromised by hostility toward African and Jewish competitors. American politicians and IOC members were concerned with Nazi Germany's ability to host a peaceful and tolerant Games (although it merits noting that only U.S. IOC member Ernst Jahnke suggested a boycott or at least moving the Games and was consequently expelled from the IOC before the Games). Because the 1936 Games illustrate the theme of militarism very well, let us examine the case of the Nazi Games closely.

Sports historians document that by 1931 Adolf Hitler started to remove German Jews and people of African descent from sports participation in the country.

Jewish athletes were barred from German sports clubs because the ruling Nazi party viewed them, as well as Africans and other non-Aryans, as lesser human beings. According to Hitler's Nazi philosophy:

> German sport has only one task: to strengthen the character of the German people, imbuing it with the fighting spirit and steadfast camaraderie necessary in the struggle for its existence. (Joseph Goebbels, Minister of Propaganda, April 23, 1933)

For Hitler, the association between sports and the military was clear. Hitler's government used sports as a way of showcasing the apparent strength of the Aryan race and to simulate German youth's ability to engage in hand-to-hand or other forms of combat. Furthermore, Jews and Africans were barred from competition because Hitler believed that, especially in the case of African athletes, their "primitive" and more "muscular" bodies provided them with an unfair advantage in competition.

As an extension of the Nazi regime's militaristic position on sports and eugenics, most of the German sports symbolism in the 1930s centered around white superiority and power. As the Greeks and the Romans immortalized their best soldiers and athletes through art, the blue-eyed and blond German athletes were showcased in city wall murals, paintings, and posters throughout Germany in the time leading up to the Olympics in Berlin. Given the Nazi military/social philosophy based on strength, breeding, and outright physical fitness, it made sense that they would use the Games to draw attention to the supposed superiority of the Aryan people. Hitler believed so much in the military opportunity the Games provided that his government spent a reported 20,000,000 Reichsmarks (around US$8,000,000) to stage the Olympics.

As the Nazi's political and military philosophies quickly became associated with the Berlin Games, several countries threatened to boycott—the United States was, in particular, one of the feared boycotters. The U.S. Olympic team and the Anti-Nazi League in the United States were outspoken critics of the way in which the Nazis used the Games to promote racist ideologies and the military strength of the Third Reich government. Avery Brundage urged the Americans to ignore the German military's interest in the Games and to focus on the international spirit of peace accompanying the Olympic philosophy instead. Others, including the American Jewish Committee and the religious group B'nai B'rith, also urged for peace at the Games, fearing that a mass boycott would in fact stir anti-Jewish feelings around the world. Countries such as Great Britain, Spain, France, Sweden, Czechoslovakia, and The Netherlands all discussed the possibility of a boycott but nevertheless ended up participating in Berlin at the Olympics. These nations even entertained the idea of staging a People's Olympiad (essentially an alternative Olympics) as a way of boycotting the Nazi regime in Germany.

Historians argue that, "the Olympics were a perfect arena for the Nazi propaganda machine, which was unsurpassed at staging elaborate public spectacles and rallies. Choreographed pageantry, record-breaking athletic feats, and warm German hospitality made the 1936 Olympic Games memorable for athletes and spectators. Behind the facade, however, a ruthless dictatorship persecuted its enemies and rearmed for war to acquire new 'living space' for the Aryan master race" (see the Jewish Virtual Library at www.jewishvirtuallibrary.org). For some people, the intolerance of the Nazi party was dramatically shown when Hitler broke Olympic custom and refused to shake the hands of any black or Jewish athletes who won medals at the Games. The victories of black athletes such as American Jesse Owens—who set three world records in track at the Games and won four gold medals—were called "disgraces" in the German media. These athletes were also referred to, by members of the German media at the time, as nothing more than "auxiliary" competitors and, on occasion, "non-humans."

By the time of the 1956 Games in Melbourne, Avery Brundage and other members of the IOC pressed for the cessation of all national hostilities or displays of militarism during Olympic tournaments (Roche, 2002). In the summer of 1956, however, just weeks before the Games were to begin, two military conflicts undermined Brundage's quest for peace in Australia. First, the Egyptian seizure of the Suez Canal and subsequent military response by the British, French, and Israelis drew out a series of established and outsider tensions. The Soviet Union, supported by the United States, demanded an immediate withdrawal of occupying forces from Egypt. The British and French armies eventually vacated Egypt, yet five nations still boycotted the Olympic Games in support of the Egyptians. Only a few days later, the Soviet Union mobilized battalions of tanks and other armored vehicles to occupy Budapest. Despite the promise of military support from established Western nations, including the United States and England, none arrived, and nearly 200,000 Hungarians were killed or fled to neighboring Austria. As a result of global military affairs, the 1956 Games were plagued with intense security concerns, and local organizers in Melbourne spent two weeks worrying if the malice of the battlefields would flow over to the Olympic events themselves as, indeed, they did in an extremely bloody men's semifinal waterpolo match played between Hungary and the Soviet Union, which was eventually suspended.

Throughout the first half of the twentieth century, the Olympic Games were consistently affected by broader matters of national aggression, ideological propaganda, and cultural exclusion. Members of the IOC and national organizing committees developed international programs and security systems engineered to protect the Games from military conflict and discouraged the display of military symbols at the Olympics. Behind the scenes, boycotts of the Games from nations escalated in number and veracity. Fears about the Olympics becoming a site for actual aggression against innocent audiences increased, despite the fact that the Olympic events themselves remained free of political violence.

Although the 1968 Summer Games in Mexico have not received attention as an instance of militarism, tragic events occurring just three weeks prior to the Games had clear elements of military aggression. For more than six months prior to the opening ceremonies, groups of over 5,000 middle-class and pro-Marxist university student protesters (from the Universidad Autonoma de Mexico and the Instituto Politecnico Nacional) repeatedly gathered near Olympic venues to express anger against the Mexican government's massive spending on the Games. According to these students, the Mexican government, led by President Gustavo Ordaz, had wasted over $140 million on the event, money that could have been utilized to improve pressing social matters such as education, labor opportunities, and health care programs for the large Mexican working class. Under government support, the Mexican army "cleared out" student protesters from the Plaza Tlatelolco on October 2, 1968 (just 10 days before the opening ceremonies of the Games), by firing upon demonstrators with machine guns. Thirty-two student deaths were reported by the Mexican government, with other death counts running as high as 300. Around 2,000 students were jailed following the protest, and the clearly depleted resistance movement went away before the start of the Games themselves.

However, the Olympiads of the 1970s and 1980s were relatively calm by comparison with the horrific events of Munich 1972. Security arrangements in Innsbruck (1976), Montreal (1976), and Lake Placid (1980) were unprecedented in both scope and material resources employed on-site. Perhaps a result of being held on neutral political grounds (Austria and Canada), or heavily militarized grounds (the United States), the spirit of the Olympic truce characterized each of these Games. However, the 1980 Summer Games in Moscow and the 1984 Summer Games in Los Angeles provided further evidence of the perpetual ebb and flow of military tensions that have affected the Olympics since 1896.

The Moscow Games of 1980 followed a 1979 invasion of Afghanistan by the Soviet Union. The IOC's Lord Killanin repeatedly refused U.S. attempts to have the Games moved and spent considerable time trying to convince U.S. President Jimmy Carter not to boycott, but Carter started a global campaign to boycott the Games as a gesture of solidarity among Western nations. U.S. Vice President Walter Mondale underlined the importance of a unified political response to the Soviet militarism by asserting, "What is at stake here is no less than the future security of the civilized world." The U.S. anti-Moscow lobby drew support from a dozen nations, and a widespread dropout of Olympic participation ensued. Boycotting nations warned others venturing to Moscow that, in the absence of established military superpowers like the United States at the Games, hostile attacks against Westerners could occur. Correspondingly, Soviet news broadcasters and politicians warned of a Central Intelligence Agency's plot to kill Olympic spectators through biological or chemical weapons or via explosives planted at Olympic sites. As an outsider response to the U.S. boycott, the Soviets and 13 other nation-states subsequently boycotted the 1984 Games in Los Angeles, claiming that they, too, feared for the safety of their athletes in a hostile U.S. setting.

Throughout the late 1980s and early 1990s, security issues addressed both local protests in host cities and wider global militarism. Members of the Canadian Olympic Association at the Calgary Winter Games of 1988, for example, confronted security issues caused by local protesters concerned with environmental disturbance involved in creating Olympic event sites. Later that year, the Seoul Summer Games unfolded amid fears of military conflict between North and South Korea. Similarly, in 1992, Spanish organizers of the Barcelona Games were besieged with security issues related to local Basque separatist protests (Bernstein, 2000).

FUTURE PROSPECTS

As long as military tensions exist between participating nations at the Olympic Games, it is reasonable to assume that political displays of nationalism will be inscribed therein. The mass mediation of the event and the extent to which the Olympics are enmeshed within international struggles between nation-states has transformed the modern Games into a social platform for highlighting and disseminating political ideologies.

See also International Olympic Committee; Terrorism and the Olympics.

Further Reading: Bernstein, A. (2000). Things You Can See From There, You Can't See From Here. *Journal of Sport and Social Issues* 24: 351–369; Guttmann, A. (2002). *The Olympics: A History of the Modern Games.* Chicago: University of Chicago Press; Roche, M. (2002). The Olympics and Global Citizenship. *Citizenship Studies* 6: 165–181; Zarkos, J. (2004). Raising the Bar: A Man, the Flop and the Olympic Gold Medal. *Sun Valley Guide* (May 17): 28.

Michael Atkinson

MISSILE THROWING

Missile throwing refers to the projection of objects onto a field of play or at participants in a sport by sports fans. Missile throwing is historically quite common in North America. Players in professional and amateur sports in North America have complained of being the targets of cans, bottles, coins, and stones hurled by sports fans as far back as the 1930s. While incidents of missile throwing were taken very lightly by stadium officials and police until the 1960s, serious incidents in professional baseball and basketball during the 1970s prompted sports leagues to alter their approaches to missile-throwing control.

BACKGROUND

Most professional sports in North America, at one time or another, have been affected by missile throwing. However, mass spectator field sports such as baseball and football are most commonly cited as the problematic sports. Fans have used any number of objects as missiles, such as golf balls, marshmallows, nails, batteries, coins, keys, event programs and magazines, bottles, and ice shards.

While fans have sporadically thrown missiles onto fields of play, specific missile-throwing traditions arose as cultural norms in several North American sports. In particular, professional ice hockey fan cultures have practiced missile throwing for some time. One of the first, and certainly most tame, types of missile throwing occurs after a player scores three goals during a game; referred to in ice hockey as a *hat trick*. The term was first used during the 1870s in British cricket culture and referred to the occasion when a cricket bowler took three wickets with three successive balls. The bowler was then awarded a new hat by his club to mark his success. Ice hockey cultures apparently borrowed the practice in the late 1940s. The hat-trick custom in ice hockey started in Guelph,

Ontario, with the Guelph Biltmore Mad Hatters sponsored by Biltmore Hats. A member of the Biltmore Hat Company would throw a top hat onto the ice for the player that scored the goals. Fans soon followed his lead and offered their hats to the player as well. Today, hundreds of fans will throw their hats onto the ice in celebration of a hat trick.

Fans of the Detroit Red Wings National Hockey League (NHL) team started a far more controversial missile-throwing tradition in 1952. They initiated the practice of throwing dead octopuses onto the ice following a Red Wings' goal during playoff games. Despite protests from animal rights organizations, Red Wings fans still engage in the tradition. Fans of the NHL's Florida Panthers emulated the playoff ritual in 1996 by throwing plastic rats onto the ice following a playoff goal. Minutes prior to a home game in early 1995, a rat scurried across the Florida Panthers' locker room floor. Scott Mellanby of the Panthers reacted by shooting the rat against the wall with his hockey stick, killing it. That night he scored two goals, which Panthers' goalie John Vanbiesbrouck laughingly called a "rat trick." Two nights later, a few Florida fans threw rubber rats on the ice in celebration of a goal. The rubber rat count escalated from 16 in the Panthers' third home game to over 2,000 during the 1996 playoffs. In 2006, fans of the NHL's Nashville Predators would throw dead catfish onto the ice after one of their players scored a hat trick. The throwing of dead animals in the NHL has been curtailed in the recent past because of new rules and policies that heavily fine spectators for such delays of the game.

In the last three decades of the twentieth century, missile-throwing incidents in ice hockey and other professional sports took a more serious, and unruly, turn. Players and referees became the specific targets of missiles with greater frequency, and missiles were used (especially beer cups and game programs) as collective protests of poor officiating or as gestures of hostility toward the opposing team's players. Missile throwing by fans is also tactically used to stall a game and thus provide the home team with a rest or break from intense play.

Of course, academic experts and sports enthusiasts have weighed in with opinions about the cause of missile throwing and its outcomes. Some feel that being in a mass crowd at a sports contest may have the impact of stirring intense emotions of anger, frustration, despair, and invincibility in people. People describe being "caught up" in the collective emotion of a mob and describe a sense of invisibility therein. Fans, it is believed, experience a sort of crowd "contagion" where a feeling of "anything goes" emerges, and they may engage in types of unruly behavior that they would not normally engage in in other spheres of life. Another psychological explanation of the behavior is that the ritual pelting of either the field or players with missiles serves as a form of collective catharsis for people. Here, the release of emotional and psychological tension fans feel and bring to a stadium (i.e., that they experience in everyday life) is facilitated in the sporting arena via the thrill of "illegal" missile throwing. Some have cited that the overwhelming majority of missile throwers are working-class, young males and, therefore, that missile throwing is tied to a rough and risk-taking type of working-class masculinity. Other far more simple explanations of missile throwing cite alcohol or drug consumption as the primary cause of the behavior.

MAJOR MISSILE-THROWING EVENTS

2004—Near the end of an Indiana Pacers–Detroit Pistons game, fans and players threw punches; spectators tossed a chair, beer, ice, and popcorn. Four players—Ron Artest, Jermaine O'Neal, Stephen Jackson, and Ben Wallace—were suspended indefinitely for a fracas commissioner David Stern called shocking, repulsive, and inexcusable.

2001—Bottles thrown by Cleveland Browns fans hit players on both teams and people in the stands. Hundreds of bottles were plastic, but many were filled with beer. Referees stopped the game with seconds still remaining on the clock.

2000—A fight involving Los Angeles Dodgers players and Chicago Cubs fans at Wrigley Field began when a spectator grabbed and threw the hat of Dodgers backup catcher Chad Kreuter. Kreuter went into the stands, and several Dodgers followed, trading punches with fans.

1999—Members of the Oakland Raiders were pelted with snowballs, some spiked with batteries, at Denver's Mile High Stadium. Oakland player Charles Woodson allegedly threw a snowball that struck a female fan in the face, and teammate Lincoln Kennedy went after a fan who hit him in the face with a snowball.

1995—Football fans at Giants Stadium in New York hurled dozens of snowballs at the San Diego Chargers' sideline, interrupting a game between San Diego and New York. One snowball knocked San Diego equipment manager Sid Brooks unconscious.

1986—California Angels first baseman Wally Joyner was hit in the arm by a knife thrown from the upper deck at Yankee Stadium but was unhurt.

1979—Boston Bruins forward Stan Jonathan was hit in the face by an object thrown by a fan, and Bruins' rightwinger Terry O'Reilly was harassed by a stick-wielding fan at the end of a 4–3 victory at the New York Rangers. Several Boston players, including O'Reilly and Mike Milbury, went into the stands to fight with spectators.

1974—Nickel Beer Night in Cleveland drew 25,134 fans but turned into a forfeit victory for the Texas Rangers. Players rushed off the field to escape flying beer bottles and drunken fans before the forfeit was called in the last of the ninth inning.

1934—After St. Louis Cardinals' player Joe Medwick slid hard into Mickey Owen at third base for a triple during World Series Game 7 at Detroit, fans threw tomatoes at Medwick when he took his position in left field for the bottom of the inning.

KEY EVENTS

While there are dozens of high-profile missile-throwing incidents in North American sports, there are three particularly infamous cases.

In 1955, Montreal Canadiens superstar forward Maurice Richard was banned from the 1955 playoffs, stemming from a March 13, 1955, incident in a game against the Boston Bruins. Richard was given a match penalty for intentionally injuring Hal Laycoe during the game against the Boston Bruins. Richard slashed Laycoe in the face and shoulders with his stick. The linesmen attempted to restrain Richard, who repeatedly broke away from them to attack Laycoe, even breaking his stick over his back. Moments passed and linesman Cliff Thompson restrained Richard by holding both his arms in a lock. Richard broke loose and punched Thompson twice in the face, knocking him unconscious. The NHL commissioner Clarence Campbell suspended Richard for the remainder of the season, ending Richard's chance at winning the overall league scoring title.

Despite incredible public protest, Clarence Campbell did not repeal the suspension and announced that he would attend the Canadiens game against the Red Wings (only a few days after the suspension). Midway through the first period, Campbell arrived at the Montreal Forum with his fiancée. Canadiens fans immediately began pelting them with eggs, vegetables, and sundry garbage, with more being thrown at him each time the Red Wings scored; they built up a 4–1 lead. The continuous pelting of various objects stopped when a tear gas bomb was set off inside the Forum not far from where Campbell was sitting. The Forum was evacuated, and Campbell ruled the game forfeited to the Red Wings. The tear gas bomb and forfeiture altered the mood of the incident, turning it destructive and violent. A riot ensued outside the Forum, causing $500,000 in damage to the neighborhood and the Forum itself. Hundreds of stores were looted and vandalized within a 15-block radius of the Forum. Twelve policemen and 25 civilians were injured. The riot continued well into the night, with police arresting people by the hundreds. Local radio stations, which carried live coverage of the riot for over seven hours, were forced off the air.

"Ten Cent Beer Night" was an ill-conceived promotion held by the Cleveland Indians baseball team during a game against the Texas Rangers at Cleveland Municipal Stadium on June 4, 1974. The idea behind the promotion was to offer as many eight-ounce cups of beer as the fans could drink for just 10 cents apiece, thus increasing ticket sales.

The beer night promotion induced over 25,000 fans to come to Municipal Stadium for the Rangers/Indians game. As the game progressed and the crowd became more inebriated, fans ran onto the field and caused problems. Rangers' player Mike Hargrove was pelted with hot dogs and spat upon, and at one point he was nearly struck with an empty wine bottle. The Rangers later argued with an umpire's call, and the Rangers angry response to this call enraged Cleveland fans, who again began throwing objects onto the field. In the bottom of the ninth inning, the Indians managed to rally and tie the game at five runs apiece, but with a crowd that had been consuming as much alcohol as it could for nine innings, the situation finally boiled over. After Texas outfielder Jeff Burroughs violently reacted to a fan stealing his glove and cap, the Texas players, led by manager Billy Martin, charged onto the field with bats. A huge number of intoxicated fans, some armed with knives, chains, and portions of stadium seats that they had torn apart, surged onto the field; others hurled bottles from the stands. Realizing the Rangers might be in danger of their lives, Ken Aspromonte, the Indians' manager, ordered his players to grab bats and help the Rangers. Rioters began throwing steel folding chairs, and Cleveland relief pitcher Tom Hilgendorf was hit in the head by one of them. Hargrove, involved in a fistfight with a rioter, had to fight another on his way back to the Texas dugout. The bases were pulled up and stolen (never to be returned), and many rioters threw a vast array of objects including cups, rocks, bottles, batteries from radios, hot dogs, popcorn containers, and folding chairs. As a result, umpire crew chief Nestor Chylak, realizing that order would not be restored in a timely fashion, forfeited the game to Texas. He, too, was a victim of the rioters as one struck him with part of a stadium seat, cutting his head. His hand was also cut by a thrown rock.

"Disco Demolition Night" was another ill-conceived promotional event that took place on July 12, 1979, at Comiskey Park in Chicago. It was held during a scheduled doubleheader between the Chicago White Sox and the Detroit Tigers. During the event, fans surged onto the field, and a near riot ensued.

Local Chicago radio station WDAI went to an all-disco format in 1979 and, in the process, fired popular disk jockey Steve Dahl. Dahl was subsequently hired by rival station WLUP. He created a mock organization called "The Insane Coho Lips Anti-Disco Army" to oppose disco in which Dahl and partner Garry Meier regularly mocked and heaped scorn on disco records on the air. Dahl and Meier, in conjunction with both Mike Veeck (son of Chicago White Sox owner Bill Veeck) and Jeff Schwartz of WLUP promotions, devised a promotion that involved people bringing their unwanted disco records to the game in exchange for an admission fee of 98 cents. The records would be collected by stadium staff, placed in a large crate in center field, and then blown up by Dahl. The turnout for this promotion far exceeded all expectations. Fans began to throw their records from the stands during the game, and the records often struck other fans. The fans also threw beer and even firecrackers from the stands.

Dahl, dressed in army fatigues and a helmet, along with a female sidekick named Lorelei, exploded the crate of records. When it exploded, the bomb tore a hole in the outfield grass surface, and thousands of fans immediately rushed the field. Some lit fires and started small-scale riots. The batting cage was pulled down and wrecked, and the bases were stolen along with portions of the field itself. Eventually, the field was cleared by the Chicago Police in full riot gear. Six people reported minor injuries, and 39 were arrested for disorderly conduct.

FUTURE PROSPECTS

Missile throwing continues to be a problem both within and outside of North American sports stadiums. Leagues and teams continue to pursue ways of managing fans' abilities to throw missiles onto fields or at players (i.e., by raising nets or barricades) around particular sections of stadiums, attempt to control alcohol consumption by fans, and often try to section fans of opposing teams in locations in the stadium out of throwing distance. In a post–September 11, 2001, world, where issues in security and violence are on the minds of every sports event organizer, teams, leagues, and local police have moved toward a zero tolerance policy regarding missile throwing. Nevertheless, there is little evidence to suggest the problem will be completely controlled in North American sports.

See also Criminal Violence During Competition; Field Invasions; Player–Fan Fighting.

Further Reading: Atkinson, M., and Young, K. (2008). *Deviance and Social Control in Sport*. Champaign, IL: Human Kinetics; Dunning, E. (1999). *Sport Matters*. London: Routledge; Young, K. (2002). Standard Deviations. An Update on North American Sports Crowd Disorder. *Sociology of Sport Journal* 19 (3): 237–235.

Michael Atkinson

O

OPENLY GAY ATHLETES

In the realm of sexual equality, professional sports is a final frontier. The world of professional sports has been called one of the last "closets" in North America because the presence of gays and lesbians is largely stigmatized as intolerable therein. Few athletes, either men or women, have participated as openly (i.e., publicly known) gay or lesbian athletes in any sport around the world as a result. Players who have "come out" after their sports career often proclaim that they could not declare their sexual identity earlier because they feared ostracism, suspension from play by teams or coaches, loss of wages or sponsorships and endorsement deals, and even physical injury. Despite several waves of gay rights' movements and changing sociocultural rules to produce greater degrees of tolerance in North American society, one must question why sports remains a final, and incredibly divisive, social battleground.

BACKGROUND

Openly gay athletes in elite amateur and professional sports are few and far between. Over the course of the entire twentieth century, only a handful of athletes have been publicly "outed" as gay or have disclosed their sexual orientation while still an active player. While the relative small number of gay athletes might be a mere statistical chance, sociocultural critics of sports, such as Varda Burstyn, have long argued that the hypermasculine, heterosexually dominant cultural philosophies of modern sports discourage many gay athletes from being themselves in locker rooms or on sports fields. Sports have been, and continue to be, some of the main social places for young boys to establish their masculinity (i.e., the tough, aggressive, authoritarian, winning-oriented, and domineering male) and distance themselves from being considered soft or feminine. Additionally, sports are believed to be primary zones wherein male and female bodies are disciplined into conforming to the expectation that close contact with others of the same sex should be completely asexual in nature.

Between 1900 and the 1980s, only a very small number of the hundreds of thousands of athletes to play amateur or professional sports in North America (or elsewhere) were "out." In the 1920s, rumors held that U.S. men's singles tennis player Bill Tilden was gay. Tilden did not ever publicly deny being gay, but neither did he confirm the persistent rumors. It was not until 1968 when American Tom Waddell, an Olympic decathlete, became the first publicly gay athlete. In 1975, David Kopay, a National Football League (NFL) running back who played for five teams (San Francisco, Detroit, Washington, New Orleans, and Green Bay) between 1964–1972, became the first professional team sport athlete to come out; but he did so three years after retiring. He declared his gay identity during an interview with the now-defunct *Washington Star*. Wadell's and Kopay's public admissions did not, however, seem to impact the heterosexist culture of sports or the mass public belief that sports should be a socialization ground for "straights only."

Over the course of the 1980s, opportunities for women to enter into sports increased as a result of institutional policies in universities and federal funding laws such as Title IX, as women's rights groups pressed for equality in sports, and as media found new marketing opportunities in women's sports. But the strong cultural association between sports and masculinity confirmation in boys and men was not similarly shifted. It was generally regarded that women who elected to participate in male-dominated social pastimes must, themselves, wish to adopt male characteristics and traits, including, of course, their sexual preferences. Women who chose to enter sports such as golf, for example, were pejoratively called "dykes with spikes" (Crossett, 1995). Women tennis players were especially targeted in the antiwomen backlash in sports of the 1980s. Cases of "documented" lesbians in sports only fueled such debates and associations. In 1981, Billie Jean King was outed when ex-lover Marilyn Barnett sued her for "galimony" while Billie Jean was still married to Larry King. Later that year, Martina Navratilova publicly revealed that she was a lesbian during an interview with the *New York Daily News*.

The negative press coverage gays and lesbians received through the 1980s, partly due to the rise of HIV/AIDS and mistaken cultural assumptions about the disease as strictly "gay related," worsened the sexual rights climate in most professional and amateur sports. In 1985, for example, gay athlete Ed Gallagher, an offensive lineman for the University of Pittsburgh football team (1977–1979), jumped from a dam 12 days after his first sexual encounter with another man. Gallagher had been unable to reconcile the image of himself as an athlete and a gay man. In 1988, Dave Pallone, a National League baseball umpire, was fired for his alleged involvement with a sex ring. According to Pallone, the real reason he was fired was because he was gay. The last year of the decade involved one of the most direct statements against the acceptability of "sexual deviance" in

A STATISTICAL RARITY?

The 2004 Summer Olympics in Athens, Greece, hosted 10,500 athletes from 199 countries, but there were only 11 openly and publicly gay athletes among them. The 11 were: Robert Dover (American equestrian); Guenter Seidel (American equestrian), Carl Hester (British equestrian); Blyth Tait (New Zealand equestrian); Rob Newton (British hurdler); Amelie Mauresmo (French tennis player); Conchita Martinez (Spanish tennis player); Martina Navratilova (Czechoslovakian tennis player); Johan Kenkhuis (Dutch swimmer); Judith Arndt (German cyclist); and Imke Duplitzer (German fencer).

The law of "gay averages" in the United Sates will tell you that many more gay or lesbian athletes actually competed in the Games. If we accept academic and cultural assumptions that 10 percent of the population is gay/lesbian that accounts for approximately 1,000 athletes in Athens. Even at a conservative 5 percent, that means 500 athletes. Even at a hyper-conservative 1 percent that leaves 100; at 0.5 percent, that means 50 gay or lesbian athletes at the Games. Imagine the public attention if even 50 athletes held a press conference in Athens to declare their homosexuality to the world!

---

sports cultures: Rene Portland, Penn State University women's basketball coach, said publicly that she practiced a personal policy forbidding lesbians from playing on any team she coaches.

Other athletes were able to reconcile their gay identities after retiring. In the 1990s, Matthew Hall, a figure skater on the Canadian National Team, came out. Roy Simmons, an ex-offensive guard for the New York Giants and the Washington Redskins football teams, revealed he was gay during an appearance on *The Phil Donahue Show*. Glenn Burke, former outfielder with the Los Angeles Dodgers and the Oakland A's who was known for popularizing the high five, came out. Greg Louganis, four-time Olympic gold medalist in diving who became HIV-positive, came out in public at the Gay Games. Ian Roberts, one of Australia's most popular rugby players, became the first major sports figure in Australia to come out. Other American athletes including Rudy Galindo (figure skating), Doug Mattis (figure skating), David Pichler (diving), Patrick Jeffrey (diving), and Canadian Brian Orser (figure skating) all came out, or were outed, during the 1990s as well.

Sports insiders have commented that despite rights' advancement for gays and lesbians in most social institutions over the past 20 years—including marriage rights, paternity leave rights, adoption rights, and others—sports is still a socially protected terrain for homophobia. In an era where the professional athlete is idolized by millions and typically showcased as a positive role model, it is more than ironic that particular athletes are taught to be ashamed of their true identities while they are simultaneously being cheered.

KEY EVENTS

A number of high-profile cases of players coming out in the 1990s placed a social spotlight on the depth of heterosexism in sports cultures and the relative lack of progression gay rights advocates have made in most sports organizations.

Justin Fashanu was the first player of African descent to receive a £1 million salary in British soccer. He shot to prominence as a promising young player in 1980 and signed an unprecedented deal with the Nottingham Forest F.C. Shortly after signing for Nottingham, however, rumors of his homosexuality affected coaches' and teammates' treatment of him. Amid alleged homophobic and racist taunting by Nottingham staff and supporters, several on-field injuries, and media hounding, Fashanu failed to perform as a player. He spent the bulk of the 1980s being transferred from club to club in the United Kingdom (Southampton, Notts County, Brighton and Hove Albion, Manchester City, West Ham United, Ipswich Town, Leyton Orient, Southall, Leatherhead, Newcastle United, Toquay United, Heart of Midlothian, and Plainmoor), North America (Los Angeles Heat, Edmonton Brickmen, Atlanta Ruckus, and Maryland Mania), Sweden (Trelleborg), Australia (Adelaide City), and New Zealand (Miramar Rangers).

Fashanu eventually came out in 1990, becoming the first prominent player in English soccer to disclose a gay identity while still playing. Colleagues lashed out in anger, and his brother John publicly labeled him a *poof.* Fashanu spent the 1990s attempting to find a welcoming home in the professional game, but he constantly met with open discrimination and hostility. Following allegations of sexual assault made in 1998 by a 17-year-old American male, Fashanu hung himself in a garage in London. His life and death serve as a reminder that gay and lesbian lifestyles remain intensely taboo in mainstream sports.

Billy Bean played major league baseball from 1987 through 1995. He broke into the major leagues with the Detroit Tigers and tied a major league record with four hits in his first major league game. He went on to play for the Los Angeles Dodgers and the San Diego Padres. After years of living secretly, Billy came out publicly in 1999, three years after he retired from professional baseball. His story was front-page news in the *New York Times* and subsequently on a nationally televised story with Diane Sawyer. He chronicled his own battles about hiding his gay identity in sports in his book *Going the Other Way.*

In the prime of his career, Billy walked away from baseball in 1996. After years of denying his sexual preferences, hiding a long-term relationship with his partner, Sam, and feeling discriminated against in a homophobic sports culture, Bean had enough. In his book, Bean describes the event that pushed him over the edge. Following the death of his partner, Sam, Bean was instructed by team management of the San Diego Padres (who suspected his relationship) not to attend the funeral or acknowledge the death publicly. Bean played for a full season after Sam's death without ever expressing his grief openly to sports insiders.

Bean is the only living former major league baseball player to acknowledge his homosexuality. Since 1999, Bean has been working actively to try and dispel the myth and stereotypes that follow people of diversity. He was a featured spokesman for the Democratic National Committee in 2000 on behalf of their national Human Rights Campaign.

Bean's accounts of the culture of silence for gay players and the many informal means by which gays are treated as intolerable in sports were even more poignantly summarized by ex-professional football player Esera Tuaolo, who in 2002 became only the third NFL football player to publicly announce his gay identity to the world. Media and public interest in Tuaolo's declaration was, in a word, immense, and it stirred substantial public debate regarding the place of gays and lesbians in sports and the myriad human rights violations regarding one's sexuality and freedom present in a full range of sports cultures.

Esera Tuaolo, a Samoan born in Hawai'i, played defensive tackle for five NFL teams (Carolina Panthers, Atlanta Falcons, Jacksonville Jaguars, Minnesota Vikings, and Green Bay Packers) in his nine years as a professional, spending the longest time with the Minnesota Vikings. He was drafted in the second round by the Green Bay Packers in 1991 after a standout career at Oregon State. His NFL career, while long, was not particularly noteworthy. He has commented to people that he never played up to his potential, primarily for fear that being a star would have raised his profile, brought more scrutiny, and perhaps led to his being outed. Instead of pressing for equality in a sport so heavily cleaved along sexist, macho lines, Tuaolo hid his sexual identity through a series of masculine overcompensating behaviors (e.g., binge drinking, partying, sexual conquests of women, and homophobic jokes) designed to curry favor with straight athletes. Tuaolo's autobiography, *Alone in the Trenches: My Life as a Gay Man in the NFL* (2006), indeed paints a depressing portrait of life in professional sports for a gay man. He describes on more than one occasion how the culture of professional football is so intolerant toward deviations from heterosexual norms that gay players even fear for their lives, thinking that if they are outed a fellow teammate will either "take them out" in practice or fail to protect them during play.

FUTURE PROSPECTS

As long as sports organizations practice a "don't ask, don't tell" cultural and structural policy related to sexual orientation, we can only assume that gay and lesbian players in most amateur and professional sports will continue to be silenced, teased, degraded, overlooked, and threatened. Changing the relationship between masculinity, femininity, and heterosexuality in sports is not an easy task, and as long as sports is viewed as a primary site for achieving normative gender/sex identities for young boys and girls, a culture of intolerance toward gays and lesbians will likely continue. Perhaps only when a major sports organization or league is successfully sued by a high-profile gay or lesbian athlete will people on the inside of professional sports realize that discriminating against or intimidating a player on sexual grounds in unacceptable.

See also Gay Games; Gender and Game Rules; Homophobia; Men in Women's Sports; Transsexual Athletes; Women and the Apologetic; Women in Men's Sports.

Further Reading: Bean, B. (2004). *Going the Other Way: Lessons from a Life In and Out of Major League Baseball.* Washington, D.C.: Marlowe and Company; Bursytn, V. (1999). *The Rites of Men.* Toronto. University of Toronto Press; Crossett, T. (1995). *Outsiders in* the Clubhouse: The World of Women's Professional Golf. Albany: State University of New York Press; Lenskyj, H. (2003). *Out on the Field: Gender Sport and Sexualities.* Toronto: Women's Press; Tuaolo, E. (2006). *Alone in the Trenches: My Life as a Gay Man in the NFL.* Naperville, IL: Sourcebooks.

Michael Atkinson